Strengthening Electoral Integri.,

Today a general mood of pessimism surrounds Western efforts to strengthen elections and democracy abroad. If elections are often deeply flawed or even broken in many countries around the world, can anything be done to fix them? To counter the prevailing ethos, Pippa Norris presents new evidence for why programs of international electoral assistance work. She evaluates the effectiveness of several practical remedies, including efforts designed to reform electoral laws, strengthen women's representation, build effective electoral management bodies, promote balanced campaign communications, regulate political money, and improve voter registration. Pippa Norris argues that it would be a tragedy to undermine progress by withdrawing from international engagement. Instead, the international community needs to learn the lessons of what works best to strengthen electoral integrity, to focus activities and resources upon the most effective programs, and to innovate after a quarter century of efforts to strengthen electoral integrity.

Pippa Norris is the McGuire Lecturer in Comparative Politics at the John F. Kennedy School of Government, Harvard University, and Laureate Fellow and Professor of Government and International Relations at Sydney University. She is the director of the Electoral Integrity Project. Recent books by this award-winning author, also published by Cambridge University Press, include *Driving Democracy* (2008), *Cosmopolitan Communications* (2009), *Democratic Deficit* (2011), *Making Democratic Governance Work* (2012), and the present volume completes her trilogy with *Why Electoral Integrity Matters* (2014), and *Why Elections Fail* (2015).

Also by Pippa Norris from Cambridge University Press

Political Recruitment: Gender, Race and Class in the British Parliament, Pippa Norris and Joni Lovenduski (1995)
Passages to Power: Legislative Recruitment in Advanced Democracies, Pippa Norris, Ed. (1997)
A Virtuous Circle: Political Communications in Postindustrial Democracies, Pippa Norris (2000) (awarded the 2006 Doris Graber award by APSA's political communications section)
Digital Divide: Civic Engagement, Information Poverty, and the Internet Worldwide, Pippa Norris (2001)
Democratic Phoenix: Reinventing Political Activism, Pippa Norris (2002)
Rising Tide: Gender Equality and Cultural Change around the World, Ronald Inglehart and Pippa Norris (2003)
Electoral Engineering: Voting Rules and Political Behavior, Pippa Norris (2004)
Radical Right: Voters and Parties in the Electoral Market, Pippa Norris (2005)
Driving Democracy: Do Power-Sharing Institutions Work? Pippa Norris (2008)
Cosmopolitan Communications: Cultural Diversity in a Globalized World, Pippa Norris and Ronald Inglehart (2009)
Sacred and Secular: Politics and Religion Worldwide, 2nd edition, Pippa Norris and Ronald Inglehart (2011) (first edition awarded the 2005 Virginia A. Hodkinson prize by the Independent Scholar)
Democratic Deficit: Critical Citizens Revisited, Pippa Norris (2011)
Making Democratic Governance Work: How Regimes Shape Prosperity, Welfare, and Peace, Pippa Norris (2012)
Why Electoral Integrity Matters, Pippa Norris (2014)
Why Elections Fail, Pippa Norris (2015)

Strengthening Electoral Integrity

PIPPA NORRIS
Kennedy School of Government, Harvard University

CAMBRIDGE
UNIVERSITY PRESS

University Printing House, Cambridge CB2 8BS, United Kingdom

One Liberty Plaza, 20th Floor, New York, NY 10006, USA

477 Williamstown Road, Port Melbourne, VIC 3207, Australia

4843/24, 2nd Floor, Ansari Road, Daryaganj, Delhi – 110002, India

79 Anson Road, #06–04/06, Singapore 079906

Cambridge University Press is part of the University of Cambridge.

It furthers the University's mission by disseminating knowledge in the pursuit of education, learning, and research at the highest international levels of excellence.

www.cambridge.org
Information on this title: www.cambridge.org/9781107052604
DOI: 10.1017/9781107280656

First published 2017

Printed in the United States of America by Sheridan Books, Inc.

A catalogue record for this publication is available from the British Library.

ISBN 978-1-107-05260-4 Hardback
ISBN 978-1-107-68166-8 Paperback

Contents

Figures

Tables

Preface and Acknowledgments

This book is the final volume of the trilogy on the challenges of electoral integrity around the world, including why it matters, why electoral integrity fails, and what can be done to address these problems. This volume focuses upon what the international community can and does do in partnership with local stakeholders in efforts to implement reforms designed to strengthen electoral integrity around the globe.

The book is the culmination of the first phase of the Electoral Integrity Project (EIP), founded in 2012. Research has been generously supported by the award of the Kathleen Fitzpatrick Australian Laureate from the Australian Research Council, as well as grants from International IDEA, Global Integrity, the Australian Research Council, the Association of World Electoral Bodies (A-WEB), the University of Sydney, (and at Harvard) by the Weatherhead Center for International Affairs, the Roy and Lila Ash Center for Democratic Governance and Innovation, and the Australian Studies Committee. I am also most grateful to the World Values Survey Association for including the electoral integrity battery in the sixth and seventh wave surveys.

The EIP project is based at Harvard University's John F. Kennedy School of Government and the Department of Government and International Relations at the University of Sydney. I am indebted to Michael Spence, Duncan Ivison, Simon Tormey, Allan McConnell, Colin Wight, and Graeme Gill for facilitating the arrangement in Sydney, as well as to all colleagues in the department. The book would not have been possible without the research team at Sydney, who have played an essential role in stimulating ideas, providing critical feedback and advice, generating related publications, and organizing events, especially developing the Perception of Electoral integrity (PEI) dataset. Throughout the lifetime of the project, I owe an immense debt to all the research team – Ferran Martinez i Coma, Richard W. Frank, Max Grömping, Jeffrey Karp, Alexandra Kennett, Alessandro Nai, and Andrea Abel van Es – as well as all the fellows and interns visiting the project. In particular, I am most grateful to Max Grömping, the PEI manager, for producing all the maps used in the book.The intellectual foundations for this study build upon a series of earlier books for Cambridge University Press that have compared electoral institutions, voting behavior, political culture, and processes of democratization, particularly the previous volumes in the trilogy, *Why Electoral Integrity Matters* (2014) and *Why Elections Fail* (2015).

Specific chapters also owe an immense debt of gratitude for work with collaborators who helped with data collection, conference papers presenting the initial results. This includes the invaluable contribution of Holly Ann Garnett (McGill University) for collaborating on Chapter 9. Chapter 6 is based on a paper for APSA 2014 in Washington, DC, coauthored with Drude Dahlerup in the Department of Political Science at Stockholm University. The chapter draws on the Gender Quota Database (GQD, Stockholm: Stockholm University, Release May 2014) with help from Alma Jonssen and Vaselis Petrogiannis, students of political science at Stockholm University. The project would also not have been possible without the help of several interns who worked with the Electoral Integrity Project over the years.

As always, this book also owes immense debts to many friends and colleagues. I also appreciate all colleagues and friends who provided encouraging comments about this project during its gestation, including Sarah Birch, David Carroll, Ivor Crewe, Larry Diamond, Jorge Dominguez, Jörgen Elklit, David Ellwood, Annette Fath-Lihic, Mark Franklin, Ben Goldsmith, Judith Kelley, Alex Keyssar, Thad Hall, Carolien Van Ham, Susan Hyde, Larry LeDuc, John Keane, Ian McAllister, Jane Mansbridge, Marc Plattner, Andy Reynolds, Carolien van Ham, Sidney Verba, and Chad Vickery. The book has also been shaped by many students who have taken my Harvard classes over the years, where we discuss challenges of electoral integrity, theories of democratization, and measures of the quality of democratic governance, and the most effective policy reforms that address these issues. Invaluable feedback has been received at several international workshops and meetings, including the Poznan International Political Science Association World Congress and EIP Workshop in July 2016, the American Political Science Association annual meeting and EIP workshop in Philadelphia in August 2016, and faculty seminars at Harvard's Kennedy School and the Government Department.

I have also learned a tremendous amount from working closely with colleagues based in many other international development agencies and academic teams linked with the Electoral Integrity Project, including the United Nations Development Program, the United Nations Electoral Assistance Division, the Australian Election Commission, the Carter Center, the International Foundation for Electoral Systems (IFES), International IDEA, the Organization for Security and Cooperation in Europe, the Organization of

American States, the Kofi Annan Commission, the Sunlight Foundation, the National Democratic Institute, USAID, the UK Electoral Commission, the Varieties of Democracy project, and many others.

Finally, as always, the support of Cambridge University Press has proved invaluable, particularly the patience, efficient assistance, and enthusiasm of my editor, Robert Dreesen, as well as the helpful comments of the reviewers.

PART I

INTRODUCTION: DOES ELECTORAL ASSISTANCE WORK?

1

The Pragmatic Case for Electoral Assistance

The previous books in this trilogy have analyzed why electoral integrity matters and how elections can be derailed through numerous types of flaws and failures. In some contests, opponents are disqualified. District boundaries are gerrymandered. Campaigns provide a skewed playing field for parties. Independent media are muzzled. Citizens are ill-informed about choices. Balloting is disrupted by bloodshed. Ballot boxes are stuffed. Vote counts are fiddled. Opposition parties withdraw. Contenders refuse to accept the people's choice. Protests disrupt polling. Officials abuse state resources. Electoral registers are out of date. Candidates distribute largesse. Votes are bought. Airwaves favor incumbents. Campaigns are awash with hidden cash. Political finance rules are lax. Incompetent local officials run out of ballot papers. Incumbents are immune from effective challengers. Rallies trigger riots. Women candidates face discrimination. Ethnic minorities are persecuted. Voting machines jam. Lines lengthen. Ballot box seals break. Citizens cast more than one ballot. Legal requirements serve to suppress voting rights. Polling stations are inaccessible. Software crashes. "Secure" ink washes off fingers. Courts fail to resolve complaints impartially. Each of these diverse problems can generate contentious elections characterized by lengthy court challenges, opposition boycotts, public protest, or, at worst, deadly violence.[1] In some cases, failures are intentional; elsewhere they arise through technical accident and human error, although it is difficult to nail down which is which. These challenges make democratic institutions more vulnerable and undermine electoral legitimacy in the United States and Europe. They heighten the threat of authoritarian resurgence in countries around the world.

Earlier volumes used comparative evidence from countries around the globe to diagnose the underlying causes of these problems and to demonstrate how flawed contests undermine democracy.[2] Like the fish rotting from the head, any corrosion of public confidence in elections can gradually spread to weaken trust in the core representative institutions of political parties, parliaments, and governments, to erode civic engagement and voting turnout, and to encourage losers to reject the fairness and legitimacy of the outcome. The role of elections should not be exaggerated; even free and fair contests by themselves are not sufficient for liberal democracy to work well by any means. Many other institutions need to be effective as well – robust parliaments, independent courts and rule of law, good governance, pluralistic news media, and active civil society organizations. But elections are the concrete and steel foundations upon which democracies rest.

If elections are often deeply flawed or even broken in many countries around the world, as widely recognized, what can be done to fix them? Here we confront some tough and tricky issues. This book evaluates the effectiveness of several practical remedies, including efforts designed to reform electoral laws, strengthen women's representation, build effective electoral management bodies, promote balanced campaign communications, regulate political money, and improve voter registration. Numerous other solutions have often been tried. This list is incomplete, but these represent some of the most common approaches widely used to strengthen electoral integrity. In each case, chapters address three questions:

(i) *In general, how effective are these programs, judged by whether these strengthen electoral integrity, the institution at the heart of liberal democracy?*
(ii) *In turn, how can we evaluate the general impact of programs of electoral assistance offered by the international community, and what are the appropriate benchmarks and measures for assessing success or failure?*
(iii) *And finally, using the SWOT analysis model, what are the Strengths and Weaknesses of each of these programs when seeking to improve the performance of elections, and what Opportunities and Threats do actors face in achieving these goals in different contexts?*

It is important to address these issues because the contemporary mood today among scholars and policymakers is one of widespread skepticism, and even fatalistic cynicism, about the value of the democracy agenda. In the West, public impressions about processes of regime change have been heavily colored by headline events in a few states: the prism of instability and corruption following military intervention against the Taliban in Afghanistan; heightened sectarian conflict and the metastasizing of ISIS in Iraq; the downfall of Mubarak but replacement by Sisi in Egypt; the erosion of democracy in Venezuela, Poland, the Philippines, and Hungary, the civil war and humanitarian crisis in Bashir's Syria; the repression of human rights in Turkey; and bloody tribal conflict and chaos following Gaddafi's fall in Libya. Many revolutionary upheavals seeking to overturn repressive regimes have failed to generate peaceful and stable states, let alone democratic institutions.

Moreover, a tidal wave of populism has risen within many Western societies, symbolized in 2016 by the outcomes of the United Kingdom's Brexit referendum deciding to withdraw from the European Union and the election of President Trump in the United States. Populist authoritarians in the West directly threaten liberal democracy at home, by challenging the core values of pluralism, social tolerance, rule of law, human rights, and freedoms. They also threaten Western efforts at supporting democracy abroad by doing business with authoritarian leaders, advocating disengagement from the institutions of global governance, and cutting development budgets.[3] Overall, the mood of the international community towards opportunities for democracy promotion shifted from the predominantly sunny optimism that prevailed in the late 1980s and early 1990s (around the time of the fall of the Berlin Wall) to reflect more pessimistic expectations in an increasingly chilly climate.

Is the more pessimistic zeitgeist well founded? This book considers pragmatic arguments about the value of international efforts at democracy promotion and presents empirical evidence to assess the effectiveness of several common types of programs providing electoral assistance. Today these types of programs have been supported by Western donors and implemented by aid workers in most developing countries, working in partnership with local stakeholders. This has become established as a multibillion dollar sector of development. Contrary to the prevalent mood of skepticism, successive chapters in this book suggest where international organizations and bilateral donors support the efforts of local stakeholders, effective programs commonly do have the capacity to achieve their goals. The evidence demonstrates that the recommendations in electoral observer reports published by the OAS are often implemented by member states; well-designed gender quotas laws advocated by UNWomen usually do boost the number of women in elected office; professional training supported by UNESCO shapes how journalists see their roles; regulations supported by integrity NGOs like Transparency International make campaign finance more transparent; and more convenient electoral procedures implemented by electoral management bodies generally improve turnout.

At the same time, the success of many common types of electoral assistance programs should not be exaggerated. We need to be cautious in assessing their more diffuse impacts on electoral integrity and the broader quality of democratic governance, as this remains indeterminate. For example, it is far easier for quota laws to increase gender equality in elected office and the number of female legislators than it is to ensure women's empowerment in leadership roles. It is more straightforward to lower the procedural and administrative barriers to registration and voting than it is to deepen political trust and civic engagement. It is simpler to pass new campaign finance disclosure laws than it is to enforce them. It is easier to provide professional training for journalists than it is to alter the deeply ingrained cultural practices of newsrooms, and so on. The challenge facing any evaluation of development programs is to develop credible evidence-based assessments, which do not encourage cynicism by specifying impossibly ambitious goals, while avoiding Panglossian happy talk that everything works, which is both implausible and unconvincing. Where common programs of electoral assistance usually achieve their specific goals, however, then their cumulative long-term effects are likely to strengthen the overall integrity of elections and liberal democracy.

Not everything works, by any means. Chapters suggest that electoral assistance has proved most effective where the strengths and weaknesses of international agencies and programs match the threats and opportunities facing each society. International programs supporting free and fair elections are commonly used as part of peace-building initiatives in some of the most challenging contexts around the world – war-torn Iraq, the Democratic Republic of Congo, Burundi, and Afghanistan – all contexts carrying the highest risks of failure. Expectations about what can be achieved are often exaggerated where glossy reports by aid agencies make inflated claims to potential donors. Researchers need far more credible independent evidence to evaluate a range of programs – and organizations need to be open to learning from the results of successes *and* failures to improve their strategic plans. But this does not mean that international attempts to strengthen elections should be reduced or even abandoned, as transactional realism suggests. Since the end of World War II, and especially since the early 1990s, the United Nations and the broader international community have been committed to supporting the values and principles of electoral rights and freedoms through responding to requests for assistance. The transactional "America first" foreign policy advocated by the Trump administration, and populist forces in Europe, threaten to overturn principles that have supported building electoral democracies around the globe for around seven decades. It would be a tragedy to undermine the progress that has been achieved by slashing international support for electoral assistance and democratic governance and downplaying people's right to self-determination, thereby capitulating to authoritarian forces at home and abroad. Failing to support democratic elections at home and abroad is a betrayal of human rights and Western values.

To develop the foundations for this argument, the first part of this chapter discusses why it is important and timely to assess the role and impact of electoral assistance programs. To counter critical skeptics, this sector faces strong pressures to demonstrate aid effectiveness and justify its work. The second part describes how to assess the effectiveness of electoral assistance and unpacks the core arguments. The final part summarizes the plan for the rest of the book.

WHY ASSESS ELECTORAL ASSISTANCE PROGRAMS?

As electoral assistance is under growing challenge, it is timely and important to assess the overall impact of these activities in strengthening electoral integrity. Many claims about these activities are common when implementing agencies report to donors. To demonstrate the impact of their work, aid workers typically highlight "best practices" in the field; for example, in their 2015 annual report, the United Nations Development Program (UNDP) emphasized their role in providing electoral assistance to many African states:

> UNDP's goal is to ensure that elections are carried out fairly, credibly and transparently in an atmosphere of peace and security, and with a commitment to social and political inclusion.
>
> In Guinea-Bissau, that assistance helped achieve a voter turnout of 88 percent in the first round—the highest in the country's history. In Malawi, UNDP helped to register 7.4 million people to vote. In Sao Tome and Principe, UNDP assisted the National Electoral Commission with new biometric technology to enroll thousands of voters, many of them women who had never previously cast ballots. In Mali, where UNDP helped authorities to restore public services and reopen courthouses and town halls in the recently turbulent Timbuktu region, our local election specialists also helped to lay the groundwork for the next cycle of municipal elections—a key step towards restoring public trust and security ... UNDP worked with the AU's Democracy and Elections Assistance Unit to train and deploy AU election observers in countries throughout the continent ... In Nigeria, UNDP helped to organize training programmes for more than 100 first-time women candidates at the state and national levels. And in Addis Ababa, UNDP convened a pan-African gathering of prominent women parliamentarians to discuss challenges they face in the region.[4]

But is there credible evidence that the UNDP programs did indeed serve to boost turnout in Guinea-Bissau, strengthen public trust in Mali, or empower women in elected office in Nigeria? In general, are agencies and programs designed to strengthen electoral integrity both at home and abroad effective in meeting their goals? Which types of interventions are most successful? And which fail to deliver?

The Retreat from Democracy Promotion Among Western Aid Donors

We need to reexamine the evidence for these issues because doubts about democracy's promise have deepened in recent years, with new vulnerabilities apparent in many Western states and authoritarian resurgence around the globe.

Over a century ago, on April 2, 1917, during a speech asking Congress to declare war on Germany, Woodrow Wilson delivered one of the most resonant lines in the history of the presidency: "The world must be made safe for democracy."[5] In 1941, Franklin D. Roosevelt and Winston Churchill issued the Atlantic Charter, committing the World War II allies to protect "the right of all peoples to choose the form of government under which they will live."[6] The United Nations endorsed the rights to self-determination and fundamental freedoms in the 1948 Universal Declaration of Human Rights. Since then, Western leaders have expressed commitment to the value of fostering the spread of the institutions and ideals of liberal democracy and human rights abroad.[7] In 1961, John F. Kennedy's inaugural issued his stirring call that the torch has been passed to a new generation of Americans "unwilling to witness or permit the slow undoing of those human rights to which this nation has always been committed, and to which we are committed today at home and around the world."[8] In the most famous passage, Kennedy called for American self-sacrifice to promote these ideals: "Let every nation know, whether it wishes us well or ill, that we shall pay any price, bear any burden, meet any hardship, support any friend, oppose any foe to assure the survival and the success of liberty." The promotion of democracy and human rights abroad has often proved more rhetorical than real in numerous cases of US foreign policy where these values have clashed with other economic or military priorities, especially in Latin America.[9] The United States has lagged behind other democracies in endorsing several major human rights treaties, such as CEDAW, and used double standards by claiming exemption from bodies such as the International Criminal Court, as well as dismissing UN criticisms of its own record.[10] Nevertheless democratic ideals have been articulated in speeches by successive presidents as diverse as Jimmy Carter, Ronald Reagan, George Bush, Bill Clinton, and George W. Bush. For example, in his inaugural address in 1981, President Ronald Reagan spoke to "those neighbors and allies who share our freedom, we will strengthen our historic ties and assure them of our support and firm commitment." The end of the Cold War ushered in the so-called "end of history" era; during the 1990s, it was commonly assumed that democratic forces would eventually triumph worldwide and authoritarianism would crack and crumble like the concrete Berlin Wall.[11]

The legitimacy of state-building and democracy promotion efforts were undermined when the Bush administration adopted this rhetoric as a post-hoc justification of military intervention in Afghanistan and Iraq, and these wars generated further instability, terrorism, and conflict within the region and elsewhere in the world.[12] By the time of the Obama administration, more sober and cautious assessments about the role of democracy promotion in US foreign policy priorities had come to prevail. During the Arab uprising, events in Tunisia in 2010/11 initially gave grounds to believe that the Middle East and North Africa might emulate the developments in Central and Eastern Europe when overthrowing entrenched leaders a decade earlier. But these expectations were quickly dashed by subsequent bloodshed, disorder, and turmoil in the MENA region, with resurgent dictators and further repression in many states following the upheavals in Egypt, Libya, Bahrain, and Syria.[13] Even Tunisia suffered from poor economic performance, weakening confidence in democracy. The events have triggered chaos and insecurity in the Middle East and North Africa, heightened terrorist risks within the region and in the rest of the world, and catalyzed the massive humanitarian crisis and the flood of refugees and migrants across borders.[14]

US Foreign Policy During the Obama Years

By the time that President Obama was elected in 2008, these developments had spurred a general mood of pessimism about the broader enterprise of democracy promotion and deepened skepticism in the public mind about the general effectiveness of attempts to provide electoral assistance in the Middle East and elsewhere in the world. The Obama years saw a counterreaction in American foreign policy to the Bush era, embracing a more cautious approach than under the neoconservatives, with the State Department rejecting reckless military adventures and displaying growing reluctance to engage overseas – notably in the bloody and disastrous civil war in Syria.[15] Grandiose dreams of democracy promotion, regime change, and state-building by force under the neoconservatives sank in the bloody sands of Iraq, the mountain caves of Afghanistan, and the streets of Aleppo in Syria. The spread of ISIS terrorist risks to Western countries reinforced doubts and weariness about the whole enterprise of state-building and democracy promotion. Thus during his first term in office, President Obama acknowledged the importance of human rights in several major speeches, but he also downplayed the inflated rhetoric of promoting democracy and freedom in US foreign policy that characterized the previous administration of George W. Bush.[16] In practice, realism often prevailed in the State Department. For example, substantial military aid was channeled to repressive regimes in Egypt, Ethiopia, and Pakistan, and American power was not consistently used to advance opportunities for democracy abroad.[17] As one important indicator of changing priorities, the total amount of foreign assistance allocated for democracy, human rights, and governance dropped by half under the Obama administration, from US$3.52Bn in 2010 to $1.92Bn in 2015, before recovering slightly to $2.72Bn in Obama's final year of office.[18] At home as well, the US record of complying with international treaties and protecting human rights fared poorly compared to many other liberal democracies on issues of national security, criminal justice, social and economic rights, and immigration policy.[19]

Growing American doubts about the broader enterprise of democracy promotion, before Trump's presidency, reflected shifts in foreign policy among other Western donors who had previously championed this cause. Major bilateral donors, including the United Kingdom, Germany, Sweden, and France, reallocated a large proportion of their development assistance budget, with spending priorities shifting in 2015 from supporting democracy to programs designed to support the reception of refugees, border controls, and the fight against terror.[20] States in the Nordic region had previously been at the forefront of championing human rights, but development aid was also diverted to dealing with the domestic influx of refugees and migrants in Sweden, Denmark, and Norway, leading to major cuts in the global funds available for the United Nations work on good governance, democracy, and human rights.[21] European priorities shifted to tackling major challenges at home: protecting citizens from terrorist threats, coping with floods of migrants and refugees, dealing with the loss of manufacturing jobs, mitigating the risks arising from climate change, maintaining the European Union, and maintaining NATO as the bulwark against threats from a newly assertive Russia. Western governments also adjusted their priorities in part to reflect a popular mood of growing isolationism among their citizens. There is a growing feeling that, despite well-meaning international attempts to support democracy abroad, and the continued importance of democratic ideals, most of the programs done in this name may prove wasteful, inefficient, unappreciated, or even damaging.[22] In America, the public (especially Republicans) have increasingly favored nationalism and isolationism, according to the polls, where the United States focuses on its own problems with many wary of global humanitarian engagement.[23]

The Trump Era of American Foreign Policy

Democracy promotion therefore slowed under Obama. After the election of President Donald Trump, however, there are reasons to believe that, after a century, the Wilsonian commitment to America's leadership role in defending human rights and promoting democracy around the world is under serious threat of being swept away. The 2016 US Presidential election campaign highlighted a marked shift questioning America's continued engagement in the post–World War II foreign policy architecture, including within NATO, NAFTA, and the UN. In his campaign speeches, Trump criticized America's historical mission to promote democracy abroad, calling attempts to build democracy from Iraq to Egypt to Libya a dangerous mistake that has triggered instability and chaos.[24] Trump's rhetoric challenges basic principles of human rights and international law, such as the obligation to accept refugees fleeing from civil wars and to refrain from the use of torture. He praised authoritarian leaders abroad with a track record of repression, including Russia's Vladimir Putin, Turkey's Recep Tayyip Erdogan, the Philippines' Rodrigo Duterte, Saudi Atabia's King Salman, and Egypt's Abdel Fattah el-Sisi. Indeed, Trump continued to defend President Putin ("doing a great job") long after the US intelligence community concluded that Russian hacking and disinformation had threatened cybersecurity and spread disinformation during and after the 2016 elections. By contrast he has been tepid towards America's allies, like Angela Merkel, for example, hectoring NATO leaders about defense spending.

Populist authoritarians advocate abandoning attempts to expand democratic freedoms around the world in favor of a narrow transactional realism approach to allies and foes; in any relationship with another country, Trump asks not what advances values of freedom, democracy, and human rights, but what's in it for American interests, defined narrowly as jobs and security. His inaugural address was silent about the core values that have guided America's vision of its ideal leadership role in the world for more than a century by promoting freedom and democracy.[25] After Kennedy's inaugural speech, the concept of freedom has been key not only to the America's conception of itself but also to its view of the wider world and what the United States has tried to achieve in its global role.

Western Europe has fully embraced this commitment. Following President Trump's election, Angela Merkel, the de facto leader of Europe, said Germany looked forward to cooperating with America based on common values: "democracy, freedom and respect for the rule of law and the dignity of man."[26] After the first NATO meeting which Trump attended, however, Merkel's tone changed, and this ever-cautious leader commented to Europeans: "The times when we could completely rely on others are, to an extent, over."

Trump's bleak and dark inaugural address was silent about the value of protecting freedoms, democracy, and human rights; instead, he said, America would not "impose our way of life on anyone," while declaring "From this moment on, it's going to be America first. Every decision on trade, on taxes, on immigration, on foreign affairs, will be made to benefit American workers and American families."[27] Trump's "America First" rhetoric, his early diplomatic initiatives with world leaders, and the executive actions his administration has prioritized, signal a radical break from the past, which threatens the long-standing commitment of the West to defend and advance human rights, to provide development assistance to help poorer nations, to maintain security through the NATO alliance, to stand up against abuses by dictators, and to collaborate diplomatically with member states through the United Nations and the agencies of global governance. Instead, he has expressed willingness to lift sanctions imposed on Russia after their annexation of Crimea, to refuse Syrian refugees and ban Muslims in several countries from entry into the United States, he praised repressive strongman rulers, and he has signed the executive order to build a wall on the US-Mexican border. In speeches, he has disparaged African Americans, Mexican Americans, women, and people with disabilities.

So far Trump's foreign policies largely reflect the realist rhetoric, and it seems likely that the legitimacy of the postwar world order will come under strong challenge in the next few years. For example, in January 2017, several House Republicans proposed a bill terminating US membership of the United Nations. Trump's speeches reflect the principles of transactional realism guiding his philosophy of foreign affairs while his Secretary of State, Rex Tillerson, displays little awareness of the need for America to defend human rights. Time will tell how the State Department acts under the Trump administration, and how words translate into foreign policies. But as America has been one of the leading actors promoting democracy and human rights worldwide, Trump's rhetoric sends damaging diplomatic signals about America's priorities, downgrading the protection of human rights and liberal democracy abroad.[28] The foreign policies of the new administration are not yet clearly established but they are expected to accelerate a new reverse wave, indicated by declining numbers of democratic regimes around the world and the resurgence of authoritarianism, encouraging a newly assertive Russia.

Populist Threats to Western Liberal Democracies

The Trump presidency has also deepened widespread concerns about how well American democracy is performing at home and whether the future of liberal democracy is under serious threat from the spread of populist authoritarianism in Western countries. The 2016 Economist Intelligence Democracy Index reported that America slipped from a "full" to a "flawed" democracy in 2016, largely due to declining trust in political institutions. Evidence continues to be gathered and carefully sifted, but anxieties are reinforced by bitter party polarization over major policy issues, mass protests against the Trump inauguration mobilized across America (and in countries worldwide) on a scale never witnessed before in a single event, historically record-breaking low approval ratings of an incoming president, and eroding confidence in political institutions, especially Congress and the media.[29] During the campaign, and even after his victory in the Electoral College, President Trump repeatedly falsely alleged widespread electoral fraud involving "millions of people who voted illegally," launching an official investigation by the Justice Department. Despite the lack of any systematic evidence supporting these claims, the Trump administration's arguments help to justify longstanding efforts by Republican state lawmakers to suppress minority voters by purging voting rolls, imposing onerous identification requirements, and curtailing early voting.[30] The President's repeated claims have potentially damaging consequences for American faith and confidence in the legitimacy of their electoral process.[31] If public skepticism about the US government and politics is gradually curdling into deep cynicism, this can be expected to have a major impact, not least by further weakening levels of voting turnout and civic engagement, eroding feelings of political legitimacy, and undermining public perceptions of how well democracy works in America.

European societies are also now feared to be under serious threat of sliding into authoritarianism due to the populist challenge at home, and a crisis of legitimacy challenging the authority of the established institutions at the heart of liberal democracy. This includes an erosion of public confidence in established parties on the left and right, the belief that elected leaders and members of parliament are out of touch with ordinary people, lack of trust in information provided by traditional mass media, experts, scientists, and intellectuals, and a backlash against the European Union.[32] Populist authoritarianism is nothing new. On April 21, 2002, Jean-Marie Le Pen defeated France's socialist Prime Minister Lionel Jospin in the first round of the French presidential elections. That shocked Europe. One of the best-known radical right leaders, Le Pen dismissed the Holocaust as a "detail of history." All over France, millions of people protested at massive anti- National Front demonstrations. His mantle was taken up by his daughter Marine Le Pen, contesting the 2017 French presidential elections. She was defeated by Emmanuel Macron but she still managed to double her share of the second round vote. In the Netherlands, on May 6, 2002, Netherlands's flamboyant and controversial Pim Fortuyn was assassinated for his anti-immigrant and anti-Muslim views, leading to a sudden surge of support for his party in the general election. The anti-immigrant Lijst Pim Fortuyn, formed just three months before the election, suddenly became the second largest party in the Dutch parliament and part of the governing coalition. The populist leader inheriting this mantle in the Netherlands is Geert Wilders's Party for Freedom, who was prosecuted for hate speech against Muslims. His party failed to win the March 2017 parliamentary elections but still came second and increased its vote share.

Nor are these isolated occurrences. During the last two decades, parties led by populist authoritarian leaders have surged in popularity in many nations, gaining legislative seats, reaching ministerial office, and holding government power. Notable gains have been recorded by the Swiss People's Party, the Austrian Freedom Party, the Swedish Democrats, and the Danish People's Party. Both the center-left and center-right in Italy are concerned about the current popularity of Matteo Salvini's Northern League and the Five Star Movement. In Hungary, the success of the neofascist Jobbik party pushed the ruling Fidesz party even further to the right; Hungary's government built a wall against the waves of migrants flooding across Europe. It's not just Europe, either. Latin America has its radical populism, with charismatic leaders such as Hugo Chavez in Venezuela and Evo Morales in Bolivia. Some populist leaders and parties rise temporarily in opinion polls then plummet equally rapidly. In Britain, for example, the UK Independence Party won only a single seat in the May 2015 general election and they lost this in the following 2017 general election when their vote fell to 1.8 percent. But even flash parties can infect the political culture and mainstream parties; the UKIP fueled more rabid anti-European sentiments, and this was one of the main reasons Conservatives called the EU Brexit referendum. Populist authoritarian parties challenge the values and institutions at the heart of liberal democracy, including tolerance and respect for social diversity and minority rights, the benefits of open borders for trade, markets, labor, and cultural exchange, and the postwar architecture of global governance and international relations. If established liberal democracies are seen as less successful, this also erodes their attraction as role models to be emulated by other states.

The Critique of Democracy Promotion Among Scholars

Beyond political developments, the consensus in the previous research literature assessing international efforts at democracy promotion also suggest considerable grounds for caution about its effectiveness, at best, with some warning about negative side effects. Systematic evidence remains limited in this sector. Specific cases of success and failure can always be quoted. Implementing agencies commonly claim progress when reporting to executive boards and funders, but this is often based on selected case studies and soft evaluation techniques in specific projects, such as interviews with local stakeholders.[33] Aid spending in the sector on democracy, governance, and civil society grew rapidly in recent decades, as discussed in the next chapter, yet reliable evidence about its impact remains scarce and inconclusive. One reason for example, is that it is difficult to generalize from assessments of specific projects (building the capacity of women leaders in Burkina Faso, encouraging young people to participate in Ghanaian elections, training journalists in Cambodia) to judge the value of broader programs on democracy in diverse contexts. Annual reports from aid agencies typically provide bean-counting lists of activities (the number of workshops, the number of publications, the number of participants), but they commonly fail to address their outcomes and impacts. By contrast, academic research has typically focused on national indices, for example, analyzing whether amounts of foreign aid received by each country are correlated with subsequent improvements in levels of democracy and governance.[34] But, even if the findings of the econometric analysis are derived from technically well-specified, reliable, and robust models, this approach is far too broad-brushed to be useful in helping aid workers and managers to judge strategically what programs of electoral assistance work best in diverse cultures and contexts.

Much of the academic literature on aid effectiveness in the sector of democracy promotion and electoral assistance also suggests cautiously that, in most cases, researchers simply do not know enough to be able to provide useful practical advice for aid organizations with any degree of confidence. Experienced observers of this sector commonly emphasize that any impact from programs is complex to assess, contingent upon circumstances, and therefore it remains difficult, or even impossible, to provide any hard and fast conclusions. Hence, Thomas Carothers concludes that although the United States has spent several billion dollars on democracy assistance during the past two decades, nevertheless "surprisingly little is known about the actual effects of these efforts."[35] He believes that there are largely mixed results, as election aid has helped many elections go more smoothly and expanded respect for free and fair contests, but this cannot guarantee good outcomes. Observers of European efforts are similarly cautious; Peter Burnell asks whether international democracy promotion works, concluding that the answer is "Both yes ... and no ... and it all depends."[36] He suggests many reasons why it remains difficult to give more definitive answers about the impact of democracy assistance, including the challenges of determining the direction of causality given the complex interaction of multiple factors, the lack of measurable objectives, and inadequate capacity to gather and analyze suitable evidence.[37] One of the most thorough overviews by Krishna Kumar argues that policy evaluations in any sector are often hard but the situation of democracy assessments is even worse, since the intervention model for many programs remains questionable; it is difficult to assess outcomes and their long-term effects; and in many cases the political environment is not conducive to collecting necessary information.[38]

Other scholars have been more critical of the effectiveness of these aid efforts. Hence Sarah Sunn Bush notes that many democracy programs today provide short-term technical, material, and financial assistance, as well as project aid.[39] This has spurred the growth of training activities and NGOs that excel in organizing workshops and seminars, she argues, but these projects often prove unsustainable once aid is withdrawn. Bush concludes that American agencies such as USAID have increasingly pursued "tame" forms of democracy-assistance programs, seeking measurable but ultimately trivial results that can be reported to Congress, rather than confronting dictators with more aggressive policies that would threaten the survival of autocratic regimes.[40] Jeroen de Zeeuw believes that aid projects have been unable to build democratic institutions, especially for strengthening the state, security, and rule of law in the most challenging and volatile conditions of postconflict societies.[41] Lincoln Mitchell warns that the United States faces almost inevitable failure by providing democracy assistance programs in authoritarian states, such as Iraq and Afghanistan, that are fundamentally hostile to these reforms.[42] Flawed and unrealistic assumptions, he suggests, doom these attempts to founder. Moreover, although US foreign policy speeches often include reference to the rhetoric of democracy promotion and human rights, in practice other strategic priorities commonly prevail at the US State Department. Mitchell estimates that the annual budget for democracy promotion is only around 1 percent to 1.5 percent of the overall U.S. annual budget (or around US$1.6 to $3.4 billion per annum). The risks of democracy promotion are greatest following the unstable period of regime transitions from autocratic rule, as well as when this is attempted in some of the world's poorest societies and in fragile states such as South Sudan, Afghanistan, Haiti, and Libya. There are also grounds to believe that successful and effective institutional reforms are hard to achieve even in the relatively favorable conditions of affluent postindustrial societies and long-established democracies like the United States and Britain. Hence, for example, Bowler and Donovan caution that the impact of a range of reforms to electoral laws and voting regulations that have been implemented in Western democracies commonly fall well short of the promises of their proponents, with unintended consequences.[43]

Moreover, well-meaning attempts at supporting democratic transitions from autocracy, including by providing electoral assistance, carry the potentially risks of unintentionally worsening government stability, security risks, and conflict. Mansfield and Snyder argue that it is hazardous to hold competitive elections at an early stage of the transition from autocracy. They argue that transitional elections, which typically have weakly institutionalized party organizations and patterns of party competition, strengthen the incentives for vote-seeking politicians to play the "nationalist card," thereby heightening intercommunal ethnic tensions and the risks of civil war.[44] Naïve efforts by aid workers to support democratic elections in transitional regimes may thereby generate harmful side effects. For example, Brancati and Snyder predicted in 2011 that rushing to the polls within post-Gaddafi Libya would be a recipe for disaster in the atmosphere of ethnic conflict and anarchy, where real power remained in the hands of rival factions and armed rebels.[45] Similarly, others argue that presidential contests have deepened the culture of corruption in post-Taliban Afghanistan, as the spigot of Western aid encouraged practices of patronage politics.[46]

THE PRAGMATIC CASE FOR ELECTORAL ASSISTANCE

Therefore, during the last decade, the zeitgeist has gradually become far more skeptical about both the value and the effectiveness of international efforts at democracy promotion. The withdrawal from democracy promotion, which started under the Obama administration, has been sharply accelerated by the authoritarian values, nationalist xenophobia, and isolationist foreign policies unleashed by populist forces and leaders. Much of the scholarly literature echoes popular doubts.

But have efforts failed? To counter the prevailing skepticism, the pragmatic argument presented in this book, and the evidence which is scrutinized in successive chapters, suggests several reasons for providing technical assistance and external support designed to strengthen electoral institutions, processes and practices, as a central part of democracy promotion efforts. Electoral assistance involves the international community working with local stakeholders to strengthen the professional skills, operational knowledge, long-term capacity, and institutional structure of agencies engaged in this sector. Far from retreating from this enterprise, or shrinking aid in this sector, the international community supporting elections – involving cooperative networks of UN agencies, regional intergovernmental bodies, bilateral donors, and international nongovernmental organizations (NGOs) – has a responsibility to respond positively to local requests for electoral assistance, even in challenging and risky contexts. Electoral assistance designed to strengthen the efforts of domestic actors is a form of soft power that differs strategically from the coercive use of either military force or aid conditionality. The characteristics of soft power are its ability to attract and persuade, highlighting international cooperation, human rights ideals, and knowledge about best practices.[47] Electoral assistance can also be conceptualized as an important form of Western linkage, deepening the density of political ties and the cross-border flows of ideas connecting developing countries with multilateral networks.[48] The popular backlash against all forms of democracy promotion, and the sense that Western efforts are futile, has gone too far. Any retreat risks abandoning fragile democratic gains and deepening the revival of authoritarianism around the globe. Three distinct arguments can be made to justify international electoral assistance.

Normative Values

The *normative* right-based case for elections rests on recognizing the essential role of these institutions as the foundation for liberal democracy and fundamental freedoms. Amartya Sen presented one of the most influential contemporary arguments, where human development and security are conceptualized as intrinsically bound up in the pursuit of democratic freedoms.[49] The human rights argument reflects a long tradition of liberal thought. The international community endorsed these claims in Article 21 of the Universal Declaration of Human Rights (1948), where all citizens are recognized as having a fundamental right to participate in their own governance through elections: "The will of the people shall be the basis of the authority of government; this will shall be expressed in periodic and genuine elections which shall be by universal and equal suffrage and shall be held by secret vote or by equivalent free voting procedures." Human rights established in the International Covenant of Civil and Political Rights (1966) include fundamental freedoms of expression, association, and peaceful assembly, all essential underpinnings for competitive free and fair elections.[50] A long series of subsequent human rights treaties and international agreements among UN and regional intergovernmental organizations have strengthened and expanded these core principles.[51] Endorsing states have a duty to respect and ensure these rights and incorporate them into domestic laws. It is widely recognized that free and fair elections are vital for fundamental rights to self-determination, as well as an essential foundation, although far from sufficient, for legitimate, transparent, and accountable government. As human rights are universal, it is inappropriate to make pragmatic arguments that elections in fragile states need to be delayed "until the time is ripe" or conditions are "more favorable."[52] The normative case suggests that it is important for the international community to support requests for assistance from governments in nation-states and local actors seeking to advance the quality of elections in countries around the world, thereby advancing liberal values of democracy and freedom, while mitigating the risks of failure.

Instrumental Interests

The *instrumental* argument promotes democratic governance and provides electoral assistance on the grounds that these institutions further development goals, including prosperity, human welfare, and security.[53] This general perspective reflects the findings demonstrated in the first volume of the trilogy, indicating that electoral integrity has important consequences for public trust and confidence in the electoral process and institutions, support for democracy, civic engagement, and political stability.[54] By contrast, where citizens believe that widespread malpractices have occurred – whether falsely or correctly – then this corrodes citizens' trust in the electoral process, political parties, parliaments and governments, and confidence in democracy, depresses voter turnout and civic engagement, and thereby undermines channels of political representation.[55] In established democracies, minor malpractices can often be remedied through legal and administrative reforms to electoral institutions and voting procedures without undermining support for the regime or destabilizing the state. In more challenging contexts, however, such as in transitional regimes, divided societies emerging from conflict, and fragile states, simple minor flaws – or even major failures in elections – can have far more serious impact, by potentially fueling social instability, riots, and violence in contentious elections, undermining fragile gains in democratization, and triggering popular uprisings and intercommunal conflict seeking revolutionary change.[56] As the 2015 UN Secretary General's report summarized the instrumental argument:

> Both types of situations – those where there is real electoral fraud and those where fraud is merely alleged – can undermine electoral processes in a very fundamental way, as they erode confidence in the existing political system. This can lead to polarization, unrest, a breakdown of political dialogue and, possibly, the outbreak of violence. The credibility of an election is closely related to the extent to which (a) the democratic principles of universal suffrage and political equality and other international obligations are respected and (b) the election is professional, accurate, impartial and transparent in all stages of its administration.[57]

Instrument arguments emphasize that holding free and fair elections deepens the principles and procedures of liberal democracy, reinforce human rights, improving social welfare, and strengthen security.[58] As an essential mechanism for civic participation, elections link citizens with their leaders. Competitive contests check the egregious abuse of power and provide periodic opportunities to "throw the rascals out," if they fail to deliver, making leaders ultimately accountable to the people. Electoral outcomes facilitate peaceful and stable transfers of power, encourage losers to accept the will of the people, and crown winners with the legitimate mantle to govern through rule of law. Democratically elected governments have a better (though imperfect) track record at avoiding abuses of human rights and man-made humanitarian disasters; at minimum, they do not commit the worst acts of state repression and outrageous war crimes against their own people by using barrel-bombs, committing genocide, throwing opponents into jail, or censoring critical voices – and stay in power.[59] Where elections make officials more accountable to ordinary people, governments are more likely to deliver goods and services responsive to social needs. For example, Halperin, Siegle, and Weinstein argue that democratic processes deliver concrete benefits in developing societies by reducing poverty, building schools, and expanding longevity.[60] There remains room for debate about the evidence, but the general consensus in the research literature is that the average economic record of democracies is also generally equivalent to autocracies, no better, no worse.[61] The well-known "democratic peace" proposition maintains that democratic states have never, or rarely, fought each other. Bruce Russett suggests that this enduring phenomenon developed towards the end of the nineteenth century: "There are no clear-cut cases of sovereign stable democracies waging war with each other in the modern international system."[62] Democracies are also more likely to support multilateral cooperation through the agencies of global governance, respect for UN treaties and international law, and ties through trade, investment, and alliances.

The Pragmatic Argument

The arguments for democracy based on values and interests are important, as I have explored in depth elsewhere.[63] But even if acknowledged as important, the claims may still not prove persuasive among those skeptical about whether international efforts at democracy promotion and electoral assistance actually work. Successive chapters of this book present persuasive evidence for the pragmatic case that well-designed programs of technical electoral assistance can strengthen integrity. The positive impact of several common programs is exemplified by programs where: 1. international agencies promote gender equality norms, and share knowledge about the design of legal gender quotas to strengthen women's representation in elected office, 2. they provide policy advice about effective reforms to regulate campaign finance, and 3. they expand the technical capacity of electoral authorities to manage complex processes of voter registration and balloting.

But how do we know when interventions succeed? Is the glass half-full or half-empty? What benchmarks are available? Programs by international agencies can be judged against multiple goals by different actors. For example, aid organizations may be concerned with organizational efficiency and therefore whether their aid budgets provide value-for-money. Similarly, based on the techniques of results-based performance, project managers commonly regard their work as successful if they can report specific outcomes that are consistent with their organization's strategic plans and mission statement. Evaluations are also often seen as positive if a range of local stakeholders in recipient countries report that they were satisfied with the program, such as participants in capacity-building workshops.[64] Bilateral donors may judge their programs as effective if activities strengthen their country's interest, such as by furthering diplomatic ties, trade, and investment with recipient countries. These sorts of criteria can be valid and useful for judging organizational performance and bureaucratic efficiency, such as typically in the annual reports presented to executive oversight bodies. But these outcomes can each be met without necessarily forwarding the broader goal of advancing human rights and democratic governance.

By contrast, this book uses a chain-of-results framework (see in Figure 1.1). Chapter 3 outlines each stage in this sequential process in more detail, including the initial SWOT problem assessment matching the Strengths and Weaknesses of international agencies with the Threats and Opportunities for local interventions designed to improve elections in each country. Subsequent steps involve the definition of specific program goals and targets, the design of

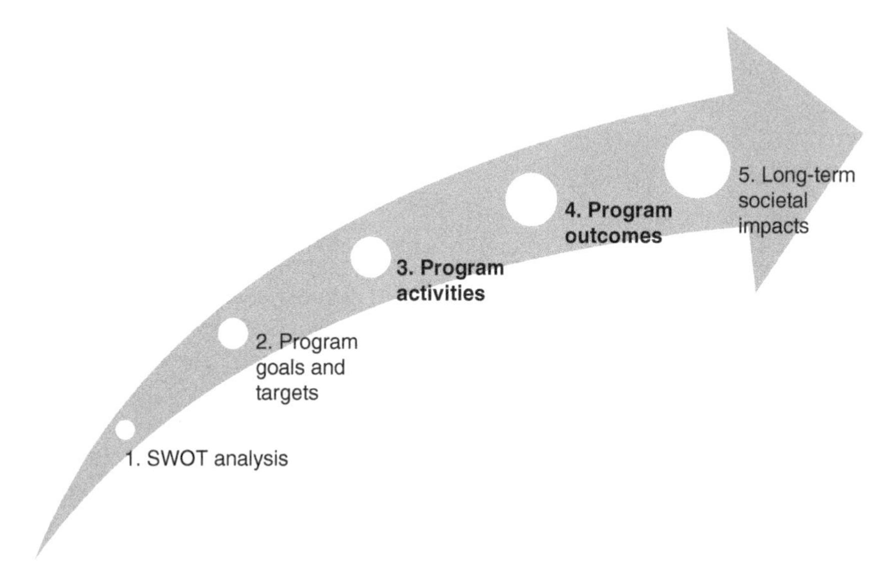

FIGURE 1.1. The chain-of-results framework for program evaluation.

program activities, the assessment of program outcomes, and the evaluation of their long-term and cumulative societal impacts. This book focuses primarily upon the middle stages of the framework, in steps 3 (program activities) and 4 (program outcomes), to evaluate whether there is systematic and credible evidence that international agencies implementing typical types of electoral assistance actually achieve specific positive outcomes that strengthen electoral integrity.

In turn, the concept of electoral integrity refers to how far contests meet international principles and global standards that have been established since the mid-twentieth century as the basis of international law, through endorsement by the world's governments in a series of written conventions, treaties, protocols, and guidelines. Countries have signed international and regional agreements and treaties. The aim of electoral assistance by the development community is to support partner countries in meeting their international commitments and obligations to which member states are committed by ratifying these agreements.[65] As recognized in the 2015 report by the UN Secretary General, endorsed by the UN General Assembly:

> The notion of integrity in elections – referring to adherence to international obligations and commitments – and to professionalism, impartiality, accuracy and transparency in electoral administration – has developed into an important and useful reference point in electoral administration. The United Nations continues to encourage and support the efforts of Member States to promote electoral integrity by complying with their international commitment, including, as relevant, those set out in the Universal Declaration of Human rights, the International Covenant on Civil and Political Rights,

and the Convention on the Elimination of All Forms of Discrimination against Woman."[66]

The key normative principles are derived from international law and recognized by the UN and its member states. In practice, electoral assistance programs should also ideally seek to meet the principles of sustainability, national ownership, cost-effectiveness, and transparency. In the past, short-term technical assistance projects used to focus traditionally upon temporary solutions to problems occurring at the ballot box and count, such as impersonation, ballot-stuffing, and vote-buying, where elections are treated as discrete events.[67]

By contrast, the broader concept of electoral integrity, which has been widely accepted today, emphasizes that universal standards need to be upheld and support provided not just on polling day but throughout all stages throughout the whole electoral cycle, including during the preelectoral period, the campaign, on polling day, and in its aftermath. Thus, ineffective and incompetent electoral management bodies, lack of equitable access to campaign money and media, and inaccurate or incomplete electoral registers can all undermine the quality of contests as much as any intentional acts of ballot-stuffing, fraudulent counts, or vote-buying on polling day. The principles of sustainability and national-ownership mean that ideally the international community should support local requests for institutional capacity development so that development aid and international assistance gradually become redundant. Programs should also be cost-effective, to maximize the use of scarce human, financial, and technological aid resources. Much of the work providing electoral assistance is focused upon building strong, independent, and professional electoral management bodies, with the capacity to organize credible and legitimate elections. This typically involves external support to processes of electoral administration, procurements, budgets, and planning, voter registration, civic education, drafting electoral laws and regulations, training officials, compilation of the results, and similar tasks. Multiple actors are engaged in elections, and support is also provided to strengthen diverse civil society groups, the news media, political parties, the security forces, and judiciary.

The pragmatic case becomes more plausible from evidence-based evaluations. Overreliance upon rule-of-thumb, past experience, and anecdotal evidence without assessing the results may lead aid agencies to continue with unworkable programs, as Carothers charges, wasting limited resources and thereby failing in their overall mission.[68] Robust, independent evaluation of development programs seeks to inform donors, development officials, and local stakeholders about what works, what does not, and why. Learning can improve the effectiveness of aid, stimulate innovation, and hold actors accountable for results. Anticipating programmatic weaknesses, and what can be done about these, is also essential to mitigate risks of failure.

At the same time, a cautious interpretation of the pragmatic case for electoral assistance is needed before claiming that these efforts consistently achieve their broader goals. The available evidence does not suggest a black-and-white picture of inevitable progress towards achieving more democratic contests. Assistance does not strengthen electoral integrity equally well in every country – nor with every type of agency and program. Successful intercessions are analyzed in this study, using the well-known SWOT matrix, explained further in Chapter 3. The positive impact of electoral assistance programs is understood to be conditioned by both the external Opportunities and Threats that elections face at societal-level, as well as by the internal Strengths and Weaknesses of the agencies and the types of programs that are implemented.

Therefore, genuine room remains for debate about the effectiveness of international efforts in all sectors of development. The contemporary zeitgeist in the United States and Europe suggests that the West should retreat from failed efforts at electoral assistance and democracy promotion abroad and instead seek to fix their own ills at home. This mood has been reinforced by indications that the last decade has seen the emergence of dangerous new threats to Western democracy at home – with populist leaders mobilizing discontent about social inequality and migration flows, evidence of widespread civic disengagement through conventional channels of participation, and disaffection with parties, parliaments and governments. Pervasive doubts reinforce the view that development agencies should readjust their priorities by tackling other urgent problems around the world which are thought to be more amenable to aid investment and practical technical assistance – building schools, clinics, and roads, improving crops to eradicate hunger, fighting tropical diseases, resettling migrants, and confronting climate change. Nevertheless, the core argument and evidence presented in this book suggest that effective programs can indeed improve electoral integrity and thus the quality of democratic governance – while also acknowledging that aid agencies need to be more strategic and coherent to make interventions work better.

THE PLAN OF THE BOOK

To understand these issues, this study builds upon the earlier books in this trilogy, which laid the foundation for understanding the phenomena of electoral integrity.[69] The first volume analyzed the consequences of problems of electoral integrity for public confidence in representative institutions, for civic engagement and voter turnout, and for democratic legitimacy and processes of regime change. The second book used worldwide comparisons to identify general reasons why elections are flawed or fail to meet international standards, comparing explanations based on structural constraints, international forces, institutional checks, and electoral management. Using this underpinning, this final volume takes the next logical step by confronting the final and most complex issue – what works – blending insights from diverse types of evidence to evaluate the impact of some of the international community's most common types of electoral assistance.

Chapter 2 clarifies the core concept and documents the international market for electoral assistance. The first section suggests several factors on the demand side leading towards the growth of local requests for support, as countries struggle to expand the resources and technical capacity needed to manage elections and avoid contentious and flawed contests. The second section describes the supply-side provision of assistance involving a complex network of multilateral organizations, bilateral donors and NGOs, fulfilling different roles. The chapter documents how activities by donors expanded substantially since the early 1990s as this sector moved from the margin to the mainstream of foreign aid. One important indicator is that as a proportion of all Overseas Development Assistance (ODA) spending, the amount devoted to this sector tripled from around 4 percent to 12 percent during the last decade. Today around $20 billion a year in ODA is invested in electoral assistance. The third section presents a summary overview and typology of what programs are typically used to strengthen electoral integrity. It identifies the main types of policy options and strategies most commonly used in this sector, including the sequential process of advocating reform of legal regulations, capacity building for implementing agencies, monitoring performance, and strengthening accountability and oversight mechanisms.

Chapter 3 considers the challenges of program evaluation. The first section expands upon the reasons why it is important to establish better evidence that could help to evaluate the impact of programs of electoral assistance. It is particularly important to assess the impact and outcome of this spending at a time of increased pushback by authoritarian regimes and growing doubts about democracy promotion efforts among Western donors and publics. The argument suggests several reasons why evaluation is useful, such as the way that this process can better inform choices by development agencies about alternative policy options; provide donors with evidence of aid effectiveness, improve transparency, feedback, and accountability to oversight agencies, and promote organizational learning among program managers. The chapter describes the chain-of-results methods for policy evaluation used in this study.

The second section describes the sequential process used in the book for analyzing impact effectiveness in subsequent chapters. The chain-of-results logic is a heuristic model that involves five stages. The first involves problem assessment. This book adopts the standard SWOT model, which seeks to identify the key threats and opportunities facing elections in any country context, as well as the strengths and weaknesses of agencies and electoral assistance programs seeking to overcome these problems. In particular, drawing upon the previous volume in the trilogy, the study theorizes that elections commonly face challenges arising from a combination of structural constraints, weak international linkages, the inappropriate design of political institutions, and lack of capacity by electoral agencies. It is essential to identify the opportunities and threats which program managers, NGOs, and aid workers face in attempts to support elections in any particular country. The third section describes the methods and evidence useful in the SWOT matrix program evaluations.

Chapter 4 describes the diagnosis process used to assess the threats and opportunities facing elections in any context, the first needs-assessment and problem-definition stage of the policy analysis process. What criteria are available to define flawed and failed elections? What benchmarks and evidence are available? How can success be measured in this contentious arena? The first section explains the methods and primary sources of evidence used to evaluate the strengths and weaknesses of national elections in this study. For cross-national comparisons, the book draws upon the Perceptions of Electoral Integrity index (PEI-4.5), based on an expert survey, providing detailed evidence about the quality of elections and diagnosing particular malpractices at national and election levels. Other macrolevel indicators are drawn from official statistics and related sources, including datasets specially constructed for different chapters in the book. The second section presents the results of the PEI analysis, describing the threats and opportunities facing elections within societies around the globe, as well as identifying which type of emerging malpractices are most common.

THE IMPACT OF ELECTORAL ASSISTANCE PROGRAMS

Reforming Electoral Laws and Procedures

Building upon this foundation, subsequent chapters scrutinize evidence to establish the impact of specific types of agencies and programs seeking to overcome common problems and thereby strengthen electoral integrity. Chapter 5 starts by considering reforms to the legal framework governing elections. These are often problematic, and there is a wealth of evidence that laws matter for how well elections work. But how can the international community encourage member states to implement effective legal reforms? The chapter seeks to understand the role and impact of regional organizations in this regard, such as programs on electoral assistance offered by the Organization of American States (OAS), the European Union, the Organization for Security and Cooperation in Europe, and the African Union. These organizations typically collaborate with member states to strengthen electoral integrity through three main types of activities: serving as watchdogs monitoring elections; advocating human rights through establishing agreement over standards and norms; and providing policy advice through technical advice and cooperation.[70] Election monitors observe elections, focusing upon the campaign and polling day, and then publish their evaluation reports and issue press releases immediately after the declaration of the results. Since 1962, for example, the Organization of American States has monitored over 200 elections in more than thirty countries, deploying more than 5,000 international observers. The monitoring reports provide a retrospective evaluation of the quality of elections, with the aim of highlighting malpractices and thereby deterring the potential abuse of power. Studies using observational and experimental data have examined whether the deployment of international observers deters flaws and malpractices in local polling stations and the count, such as acts of ballot stuffing, fraudulent tallies, maladministration of voter registers, and voter impersonation.[71]

Nevertheless, the broader impact of international agencies as policy advisors remains less clearly established, especially the role of recommendations for legal and administrative reforms published in the observer reports. Many major malpractices arise throughout the electoral cycle, not simply on election day in polling places and the count. Monitors commonly suggest a range of procedural improvements to address these issues, such as recommending improvements to strengthen the accuracy of voter registries, the independence of election management bodies, the adoption of gender quotas, and the regulation of campaign finance. Reports may recommend occasional wholesale reforms to electoral systems, but more commonly this process involves suggesting a series of minor technical amendments.

The question arising from these activities concerns the effectiveness of the recommendations published in observer reports. Ideally, if the monitors achieve their goals, following publication, electoral authorities and parliaments will seek to revise the legal framework and the administrative procedures used for regulating elections in line with the recommended advice. In long-standing democracies, electoral systems used to be regarded as fairly stable institutions, which experienced only occasional minor adjustments, such as amendments to the basic electoral formula used for translating votes into seats or adjustments to district magnitude.[72] In recent years, however, a range of minor and major reforms to electoral systems and processes have become more common.[73] For example, Colomer's study of electoral systems in 94 democracies since the early nineteenth century monitored no fewer than 82 major changes in the electoral system used for legislative contests (for example from majoritarian to mixed or from mixed to proportional formula).[74] Golder compared 125 countries that had held democratic elections from 1946 to 2000, concluding that more than half experienced a significant change in their electoral system during these years, measured by either shifts in district magnitude or assembly size of 20 percent of more, the introduction of presidential direct elections, alterations to electoral tiers or electoral formula, or the breakdown or reintroduction of democratic regimes.[75] To examine the role of observer organizations in this process, this chapter analyzes new evidence concerning the contents of over 1,000 recommendations made by the OAS during 1999–2015 covering 71 national elections in 25 countries. The recommendations are compared against the record of subsequent changes implemented through electoral laws and procedures in these states.

Inclusive Representation: Quotas, Women, and Minorities

Chapter 6 examines the related issue of the international community's role in promoting gender equality and women's empowerment in elected office, especially through the diffusion of awareness about quota policies, and which designs work most effectively for inclusive representation. The international community has sought to strengthen social inclusion in elected and appointed offices, including measures designed to bring about gender equality and the representation of women in parliaments.[76] This issue has become a global norm endorsed by international organizations and national governments around the world. Since the world community met in Beijing in 1995, the proportion of women in the lower house of national legislatures has doubled (from around 10 percent in 1995 to 22 percent in 2016), an unprecedented leap, although far from parity.[77] Many policies can affect how social inclusion, through strengthening constitutional rights, reforming electoral systems, establishing legal gender quotas and reserved seats, reforming internal party recruitment procedures and rules, expanding the skills and resources of candidates in the pipeline for elected office, and revising parliamentary procedures. *The Gender Quota Database* (GQD-1.0) is used in this chapter to analyze patterns of quota adoption and revision around the globe from 1990 to 2014.[78] In countries as diverse as New Zealand, India, and Lebanon, the rights of ethnic minorities are also recognized through reserved seats and similar measures.[79] Based on cross-national evidence, as well as selected case studies of quota reform, this chapter will assess the effectiveness of these strategies and under what conditions they work for generating more socially inclusive and diverse parliaments for both women and ethnic minorities.

Independent Media

Turning to the campaign stage of the electoral cycle, the previous volume in the trilogy demonstrated that among all types of political institutions, the independent media plays a major role in helping to safeguard electoral integrity.[80] This confirms findings observed in other studies.[81] Chapter 7 seeks to examine the diverse roles of the news media in campaign communications. Ideally as *watchdogs*, the independent news media helps to guard the public interest, ensuring the accountability of electoral officials by highlighting cases of malfeasance, misadministration, or corruption, thereby strengthening the transparency and effectiveness of electoral governance.[82] As *agenda setters*, the news media highlights issues in any contest, informing citizens and representatives, thereby strengthening policy responsiveness. As *gatekeepers*, the news media seeks to reflect and incorporate the plurality of viewpoints and political persuasions in reporting the campaign, to maximize the diversity of political perspectives and arguments heard in campaign debates, and to enrich the public sphere.

Many NGOs and international organizations, such as UNESCO, the Soros Foundation's Open Society Institute, and the Knight Foundation, seek to strengthen the roles of the independent news media in their electoral coverage, most commonly through providing capacity building and technical assistance for journalists, as well as thorough recommending legal reforms to the regulatory environment governing freedom of expression and access to information, supporting media-watch NGOs, and expanding the use of social media technologies in developing countries. Most evaluations of media assistance have been very simple assessments of the short-term outputs of activities. For example, a series of workshops are typically assessed by project staff counting the number of journalist trained, or by consultants using a simple standard checklist to measure satisfaction among participants after these events. The results are commonly used for donor reports or to satisfy the agencies' standard accountability systems, but it is not clear that this formal process achieves rigorous evidence or in-depth insights that could be used to improve future activities.[83] This chapter therefore analyzes PEI cross-national evidence and a large-scale survey of journalists in over 60 countries to identify the most effective programs and policy interventions that strengthen the roles of the independent media during election campaigns.

Regulating Campaign Finance

Chapter 8 considers the most effective strategies for regulating political finance. Money is essential for electoral politics yet regulating its appropriate use raises complex and controversial challenges in countries around the world. Affluent societies and long-established democracies have been sporadically rocked by major problems of financial malfeasance, exemplified by the "Recruit" scandal in Japan, the misuse of "Westminster expenses" in Britain, and "Watergate" in the United States. Problems of graft, corruption, and cronyism have also commonly plagued many emerging economies, including those of India, Russia, Brazil, South Africa, and Indonesia.[84] To understand policies addressing these problems, the study identifies four main categories of regulation, which can be employed singly or in combination – including disclosure requirements, contribution limits, spending caps, and public subsidies – each with several subtypes. These policies are measured across nations using an integrated political finance regulation scale, derived from the International IDEA database on political finance, ranging from the most laissez-faire policies to those involving the highest degree of state regulation.[85] The chapter then tests the impact of this measure and the types of policies employed on public perceptions of electoral corruption derived from the 6th wave of the World Values Survey, as well as on expert assessments of Perceptions of Electoral Integrity. Case studies also describe and evaluate specific projects designed to curb the abuse of money in politics in several countries.

Voter Registration: Convenience Versus Security

Finally, it is also important to consider the act of voting and its aftermath, where many irregularities can occur. Chapter 9 examines the process of registering voters and trade-off values between the introduction of "convenience" ballots, designed to maximize citizen participation, and the potential risks for security that easier procedures entail. Recent decades have seen widespread concern in many established democracies about either persistently low or declining voter turnout since the 1980s.[86] Election management bodies have sought to address this problem through introducing a variety of forms of "convenience voting," which are designed to make registration and balloting easier. This includes the use of vote-by-mail or postal ballots, absentee ballots, in-person early voting, and proxy voting.[87] The role of new information and communication technologies, particularly the opportunities this generates for remote internet voting and registration, has aroused considerable interest. Registration and voting procedures for overseas citizens, and more accessible facilities for the disabled, have also received growing attention.

The spread of convenience voting has also raised concern, however, about potential security risks, thereby weakening public confidence in the electoral process and authorities. In addition, studies that have examined the effects of the use of different forms of convenience balloting have often reported only a modest boost to overall levels of political participation.[88] One reason is that these facilities are often most likely to be used by engaged citizens, but this does not necessarily serve to close any social gaps in turnout arising from age, socioeconomic status, education, ethnicity, or sex. Indeed some scholars report that in the US, such facilities may have the perverse effect of exacerbating socioeconomic inequalities in voting participation.[89] The effects of different types of reforms have also been found to vary. For example, studies report that in the United States early voting tends to depress turnout, while by contrast election-day registration has a positive effect.[90]

One way to examine these issues is to compare recent changes to electoral laws and procedures in US states when they have adopted either more lenient or stricter electoral procedures. What have been the consequences of implementing these laws? Heated partisan debate surrounds whether these reforms have either heightened the risks of voter suppression or opportunities for voter fraud. To consider new evidence, the chapter studies variations in the logistical costs of registration and balloting in state laws to generate the most appropriate within-country comparison. After setting out the conceptual and theoretical framework the chapter describes the evidence from an expert survey of Perceptions of Electoral Integrity conducted in 21 US states immediately after the 2014 US Congressional elections (PEI-US-2014). This data is combined with a new Convenience Election Laws Index (CEL) summarizing variations in the leniency of state laws for registering and voting. Multilevel (HLM) analysis is used to compare the state-level CEL index against expert evaluations of the integrity of the registration and voting process. The conclusion draws together the major findings and considers their broader implications.

Conclusions: Lessons Learned

Finally, Chapter 10 recapitulates the overall theoretical argument, summarizes the main findings concerning the core propositions, and considers practical policy recommendations that should be advanced to make electoral integrity work better. In general, previous accounts by scholars and practitioners remain divided in their assessments of the practical effectiveness of electoral assistance. There are several schools of thought debating these issues within the research literature and the policy community. By contrast to skeptics and critics, proponents commonly claim that programs in this sector have usually made a positive contribution towards strengthening electoral integrity and thereby met important development goals. The annual reports and evaluation studies published by the major development agencies engaged in this sector often claim the effectiveness of these initiatives, whether in terms of strengthening civic engagement and literacy, improving the capacity of electoral management bodies, or encouraging more inclusive and representative electoral processes. For example, many studies report that the international community's advocacy of women's rights and gender equality policies has encouraged the global diffusion of gender quota laws and the implementation of these policies has increased the number of women in elected office in many parts of the world.[91] The conclusion addresses the arguments of both critics and proponents of electoral assistance and summarizes the key findings and lessons from the evidence presented in this book. While there are major risks in the enterprise in many societies, this book contends that the skeptical conclusion that attempts at providing electoral assistance should be reduced or even abandoned would be unduly pessimistic. Instead, the pragmatic case argues that the international community needs to learn the lessons of what works best to strengthen electoral integrity, to focus activities and resources upon the most effective programs, and to innovate after a quarter-century of efforts to strengthen electoral integrity.

PART II

EVALUATING ELECTORAL ASSISTANCE

2

What Is Electoral Assistance?

To lay the foundations for the book, the first section clarifies the typical agencies and programs that fall under the area of electoral assistance. This subfield has become a rapidly growing part of foreign policies, development aid budgets, and democracy promotion activities. Studies commonly seek to understand the supply-side of democracy promotion from the perspective of Western donors, such as debating whether international and bilateral agencies providing assistance are motivated by the promotion of their ideological values or national interests.[1] By contrast, this chapter considers the global market for electoral assistance where the core stakeholders engaged in this sector can be loosely divided into the supply-side (multilateral agencies providing assistance) and also the demand-side (states requesting support). The first section documents trends in the demand-side of the equation, reflecting requests from countries for international electoral assistance from the UN. This phenomenon rapidly accelerated following the spread of competitive contests around the globe, despite the persistence of contentious outcomes following common flaws and failures to hold genuine and credible contests. The second section describes the roles of the main actors engaged in the supply-side of this sector, engaging cooperation among a complex network of UN agencies and bureaus, regional intergovernmental organizations, bilateral donors, and nongovernmental bodies. Turning to what types of activities are typically supported in this sector, The third section presents a typology of common programs in the field of electoral assistance. This includes encouraging legal and procedural institutional reforms, supporting individual and institutional capacity building, using forms of external monitoring, such as international observer missions and expert-based indices, and strengthening internal accountability and oversight mechanisms. This lays the foundations for the next chapter, which goes on to consider what methods and evidence are useful for evaluating the impact of electoral assistance.

THE CONCEPT OF ELECTORAL ASSISTANCE

What is electoral assistance? This sector concerns legal, operational, and logistical support offered by the international community to improve electoral laws, procedures, and institutions. Programs of electoral assistance typically address areas such as electoral administration, logistics, budgeting and planning; the review and reform of constitutional principles, electoral laws and regulations; boundary delimitation; voter registration; the electoral use of information and communication technologies; the training and capacity building of electoral officials and other stakeholders such as parties and the media; civic education, information, and engagement, especially the inclusion and participation of underrepresented groups such as women, young people, and ethnic minorities; the role of journalists and the news media; the regulation of political finance; the structure, organization, and funding of political parties; the role of the police and armed forces in providing electoral security and preventing conflict; processes of balloting and vote count facilities; and the role of the judiciary and intermediary bodies in dispute resolution processes.

The UN-Electoral Assistance Division (UNEAD) within the Department of Political Affairs, the core focal point for United Nations electoral support, highlights a related set of activities when defining the area:

> Technical assistance covers a wide range of short and long term expertise provided to national authorities in charge of administering elections in their country. Advice and support are provided in all sectors of electoral administration, and have expanded as experience has grown and as Member States' requests have become more sophisticated and specific. Technical assistance can be provided in areas such as electoral administration and planning, review of electoral laws and regulations, electoral dispute resolution, boundary delimitation, voter registration, election budgeting, logistics, procurement of election materials, use of technologies, training of election officials, voter and civic education, voting and counting operations, election security and coordination of international donor assistance.[2]

Similarly, the EU offers an equivalent definition when describing the subfield:

> Electoral assistance may be defined as the technical or material support given to the electoral process. It may imply support to establish a legal framework for the elections. It may also take the form of a general input to the national electoral body, such as providing voting material and equipment, or helping in the registration of political parties and candidates and the registration of voters. It may also imply support to NGOs and civil society in areas such as voter and civic education or training of domestic observers, as well as support to media monitoring and training of journalists.[3]

Electoral assistance is provided by international agencies as a subcategory of foreign aid programs in the sector on democracy, human rights and governance. The organizational framework and thematic priorities vary across agencies, however; for example, USAID, which administers most American democracy assistance, targets work on the rule of law and human rights, competitive elections and political processes, civil society and accountable governance. In many international organizations, electoral assistance usually works in conjunction with closely related programs that focus upon bolstering the rule of law, access to justice, and human rights, building effective political institutions such as parliaments, courts, and decentralized governments, strengthening civil society, and improving transparent and accountable processes of governance and public administration.

From the perspective of international relations scholars, this overall strategy focuses upon external agencies generating positive incentives ("carrots") designed to improve the quality of elections within countries. This can be conceptualized as a form of "soft power," reflecting the ability of external agencies to attract and co-opt rather than to influence states by the use of coercion.[4] Soft power is particularly useful for issues requiring multilateral cooperation among states. Electoral assistance thereby supplements the alternative mechanisms commonly used by the international community, regional organizations, and the foreign policies of bilateral donors to encourage states to comply with international standards. These techniques include the enforcement ("sticks") mechanisms of election monitoring (where observers seek to deter and highlight any electoral malpractices); aid conditionality (where strings are attached before or after the provision of benefits such as loans, debt relief, or aid); economic sanctions (involving various forms of trade barriers, tariffs, embargoes, and restrictions on financial transactions); diplomatic mediation (especially interventions seeking to resolve cases of postelection conflict); and the deployment of peacekeepers or the use of military force.[5] For example, after the historic May 2016 elections in Myanmar, trade sanctions were partially lifted. By contrast, the following month the UN Security Council voted to renew sanctions against the Democratic Republic of Congo to pressure the regime to hold scheduled elections by the end of the year, following the arrest of opposition leaders and fears that President Joseph Kabila was trying to cling to power.[6]

In the useful conceptual distinction made by Levitsky and Way, electoral assistance can be regarded as a form of Western "*linkage*" (strengthening cross-border ties of interdependence connecting societies to Western democracies) rather than "*leverage*" (reflecting state vulnerabilities to external democratizing pressures).[7] From the perspective of developing countries, however, this process can be regarded as a way to request financial resources, technical know-how, and policy advice from the international community about the most effective ways to manage the large-scale and complex tasks of managing elections, especially in countries lacking experience, skills, and capacity to manage genuine and credible contests.

International assistance is typically supported by donors, and requested by states, because in the ideal model, when elections work well, they can potentially fulfill multiple functions.[8] Elections are not sufficient for liberal democracy – but they are essential. Competitive contests provide opportunities for voters to select parties and leaders. The electoral process helps to determine priorities on the policy agenda. Elections link citizens (as principals) with representatives (as agents), and thereby confer the mantle and authority of democratic legitimacy on elected officials. Contests hold leaders periodically to account for their decision and actions, strengthening government transparency and facilitating orderly processes of elite succession. They also provide the main opportunity for most ordinary citizens to have a voice in politics as the primary avenue of public participation. In the ideal model of competitive multiparty elections, political parties seek to mobilize popular support by appeals based on their positions on alternative policy issues, their core ideological values, and their past record in government and opposition, as well as the background, social identities, and experience of their leaders and candidates. In theory, popular preferences expressed in ballot choices are translated through the electoral system into the selection of officeholders – helping to reinforce responsive and accountable democratic governance.

In practice, however, it is well established that multiple problems commonly undermine the electoral process.[9] Malpractices are not simply confined to intentional techniques of ballot stuffing, vote-buying, threats, or fraud in polling places and the count – shortfalls can occur throughout the whole electoral cycle. In many countries, as Chapter 4 demonstrates, the expression of free electoral choices is severely limited by laws restricting opposition parties and candidates. Rival leaders are imprisoned. Voting rights are suppressed. Electoral registers are inaccurate. Incumbents dominate the airwaves. Free speech is muzzled. Thugs threaten voters. Campaigns are awash with money. Ballot-stuffing fakes the count. Electoral officials favor the government. Dispute resolution mechanisms are broken. These types of irregularities matter. Rigged elections reinforce the legitimacy of corrupt and repressive leaders, solidifying their hold on power. Electoral malpractices directly violate human rights, restricting choices, and distorting the translation of popular votes into seats. Problems also indirectly deepen public mistrust of electoral authorities, political parties, and parliaments. This in turn affects citizen behavior by depressing voter turnout and catalyzing protest activism.[10] Since elections are the heart of the representative process, flawed contests have the capacity to damage competition, democratic governance, and responsive and accountable parties.[11] When elections go well, they may have limited power to rebuild trust and intercommunal tolerance in deeply divided societies emerging from conflict. When they go wrong, however, then there easily can be disastrous consequences for peace and prosperity, as illustrated by diverse cases of hybrid regimes (in the middle ground as neither full democracies nor autocracies) exemplified by the cases of Kenya, Ukraine, and Thailand, all of which saw violence, instability, and the repression of democracy and human rights after recent contentious elections.

Electoral assistance programs typically seek to mitigate or eradicate malpractices by providing positive inducements to improve elections, including where development agencies support local actors with technical support and knowledge exchange, capacity building, and training, and the provision of financial aid and material resources. In earlier decades, assistance programs traditionally used to focus on short-term activities focused upon balloting on polling day and the vote count. This led to the dangers of trying to support rushed elections in volatile crisis contexts, where officials lacked administrative capacity and experience, without adequate planning and preparation for complex logistical tasks such as preparing accurate electoral registers and mobilizing citizens through civic education, and with bottlenecks, waste, and inefficiencies arising from the sudden influx of development aid.[12] Since 2005, however, reflecting a broader understanding of how contests fail and recognizing the need to build sustainable, long-term processes, programs commonly address problems occurring throughout all stages of the election cycle, including during the preelection period, the campaign, on polling day, and its aftermath.[13] This sequential process can be further subdivided into eleven sequential steps, as illustrated in Figure 2.1. Programs focus upon each stage, for example by strengthening the design of electoral laws and

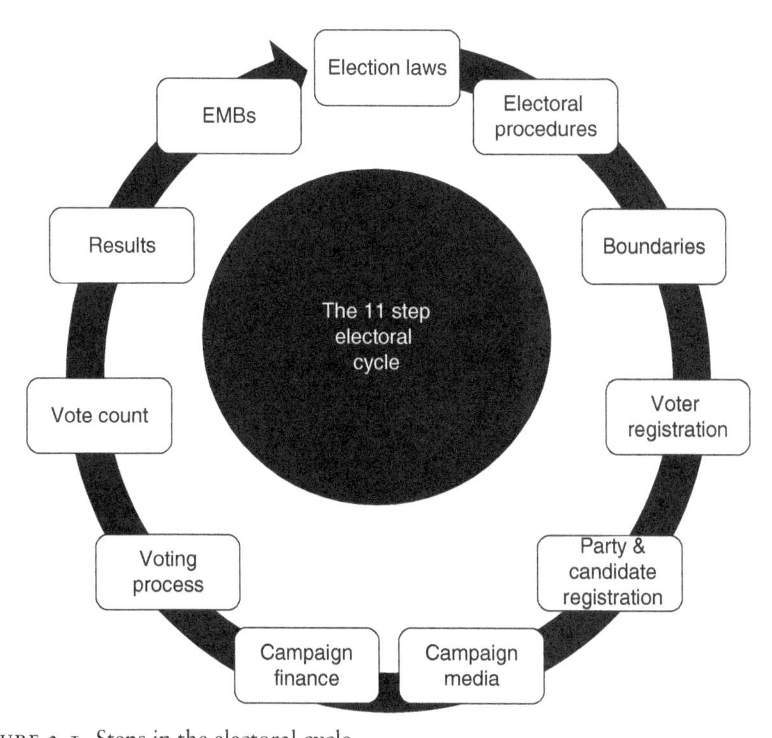

FIGURE 2.1. Steps in the electoral cycle.

administrative regulations; the procedures used for redistricting of constituency boundaries; the registration of parties, candidates, and voters; the regulations governing equitable access to campaign media and political finance; the procedures used for balloting, tabulation, and the announcement of the results; as well as the overarching role of official bodies administering the electoral process.

The sector of electoral assistance expanded rapidly since the early 1990s, spreading from a specialized niche concerning a limited number of international organizations into a substantial, well-institutionalized mainstream domain of electoral assistance and development aid that affected almost every corner of the globe by the end of the 20th century.[14] During the first decades of the twenty-first century, this sector gradually moved from the margin to the mainstream of foreign aid.

THE DEMAND FOR ELECTORAL ASSISTANCE

What triggered these developments? The market for electoral assistance can be understood to reflect both the growing demand among member states as well as the supply of electoral assistance programs by the donor community within the broader context of changing global norms and international priorities.

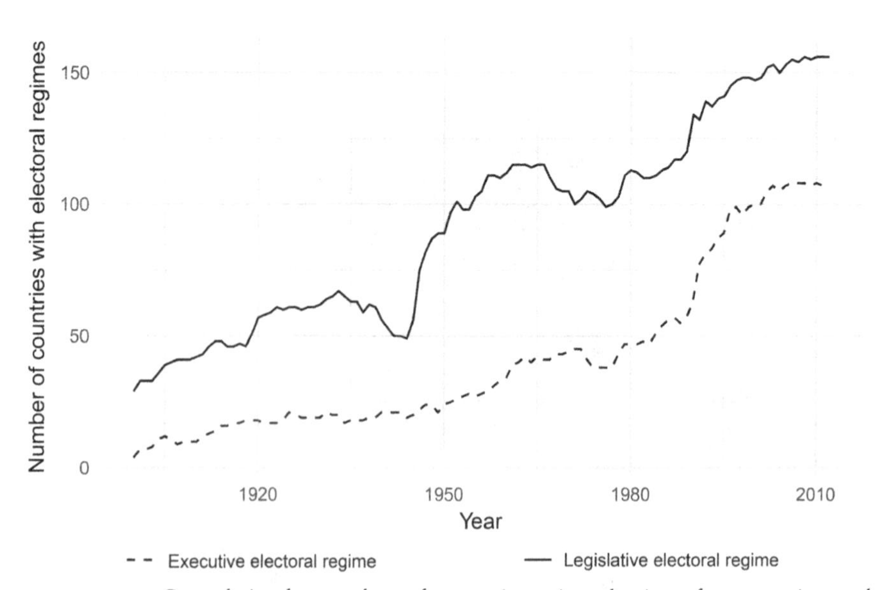

FIGURE 2.2. Growth in the number of countries using elections for executive and legislative office.
Source: Varieties of democracy (V-Dem) Version 6.2.

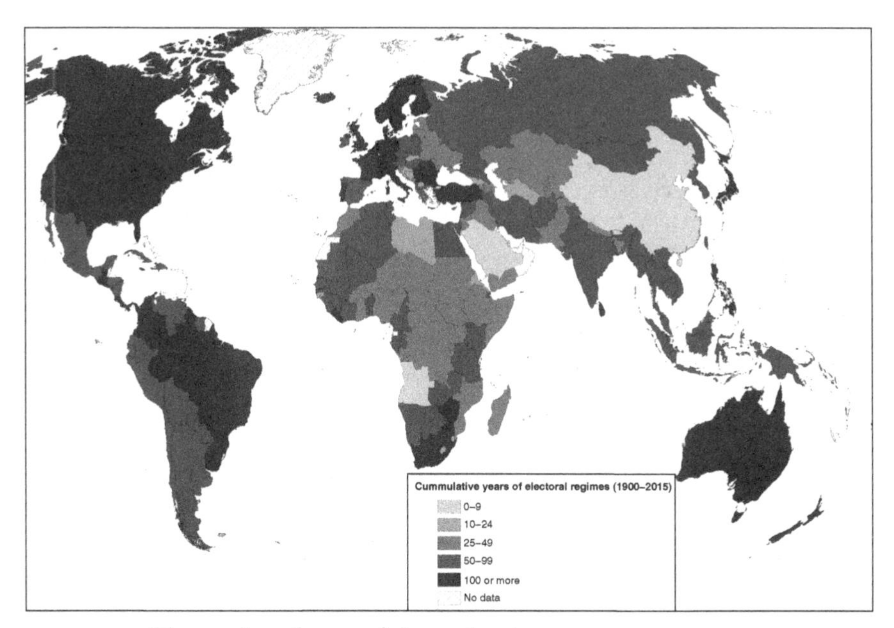

FIGURE 2.3. The number of years of electoral regimes.
Note: An electoral regime is defined as a country where there have been a regular series of annual elections, irrespective of their quality or degree of electoral competition.
Source: Varieties of democracy (V-Dem) Version 6.2.

The growth of elections, the core institutions at the heart of representative democracy, is the major development fueling the demand for electoral assistance. As illustrated by Figure 2.2, trends closely mirror the ideas and periodization of waves of democratization, identified by Samuel Huntington.[15] In the early twentieth century, elections were largely confined to the US, Western Europe, and several ex-British colonies. The first wave of democratization during the 1920s saw the gradual growth of elections for legislative office, but this trend was halted and then reversed by the aftermath of the Great Depression, economic dislocation, and the rise of fascism in the first reverse wave during the 1930s. By the end of the Second World War, as illustrated by Figure 2.3, around fifty independent nation-states had a popularly elected legislature with different degrees of party competition, but, with some notable exceptions, this excluded large swathes of the African continent, Asia, the Middle East, and most of Latin America.[16]

The second wave of democratization spreading legislative elections occurred from the end of WWII until the mid-1960s, when many newly independent nation-states in the Caribbean, Latin America, Asia, and sub-Saharan Africa adopted constitutions reflecting European parliamentary democracies, including multiparty contests. After the initial transition, these states were often destabilized by subsequent coup d'états or strongman presidential takeovers. The second reverse wave, from the mid-1960s to the mid-1970s, can be observed when many of these states saw the collapse of electoral institutions and their replacement by military juntas, personal dictatorships, and one-party states. As shown in Figure 2.3, the start of the "third wave" era in the mid-1970s saw democratic transitions in Mediterranean Europe and most of Latin America, and elections have spread to several states in Southeast and North Africa, as well as in Asia.

Today, by contrast, few parts of the world have remained untouched by the dramatic expansion in the use of direct elections for national office, with the aftermath of the fall of the Berlin Wall in 1989 triggering a further surge in multiparty contests in Central and Eastern Europe. The Arab Uprisings after President Zine El Abidine Ben Ali fled Tunis in January 2011 expanded the use of elections in the Middle East, although subsequent events in Egypt, Libya, Bahrain, and Syria saw further repression, where flawed elections were manipulated to legitimate authoritarian rulers. As a result of all these successive waves, out of 193 independent nation-states worldwide today, 95 percent (185) hold direct elections for the lower house of the national legislature.[17]

Several commentators have warned that recent years have seen a reversal underlying trends in democratization following a resurgence of authoritarianism.[18] If we compare the last decade, among states classified by Freedom House as democratic in 2005, the core institutions safeguarding political rights and civil liberties have not (yet) declined in Western states. Nevertheless by 2016 significant losses were registered in Mali (following the coup d'état), Hungary (under the new constitution brought in by Viktor Orbán's Fidesz government), Poland (under the Law and Justice party), the Dominican Republic (following restrictions on human rights), Mexico (destabilized by narco-crime), and Nauru (after restricting the judiciary and media).[19] Some of the worst backsliding during the last decade has happened in states classified in 2005 as hybrid regimes (or "partly free," using Freedom House's categorization), exemplified by Russia, Venezuela, Kenya, and Turkey. Hybrid regimes, in the grey zone of neither being full democracies nor absolute autocracies, are often the least stable politically, and at high risk of social conflict, with competitive elections but weak institutionalized checks and balances on executive power and poor-quality governance. But the last decade also saw some counter-balancing gains for democracy that do not always merit as much attention in international headlines, notably in Mongolia, Nepal, Bhutan, Tunisia, and Côte d'Ivoire. Elections have been suspended following reversals in several states, such as after the military coups in Thailand and in Egypt, but contests are commonly postponed rather than abandoned.

In recent decades, however, even where the quality of democracy has been eroded, around the world popular contests have become more widely used for executive office, and for directly elected assemblies at local, provincial, and supranational levels, plebiscites, and referendums. Figure 2.4 shows the number of years since 1900 for which countries can be classified as electoral regimes,

The world elections, 1944 (V-Dem)

The world elections, 1976 (V-Dem)

The world elections, 2012 (V-Dem)

FIGURE 2.4. The world of elections in 1944, 1976, and 2012.
Source: Varieties of democracy (V-Dem) Version 6.2.

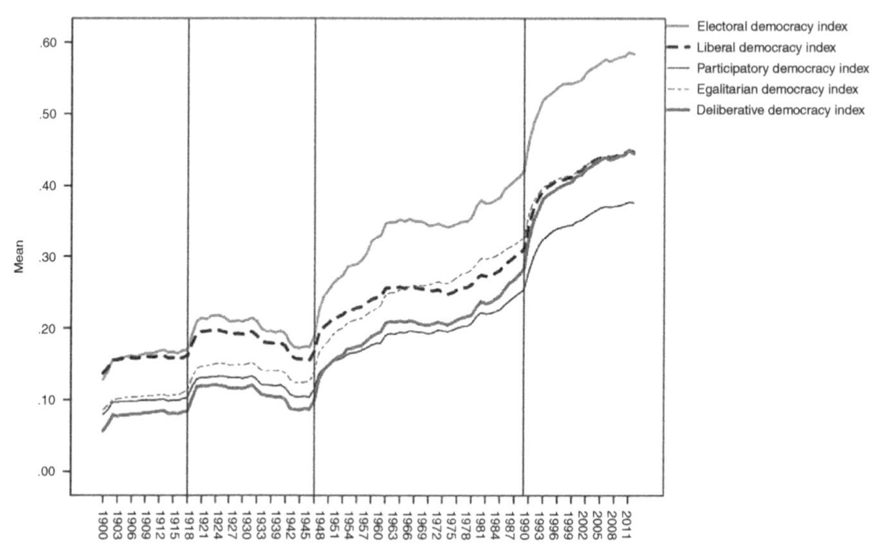

FIGURE 2.5. Trends in varieties of democracy, 1900–2014, V-Dem.
Note: For the components of each of the elements of the alternative models of democracy, and how these are measured, see the Varieties of Democracy Codebook Version 6 – Mar 2016.
Source: Varieties of democracy dataset, V6.

meaning that there have been a regular series of annual elections, irrespective of their quality or degree of electoral competition.

Waves of democratization around the world closely match the spread of elections. Annual indicators documenting these trends are provided by several leading organizations including the Varieties of Democracy project, Freedom House's *Freedom around the World*, Polity IV, and the Economist Intelligence Unit's Democracy Index.[20] The Varieties of Democracy project provides the most comprehensive time-series using expert judgments to construct cross-national trends in several conceptually distinct types of democracy since 1900, including electoral, liberal, participatory, egalitarian and deliberative democracies. The trends in the electoral democracy index in Figure 2.5 closely reflect the observed expansion in the use of elections, including the first wave of democracy evident after the end of the First World War, followed by a gradual erosion in the interwar years and the Great Depression. The aftermath of the Second World War saw the second wave of democratization, following decolonization in Africa and Asia and the growth of independent states, a process halted and reversed in the second reverse wave during the mid-1960s, as newly created constitutions and parliamentary institutions foundered under the assault of military-based strongman rulers. Finally, the third wave era saw an expansion in democratization, a process which greatly accelerated around 1989, before slowing to a more modest upwards trajectory.

Requests for Electoral Assistance

The spread of elections around the world generated more requests for international assistance and aid among UN member states. Which countries are most likely to ask for support? Demand can be illustrated by focusing upon the activities of the United Nations in this process. The UN Electoral Assistance Division (UN-EAD) functions as the official focal point within the UN system to receive requests from governments in member states or the mandate of the Security Council. Once requests are approved by UN-EAD, programs are subsequently implemented by a range of UN agencies, notably the United Nations Development Programme (UNDP), as well as UN-Women, UN Volunteers, and the UN Department of Peacekeepers. As discussed later in this chapter, numerous other international organizations and bilateral donors are involved in the provision of technical electoral assistance, so only a fraction of the demand is channeled through the UN. Inken van Borzyskowski documented the number of developing countries requesting and receiving technical electoral assistance from UN-EAD from 1990 to 2003.[21] Her data suggests that out of 130 developing countries, around 28 percent of member states requested technical assistance from the UN, with significantly stronger demand from poorer societies, postconflict states, and those low in

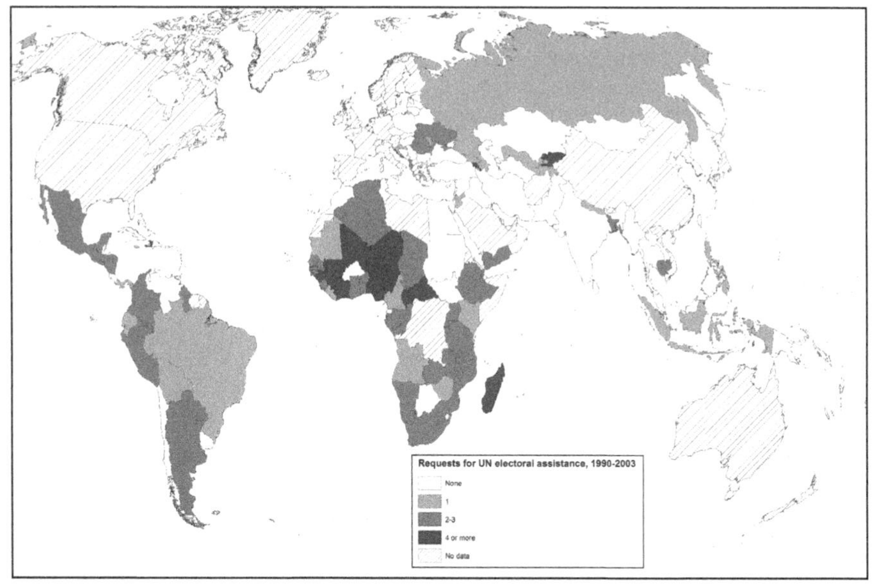

FIGURE 2.6. Requests for UN electoral assistance, 1990–2003.
Source: Data from Inken van Borzyskowski. 2016. "Resisting democracy assistance: Who seeks and receives technical election assistance?" *Review of International Organizations* 11(2): 247–282.

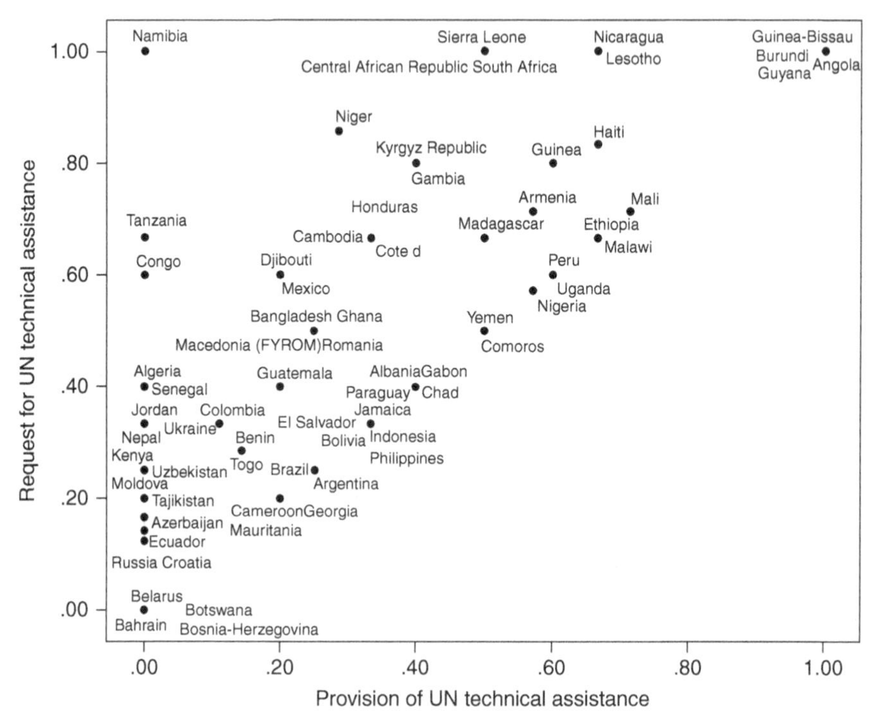

FIGURE 2.7. The supply and demand for UN electoral assistance, 1990–2003.
Source: Data from Inken van Borzyskowski. 2016. "Resisting democracy assistance: Who seeks and receives technical election assistance?" *Review of International Organizations* 11(2): 247–282.

administrative capacity. The global patterns for demand during the 1990s are illustrated in Figure 2.6. Many requests come from the poorest countries in West Africa, as well as from the Southern Cone of Africa, Latin America, and Asia.

To compare the demand for assistance with its supply, Figure 2.7 illustrates the links, with autocracies such as Russia, Belarus, and Azerbaijan making few or no requests from the UN and receiving little or no support. By contrast many of the poorest African states with a recent history of conflict, such as Burundi, Angola, and Guinea-Bissau, made multiple requests for assistance during this period, and they consistently received UN support. The overall estimates suggest that in total, about 18 percent of member states received UN assistance, with priority given to hybrid regimes and poorer developing states with little administrative capacity to manage these complex logistical operations.

WHO ARE THE CORE ACTORS SUPPLYING ASSISTANCE?

Several factors may have been important for shaping why international agencies responded to growing demand in this sector during the last quarter century. One possible explanation could be the evolution of international norms. However, the sequential timing of developments fits this account relatively poorly since the expansion of electoral assistance only started in the early 1990s as new opportunities arose during the third wave era, whereas the major conventions governing the framework of electoral rights were established decades earlier, including the 1948 Universal Declaration of Human Rights and the 1966 International Convention on Civil and Political Rights. It seems more likely that changes in foreign policies and developmental priorities among major Western donors, led by the United States, Scandinavia, and Western Europe, reflected a response to the new imperatives arising from transitions from authoritarianism and opportunities for democratization and diplomatic engagement following the collapse of the Soviet Union and the end of the Cold War, and the readjustment of security concerns and regional priorities following the events of 9/11. Neoconservatives in the George W. Bush administration coupled the aggressive expansion of free markets with the muscular promotion of democracy, regarding both as ways to advance both American values and security interests.[22] The mid-1990s also saw changing philosophies of development and growing recognition, championed by the World Bank, of the importance of strengthening accountable governance and fighting corruption to ensure the effective delivery of aid.[23]

United Nations Agencies and Bureaus

The way that international agencies responded to these new opportunities, and their diverse organizational strengths and weaknesses, can be illustrated. The United Nations has long been engaged in providing electoral assistance. The mandate for this work was first laid down in Article 21 in the 1948 Declaration of Human Rights and then reinforced by the 1966 International Covenant on Political and Social Rights and a long series of subsequent treaties and conventions. The UN's involvement with electoral activities began in earnest in the 1960s and 1970s, when the Trusteeship Council assisted with the observation or supervision of some thirty plebiscites, referenda, or elections in various regions of the world.

Early work was also pioneered by agencies such as Amnesty International (founded in 1961), US Agency for International Development (USAID, founded in 1961), Human Rights Watch (founded in 1978), the US National Endowment for Democracy (NED, founded in 1983), and several German political party organizations promoting democracy abroad, such as the Friedrich Ebert Foundation. Activities during this period emphasized monitoring human rights, electoral observation missions (exemplified by the activities of The Carter Center), and support for political parties and civil society organizations (such as by the National Democratic Institute and the National Republican Institute). In 1987 USAID established the International Foundation for Electoral Systems (IFES) to provide technical assistance.

The end of the Cold War in the late 1980s represented a critical tipping point in the number of UN member states with elected governments. Around this time the UN engaged in three types of major electoral missions – the organization and conduct of elections (such as through the United Nations Transitional Authority in Cambodia in 1993); the supervision and control of elections (such as in Namibia in 1989); and the verification of electoral processes (such as in El Salvador in 1994). These activities, along with rising demand from Member States for technical assistance by the UN, led to the introduction in December 1991 of a General Assembly (GA) Resolution 46/137 on "*Enhancing the Effectiveness of the Principle of Periodic and Genuine Elections.*" Since then, the UN has passed a series of biannual resolutions authorizing the role of the United Nations to respond to requests by member states for assistance in enhancing periodic and genuine elections and (since 1995) the promotion of democratization, while respecting principles of national sovereignty.[24] Since 1991, UN work in enhancing the effectiveness of elections has been coordinated by the United Nations Electoral Assistance Division (UNEAD). Electoral assistance is part of broader UN programs seeking to reinforce processes of democratic consolidation, expand civic participation, strengthen government accountability, and reduce sources of conflict in hybrid regimes.[25] During 2015 alone, for example, UNEAD estimated that they supported UN electoral assistance in 67 countries (roughly one-third of all member states), including Burundi, Nigeria, Afghanistan, the Central African Republic, Myanmar, and Papua New Guinea, involving in total expenditures of US$1.2 m.[26]

Further international endorsement came in 2000 with the UN Millennium Development Declaration, where world leaders resolved to "spare no effort to promote democracy and the rule of law."[27] In response to this mandate, agencies within the international community have sought to reinforce prospects for more open societies and effective governance by working with national stakeholders to deploy a wide range of initiatives in democratic governance. During recent decades, the donor community has supported programs designed to improve political institutions and processes, from elections, parliaments, and the judiciary to political parties, civil society groups, local governments, and public sector administration.[28] This includes a range of initiatives seeking to improve the quality of elections, commonly regarded as one of the first steps in successful regime transitions and peace-building in societies such as Afghanistan, Burundi, the Democratic Republic of the Congo, Iraq, Nepal, Sierra Leone, and Sudan. The most recent statement endorsing these activities comes from the outcome document of the post-2015 negotiations, *Transforming Our World: the 2030 Agenda for Sustainable Development*, adopted by member states on September 25–27, 2015. Although the language remains opaque and open to alternative interpretations, this agreement reaffirms the UN commitment to a world in which "democracy, good governance and the rule of law as well as an enabling environment at national and international levels, are essential for sustainable development."[29]

The mandate for UN electoral assistance by all these agencies and bureaus is rooted in the principles established in the Universal Declaration of Human Rights, notably that the will of the people, as expressed through periodic and genuine elections, shall be the basis of government authority. Electoral assistance by the UN recognizes the principles of state sovereignty and national ownership of elections and that UN agencies assist at the request of national governments. The UN also recognizes that there is no single model of democracy or system of elections. The main goal of United Nations electoral assistance is to support Member States in holding periodic, inclusive, and transparent elections that are perceived as credible and establishing nationally sustainable electoral processes. Today, the United Nations provides electoral assistance to approximately sixty countries each year, or one-third of all member states, at the request of national governments or a UN General Assembly or Security Council mandate. The primary strengths of the United Nations in this sector are its legitimacy and reputation for neutrality in supporting member states, as well as its local capacity and resources to implement and coordinate programs in developing countries around the world. By contrast, its weaknesses are perhaps that in most contexts, in respecting the principles of state sovereignty it can only go as far as member states permit, and the sheer size and diversity of the organization means that its capacity to deliver programs and services remains uneven.

Within the UN, under this mandate, a complex network of UN agencies and bureaus are centrally engaged in strengthening democratic governance and elections in member states, each playing a slightly different role.[30] This is coordinated by the UN Electoral Assistance Division located in the Department of Political Affairs (DPA) of the Secretary General (the core UN focal point) and implemented by the United Nations Development Programme (UNDP), the United Nations Democracy Fund (UNDEF), the Department of Peacekeeping Operations (DPKO), the Office of the High Commissioner for Human Rights (OHCHR), UN Volunteers, the United Nations Entity for Gender Equality and the Empowerment of Women (UN Women), the UN Educational, Scientific and Cultural Organization (UNESCO), the UN Peace-building Fund, as well as more broadly the Department of Economic and Social Affairs (UN DESA), and the World Bank's programs on good governance and public sector reform.[31] These activities fall under the UN's broader mandate in promoting human rights, development, and peace and security.

The Electoral Assistance Division, within the Secretary General's Department of Political Affairs (DPA), plays the lead role to ensure system-wide coherence and consistency in the provision of UN electoral assistance.[32] This includes undertaking electoral needs assessments, recommending parameters for all United Nations electoral assistance, advising on the design of projects, developing electoral policy, maintaining institutional memory, and coordinating technical guidance and support in the implementation of electoral projects.

The United Nations Development Programme (UNDP) is the UN's main provider of technical electoral assistance outside of peacekeeping or postconflict environments. This work is delivered as part of UNDP's mandate to provide democratic governance assistance at the country level. UNDP supports the development of electoral institutions, legal frameworks and processes. The United Nations Development Program is the largest boots-on-the-ground UN agency working on democratic governance in all developing countries. Under the leadership of Mark Malloch Brown, in 2002 the organization established the Democratic Governance practice, including a core pillar of work on electoral systems and processes.[33] During 2013 alone, UNDP provided electoral assistance to 68 countries in Africa, the Arab States, Asia Pacific, Latin America, and the Caribbean, and Europe.[34] Typically UNDP works with local national partners on activities such as promoting legal reforms, building the capacity of independent and permanent electoral management bodies, implementing systems for election planning, monitoring and budgeting, supporting voter and civic education on democratic rights and responsibilities, coordinating electoral assistance among donors, promoting women's participation in elections as voters and candidates, encouraging political participation of vulnerable and marginalized groups such as youth, women, persons with disabilities and minorities, and preventing electoral conflict and violence.[35]

UNDP collaborates with more specialized UN agencies on specific topics. UNWomen is mandated to provide guidance and technical support on issues of gender equality in elected office, the empowerment and rights of women, and gender mainstreaming. The Department of Peacekeeping Operations (DPKO) is the agency responsible for electoral security in peacekeeping and postconflict settings, such as the military and police components of field missions supporting national law enforcement agencies. The office of the UN High Commissioner for Human Rights (OHCHR) provides training and advice on human rights monitoring in elections, supports campaigns for violence-free contests, advocates electoral laws and institutions that are compliant with human rights, and monitors human rights violations during elections. The UN Educational, Scientific and Cultural Organization (UNESCO) is responsible for promoting and supporting freedom of expression, press freedom, and freedom of information. This includes strengthening the capacity of the news media to provide fair and balanced coverage of election campaigns. Other agencies provide additional support and resources, including the UN Democracy Fund, the Peacebuilding Fund, and the UN Volunteers program. Member states are supported at their specific request or through a Security Council mandate. All the UN agencies and bureaus work closely in partnerships with the broader networks of regional intergovernmental organizations and with election management bodies and domestic NGOs within countries. Electoral assistance is complimentary to other UN activities supporting peaceful transitions, democratic governance, the rule of law, human rights, and gender equality.

Intergovernmental Agencies and Regional Organizations

Beyond the United Nations, electoral assistance engages a complex and diverse network of institutions. This includes intergovernmental agencies for regional cooperation, epitomized by the European Union (EU), the European Commission, the Council of Europe, the Organization for Security and Cooperation in Europe (OSCE), the African Union, the Inter-American Development Bank, the Organization for Economic Cooperation and Development (OECD), and the Organization for American States (OAS), as well as by the International Institute for Democracy and Electoral Assistance (IDEA), the Inter-Parliamentary Union, the Community of Democracies, and the World Association of Electoral Bodies (A-WEB).

Governmental Donor Agencies

Multiple development agencies, bilateral donors, and nonprofit foundations provide resources and technical assistance to strengthen competitive elections. Activity in this subsector has grown substantially since at least the mid-1990s. Official agencies for international cooperation and development and Ministries of Foreign Affairs play a major role in funding bilateral and multilateral initiatives in this sector, exemplified by the work of US Agency for International Development (USAID), the Canadian Department of Foreign Affairs, Trade and Development, the Netherlands Ministry for Foreign Affairs, and the UK's Department of International Development (DfID). Today, nearly every Western government gives some aid for electoral assistance, whether through its foreign ministry, bilateral-aid agency, or other institutions.[36]

Figure 2.8 shows the diversity among the leading countries spending the most on governance and civil society in 2013, as a proportion of total ODA. The biggest donors in the governance and peace sector, measured in absolute dollar contributions, include the United States, European Union, Germany, the United Kingdom, the Netherlands, Australia, Sweden, Norway, and Canada. As of 2013 (the latest year available at this writing), the OECD donors contributing the highest proportion of ODA to this sector include the Nordic

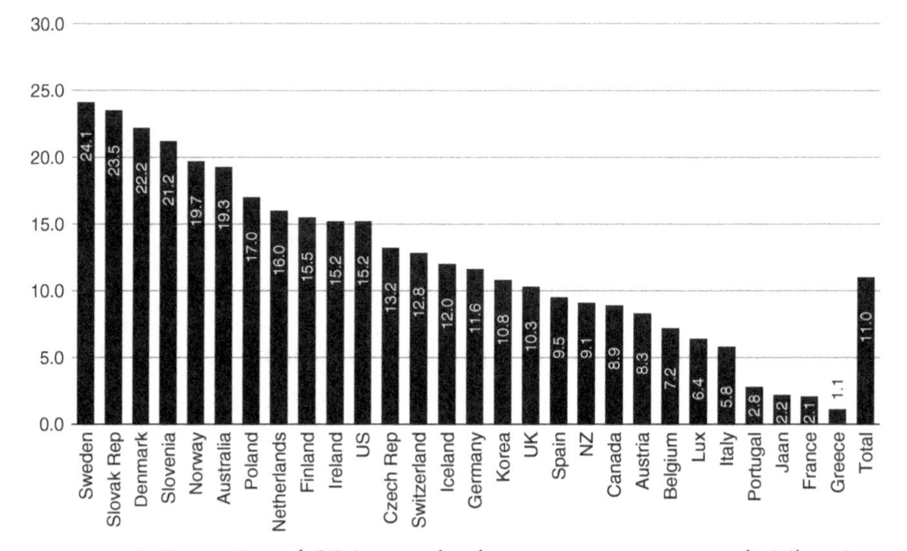

FIGURE 2.8. Proportion of ODA spent by donors on government and civil society, OECD-DAC 2013.

Notes: The estimates are based on the OECD Creditor Reporting System categorizing Official Development Assistance (ODA) by the purpose of aid, signifying the sector of the recipient's economy that the aid activity is designed to assist. Category 151 refers to "Government and Civil Society, total" including assistance to strengthen the administrative apparatus and government, public sector management, decentralization, anticorruption, legal and judicial development, democratic participation and civil society, elections, legislatures and political parties, media, human rights, and women's equality. Data are collected from individual projects and programs. Coding for elections is contained in subcategory 15151, including election management bodies, electoral observation and voter education.

Source: http://stats.oecd.org/ DAC5 ODA by Sector; CRS Coding Guide (April 2016). www.oecd.org/dac/stats/documentupload/2015%20CRS%20purpose%20codes%20EN_updated%20April%202016.pdf.

nations (led by Sweden, Denmark, Norway), but a diverse range of other countries also contribute heavily, including older democracies such as Australian and the Netherlands, as well as third-wave democracies such as the Slovak Republic, Slovenia, and Poland. The United States is in the middle of the pack, as a proportion of ODA spent on this sector. By contrast, several countries in Mediterranean Europe contribute the lowest proportions to this sector, including Greece, Portugal, and Italy, partly reflecting tough domestic economic conditions following the 2008 financial crisis, although Japan and France also fall into this category. Overall, around 11 percent of ODA is invested in this sector. The level of expenditure suggests that popular contests are widely understood by many ministries of development and foreign affairs within the donor community as the essential foundation for electoral accountability in democratic governance. allowing corrupt leaders to be thrown out of office by their citizens, as well as being essential for strengthening the legitimacy and stability of elected governments in fragile states. Elections are the basis for sustainable transitions from the legacy of authoritarianism.

International and National NGOs

A dense network of international and national nongovernmental nonprofit organizations function as advocacy, think-tank, monitoring, and implementation agencies. Leading organizations in this sector includes the US National Endowment for Democracy (NED), the Asian Network for Free Elections (ANFREL), the International Foundation for Electoral Systems (IFES), the Carter Center, Democracy International, Transparency International, the Open Society Institute, the Electoral Institute for Sustainable Democracy in Africa (EISA), the World Movement for Democracy, the Netherlands Institute for Multiparty Democracy (NIMD), the Oslo Centre for Peace and Human Rights, and the Danish Institute for Parties and Democracy. Hundreds of international think tanks and advocacy groups have local branches in many countries, including Amnesty International, Human Rights Watch, the Open Society Foundation, the Hans Seidel Foundation, the Ford Foundation, the Bertelsmann Foundation, the Carter Center, the Konrad-Adenauer-Stiftung, and Freedom House. Independent research institutions and university-based study centers buttress this work.[37] These organizations collaborate closely with national partners in the public sector, especially election management bodies, as well as a wide range of grassroots nongovernmental organizations involving human rights activists, political parties, the news media, and democratic social movements.

Trends in Democracy Assistance Spending

The expansion in assistance can be vividly illustrated by the growth in the billions of dollars spent by development programs seeking to strengthen democratic governance. This is understood both as a development outcome in its own right, as well as critical for delivering other developmental goals for the well-being of citizens. The size of initiatives in this sector are illustrated by the most comprehensive annual statistics on development assistance compiled by the Organization for Economic Cooperation and Development/Development Assistance Committee (OECD/DAC), which estimates the proportion of Official Development Aid (ODA) allocated annually by sector for all recipient countries by all donors.[38] Trends in aid spending in Figure 2.9 are standardized to constant US dollars, to compare like-with-like, allowing for inflation. These estimates suggest that during the Cold War era, from 1971 to 1998, spending on

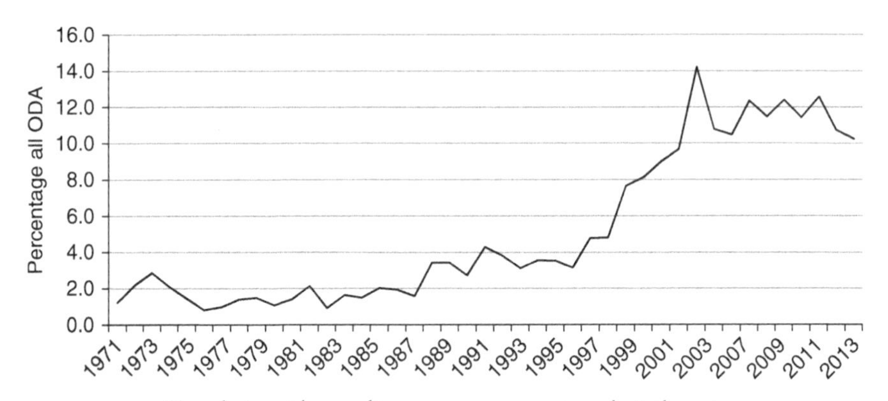

FIGURE 2.9A. Trends in aid spending on government and civil society, 1971–2013 (constant $US).
Note: Official Development Assistance, all donors, constant US$, millions, 1.5 Government and Civil Society.
Source: http://stats.oecd.org/ DAC5 ODA by Sector.

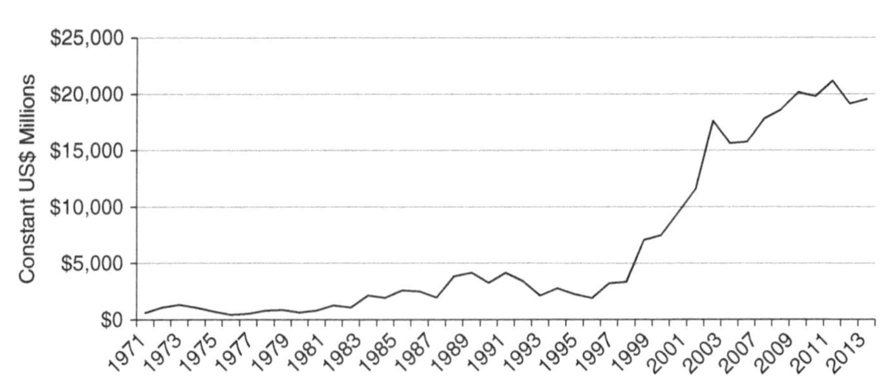

FIGURE 2.9B. Trends in aid spending on government and civil society as a proportion of all ODA, 1971–2013 (constant $US).
Note: Official Development Assistance, all donors, constant US$, millions, Spending on 1.5 Government and Civil Society as a proportion of all ODA.
Source: http://stats.oecd.org/ DAC5 ODA by Sector.

the government and civil society sector fluctuated under $5 billion a year, representing less than 4 percent of all ODA. The pattern was transformed after the fall of the Berlin Wall and then the events of 9/11, when spending on this sector rapidly surged, reaching a peak of around US$20 billion (in constant US dollars) in 2011, before falling slightly in the following years (see Figure 2.9a).[39] Of course all aid spending rose during recent years, but as a proportion of all ODA, the investment in this sector tripled from around 4 percent in 1998 to 12 percent in 2011 (see Figure 2.9b).

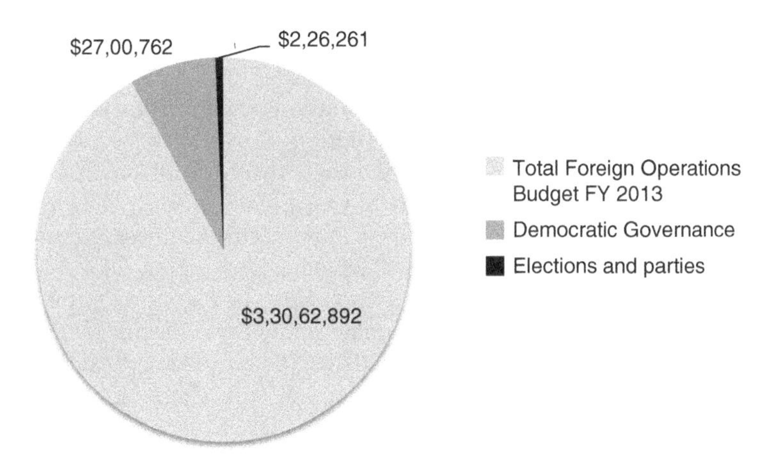

FIGURE 2.10. US Foreign Operations Budget FY 2013.
Note: U.S. Foreign Operations FY 2013 Performance Report.
Source: USAID www.usaid.gov/sites/default/files/documents/1870/USAID_FY2013_APR.pdf.

Broken down among the leading agencies, the United Nations Development Programme (UNDP) invested around US$1.2bn on democratic governance programs in 2012 (around one-quarter of the UNDP's total annual budget) in more than 170 countries.[40] Another major contributor, USAID, has supported democracy and governance (DG) programs in approximately 120 countries and territories since 1990, spending an estimated total of $8.47 billion (in constant 2000 US dollars) between 1990 and 2005.[41] In 2013 alone, the United States foreign assistance budget for activities by the US Agency for International Development (USAID) and State Department devoted US$2.7bn (1.56 percent of its budget) in 2013 to this area, clustered into programs on rule of law and human rights, good governance, political competition (including spending on elections and political parties), and civil society.[42] The amount devoted to governance and to elections can be regarded as a relatively small proportion of the overall foreign assistance budget (see Figure 2.10), although it is not an inconsiderable amount in real terms, similar in size to investments in programs on antituberculosis or clean water and sanitation. Similarly, the UK Department of International Development (DFID) devoted just over US$1.2bn in total on government and civil society in 2011 on bilateral and multilateral initiatives.[43] The European Instrument for the Promotion of Democracy and Human Rights spent about $176 m a year to promote civil society efforts in recent years, with direct expenditure by European development agencies in member states adding substantially to this pooled EU fund.[44]

Electoral assistance is only one part of the far broader package of initiatives concerning democratic governance, however, and not necessarily the program area with the highest spending within this sector. For example, building capacity through professional training of thousands of staff employed in public sector management across national and local governments, to provide efficient public services and reduce corruption in fragile states such as South Sudan and Afghanistan, can vastly outweigh the costs of aid for elections. In 2012, OECD/DAC calculate that US$17.4 billion of Official Development Aid was disbursed to support all activities in the sector on government and civil society (coded 151) and peace (152). Breaking down this total amount by subsector suggests that almost one-fifth was allocated to public sector management (US$3.3 billion), and a similar amount was disbursed to legal and judicial development, while 15 percent was given to democratic participation and civil society programs, and 9 percent to civilian peace-building, conflict prevention, and resolution. All these subsectors far outweigh the money spent on elections, estimated to be around US$468 million in 2012 (2.7 percent of the total amount spent on governance and peace). The proportion of ODA disbursed for elections has remained relatively steady during recent years (at around 3–4 percent). Most of the funds are allocated to projects and invested in two global regions (Central and South-Asia and sub-Saharan Africa), which account for almost half (47 percent) of the total ODA for governance and peace. Overall, therefore, aid spending on elections remains a relatively modest area of official development aid. It is estimated that in 2010 multilateral organizations invest an estimated US$5 billion annually to assist states seeking to strengthen democratic governance, a growing total, although still relatively modest as a proportion of the overall development aid budget.[45]

WHAT ELECTORAL ASSISTANCE PROGRAMS ARE OFFERED?

What types of programs are most commonly supported in this sector? The most common types of policy interventions are depicted in Figure 2.11, depending upon the specific problem that needs to be addressed in each context and also the role, mission, and mandate of development agencies.[46] The primary types of interventions, in a sequential policy implementation process, concern *establishing rules meeting international standards* (by reforming the constitutional principles, legal policies and regulatory framework governing elections); *implementing policies* (by building capacity, which enables official agencies to carry out these policies); *ensuring compliance* (by strengthening independent oversight and accountability mechanisms, especially through parliament and the judiciary); and, finally, *monitoring performance* (expanding transparency through international observer missions, comparative indicators, and domestic watchdog agencies). Depending upon their role and focus, programs of electoral assistance are targeted at diverse agencies involved in different stages of this policy implementation process, notably legislatures empowered to revise electoral laws and pass regulatory reforms, electoral management bodies and official government regulatory

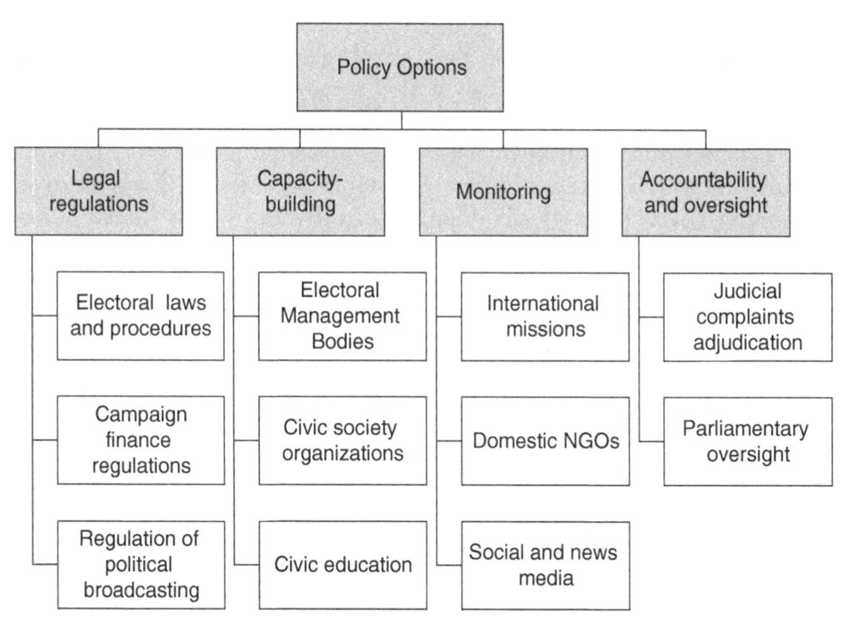

FIGURE 2.11. The typology of policy options designed to strengthen electoral integrity.

agencies concerned with implementing policies, parliaments and the judiciary exerting oversight and accountability, and diverse actors monitoring performance, including political parties, civic society organizations such as transparency and human rights NGOs and think tanks, and the news media and social media. Programs seeking to strengthen electoral integrity are perhaps the most visible, although not the most expensive, part of a much larger set of initiatives designed to strengthen democratic governance.

Establishing Rules: Reforming Constitutional, Legal, and Regulatory Frameworks

As part of its role in providing policy advice and technical assistance for EMBs, agencies in the international community, including International IDEA, IFES, the OAS, and the ACE project, have simultaneously sought to compare practices and legal regulations of electoral administration, campaign finance, and campaign broadcasting in countries around the world.[47] Revisions may be made to constitutions, which contain important clauses regulating the conduct and management of elections, as well as to electoral laws and administrative procedures and regulatory codes. A large research agenda is required to compare the constitutional and legal frameworks governing each of these areas and determining the most appropriate regulations that meet international standards.[48]

The United Nations has been committed to strengthening human rights and elections ever since Article 21 in the 1948 Universal Declaration of Human Rights, which declares that "the will of the people shall be the basis of the authority of government; this will be expressed in periodic and genuine elections which shall be by universal and equal suffrage and shall be held by secret vote or by equivalent free voting procedures" guaranteeing everyone "the right to take part in the government of his country, directly or through freely chosen representatives."[49] These principles have been elaborated and endorsed in many subsequent international treaties and instruments, notably the International Covenant on Civil and Political Rights, and the International Covenant on Economic, Social and Cultural Rights which entered into force in 1976.[50] The General Assembly underscored the United Nation's active support for representative democracy on February 21, 1991 by passing a resolution declaring that "periodic and genuine elections" are a "crucial factor in the effective enjoyment ... of a wide range of other human rights." A series of similar resolutions have been passed periodically by the General Assembly over the years.[51]

The core principles have been long endorsed by the international community, but unless the standards of elections reflect these principles, by eliminating common malpractices, contests will fail to strengthen democracy and reduce conflict. One major challenge is that international conventions are often not yet fully integrated into domestic laws, so that official endorsement has not been translated into practice. Equally importantly, there are many important components of electoral rights, including the role of campaign finance and campaign communications, which are still not covered by any international treaty, even though regional organizations are laying the foundations for a broader agreement. Therefore, human rights organizations, such as Human Rights Watch and Amnesty International, seek to monitor compliance with existing conventions, and norm advocates, NGOs. Leading regional organizations also seek to expand agreement about appropriate standards, such as for regulating money and media during election campaigns.

Implementing Policies: Capacity Building and Technical Assistance

Another major set of initiatives has sought to strengthen the capacity of electoral management bodies and local electoral officials so that they can implement the legal and regulatory policies through supporting training programs and providing technical assistance. The UN established a permanent Electoral Assistance Division to provide countries with technical advice for holding elections. This division is deeply involved in postconflict peace-building activities and it was even briefly under UN Department of Peacekeeping Operations supervision before moving to the Department of Political Affairs. Since 1991, more than 100 countries have requested and received UN assistance with holding referendums, plebiscites, and elections.

Technical assistance is provided in areas such as electoral administration and planning, review of electoral laws and regulations, electoral dispute resolution, boundary delimitation, voter registration, election budgeting, logistics, procurement of election materials, use of technologies, training of election officials, voter and civic education, voting and counting operations, election security, and coordination of international donor assistance.

Similarly, during the last decade, the United Nations Development Program stepped up its technical assistance to strengthening electoral processes and management, as did many regional agencies and multilateral organizations and NGOs. UNDP has identified ten main entry points, which currently guide how the organization provides electoral assistance: electoral system reform, strengthening electoral administration, building sustainable electoral processes, mobilization and coordination of resources, civic and voter education, electoral dispute resolution, support to domestic observation, working with political parties, media strengthening, and increasing women's participation. UNDP provides both event- and process-driven support during the electoral cycle. During the last decade, the UNDP alone has invested from US$1.2 billion to $1.5 billion every year to programs strengthening democratic governance in 130 developing countries worldwide, out of a total UNDP annual budget of around $5 m. In total, UNDP has assisted 83 countries with elections with expenditures of approximately $2.2 billion between 1999 and 2011.[52] The total cost fluctuates a lot annually, however, with the highest spending during years of large-scale international efforts to support postconflict elections, such as in Afghanistan, Sudan, Nigeria, and Burundi. In the context of electoral assistance, the largest UNDP focus area has been upon strengthening electoral administration, accounting for approximately one-quarter of the total effort. Initiatives by the UNDP included launching the Global Programme for Electoral Cycle Support (GPEC) in 2009, designed to help countries improve their electoral laws, processes, and institutions and to enhance the participation of women in electoral processes.[53]

Many international agencies have also aimed to expand the capacity and professional standards of independent election management bodies (EMBs). This includes technical assistance provided by the International Institute for Democracy and Electoral Assistance (IDEA), the International Foundation for Election Systems (IFES), the National Democratic Institute for International Affairs (NDI), and United Nations Development Programme (UNDP), and the Carter Center, in partnership with regional organizations such as the European Union and Organization of American States, bilateral partners, and local stakeholders.[54] Elections are large-scale, complex and sensitive operations, as observed earlier with the Indian case, and EMBS need the logistical capacity to develop strategic and operational plans; to assess election costs and prepare budgets; to improve voter registration processes; to implement procurement plans, to manage the vote count, and to handle any complaints and disputes. International agencies, regional organizations, and bilateral donors have also worked with local stakeholders to strengthen political parties and the independent media, to address judicial dispute resolution mechanisms, to increase the participation of women, young people, and minorities, and to improve civic education.

In response to these challenges, a growing body of applied policy analysis has developed to study the framework for electoral law and administration, drawing upon comparative political science, legal studies, and public sector management. Work has focused upon the institutional framework surrounding election rules, including the design and reform of constitutions, electoral laws, and procedural regulations; the role, independence, and powers of Election Management Bodies; the capacity, skills, and training of election officials; legal voter registration and polling requirements; the regulation of campaign finance and broadcasting; the provision of balloting facilities; the establishment of complaints and dispute resolution mechanisms; and the deployment of new voting technologies, including online polling. Ever since the Florida controversy in the 2000 race, and the polarization of issues of voter registration and flaws in voting technologies, interest in electoral administration has grown among American scholars.[55] New research has evaluated the effects of moving from localized to state-coordinated voter registers, the introduction of new electronic voting machines replacing mechanical models, and the use of convenience voting (such as early in-person voting, voting by mail, absentee voting, electronic voting, and voting by fax) and election-day registration. While work has focused on the effects of these reforms on differential patterns of turnout among social groups, less is known about their impact on campaigns, costs, fraud, security, and party support.[56] Elsewhere, the impact of independent Electoral Management Bodies on the public confidence and the quality of democracy has started to be examined in developing countries in sub-Saharan Africa and in Latin America.[57]

Ensuring Compliance: Strengthening Accountability and Oversight Mechanisms

When establishing the legal and regulatory policy framework to ensure effective implementation by official agencies, it is also important to build in mechanisms ensuring accountability through independent oversight. Here both parliaments and the judiciary can play important roles, although little systematic research has explored the process of oversight for electoral authorities and dispute resolution mechanisms. Despite important advances in recent years, it has been recognized that far too many elections have ended with the major protagonists at loggerheads, parties bitterly disputing the results, and conflict spilling over onto the streets.[58] Cries of fraud are commonplace, especially among losers in tight winner-take-all presidential races. Protests have generated contentious outcomes in many places.[59] Accusations of vote rigging, corruption and stolen elections are particularly common in cultures stamped by a long history of past malpractices, undermining public confidence in the process, associated with Mexican practices of vote-buying by the PRI, overwhelming progovernment coverage in the Russian airways, and outbreaks of intercommunal violence in Nigeria. Therefore, forms of legislative and judicial oversight should be established to make sure that electoral authorities meet international standards and that resolution mechanisms, including the judiciary and courts, are able to resolve any disputes occurring during or immediately after elections through peaceful and legal processes.

Monitoring Performance: International and Domestic Observer

The final type of program involves ensuring that elections perform in accordance with international standards and with domestic legal and regulatory frameworks. Traditionally, as discussed in Chapter 5, this has been done through the deployment of international monitoring missions. Regional organizations and development agencies have sought to strengthen the transparency of election procedures and to monitor the implementation of internationally agreed standards and principles. Thousands of international and domestic observers have been deployed in election missions, most commonly by regional organizations, including the Carter Center, IFES, the Organization of Social and Economic Cooperation (OSCE), the African Union (AU), the European Union (EU), and the Organization of American States (OAS).[60] Domestic election watchdog NGOs supplement these activities, along with attempts to strengthen the independent media and civil society organizations.

The number of electoral observer missions gradually expanded from the start of the third wave era in the mid-1970s, followed by a sharp increase during the late 1980s. Today about two-thirds of all elections have international observer missions. A growing body of research has sought to evaluate the effectiveness of this development. In particular, scholars have analyzed whether the presence of observers in certain electoral districts successfully reduces, or else simply displaces, fraudulent practices.[61] Nevertheless, while international monitors have been scrutinized, less has been established about the impact of domestic monitors, media watch, and "crowd-sourcing" social media initiatives, as well as many other strategies and programs.

In general, programs focusing upon election observing are part of a broader set of initiatives concerning transparency. In the field of development, greater transparency and accountability are generally thought to help plug the leaky pipes of corruption and inefficiency, channel public spending more efficiently, and produce better services. In the field of electoral governance, openness about the rules and procedures, outcomes, and decisions processes used by electoral authorities is widely assumed to build public trust, improve policy-making, and facilitate accountability.[62] By revealing problems, such as ballot stuffing, vote-rigging, and bribery, it is generally believed that the reports published by election observers will pressure government officials to implement reforms and deter malpractices in future contests by increasing the risks of being caught red-handed. By contrast, in the words of the Open Society Institute: "Silence and secrecy are two of the most powerful tools that governments can employ to mute critics and cloak their actions from public scrutiny."[63] Even if unable to generate positive benefits, there is still a presumption in favor of open governance since, by contrast: "The absence of transparency in electoral processes invariably leads to the suspicion that fraudulent activities are taking place."[64] Whether disclosure alone has the capacity to generate these types of benefits, however, remains to be determined.[65] Meta-analysis of the empirical evidence used in several rigorous evaluation studies suggests that in general some transparency initiatives in democratic governance have indeed proved highly successful, while by contrast others have had little impact in achieving their objectives.[66]

Cases of Electoral Assistance Programs

Although the types of activities differ, in practice these programs are usually combined in complex ways, depending upon the priorities facing the country. This process can be illustrated by some descriptive examples of how the UN responded in recent contests in the cases of Libya, Mali, and Nigeria.

Libya

After Colonel Gaddafi died in October 2011, Libya held elections in July 2012 for the General National Congress, in February 2014 for the Libyan constitutional drafting assembly, and in June 2014 for the House of Representatives. The country emerged from forty years of repressive rule by Gaddafi but the violent struggle leading to his eventual overthrow left the country scarred and deeply divided. Security challenges in the House of Representatives elections included violence and intimidation, especially that directed against prominent female candidates and human rights defenders, including the shooting of one such defender on polling day. UN agencies sought to strengthen the electoral process and institutions throughout this period. In preparation for these contests, the UNDP coordinated a bucket of funds of around US$16 million for the Libyan electoral assistance project from several donors, including Spain, Sweden, Japan, the United Kingdom, Denmark, the Netherlands, Austria, and Switzerland.[67] An integrated United Nations electoral team consisting of advisers from the United Nations Support Mission in Libya (UNSMIL) and UNDP supported the Libyan authorities in their electoral operations, external relations, and public awareness campaigns. The UN electoral team facilitated professional capacity building and dialogue among Libyan electoral stakeholders, especially the High National Election Commission, which encouraged the nomination of more women candidates and also facilitated training sessions for women candidates. The UN team monitored the human rights situation during the elections and focused on strengthening Libya's legislation, processes, and institutional capacity. The United Nations Democracy Fund provided support designed to strengthen independent journalism and improve citizens' access to information. Electoral assistance projects coordinated by UNDP were designed to strengthen the logistical, management, and operational capacities of the electoral authorities, to conduct civic and voter education campaigns through fact sheets, radio and television announcements about where, when, and how to vote, to encourage the participation of marginalized groups including women, youth, minorities, and displaced refugees, to promote issue-based reporting by the national media during the election campaign, to assist the electoral authorities with the accreditation of domestic election observers, and to strengthen judicial complaints adjudication mechanisms. Despite all these activities, for the 2014 election to the 200-member Council of Representatives, out of a total Libyan population of over 6 million people, only 1.5 million registered to vote, and only 630,000 ballots were cast.[68]

Mali

Mali held the first round of presidential and legislative elections on July 28, 2013, with a second round on August 11, 2013. The United Nations provided political, technical, logistical, financial, and security support. The Special Representative of the Secretary-General worked with the United Nations Integrated Electoral Team, consisting of advisers of UNDP and the United Nations Multidimensional Integrated Stabilization Mission in Mali (MINUSMA). The team provided technical assistance and advice in a broad range of areas, including electoral operations, civic and voter education, capacity-building of the electoral management bodies, financial support for the hiring of polling staff, updating of the voter register, printing of the voter list, and resource mobilization. Other MINUSMA components facilitated the deployment of equipment and personnel of the national electoral authority and provided security support. The MINUSMA Human Rights Division monitored the human rights situation during both elections.

Despite the constraints imposed by a challenging electoral timetable and a volatile security situation, the election was held under generally calm conditions, with no significant security incidents reported. A preelectoral agreement between the Government and armed opposition groups paved the way for a peaceful process. Around 45 percent of the registered voters participated in the first round, more than in previous elections, with the number dropping to 37 percent in the second round. Only 8 women were elected, compared with the 15 elected to the previous parliament. An estimated 1.2 million citizens were not able to register and the country faced limitations in respect of the participation of refugees, despite measures taken by national stakeholders to secure inclusive participation. These challenges notwithstanding, observer groups were generally positive in their assessment of the electoral process. Overall the election helped to reestablish constitutional order, which had been suspended since the military coup in early 2012.

Nigeria

On March 28 and April 11, 2015, Nigeria held its presidential, parliamentary, and State House of Assembly elections. Governorship elections were held in all but seven States. Contests faced a challenging political and security environment amid concerns over election-related violence. The presidential elections were contested by the incumbent President, Goodluck Jonathan, facing Muhammadu Buhari. At the request of the Nigerian authorities, the United Nations initiated a broad range of political and technical engagement activities before and during the election in support of a credible and peaceful process. This included the Special Representative of the Secretary-General for West Africa, working in close coordination with regional and international actors, in particular the African Union and ECOWAS. It also included high-level engagement by other senior United Nations officials at United Nations Headquarters and in Nigeria. UNDP provided technical assistance to national authorities, including capacity-building of the Independent National Electoral Commission in the areas of planning and electoral operations, results management, and Commission-stakeholder relations. UNDP also provided support to domestic observer groups and to the National Peace Committee. A small team from the Office of the United Nations High Commissioner for Human Rights monitored the human rights situation in the national elections. The Office of the High Commissioner also assisted the National Human Rights Commission in preparing a report on preelection violence and in designing a UNDP-funded project to support the Commission's monitoring of election-related violence. The outcome was generally peaceful on polling day, although some incidents of violence were reported. Voter turnout was estimated at 47 percent. The opposition leader secured a sufficient number of votes to win the election in the first round. The peaceful transfer of power to an opposition party was celebrated as the first such event since Nigeria's transition to civilian rule in 1999.

CONCLUSIONS

The trends in international development aid demonstrate the substantial growth of spending on democratic governance and electoral assistance in recent decades. Demand was fueled during the third-wave era by the diffusion of elections around the world, growing requests from governments for the resources needed to manage these complex tasks, and the shifting balance of democratic member states within the UN. The supply of agencies offering electoral assistance expanded in part to meet demand, especially the rapid growth in the UN's technical help, along with the role of regional intergovernmental organizations, bilateral donors, and a network of NGOs. As one important indicator, the proportion of Official Development Assistance spending in the sector of programs on government and civil society (including elections) surged after 2000 to around US$20 billion a year, before falling more recently. The selected cases in this chapter illustrate many of the typical activities provided under the umbrella of electoral assistance, including supporting official election management bodies with logistical, administrative, and technical tasks associated with running elections, as well monitoring human rights and strengthening civil society groups, the media, and political parties. The central question raised by the shift in development spending concerns the effectiveness of initiatives in this sector, and what evidence is available to evaluate the impact of electoral assistance. The next chapters turn to consider these issues.

3

Evaluating Effectiveness

When assessing policy impact, evidence-based evaluations seek to determine the effects of common types of interventions on a few key programmatic outcomes and certain longer-term societal impacts, whether the results are positive or negative, and whether they are intended or unintended.[1] Reflecting this approach, the task of evaluating electoral assistance in this study can be stated relatively straightforwardly to judge what forms of support provided by the international community succeed or fail in strengthening electoral integrity. Better impact evaluations, including when, where, and why electoral assistance programs work or fail to deliver, can potentially contribute towards more informed choices by multiple stakeholders, including local officials and reform groups, development managers and aid workers, bilateral agencies, and multilateral organizations.[2] Assessments can be useful directly, through reducing the risks of uncertainty, and also prove valuable indirectly, by guiding the most effective strategic investments for international agencies providing development aid and electoral assistance. Accountability is strengthened where agencies can report credible results to bilateral donors.

Multiple forms of evidence and techniques are utilized for program evaluations, ranging from diverse case studies drawing upon document reviews, surveys of participants, interviewers with stakeholders, and more anecdotal best-practice experiences, through various more or less controlled designs and econometric models applying regression models, to randomized control trials, regarded by many scholars as the gold standard at the top of the scientific hierarchy.[3] Whatever the specific mix of methods deployed, it is challenging to achieve effective, credible, and rigorous programmatic evaluations, based on valid and reliable evidence, especially where the results can be generalized across many diverse contexts.

This chapter tackles three questions: What are the main functions of program evaluation? What information needs to be collected to determine the impact of interventions in this sector? And what analytical methods and techniques provide the most useful insights to help design, evaluate, and implement better electoral assistance programs? To lay the foundations for understanding these issues, The first section in this chapter starts by suggesting several reasons why it is important to assess the efforts of the international community in seeking to strengthen electoral integrity. This includes the way that this process can help to inform choices about alternative ways of strengthening democratic governance; provide evidence to monitor the effectiveness of aid dollars spent in this sector; address doubts about democracy promotion during an era of authoritarian resurgence; improve transparency, feedback, and accountability to donors such as governments, parliaments, and NGOs; and serve to promote organizational learning among program managers and local aid workers. The role of program evaluations should not be exaggerated, however. Even where evidence suggests that certain policies are technically optimal, the decision-making process cannot avoid or bypass complex ethical and political judgments. When deciding between alternative programs, policymakers have to juggle and weigh what is known about the effectiveness of alternative interventions against multiple alternative considerations, including considering political constraints, administrative capacity, ethical considerations, technical feasibility, time pressures, and limited finances.

On this basis, the second section considers how the impact of electoral assistance can best be evaluated. The study uses the logic of a sequential chain-of-results model broken down into five steps: diagnosing problems, identifying benchmarks, goals and targets, implementing programs, assessing specific electoral outcomes, and evaluating broader societal impacts. In this book, the overarching goals of electoral assistance programs are derived from the broader concept of electoral integrity, defined as how far contests meet international standards and global norms that have been endorsed in a series of written conventions, treaties and guidelines. As discussed in Chapter 2, electoral assistance is typically designed to address problems where electoral institutions, processes, and practices fall short of international standards, such as programs seeking to improve legal frameworks to ensure equitable competition for all parties and candidates, to expand capacity for professional, impartial, and fair electoral administration, to strengthen transparent and fair campaign finance regulations, to increase the inclusion of women and minorities in elected office, and to strengthen civic engagement and information among all sectors of the electorate. In practice, evidence-based analysis seeks to: (i) identify problems (including the strengths and weaknesses of the agency and the threats and opportunities in the environment), (ii) specify key goals and measurable benchmarks, (iii) document operational activities, (iv) assess selected outcomes that can be attributed plausibly to the programmatic interventions, and (v) evaluate the broader and more indirect societal impacts. The chain of results model provides a useful way to distinguish these different steps in program assessment.

The third section concludes that, like any tool, no single method is sufficient for dealing with all stages of impact evaluations. Instead, studies should ideally blend the most suitable techniques that are best adapted to the context and the program under scrutiny.[4] In general, mixed methods are the most appropriate strategy, adopted in subsequent chapters, where comparative evidence at the macrolevel is used to monitor the severity of electoral malpractices in each contest and the risks and opportunities for assistance arising from the broader context within each society. This can be combined with program-level evaluations of specific interventions common in this sector, with evidence derived from process-tracing "before and after" cases, interviews with stakeholders, surveys of participants, randomized control trials, and related methods.

WHY EVALUATE IMPACT?

The Intrinsic Value of Elections in Theories of Democratic Governance

To start, why is it important to evaluate program impact? This may seem intuitively obvious for rational and informed policymaking but in fact rigorous evaluations are fairly exceptional in the field of electoral assistance – many practitioners doubt their value. One major reason is that elections have long been conceived as the essential bed-rock foundation of representative democracy. They are the core institution in minimalist understandings of democracy. Classical Schumpeterian conceptions regard competitive contests and the rotation of office between government and opposition parties as the primary mechanisms of representative democracy.[5] Rival conceptions of liberal, deliberative, and participatory democracy all agree with this core assumption, although elections in these models are regarded as far from sufficient by themselves without strengthening alternative channels of political participation and accountability. Hence, liberal notions of democracy, following Robert Dahl, emphasize the critical role of political rights and civil liberties needed to buttress competitive elections, including freedom of the press, the capacity for plural civil society organizations to mobilize, and effective horizontal checks and balances on the power of the executive from the judiciary and legislature.[6] Under democratic theories, therefore, it is critical to identify which elections meet international standards and which electoral assistance programs are most effective in improving political institutions and strengthening civic culture.

Instrumental Arguments

In addition to regarding elections as valuable in themselves, the instrumental consequences of popular contests are also widely seen as important, especially to facilitate sustainable transitions from authoritarian states and long-term processes of democratic consolidation. Evidence indicates that malpractice has the capacity to undermine the legitimacy and authority of elected governments, to erode confidence and trust in elected authorities and political institutions, to deepen dissatisfaction with democracy, to weaken government accountability, and to depress voting participation.[7] Failed contests have been the catalyst for many peaceful mass demonstrations and violent protests, with popular uprisings and instability derailing fragile democratic transitions in states such as Thailand (2014) and Ukraine (2014).[8] In autocracies, the false façade of legitimacy generated by manipulated contests can weaken and fragment opposition forces, moderate diplomatic pressures for reform, and thereby reinforce the grip of rulers, such as elections in Malaysia (2013), Bahrain (2014), and Equatorial Guinea (2013).[9] Problems of flawed and failed polls are not confined to the world's least developed societies. Instead, these represent universal challenges observed in states around the world. For example, Americans often regard the United States as the leading model of liberal democracy for the rest of the world. But in fact evidence suggests that contemporary US elections rank as the worst among Western nations, with considerable room for improvement in procedures for redistricting, regulating campaign finance, and voter registration.[10]

By contrast to the negative consequences, however, free and fair contests can potentially serve multiple valuable functions for democracy.[11] This includes strengthening feelings of political legitimacy, facilitating the peaceful and orderly rotation of office between governing and opposition parties, providing authoritative processes of executive recruitment and succession, improving the accountability of elected officials to ordinary citizens, and generating inclusive forms for the expression of political voices, especially through the representation of minorities in deeply divided societies. For all these reasons, and for many more, electoral assistance programs strengthening integrity and reforming malpractices have been widely acknowledged as an urgent priority for the international community. Many agencies and bilateral donors expanded assistance in this sector from around the mid-1980s until the late 1990s, responding to growing demands for support from countries experiencing transitions from absolute autocracy.

Concern About Aid Effectiveness

Another reason for evaluation is that recent years have also seen mounting pressures for development agencies to demonstrate the efficiency of aid spending to bilateral donors – ministries of foreign affairs and international development – and thus to national parliaments with oversight powers. The 2005 Paris Declaration of Aid Effectiveness and the 2008 Accra Agenda for Action highlighted the need to gather better evidence to gauge the impact of development spending. Both these agreements recognized that aid could – and should – be producing better impacts.[12] These landmark pacts and subsequent agreements emphasize the value of measuring results and impacts, as well as reinforcing the principles of national ownership, alignment among donor countries, harmonization to share information, and mutual accountability between donors and partners for delivering development results. This was part of a quid pro quo for raising overall levels of development spending by Western donors.

In response to this shift, some development sectors have been subject to growing scrutiny seeking to evaluate aid effectiveness, including programs on health care, agricultural yields, and microfinance loans. Rigorous evaluation methods have become more common in policy evaluations, as well as in behavioral economics and experimental political science, notably through the use of randomized control trials that randomize treatments and thereby seek to isolate the underlying causal mechanisms.[13] With a few important exceptions, however, assessments of programs of democracy assistance have tended to lag behind these methodological developments. Most assessments used by development agencies typically use softer techniques and mixed methods when presenting program results.[14]

This situation persists despite the fact that electoral assistance has gradually become a mainstream sector of development, engaging multiple international and domestic agencies. Since 1991, the majority of member states have requested UN electoral assistance. The largest agency, the United Nations Development Programme (UNDP), provides assistance with elections in over 60 countries each year. Today nearly every Western government gives some international aid earmarked for support for democratic governance. As discussed in more detail later, In the late 1980s, less than US$1 billion a year of Official Development Aid (ODA) was devoted to democracy assistance.[15] By contrast by 2012, around US$14.3 billion in ODA was invested in "governance and civil society," while almost half a billion dollars was spent on election assistance alone.[16] To put these figures in perspective, around one in ten dollars in all ODA spending is allocated for "governance and civil society."[17] Numerous multilateral agencies and transnational NGOs have entered the field to deliver programs in democratic governance. Electoral assistance programs have become established as standard practice during the last quarter century, exemplified by international observer missions, capacity building training workshops for electoral officials, and voter registration projects. It is thus timely to review the key lessons learned from all these diverse types of interventions.

Western Doubts About Democracy Promotion During an Era of Authoritarian Resurgence

Addressing skeptical doubts among donor countries about aid effectiveness is especially important at a time when democracy promotion has become increasingly controversial, a target of counterattack and pushback in many parts of the globe, as discussed in the opening chapter.[18] During the last decade, growing evidence suggests that the world has been entering an era of democratic recession, with renewed resurgence from authoritarian forces within and outside Western states.[19] In authoritarian states, leaders from Robert Mugabe to Vladimir Putin to Nicholás Maduro routinely condemn democratic assistance as undue interference by the United States (and ex-colonial powers in the West) in the domestic affairs of sovereign states. Recent years have seen active attempts by several autocracies and illiberal regimes to undermine democracy promotion efforts in their countries, exemplified by crackdowns on international journalists in Sisi's Egypt, renewed attacks on leading opposition figures in Russia, and more draconian censorship of the Internet and the imprisonment of dissident bloggers in China.[20] Autocratic states have also sought to shape geopolitical events beyond their borders, notably Putin flexing his muscles by propping up Assad's regime in Syria, destabilizing Ukraine and invading Crimea, supporting Lukashenko's rule in Belarus, and using disinformation campaigns and computer hacking designed to destabilize elections in Europe and the United States. How far "black knights" actively seek to promote their own values and prevent democratic elections from taking root in neighboring countries, or whether this is an unintended by-product of other foreign policy goals, remains under debate.[21] At minimum, however, international economic investments by major authoritarian regimes have proved indifferent to the human rights record of states, thereby undermining Western pressures for these countries to democratize, exemplified by Chinese investment in sub-Saharan Africa.

Moreover, as discussed in the introduction to the book, the third-wave era of heady Western optimism about inevitable democratic progress, which surged in the early 1990s following the fall of the Berlin Wall, gradually faded and gave way to more widespread doubts in recent years. The Huntington thesis concerning the third wave of democracy emphasized that successive historical eras during the twentieth century had experienced successive periods of progress but also retreat. The contemporary weltanschauung of democratic decline among popular pundits has been heavily colored by specific events. Hence the early 1990s were dominated by a mood of heady Western optimism concerning prospects for inevitable transitions to liberal democracy and free markets following the fall of the Berlin Wall, the end of the Cold War, and the wave of regime transitions as a series of Soviet-style leaders fell in Central and Eastern Europe, with growing liberalization as well as many other states in the world. Since the turn of the 21st century, however, popular sentiments have reflected the steadily growing mood of pessimism about prospects for democracy, a zeitgeist which gradually deepened in many Western nations. This was colored by the prism of attempts to support state-building and hold competitive multiparty contests in Iraq and Afghanistan, as well as by tension and instability in the aftermath of Arab uprisings in Egypt, Syria, Yemen, and Libya, the sporadic violence spread by ISIS terrorism within and outside the MENA region, as well as more assertive authoritarian pushback against democracy promotion by leaders in Russia, China, Turkey, Egypt, and Venezuela.[22] There is renewed interest in understanding the phenomenon of so-called black knights, reflecting active attempts by Russia and other major authoritarian states to undermine political reforms in neighboring states.[23] Even established democracies are not immune from these efforts, including Russian meddling in German and American elections. Concern has been deepened by several events, including repeated headlines about persistent conflict and chaos in Afghanistan and Iraq, the instability and violent extremism following the Arab uprisings in Egypt and Libya, deadly violence and mass population migrations triggered by the Syrian civil war and attempts by ISIS to establish a caliphate spanning national boundaries, and authoritarian pushback and resurgent Cold War tensions between Russia and the West, exemplified by military intervention in Crimea and Syria.[24]

Thus development support through the provision of electoral assistance, which has become standard practice among many multilateral agencies and bilateral donors, now faces a chilly climate and renewed doubts about its effectiveness. Like a massive juggernaut, initiatives in the international community have tended to lag behind the mood turn in the zeitgeist. Liberal and neoconservative interventionists argue that democratic elections are an integral part of any long-term solution to civil conflict and political instability, so these programs should remain a standard pillar of the international community's repertoire support for postwar reconstruction and sustainable development. Yet these claims have come under increasing challenge. Realists argue that Western states should prioritize strengthening direct forms of state security and rule of law rather than elections. Reflecting contemporary events, several leading American commentators, while committed to democratic values and principles, have expressed growing doubts about the efficacy of international efforts at democracy promotion. Hence a prominent critic, Robert Kaplan, argued that holding democratic elections in many countries may unintentionally hinder efforts to strengthen ethnic peace, social stability, and economic development.[25] Fareed Zakaria suggests that in countries without liberal values, elections reinforce illiberal regimes that pose grave threats to freedom.[26] Thomas Carothers questions whether the field is learning how to produce better results, or whether practitioners are just repeating a standard repertoire of stale approaches making inflated promises that are palatable to stakeholders but ultimately fail to deliver.[27] Several prominent Western political leaders have also expressed deep doubts; President Donald Trump argues that state-building has been proven not to work, with "American First" foreign policies signaling an isolationist retreat from the democracy promotion goals advocated by neoconservatives from Ronald Reagan to George W. Bush.[28] Nor is Trump alone in these sentiments; as discussed earlier, in general, the financial crisis in 2008 and the refugee crisis, coupled with the rise of populist authoritarian parties in Europe, have reinforced isolationist and nationalistic sentiments, where politicians prioritize jobs and economic growth at home over the expenditure of blood and treasure overseas.[29]

For all these reasons, international attempts at providing electoral assistance need to prove that they are motivated by more than lofty promises and well-meaning intentions. They need to demonstrate that, under favorable circumstances, these programs can achieve their stated goals, such as by mobilizing civic engagement among citizens, expanding opportunities for gender equality in elected office, and strengthening the capacity of election management bodies. In a period of belt-tightening for aid budgets, the large-scale investment in programs of electoral assistance needs justifying to its friends and critics, not least because donors could have allocated resources alternatively for many other pressing priorities, such as assistance for displaced Syrian migrants in Lebanon and Jordan, humanitarian aid for Nepal, schooling girls and boys in Pakistan, distributing antimalarial bed nets in Burundi, or tapping village aquifers in Mali.

Organizational Learning

As well as improving accountability to donors and oversight bodies concerning the use of public funds, establishing what works in this sector has many potential benefits for development organizations, aid workers, and domestic stakeholders. Evaluation can ideally establish the most effective initiatives for strengthening the delivery of efficient and inclusive electoral services to all citizens; increase organizational feedback for program managers; and facilitate informed decisions about the most efficient deployment of financial, human and technical resources. Opportunities to engage in electoral assistance often carry serious risks that may harm prospects for sustainable democratic progress, especially contentious contests held as part of the peace-building process in the aftermath of deep-rooted conflict. Without establishing what types of policy solutions usually have the greatest impact on malpractices, and under what circumstances, ineffective programs may continue to be repeated indefinitely out of organizational inertia, while the lessons of successful innovations may not be replicated. Evaluation is often conducted at the end of major projects. But it is even more valuable and timely when used as an integral part of the implementation process, thereby facilitating incremental adjustments to fine tune program performance. In taking the Hippocratic oath, doctors are cautioned to first do no harm. Similar sentiments should govern aid workers assisting elections and democratic governance.

Difficulties in Establishing Aid Effectiveness

Unfortunately, however, systematic, comprehensive and rigorous scrutiny of programs in this sector has lagged behind many other areas of development aid, despite the acknowledged important of evaluation – and the expansion of democratic governance and electoral assistance to hundreds of projects conducted around the world. Consequently, many critical questions about the impact of electoral assistance still remain unexamined. Practitioners hope projects help, and anecdotal descriptions of positive outcomes are often used to buttress this claim. Yet there are many reasons for skepticism, and plausible evidence often remains remarkably scarce for all sorts of reasons. Compared with other sectors of development, such as food production or antimalarial treatments, it is perhaps tougher to produce solid and credible evidence demonstrating that democratic governance and electoral assistance programs achieve their substantive goals.[30] Seasoned practitioners in the field are often dubious (at best) or else hostile (at worst) about the practical value of rigorous scientific techniques seeking to determine aid effectiveness and project impacts in this sector. Program managers, aid workers, and local NGOs implementing programs may all be suspicious of being scrutinized and concerned about the risks of poor evaluations by outside agencies. Information about the activities of development organizations is often far from transparent to external observers, in part for legitimate reasons in sensitive areas, to protect the identities and activities of staff and local reformers working in dangerous regions, repressive states, and hazardous conditions where publicity could threaten their work. Even if agencies are genuinely open and committed to evaluation, with the best scientific techniques it is still challenging to generate credible and rigorous evidence demonstrating the macrolevel and long-term effects in electoral assistance programs. Difficulties surround the political sensitivity of the results, the extended chain of actions, and the multiple stakeholders involved, and the long-term period typically required for the consolidation of democratic institutions, processes, and cultures.[31] In this regard, evaluation is far more difficult than, say, assessing the impact of specific microcredit loans on household savings in Indian villages, the use of bed nets in reducing the risks of malaria in the tropics, or whether sex-segregated classrooms encourage girls' learning in Pakistan. Headline news surrounding dramatic cases of failed elections, such as those concerning claims of widespread fraud in Afghanistan or instability in Iraq, as well as media attention to deeply flawed cases such as Ethiopia, Burundi, Egypt, Cambodia, and Haiti, can drown out the quiet humdrum success of behind the scenes international electoral assistance conducted in more low-profile contests, such as in Ghana, Slovakia, or Benin.[32] Where elections succeed, agencies often seek to give the credit to local actors ("lowering the flag"), to consolidate reforms and national ownership, rather than emphasizing the role of external assistance.

HOW CAN PROGRAMS BE EVALUATED? METHODS AND EVIDENCE

Diverse methods, cases, and data therefore need to be carefully compared to piece together whether a typical range of programs and projects implemented by governments and other local stakeholders, with the support of multilateral agencies, serve to strengthen electoral integrity as the bedrock foundation for democratic governance or whether they prove ineffective. The main approaches to gathering evidence in this sector can be subdivided into comparative approaches, establishing the context at country and electoral levels, and studies evaluating the more detailed effects of specific programs within these contexts. The combination provides nested models. Evidence can be gathered from qualitative process-tracing case-studies, in-depth interviews with key stakeholders and experts, surveys of the mass public, expert elites and electoral officials, the forensic analysis of official election statistics, legal studies of electoral disputes, court cases and prosecutions, performance indices and audits, meta-analysis of the research literature, the content analysis of social and traditional media textual documents, and experimental designs.[33]

Given the arguments of aid skeptics, what approaches allow us to determine whether electoral assistance has the capacity to achieve its goals, especially by strengthening the medium-term outcomes for electoral integrity, which are the focus of this book? As the next chapter documents, there are numerous examples of contests in emerging economies and developing societies, such as in Slovenia, Chile, and Mongolia, that meet international standards, but there are also multiple cases of flawed and failed contests in places such as Togo, Zimbabwe, and Malaysia.[34] Efforts to develop systematic evaluations of development projects are part of the evidence-based policy movement and results-based performance management which swept through many public sector agencies in OECD countries during the 1990s.[35] Alas, previous attempts at systematic program evaluation have usually been unable to provide convincing and credible answers, either positive or negative, about the effectiveness of the wide array of programs seeking to strengthen democratic governance in general and, in particular, projects designed to minimize the risks of holding flawed and failed elections. Despite the growth of development aid and technical assistance programs designed to strengthen democratization and elections, and the increased emphasis on monitoring aid effectiveness, the most basic issues about the impact of electoral assistance – what it accomplishes, where it succeeds, why it fails, and how it can be improved – remain inconclusive. There are certainly country case studies providing anecdotal best-practice narrative accounts, but it is difficult to establish the reliability and generalizability of these reports.

Yet it is important to establish evidence for what works for all the reasons already mentioned, including to strengthen both elections as well as democratic governance, to select optimal interventions, to learn from experience, and to adjust and improve programs in the light of existing practices. For example, when evaluating the role of programs designed to strengthen a few key goals of electoral integrity, does technical assistance in drafting a new gender quota law lead to passage of the statute and more women in elected office in subsequent contests (as medium-term outcomes) and thus gender empowerment in elected office (as a long-term developmental impact)? Do programs training electoral officials in the use of digital registration records improve the efficiency and accuracy of the registration process (as a medium-term outcome) and thus efficient and inclusive elections (as a broader goal)? Do new political finance laws strengthen disclosure records of campaign spending by political parties and candidates (as an outcome) and thus the transparency of the electoral process (as an impact)? Does the implementation of absentee or postal ballots making voting more convenient (as an outcome) thereby boost turnout participation (as a societal impact)? Does access to a process of impartial judicial review of electoral complaints encourage political parties to resolve disputes through the legal appeal process (as an outcome) and thereby reduce conflict and violence (as the overarching goal)?

In each area covered in this book, a review of evidence-based program evaluations seeks to determine answers to these sorts of questions with some degree of confidence about the most appropriate evidence and analytical techniques and thus whether positive changes in electoral integrity can be credibly attributed to the implementation of particular policy interventions. Evidence-based evaluations are not the only consideration by decision-makers, by any means, and more intangible ethical and political considerations also come into play. Nevertheless, by expanding information and reducing risks, evidence-based analysis can assist in choices about the most appropriate and effective form of electoral assistance.

The Chain of Results Evaluation Process

When seeking to assess the work of international development agencies, studies can focus upon a larger *program* (such as the European Union's activities in training electoral observers), or a specific *project* located within a broader program (such as EU monitoring missions conducted in Nigeria or Afghanistan). To make sense of the separate steps involved in the evaluation process, this book uses a chain-of-results logic. As already discussed, evaluations are divided into stages in a sequential chain-of-results process illustrated in Table 1.1. This involves the needs-analysis identification of the risks and opportunities for intervention, establishing program goals and specific targets, reporting operational activities, analyzing medium term outcomes for electoral integrity, and determining long-term societal impacts.[36] This book focuses most attention upon evidence for the intermediate stage of determining medium term outcomes, concerning how far specific programs influence particular dimensions of electoral integrity, whether positively or negatively. This approach therefore seeks to steer a middle way between examining particular operational activities, which are concrete results for each agency but not necessarily substantively interesting, and the more diffuse macrolevel societal impacts, which are critical for development and democracy yet difficult to link credibly with particular programs.

Should Agencies Intervene? SWOT Matrix Assessments

The demand for electoral assistance has expanded substantially as these institutions spread worldwide. Since 1945, the use of direct elections for the lower house of national legislatures and for presidential office has gradually replacing other traditional nonelectoral recruitment mechanisms, including appointment and inheritance, transforming pathways to political leadership in most countries around the world. At the same time, multiple problems often undermine the transparency of their procedures, limit the accountability of elected representatives, and restrict genuine political competition. Numerous flaws are often observed and carefully documented by international monitors. As documented in the next chapter, in several cases, laws ban opposition parties. Voting rights are suppressed. Electoral registers are inaccurate. Ruling parties dominate the airwaves. Thugs threaten voters. Campaigns are awash with money. Electoral officials favor the government. Dispute resolution mechanisms are broken.

The first step in any policy evaluation is needs-assessment to diagnose the exact nature of the problems to be addressed and thus identify suitable courses of action. One useful analytical technique uses the standard "SWOT" matrix, illustrated in Table 3.1, which seeks to establish the organizational strengths and weaknesses of each agency, as well as the external environmental

TABLE 3.1 *Should International Organizations Intervene? The Strengths, Weaknesses, Opportunities, and Threats (SWOT) Assessment Matrix*

	Conditions Most Likely to Strengthen Electoral Integrity	Conditions Most Likely to Weaken Electoral Integrity
INTERNATIONAL AGENCY CAPACITIES Mission focus, technical expertise, financial and human resources, capacities, and experience	AGENCY STRENGTHS	AGENCY WEAKNESSES
LOCAL CONTEXT in each election and country: Structural constraints, international forces, and institutional arrangements	LOCAL CONTEXTUAL OPPORTUNITIES	LOCAL CONTEXTUAL THREATS

opportunities and threats of any interventions in each country, including in this case those facing the provision of electoral assistance. This approach aims to diagnose more fully the nature of any problems, to consider strategic policy remedies, and to calculate the chances for success. The capacity of the agency ideally needs to match the type of conditions on the ground. Thus, for example, the opportunities and risks facing international agencies seeking to mitigate or overcome violent electoral disputes and boycotts are going to differ substantially in, say, the environment of divided societies and fragile states with deep-rooted conflict and recent transitions from autocracy, such as Afghanistan and Libya. This is in contrast to states such as Mexico and Ghana with experience of successive contests rotating the parties in government and opposition, well-established Electoral Management Bodies, trained security officers capable of managing demonstrations peacefully, and judicial review processes. Unless program evaluations incorporate a baseline SWOT needs analysis of problems, then it becomes difficult to compare like-with-like.

What evidence is available for these purposes? International monitoring missions publish detailed reports for each contest along with summary judgments, where specific contests are deemed to have passed or failed to meet international standards. These assessments provide invaluable insights into each case and the reports can be standardized and coded to facilitate comparisons across countries and over time.[37] Cross-national annual political indicators are also widely used as proxy measures of the quality of elections, for example to compare the overall quality of political rights and civil liberties (from Freedom House), democracy and autocracy (from the series produced by Polity IV), human rights (such as CIRI), and good governance (including datasets compiled by the World Bank Institute), along with many other macrolevel indices.[38] But these are all indirect national-level measures and it is only relatively recently that more systematic, rigorous, and fine-grained indicators for the diagnosis of specific electoral malpractices have become available.

To diagnose problems arising in national parliamentary and presidential election in any country, this study draws from the Perceptions of Electoral Integrity (PEI) rolling expert survey, described in detail in Chapter 4. This compares expert perceptions about the threats and opportunities arising from all stages of the electoral cycle on a consistent basis across contemporary states around the globe. To supplement this resource, several chapters also use the 6th wave of the World Values Survey, which monitors public perceptions of electoral integrity, as well as the Varieties of Democracy and the National Elections across Democracy and Autocracy (NELDA) datasets, which facilitate the comparison of electoral trends annually from 1945 to 2012, among several indicators.[39] In combination, these datasets help us to understand the global pattern of electoral risks and opportunities, to map the global picture and time-series trends, and to identify the frequency of problems in each election that can shape strategic policy priorities for the international community and local stakeholders.

Analysis of these datasets, especially the PEI index and its subcomponents, help to diagnose the most common problems of elections in any country, and thus the threats and opportunities facing international agencies and programs offering electoral assistance. The next chapter explains the risk estimates, which are based on calculations of the structural, international, and institutional factors established in the previous volume as contributing towards electoral integrity.[40] Thus regression analysis models evaluating evidence for program effectiveness need to control for the social structural, international, and institutional factors that are associated with electoral integrity at national level. This helps to identify electoral assistance programs that underperform, and thus fall short of expectations, according to the models, and also election programs that overperform, and thus do better than anticipated based on baseline conditions.

Program Goals

The second stage of any evaluation process concerns the type of programmatic goals, and more specific project targets, that are designed to be achieved in assistance seeking to overcome problems of democratic governance and electoral integrity. For example, many electoral support programs are typically designed to strengthen the capacity and technical skills of electoral official bodies, to promote inclusive forms of parliamentary representation for women and minorities, and to improve the accuracy and comprehensiveness of the electoral register. Specific targets can be set to monitor each overall goal; hence the aim may be to increase the proportion of women in elected office to around 30 percent, reflecting the target set at the 1995 Beijing UN Convention. General goals and more specific targets are typically reported in standard annual reports by agencies in the international community to present the justification for their programmatic activities.

The foundation for international standards of electoral integrity rest upon Article 21(3) in the Universal Declaration of Human Rights (1948). This specifies that "The will of the people shall be the basis of the authority of government; this will shall be expressed in periodic and genuine elections which shall be by universal and equal suffrage and shall be held by secret vote or by equivalent free voting procedures." Agreement about the principles which should govern the conduct of elections were further specified in Article 25 of the UN International Covenant for Civil and Political Rights (ICCPR of 1966), namely the need for:

- Periodic elections at regular intervals;
- Universal suffrage which includes all sectors of society;
- Equal suffrage, in the idea of one-person, one-vote;
- The right to stand for public office and contest elections;
- The rights of all eligible electors to vote;

- The use of a secret ballot process;
- Genuine elections; and that,
- Elections should reflect the free expression of the will of the people.[41]

Other treaties provide enhanced protection of electoral rights for specific groups or extend rights by addressing additional thematic issues. Relevant treaties include the 1965 International Convention on the Elimination of All Forms of Racial Discrimination (ICERD), which refers to electoral rights without distinction or discrimination, and the 1979 Convention on the Elimination of All Forms of Discrimination Against Women (CEDAW), which includes obligations on women's political participation. The 1990 International Convention on the Protection of the Rights of All Migrant Workers and Members of Their Families (ICMW) protects electoral rights for migrants and their families, and the 2006 Convention on the Rights of Persons with Disabilities (CRPD) provides explicit rights regarding the political participation of persons with disabilities. In addition, the 2003 Convention against Corruption (UNCAC) includes provisions on the transparency of public administration bodies and campaign finance. Each of these treaties establishes a body, consisting of independent experts, to monitor the compliance of states that have ratified or acceded to them. States that ratify the treaty are obliged to respect the authority of these bodies as well as to implement rights into domestic laws.

UN and regional treaties endorsed by member states are the most important source of international law but other documents interpreting and elaborating upon treaty obligations include official reports, working documents, guidelines, and court judgments. These documents establish the fundamental rights, codified in international law, that are often discussed when defining the quality of elections. Thus the Carter Center maintains a comprehensive database of obligations for democratic elections in public international law that is designed to aid monitors assessing the quality of electoral processes.[42] The key topics are organized around the traditional principles in the ICCPR, such as universal voting rights, access to information, and rule of law. These principles of civil and political rights constitute the basic or minimal level acceptable by states which have endorsed these standards. But these are not static and frozen in the politics of earlier eras; instead global norms continue to evolve and expand within the international community through a series of multilateral treaties, human rights conventions, legal instruments, and more detailed working guidelines.[43] Advocates continue to press for the adoption of additional standards to cover contemporary issues arising on the current policy agenda, exemplified by concern about the need to achieve gender equality in elected office, the deployment of new technological facilities for electronic voting, polling access for the physically disabled, as well as the regulation of political finance and the use of public subsidies for campaigns by political parties. In turn, as norms have diffused, human rights activists and local reformers who support these agreements have sought to implement them and codify normative standards through reforming domestic legislation and regulations.

In practice, technical assistance from the international community has been provided typically throughout the electoral cycle with the aim of strengthening many stages, including electoral administration and planning, review of electoral laws and regulations, electoral dispute resolution, boundary delimitation, voter registration, election budgeting, logistics, the procurement of election materials, the use of technologies, training election officials, voter and civic education, media assistance, voting and counting operations, election security, and coordination of international donor assistance. The international community usually collaborates with local networks within each country, commonly by sharing knowledge of best practices, working with technical experts, electoral officials, government departments, and legislators to craft new laws and administrative regulations, bringing together coalitions of reform movements, fostering dialogue among rival communities and parties in divided societies, encouraging civic awareness and participation in electoral processes, strengthening gender equality and minority representation in elected office, expanding access to electoral justice, encouraging independent watchdog agencies, and implementing budgetary audits facilitating transparency in electoral administration. Technical assistance is designed to strengthen the institutions of democratic governance, concentrated especially upon electoral management bodies, the frontline troops running contests. Development aid is also intended to shape the incentives for domestic actors to implement specific policies and human rights reforms, exemplified by providing technical assistance concerning the adoption of gender quotas for elected office. Aid is also targeted directly towards civil society bodies, including independent media watchdogs and human rights monitoring organizations, as well as specific populations such as young people, women, and minorities.

Nevertheless, rigorous evaluations are easiest for development goals with specific targets that can be relatively easily observed and counted by national statistical offices. For example, how far countries are meeting the Sustainable Development Goals, which came into force in January 2016, can be gauged fairly reliably by monitoring several standard demographic and social indicators where data is available, such as in national levels of child immunization, rates of boys and girl's attendance at primary school, levels of maternal mortality, and patterns of female literacy.[44] In practice, however, there remain important gaps in data availability, quality, disaggregation, and harmonized statistics, even for core indicators in many of the world's least developed countries. The gaps are worst in fragile states and in societies lacking regular general household surveys. Most sub-Saharan African countries, and many other developing countries, still lack complete civil registration systems for reporting births and deaths.[45] Nevertheless, in principle there is a fairly broad agreement within the international community about the statistical measures that are suitable to monitor progress in the SDGs on issues such as health, education, child protection, and HIV/AIDS.

Downstream development projects are also relatively straightforward to report, such as the number of antimalarial bed nets distributed in Niger by the Bill and Melinda Gates Foundation, or the proportion of farmers planting golden rice in the Philippines.[46] It is perhaps inherently more challenging to assess the societal-level impact of programs in development which typically have broad and diffuse goals, such as strengthening inclusive participation, building impartial electoral authorities, and expanding opportunities for equitable political competition.[47] Despite these difficulties, the last decade has seen important advances in the metrics and methods used for collecting and analyzing electoral assistance that strengthen confidence in both the external and the internal validity of evaluation studies.

Operational Activities

Many alternative strategies are employed by different development agencies, ranging from soft-power technical assistance and transformative engagement to hard-power coercive strategies, such as conditionality, sanctions, and even military interventions. In the field of electoral assistance, programs typically provide capacity development and technical assistance for government bodies (emphasized by UNDP), legal advice about the implementation of international conventions and treaties into domestic laws (the focus of activities by the Council of Europe), the deployment of electoral monitoring missions (such as by OAS, OSCE, and the Carter Center), support for networks of civic society reform organizations (such as by the UN Democracy Fund and the Open Society Institute), the publication of integrity indices (such as by Transparency International and Global Integrity), and human rights monitoring naming and shaming violators (such as by Human Rights Watch, Amnesty International, and the Committee to Protect Journalists), diplomatic pressures, trade sanctions, and dispute mediation efforts (such as by the US State department), the use of conditional aid through incentives and penalties (exemplified by the European Union requirements for prospective member states), criminal prosecutions of leaders for gross human rights violations (by the International Criminal Court), and peace-keeping interventions in conflicted societies (by UN blue helmets). No single technique is appropriate for all international actors. For example, the UNDP has the legitimacy, resources, and trust to focus upon capacity building with official government agencies. By contrast Human Rights Watch has the political autonomy that facilitates critical human rights monitoring. In most countries, a blend of loosely coordinated approaches and functional roles are commonly employed by different agencies. Thus in this stage of any evaluation process, it is important to establish exactly what activities are included in technical electoral assistance program, including monitoring and reporting the investment of human, technological, and financial resources, the planning timeline, the key objectives, and the strategies used by agencies.

Many existing program and project evaluations produced by international agencies, bilateral donors, and recipient countries are concerned with monitoring the technical efficiency of interventions. Both the landmark Paris Declaration of 2005, and the subsequent Accra Agenda for Action in 2008, focused attention on results-based management as a prerequisite for achieving effective and accountable states.[48] Under this commitment, partner countries commit to work to establish results-oriented reporting and assessment frameworks that monitor progress on key indicators against selected dimensions of the national and sector development strategies. During recent decades development agencies in many OECD countries have also adopted "results based performance management" that seeks to determine whether plans are implemented by employees efficiently, cost-effectively, and in a timely fashion, as well as achieving specific practical goals and objectives. This approach is hardly novel, as it became widely used in the corporate sector in postindustrial societies by the 1950s, but performance management become more widely used by public sector agencies during the 1990s, including among OECD bilateral donors, thereby spreading to organizations in the international development community such as UNDP's strategic plan.[49] For example, a week-long training workshop designed to strengthen women's capacity for leadership roles, organized with local partners by USAID or UN Women, is commonly reported today according to benchmarks such as how many people attended the event, whether it was regarded by participants as relevant, engaging, and informative, whether the pedagogic goals achieved several learning objectives, and whether the event was carried out within its allocated budget and timeline. Similarly, agencies such as International IDEA produce a wide range of technical policy papers, handbooks, guidelines, tools, and online databases designed for electoral officials, civil society organizations, and policymakers. Topics focus on electoral processes, constitution building, political participation and representation, and democracy and development. In its annual reports, the organization documents its record of results by indicators such as the number of outreach meetings and capacity building workshops which IDEA organized, the launch and dissemination of publications, and the use of country and regional studies with local partners in specific cases.[50]

It is relatively straightforward to document program activities in results-based management systems that are now routinely used by bilateral and multilateral development agencies and NGOs, such as recording the catalog of activities implemented to assist the 2013 Kenyan presidential election, for how long and how many people participated, how much projects cost, and so on. But determining whether these programs actually achieved their goals by strengthening international standards of electoral integrity in Kenya is far more difficult to establish with any degree of certainty. Monitoring by matching organizational strategic goals, specific indicators and targets, and subsequent operational activities can be fairly precise, for example a pre- and postevent questionnaire can be implemented at a workshop to see whether participants were satisfied by the event and whether they reported acquiring new skills or awareness from different activities. To monitor the dissemination of policy papers and technical reports, we can measure online downloads, citations in the research literature, and the amount of media coverage of published reports. The causal link between the program aims and the immediate operational activities can be attributed with considerable confidence. Proponents of new public sector management argue that is important to use strategic plans and performance evaluations for administrative accountability, for example to insure that programs run by staff are cost-effective, well-run, coordinated, and delivering on their planned objectives. Results-based management is also potentially useful for organizational learning and feedback, to monitor the link between the organization's goals and activities, and adjust the latter where failing to deliver. Another potential advantage is that the development of strategic plans can encourage organizational coherence, for example to gauge how far activities are meeting specific targets when reporting to executive boards. Moreover, managerial flexibility can be encouraged; rather than following rigid one-size-fits-all bureaucratic rules, officials have considerable autonomy to decide the best way to implement activities designed to achieve strategic organizational targets within each local context, thereby potentially improving public sector service delivery.[51]

Such indicators typically monitor the efficiency of projects for achieving organizational goals but not their broader developmental effectiveness. For example, when IFES organizes a training workshop for electoral managers in Myanmar on how to improve the electoral register, or NDI train citizens groups in Quick Count or Parallel Vote Tabulation methodologies to monitor the accuracy of the declared results and prevent fraud, operational activities can be assessed by the number of participants. Also, those who attended can be studied to see if they acquired a clearer understanding of these issues when gauged by comparing before-and-after participant surveys, focus groups, or in-depth interviews. Similarly, USAID performance indicators published in their annual reports count the number of individuals receiving voter and civic education through US-assisted programs, the number of independent news outlets their programs support, and the number of domestic NGOs engaged in monitoring or advocacy work on human rights they support, and so on.[52] This type of monitoring is important for accountability and sound financial management within any organization, documenting what was done by the project and checking that budgets are met and resources deployed efficiently. It goes beyond narrative stories illustrating successful cases. Performance-based management has long been advocated under the assumption that accountability and efficiency is strengthened where organizations identify clear strategic goals and administrators are assessed by their delivery of results.

In practice, performance-based management often fails to meet these ideals.[53] For example, a review by OECD/DAC concluded that despite some efforts to develop "actionable governance indicators" for public sector management, few countries have robust and comprehensive results-oriented frameworks or monitoring systems in place for public sector reforms.[54] Those which do exist are usually task-focused and short-term, leading to incremental reforms rather than assessing overall progress and needs. When reporting results in this area, the review suggests, selected indicators often proved inconsistent, unreliable, immeasurable, or poorly specified, with overloaded frameworks, poor disaggregation, and weak theories about the drivers of change.

Organizational activities reported during and immediately after the conclusion of a project are the most straightforward component to gauge with a considerable degree of confidence, but in many ways they also provide minimal information about improvements in the quality of elections, still less the consequences for democratic governance. The record of operational activities can be reported in a mechanical fashion, without any clear rationale for the planned goals, the selected benchmarks, and resource costs, for example by failing to provide consistent information useful to compare year-by-year performance. Moreover, the output indicators are not substantively meaningful for the achievement of development goals; the fact that more or fewer participants attended a workshop, for instance, and whether they expressed satisfaction with the event, does not say anything about the broader outcome of the activity, for example whether the women who attended improved their prospects of getting nominated or elected to public office, still less whether this contributed towards their empowerment. A long list of activities says anything about the substantive quality or ultimate impact of the work on electoral integrity, such as whether workshop participants acquired new skills or insights, or whether organizations performed better following the training. The observable (and trivial) often predominates over the intangible (and important) outcomes. Certainly results-based management can be treated as a first step and organizations can follow up with further evaluation research of longer-term impacts, for example the careers of women who participated in an event can be compared with their subsequent political leadership roles many years later – but this group may have been equally successful without attending the workshop. In addition, even a program is regarded as successful according to the survey evidence, this may be due to selection effects; women who chose to attend the workshop may have already been more ambitious and motivated than their equivalent peers. Similarly, expert meetings providing technical briefings and high-level advice to senior ministers and elected officials about the options to reform the electoral process may well be associated with subsequent passage of new legislation, suggesting a positive intervention; however, selection effect are also probably at work, since governments already committed to reform are most likely to request technical assistance in drafting new policies. Thus ideally a randomized or matching control group needs to be built into the evaluation process from the launch of any program or project to determine any treatment effects. For all these reasons, results-based management needs to be treated as a preliminary stage in any more comprehensive and systematic evaluation of organizational performance, not the final endpoint. None of this bean counting says anything about the substantive quality or ultimate impact of the work on electoral integrity, such as whether workshop participants acquired new skills or insights, or whether organizations performed better following the training. Activities reported immediately after the conclusion of a project are the most straightforward component to gauge with a considerable degree of confidence, but in many ways they also provide minimal information about improvements in the quality of elections, still less the consequences for democratic governance. Where bean counting is regarded skeptically by administrators, as a managerial exercise that generates largely meaningless reports, it may also damage more credible forms of program evaluation.

Medium Term Programmatic for Electoral Integrity

Broader impact evaluations focus upon whether the results attributable to a program achieved certain medium-term developmental goals and thus whether it should be continued, expanded, or abandoned. In this book, such objectives are conceptualized and defined by whether interventions strengthen different components of electoral integrity. For example, the notion encompasses the goal of creating inclusive parliaments and gender equality in elected office. This obligation has been endorsed by the world's governments in a series of international agreements, including the Beijing Declaration in 1990 and the 2000 Millennium Development Goals.[55] Given this objective, evaluation seeks to determine whether a training program for women leaders led many participants to seek party nominations for local councils or national parliaments. If they did run for office, did they display skills in public speaking, in campaigning, or in fundraising which can plausibly be attributed to the project?

Organizations are expected to use suitable performance indicators and rigorous evaluation techniques to determine strategic policy priorities and goals, to monitor policy effectiveness, and to facilitate organizational learning.[56] It is important to utilize suitable metrics and methods because rigorous and well-designed evaluations of development aid and assistance can serve multiple functions. Evaluations can help to identify social needs and inform programmatic decision-making, improve organizational accountability and effectiveness, promote institutional learning and feedback, and increase the chances that the future investment of resources will yield effective benefits.

Advocates of evidence-based policy-making argue that this can also potentially help inform decision-makers when choosing from multiple policy options about electoral assistance, each with many specific implementation choices. The simple language commonly used in observer assessment reports of "free and fair" elections, providing "genuine" choices, and producing "credible" results disguises many complex issues. Electoral integrity is a multidimensional concept, and thus many goals can be identified as legitimate medium-term outcomes, although the effectiveness of programs in achieving these objectives remains to be determined. For example, should strategic reformers seek to revise the formal legal framework governing electoral procedures in order to maximize party competition, such as efforts to reform the electoral system, to reduce partisan gerrymandering of district boundaries, and to lower vote-seat thresholds? Or should policy makers address more minor administrative voting reforms designed to improve sagging turnout, such as by implementing convenience ballots, extending balloting hours, introducing biometric electoral registers, developing civic education programs, and expanding access to the disabled? Should projects address the effectiveness of election management bodies, for example bolstering capacity through providing professional training workshops and procedural guidelines for midlevel officials and poll workers, computerizing registration, voter identification, and balloting processes, strengthening accountability through performance indicators, and improving the accuracy and timeliness of vote tabulation procedures? Or should agencies seek to increase the transparency of the electoral process through expanding the role of independent media and observer monitors, by offering training programs for journalists, deploying international missions, and supporting civic organizations as election observers? Or should efforts be invested in encouraging more inclusive parliaments, for example through pressuring governments to adopting legal quotas for historically disadvantaged groups such as women and minorities? Are political finance regulations in urgent need of reform through the provision of public funding, spending or donor caps, or disclosure requirements? And in postconflict societies and fragile states, should the policy priorities focus on developing electoral dispute resolution mechanisms, such as programs strengthening the mediating role of the judiciary and training security forces? Finally, should regional organizations and multilateral agencies seek to expand the electoral rights recognized in international law through seeking agreement for new conventions, treaties, and guidelines within the international community, for example concerning the appropriate legal regulation of media and money in electoral politics? Alternatively, rather than prioritizing any single initiative, should a mix of all of the above be attempted on an ad-hoc basis by different development agencies in different local contexts, on the grounds that limited evidence is available to determine which strategy is the most effective, malpractice differs in severity across societies and types of regimes and key actors also diverge in their core capacities and mission goals.

Yet while program outcomes for electoral integrity are more important for development than reporting technical activities, they are also far harder to determine with any degree of confidence. One reason is that technical assistance for elections is usually a long-term process; for example, candidates often have to run for successive contests before they are eventually successful in winning a seat. Capacity building for electoral officials is also expected to accumulate as experience deepens over successive contests. One contest may see substantial gains for women in office while the next one produces setbacks, for example if parties shift fortunes. In addition, a program may achieve its specific objectives, for example by making women leaders more confident and articulate public speakers, or more effective campaigners. Nevertheless, multiple external constraints may limit opportunities for women to gain nominations for winnable seats, such as the power of incumbency, the need for independent financial resources, or the attitudes of party selectors. Thus a program's specific goals (focused on supply-side factors addressing the capacity of women to run for elected office) may be poorly matched to the problem (if the chief obstacle concerns the institutional rules and the demand-side of political recruitment). In one program by NDI, for example, the million dollar project provided technical assistance to support women's campaigns in the 2005 Lebanese elections, with the result that several women mounted campaigns to gain spots on candidate lists, but none were nominated.[57]

When elections are held in fragile states, a mélange of programs are often typically implemented by multiple partners and agencies, involving numerous international and domestic actors and types of interventions, not the outcome of a single project. For example, the donor community invested in many programs in the run-up to the 2013 Kenyan elections in the attempt to prevent a recurrence of the violence that plagued the 2007 contests, working to promote dialogue with political parties, to build the capacity and impartiality of the election commission, to develop civic education through civil society organizations, and to promote effective dispute resolution mechanisms with the judiciary. Thus diverse agencies such as USAID, IFES, the European Union, the African Union, the Kofi Annan Foundation, EISA, the International Criminal Court, and UNDP were all active in different ways when seeking to bring parties to the peace-building table after 2007 and prevent further electoral violence and instability. In the run up to 2013, the international donor community contributed approximately US $107 million to the elections.[58] This includes USAID, which alone spent $41 million on a wide range of programs during the 2008–13 electoral cycle in Kenya. These activities were subsequently evaluated by USAID through a desk review of key documentation, key informant interviews, group discussions/interviews and site visits.[59] Yet even if information from a common results framework is available, evaluation remains limited, as it is difficult to isolate the effects of any single USAID programmatic initiative in Kenya from the broader context, the overall basket of donor funds, and collaborative partnership networks.[60]

When determining the impact of programs, it is essential to be able to identify a counterfactual, namely the situation for individuals, communities, and governments had there been no program intervention, to rule out the effects of selection bias and other intervening factors. For example, what would have been the levels of electoral violence in the 2013 Kenyan contests if USAID had not sought to implement their conflict-prevention programs among security officials? How many women might have been nominated and elected to office without participating in UN Women civic education and training workshops, or without the implementation of legal quotas? Would the capacity of the Nigerian election management body have improved without the technical manuals and knowledge exchange networks assisted by International IDEA? Randomization can help to compare program participants with control groups that are not subject to the treatment interventions. This works especially well at individual and community levels, for example if participants in a training program, like polling staff, are randomized into different treatment and control groups. But for many practical reasons in the field of electoral assistance and democratic governance it is not always possible to use randomized designs. For example, this technique cannot be used to assess the effects of reforms following implementation of nationwide laws and procedures rolled out across the whole country, such as the impact on individual-level electoral turnout or public trust in the electoral process, since the reforms affected all the electorate equally.

Communities can only be compared using pre/post "natural" experiments if there is variance in laws across local authorities, states, or provinces, and even here there are challenges since the choice of reforms are not randomly distributed. For example, the US states provide a fascinating laboratory, with over 30 new state laws passed that change processes of electoral registration and balloting, some liberalizing procedures (such as through introducing postal ballots and election-day registration), others tightening procedures (such as strict requirements for official photo IDs). But the changes are strongly predicted by the party in control of the state house, so the interventions are far from random. In practice, therefore, this approach often needs to be combined with many other analytical techniques in mixed-methods designs. Alternative methods include using lab or field experiments to assess project outcomes, where a short-term effect is inferred. For example, experiments can allocate citizens randomly to groups that are offered alternative ways of casting a ballot to see whether the mode effects confidence and trust in the electoral process. Thus the UK Electoral Commission used experimental pilot studies during the May 2003 local elections where different local authorities allowed citizen to cast ballots through a variety of remote electronic voting technologies, including use of the internet from home and public access sites, interactive digital television, SMS text messaging, and touch-tone telephones. Pilot programs also used all-postal ballots, getting electronic information to voters and extended voting periods. For comparison, in the remaining areas the public cast a traditional in-person vote by marking crosses on standard paper ballots in local polling stations.[61] The results were used to monitor changes in voter turnout between the previous contest and the 2003 elections in each locality. The analysis suggested that all-postal ballots had the most positive effect upon boosting turnout.[62] It can commonly be assumed that any specific outcomes that are detected through such methods will gradually accumulate over time, but it is unclear whether it is appropriate to assume that monotonic linear developments will continue to occur.[63] For example, the novelty of casting ballots through new technologies in local elections and activities by local polling officers promoting use of these facilities could be expected to die down over time. Evaluation reports should ideally assess short-term and also any subsequent effects occurring well after the project finishes.

Finally, many forms of electoral assistance, such as building the technical and human capacity of electoral management bodies, do not lend themselves easily to clearly specified goals monitored by measurable medium-term outcomes. The quality of health care can be scrutinized quite precisely, for example where the WHO immunization programs reduce incidents of measles among children living in tropical zones. Similarly, indicators such as the ratio of girls to boys in primary and secondary schools, as an indicator of gender equality in educational opportunities, is relatively straightforward to monitor through official statistics reported in the MDGs or through local detailed studies. By contrast, the concept of electoral integrity is complex and multifaceted, engaging normative values such as inclusive parliaments, transparent and equitable campaign finance regulations, and fair electoral administration. All of these abstract global norms remain complicated to interpret and translate into specific goals and detailed indicators. Moreover, programs can succeed in their specific technical goals, such as introducing biotechnology to improve the accuracy and efficiency of electoral registration and voter identification processes, even if elections end in disputed results, claims of fraud, or widespread technical irregularities. And conversely electoral technologies can fail, while the outcome of the election remains largely peaceful and widely accepted.[64]

Long-Term Societal Impacts

Finally, programs can also be evaluated in terms of their contribution towards long-term societal impacts at the national level, such as the broader consequences of electoral integrity for democratic governance, human development, and security. This perspective concerns the more diffuse goals that the international community seeks to achieve, such as to facilitate accountable, transparent, and inclusive political institutions. Evaluation of societal impacts usually focus on the achievement of overall societal goals, including democratic governance, peace, and prosperity.

Agencies commonly claim that their programs pay substantial dividends for democracy as well as human development and peace-building. For example, USAID argues: "By helping societies protect the basic rights of citizens, we prevent conflict, spur economic growth and advance human dignity. Countries with democratic freedoms are more just, peaceful and stable – and their citizens can fulfill their potential."[65] Similarly DFID lists a series of the instrumental benefits believed to arise from their efforts to strengthen elections and democratic governance:

> The underlying requirements for poverty reduction include sustained peace, the rule of law, effective property rights, stable business conditions, and honest and responsive governments. These enable open economies and open societies to thrive ... DFID is helping to build peaceful states and societies by addressing the root causes of conflict and fragility; giving people a say in the decisions that affect them and supporting more inclusive politics; helping to create economic opportunities and jobs; and strengthening the institutions delivering security, justice and basic services.[66]

Likewise an independent evaluation concluded that technical aspects benefitted from UNDP's work in strengthening electoral systems and processes: "UNDP has contributed to more professional electoral management, more inclusive processes and more credible electoral events than would have been the case without UNDP assistance."[67] The UNDP's role, the report noted, was enhanced by its extensive field-presence throughout the world, ability to mobilize donors, and trusted impartiality. At the same time, the report concluded UNDP had been less successful in generating electoral processes with long-term sustainability and national ownership.

Agencies are not alone in making these types of claims. In the decade following the fall of the Berlin Wall in 1989, the democracy-promotion perspective was championed by a wide range of commentators such as Morton Halperin, Joseph Siegle, Michael Weinstein, Larry Diamond, Thomas Carothers, and Michael McFaul, among others.[68] This viewpoint emphasizes that holding competitive elections in the early stages of regime transitions, and providing technical assistance designed to deepen and consolidate the principles and institutions of liberal democracy, would have intrinsic benefits by reinforcing human rights and public participation. Elections are advocated to make elected officials more accountable to ordinary people and thus more responsive to social needs and political grievances. Competitive multiparty elections are thought to work through constraining the abuse of power by predatory leaders, expanding voice and participation, and empowering citizens to rid themselves of incompetent rulers. In places undergoing regime transitions – exemplified by developments in Central Europe following the fall of the Berlin Wall – democracy-promoters argued that elections are one of the first steps in strengthening civic participation, inclusive representative bodies, and party competition for its own sake. Once elections have been held, then the international community can partner with a legitimate government. In addition to these claims, commentators such as Halperin, Siegle, and Weinstein argue that democracy also delivers concrete instrumental benefits, by improving human development and security, reducing poverty, expanding educational opportunities, and building the conditions for lasting peace in developing societies.[69] From this viewpoint, elections are only one part of attempts by the international community to strengthen democratic governance and open societies but they are an essential first step.[70] The early stages of the standard sequential process following any regime transition include developing constitutional frameworks respecting human rights, strengthening competitive political parties, and holding multiparty elections meeting international principles. The standard process then moves on through a series of initiatives designed to strengthen the capacity of effective and inclusive legislatures, professionalizing independent judicial bodies and the courts, decentralizing decision-making for local government, and expanding participation in civil society organizations, NGOs, and the independent media.

But is there plausible evidence that elections, and thus by implication technical assistance attempting to strengthen popular contests, actually generate beneficial long-term societal impacts, as claimed? During the last decade these arguments came under increasing scrutiny, and a more skeptical interpretation became popular among commentators, following the attempts to hold competitive elections following regime change and attempts at peace-building in states such as Iraq, Afghanistan, Egypt, and Libya. The positive role of competitive elections has been challenged by a wide range of scholars, including Samuel Huntington, Francis Fukuyama, Simon Chesterman, James Fearon, David Laitin, Stephen Krasner, and Roland Paris.[71] From this perspective, state-building is the highest priority goal following any regime transitions in divided societies where basic human security is lacking, so that any competitive elections are delayed until conditions are ripe.

This emphasis is also echoed by several agencies in the international community, led by the World Bank, which prioritize the developmental benefits thought to accrue more generally from strengthening the institutions of so-called good governance, reflecting principles of transparency, accountability, and rule of law, rather than electoral participation per se. This perspective stresses that fragile states in some of the world's poorest developing societies inherit a long legacy of conflict and anarchy, where the central authorities have limited capacity to maintain order, to defend their boundaries against external threats, and to deliver many basic public goods and services, let alone manage the complex task of holding competitive elections meeting international standards.[72] Many states struggle to guarantee conditions of public safety (such as in Côte d'Ivoire, Somalia, Mali, Nigeria, and the Democratic Republic of Congo), to protect against the worst effects of humanitarian and natural crisis (such as following the devastating earthquake in Haiti, floods in Benin, and famine in Niger), and to provide universal access to schooling and health care for their citizens (such as to cope with the devastating effects of Ebola in Liberia and Sierra Leone). In this context, attempts to hold multiparty elections are thought to prove counterproductive, by exacerbating partisan tensions and ethnic rivalry.

State-building interventions prioritize the provision of aid and assistance designed to strengthen the core functions of executive agencies, government ministries, and the civil service, the courts and security services, local government agencies, and public sector management. This view builds on the developmental success of countries such as South Korea, Taiwan, China, Ethiopia, Rwanda, and Vietnam. The core minimum functions of the state strengthened through this process including the capacity to maintain security and rule of law within their national boundaries, to provide basic services for citizens such as emergency relief, schools, and health care, to formulate and administer budget plans, and to collect taxation revenues.[73] Cases such as Timor-Leste, Kosovo, Afghanistan, Liberia, and South Sudan exemplify the complex dilemmas raised by attempts by the international community to rebuild public sector capacity.[74] The state-building school of thought generally acknowledges the normative value of competitive elections as an abstract ideal, but this view prioritizes the pragmatic benefits of strengthening governance institutions as the overarching first priority. In the strongest version of this argument, scholars contend that in weak or fragile states, competitive elections should be deferred or postponed until conditions are ripe.[75]

The broadest objectives of electoral assistance may not be achievable during the life cycle of the project. It is difficult to establish the links in the chain of results connecting specific programs with societal impacts with any degree of confidence, even if the most rigorous scientific techniques are deployed. For example, performance indicators for the effectiveness of any strategies used by managers to reduce electoral disputes could be monitored by changes in subsequent levels of official complaints, the timeliness with which any disputes are resolved, or the number of outbreaks of conflict. The cumulative impact created by a program or specific project it is usually seen only after several years and this is the most difficult aspect to assess, given many other confounding factors which could plausibly influence development goals. Thus it is relatively straightforward for the World Health Organization to link a major immunization program with the subsequent incidence of the disease or for the World Food Programme to monitor the impact of distributing high-yielding seeds on agricultural production. It is far more complex for UNDP to establish the effects of technical assistance and training for election management bodies in Nigeria or Ghana with their subsequent performance. Establishing credible evidence for inferring causal links between the project's activities and its ultimate impact is less clear-cut than documenting specific activities and key outcomes.

CONCLUSIONS

Multiple methods of evaluation have been used in this sector, both singly and in combination.[76] The most common approach among practitioners relies upon qualitative information. UNDP recently examined the long-term effects of its electoral assistance from 2000 to 2011 through eight detailed national case studies involving interviews with key stakeholders including representatives from UNDP country offices, EMBs, main political parties, parliamentarians, CSOs, international assistance providers, and development partners. Other sources of information include UN needs assessment mission reports, project documents, evaluations, and international observer reports.[77] This approach has certain pros and cons. At a purely descriptive level, it is useful for organizations to document their project work and to listen to the views of multiple stakeholders, including grassroots participants, to promote downwards accountability. Process-tracing narrative cases allow greater transparency and organizational learning. At the same time, however, this traditional approach may be regarded by critics as making implausible claims and unduly rosy assessments of best-practice stories if it goes beyond description to make certain causal claims.

During the last decade, international organizations have increasingly adopted results-based management systems that seek to document concrete program activities: the number of workshops held, the number of participants who attended, the amount of aid spent, the number of reports published, and so on. Unfortunately, while commonly understood as "evaluation" in the language of results-based management, and while useful for internal accountability within development organizations, the reported catalog of activities is too specific to provide an indication of what concrete difference these interventions made.

A common tradition in scholarly research has attempted to determine the societal impacts of development aid and assistance, such as upon democracy or regime change, commonly through employing standard econometric models and observational evidence. For example a series of studies using these methods have sought to test how far the distribution of official development assistance in general and spending on the governance and civil society sector are correlated with the observed performance of states in achieving certain national-level political indicators, such as the Polity IV democracy-autocracy scale, the Freedom House indices of political rights and civil liberties, and Cheibub and Gandhi's regime classification.[78] In related studies, researchers have used similar techniques to analyze whether aid spending is correlated with indicators such as the World Bank Institute's measure of good governance and Transparency International's measure of Perceptions of Corruption.[79] Unfortunately, this analytical strategy is also unlikely to be fruitful for guiding strategic decisions by policymakers, since the goals are usually far too diffuse to be plausibly attributable to the impact of specific programs. Unfortunately econometric techniques have been unable to resolve debates about the impact of diffuse or specific forms of aid on democratic governance, and the overall results present mixed and inconclusive findings that are heavily dependent upon model specification.[80] When interpreting the causal direction in any observed correlations, analysts confront complex issues of endogeneity and selection effects. This issue is especially problematic where the distribution of aid is conditional upon the achievement of certain benchmarks of democratic governance, such as where lack of corruption is imposed as a condition for membership of international organizations such as the European Union or in the allocation of aid from the US Millennium Development Corporation.[81]

The difficulties of using these techniques for program evaluation can be illustrated by the Pew Trust, which has produced one of the most thorough set of electoral indicators to monitor and compare the performance of US states after each election, using data such as the availability of online registration, balloting wait times, and the registration rate within each state.[82] Some of these indices can be attributed fairly plausibly to the activities and efficiency of electoral authorities. For example, excessively lengthy queues waiting to cast a ballot may well be due to lack of contingency planning in allocating sufficient polling booths and poll workers or the use of restrictive opening hours.[83] Turnout in each state may also plausibly prove to be related to the availability of convenience voting facilities, such as vote by mail or advance voting. Yet it is difficult to link some of the Pew indicators directly to administrative performance by electoral authorities per se; for example, levels of voter turnout in a state are frequently due to multiple factors that are well beyond the scope of electoral management – such as the demographic composition of the constituency, the closeness of the race, the inclusion of hot button referenda issues on the ballot, and the efforts by parties and candidates to mobilize the electorate. Any well-specified econometric models would need to control for all the factors that have commonly been found to affect societal levels or individual levels of voter turnout, as well as including specific factors that could credibly be related to electoral administration per se, exemplified by the provision of convenience voting facilities in a locality or state.

During recent decades, methods using observational data have been supplemented by growing use of randomized methods including *laboratory* experiments (controlling the treatment in highly artificial settings), *field* experiments (typically where researchers have less control of the specific type of project intervention but where treatments are randomized among groups to monitor effects), and *natural* experiments (taking advantage of pre- and postchanges in a treatment and control group in naturally occurring real-world phenomenon). For evidence, a growing number of project evaluations have been now been conducted and published in each sector of democratic governance, including a smaller subset using rigorous techniques of field experiments.[84] Large donor organizations have spearheaded these initiatives, notably USAID, OECD-DAC, and the World Bank. In 2012, USAID adopted a new evaluation program in the Office of Democracy and Governance that included collecting evaluation reports in a public database.[85] Several networks of scholars and consultants have also promoted impact evaluations in development, notably the Poverty Action Lab (JPal) at MIT, the Network of networks on Impact Evaluation (NONIE), the International Initiative for Impact Evaluation (3ie), Experiments in Government and Politics (EGap),[86] and Innovations for Poverty Action (IPA). Yet at the same time while multiple project evaluations have flourished, it remains difficult to generalize from each of these particular studies as they lack external validity. Little has been firmly established with any certainty about the more general impact of program-level interventions in democratic governance, or how performance varies systematically across different types of agencies, programs, sectors, regimes, goals, and countries.

Rejecting each of these approaches, we use multiple methods that focus upon credible evidence to evaluate the middle stage of the chain-of-results model. In particular, chapters seek to test whether typical electoral assistance programs that are widely used in the international community generate certain specific goals and targets, notably whether they strengthen certain dimensions of electoral integrity. Taking the example of capacity building workshops, under this approach project indicators could be measured by monitoring whether electoral officials who participated in the dispute mitigation workshop subsequently undertook actions based on information gathered from the event, such as producing contingency plans, implementing institutional mechanisms, writing guidelines, training staff, and developing administrative procedures designed to deal more effectively with electoral disputes. The challenge tackled in subsequent chapters is how to identify evidence linking program activities plausibly to the specific outcomes for electoral integrity. The next chapter goes on to describe the assessment of problems in elections and the threats and opportunities in the external environment based on expert surveys. These problems generate domestic demand for support from multiple stakeholders, and the context for programs of electoral assistance provided by the international community.

4

Threats and Opportunities Facing Electoral Assistance

The first stage of any strategic risk assessment of whether electoral assistance programs are likely to be effective is to establish diagnostic evidence arising from the countries where international agencies work in order to assess the threats and opportunities that interventions face. Agencies may well decide to go ahead with providing assistance, where other considerations prevail despite the odds, such as following requests from the UN security council and from member states to support transitional elections as part of peace-building programs, or if bilateral donors are motivated by the desire to maintain diplomatic, economic and security relations. But the chain-of-results framework for program evaluation outlined in the previous chapter starts with gathering information to evaluate both the agency's strengths and weaknesses (such as what they can best offer in the form of technical expertise, policy advice, and aid resources) and the threats and opportunities arising from working within specific countries.

How do we know when elections are most likely to succeed in meeting international standards or fail to do so? Contentious elections generate heated partisan disputes.[1] To justify their defeat, sore losers often falsely allege fraud, rigged results, and stolen ballots, stirring up peaceful or violent protests among their supporters.[2] In response, government officials defend fair processes and outcomes, but the credibility of these counterclaims may be in doubt. Many contests see challenges to their illegitimacy: during the last decade, around 12 percent of all elections worldwide triggered opposition boycotts, 17 percent experienced postelection riots or protests, and 18 percent saw electoral violence involving at least one civilian fatality.[3]

Observer reports provide independent assessments into the quality of each election. But the growth of rival international and domestic monitoring organizations means that their reports can provide divergent conclusions that are unable to adjudicate any disputes.[4] Journalists and broadcasters highlight information about common problems observed on election day, such as fraud and violence. But global news coverage remains uneven and slanted towards negative problems. It remains difficult to piece together news media accounts consistently across dozens of elections every year. Eyewitness journalism is restricted in the most repressive regimes like Eritrea, Turkmenistan, and Syria, all rated poorly for press freedoms.[5] Moreover, even in more liberal regimes, the owners and editors of local newspapers may be in the pocket of the ruling party, allowing illicit malpractices to go unreported. The proliferation of social media expands transparency, as does the cacophony of rival claims and conspiracy theories surrounding contentious contests. Similar problems are raised through analyzing court cases and legal prosecutions because the police and judiciary may lack independence from powerful elites. More scientific tests associated with "electoral forensics" are used to detect anomalies in precinct-level results, but, although promising, statisticians have not yet reached any consensus about the best technical methods.[6]

To diagnose when and where elections fall short of international standards, therefore, and thus assess the threats and opportunities facing programs of electoral assistance, this study draws upon the Perceptions of Electoral Integrity (PEI) dataset. This is constructed by the Electoral Integrity Project based upon expert evaluations of whether elections meet international standards. The first section explains the methods used for constructing this dataset and summarizes tests confirming the validity and reliability of this evidence. The second section describes the results and compares a wide range of contests held across the global, as well as documenting the severity of problems raised during different stages of the electoral cycle. Building upon the previous book in this trilogy, the third section assesses the threats and opportunities facing programs of electoral assistance arising from structural conditions, international forces, and institutional contests. On this basis, subsequent chapters go on to consider the effectiveness of some of the most common types of programs of electoral assistance in addressing electoral problems.

METHODS AND EVIDENCE

Expert judgment-based measures first evolved in engineering, science, and commerce to assess the risks arising from nuclear reactor accidents, investment decisions, or military conflict.[7] As part of the data revolution, expert-based perceptual surveys in the social sciences have become widely used in recent decades as a technique useful for evaluating many dimensions of democratic governance that are hard to observe directly through other means. The technique is often employed when many other standard approaches to measurement or direct observation are lacking. Standard comparative indicators that are widely used include Freedom House's measures of political rights and civil liberties, the Polity IV measures of democracy-autocracy, the Cinganelli and Richards (CIRI) human rights data,

Reporters without Borders measures of press freedom, and Transparency International's Corruption Perception index.[8] The Varieties of Democracy project uses similar techniques,[9] as do several expert surveys comparing political party ideological and policy positions.[10]

In general, statistical indicators appeal to the desire for simplicity and clarity, becoming the standard metrics used by scholars, NGOs, international organizations, and donor agencies for comparing states and monitoring their performance. Indicators are used to highlight national compliance with international conventions, to "name and shame" violators, to encourage human rights protections, and to mobilize diplomatic pressures.[11] In the literature, "expert judgments" are also sometimes called "expert opinion," "expert forecasts," and "expert knowledge." In general, expert judgments rely upon cognitive reasoning drawing upon information and skills acquired from specialized training, technical knowledge, and experience. Judgments reflect the contemporary elite consensus on any topic, although they need to be adjusted in the light of new information. Nevertheless, any expert judgments and perceptions are open to the charge of bias arising from many sources, such as the cultural values, normative assumptions, sources of evidence, and levels of knowledge of the experts. There is no consensus in the literature about who counts as an expert, and technical methods differ considerably across indices. The external validity and accuracy of any estimates therefore need to be examined against independent evidence wherever possible.

The Perceptions of Electoral Integrity survey, used for problem diagnosis in this study, differs from other datasets in three main ways, by drawing upon (i) evaluations derived from a broader range of domestic and international experts than is commonly used; (ii) facilitating disaggregated analysis at a finer level of granularity (including comparing 49 separate indices) than many other summary indices; as well as (iii) providing comprehensive coverage of all national parliamentary and presidential elections after the event in almost all countries worldwide, not just those contests with international observer missions or news media reports.

To provide comprehensive evaluations of each stage of the electoral cycle, this study utilizes the annual Perceptions of Electoral Integrity (PEI-4.5) dataset, covering 213 national parliamentary and presidential elections around the globe for the period from July 1, 2012 to the June 30, 2016. This release covers 213 national parliamentary and presidential elections held during these years in 153 independent nation-states, excluding around a dozen microstates (with populations below 100,000), five countries that do not hold direct elections for the lower house of parliament, and three states that have constitutional provisions for direct elections for the lower house but have never held such contests since independence or within the last thirty years. Electoral competition varies; the survey includes national elections in some one-party states (such as Vietnam and Cuba) that ban all opposition parties, contests where all political parties are banned (such as Bahrain and Swaziland), elections where one specific type of party is restricted from ballot access (such as the Freedom and Justice party in Egypt), and those where candidates are restricted from standing (such as due to the vetting process in Iran). It is important to include all these types of cases, both to establish suitable benchmarks if countries subsequently liberalize, and also because electoral competition is best understood as a continuum, rather than a simple binary categorization.

The study selects a cross-section of electoral experts to participate in the survey, including both domestic and international respondents. The survey asks approximately 40 electoral experts from each country, generating a mean response rate of 29 percent across the survey with replies from 2,417 experts. "Electoral experts" are defined in the PEI study as political scientists (or scholars in related social science disciplines, such as law, history, political economy, or political sociology) who are knowledgeable on one or more of the following topics: elections, electoral systems, electoral administration, voting behavior, public opinion, campaigns, political communications, mass media, democracy and democratization, political parties and party systems, human rights, and national politics. All these topics touch on different dimensions of the underlying concept of electoral integrity. "Expertise" is defined by publication of scholarly articles, books, and conference papers or teaching at university level on these topics, and/or by membership and participation in professional research groups, disciplinary networks, and organized sections on the above topics with organizations such as the International Political Science Association.

The instrument used for the annual PEI expert survey was developed in conjunction with Andrew Reynolds and Jørgen Elklit.[12] The rolling survey relies upon multiple questions, not simply an overall pass/fail summary judgment. Social psychological research suggests that breaking estimates into their components parts, or greater granularity, usually generates more accurate answers.[13] The 49 items concerning electoral integrity contained in the questionnaire are designed to capture expert judgments about whether specific national elections meet internationally recognized principles and standards of elections. Details of the core questions in the survey are provided in Table 4.1. Respondents are not asked to report their own direct experience of elections or to provide information about legal or factual technical matters in each country, such as the level of the vote threshold to qualify for parliamentary seats, or the proportion of the eligible electorate registered to vote, which can be gathered more accurately from alternative sources including electoral laws and official statistics. Instead expert respondents are asked to report their *perceptions* about the quality of a wide range of electoral integrity and malpractice items in a specific national election held within each country. The items are derived from a series of common and universally agreed upon global norms and values reflecting the conceptual framework already discussed, such as the value of fairness, equality, inclusiveness, honesty, and efficiency in all the sequential steps in the electoral cycle. The rolling survey is conducted one

TABLE 4.1 *Questions in the Expert Survey of Perceptions of Electoral Integrity*

Period	Sections	Questions
Pre-election	1. Electoral Laws	1. Electoral laws were unfair to smaller parties 2. Electoral laws favored the governing party or parties 3. Election laws restricted citizens' rights
	2. Electoral procedures	4. Elections were well managed 5. Information about voting procedures was widely available 6. Election officials were fair 7. Elections were conducted in accordance with the law
	3. District boundaries	8. Boundaries discriminated against some parties 9. Boundaries favored incumbents order 10. Boundaries were impartial
	4. Voter registration	11. Some citizens were not listed in the register 12. The electoral register was inaccurate 13. Some ineligible electors were registered
	5. Registration process for parties and candidates to get on the ballot	14. Some opposition candidates were prevented from running 15. Women had equal opportunities to run for office 16. Ethnic and national minorities had equal opportunities to run for office 17. Only top party leaders selected candidates 18. Some parties/candidates were restricted from holding campaign rallies
Campaign	6. Media's coverage of these elections	19. Newspapers provided balanced election news

TABLE 4.1 (*continued*)

Period	Sections	Questions
		20. TV news favored the governing party 21. Parties/candidates had fair access to political broadcasts and advertising 22. Journalists provided fair coverage of the elections 23. Social media were used to expose electoral fraud
	7. Campaign finance	24. Parties/candidates had equitable access to public subsidies 25. Parties/candidates had equitable access to political donations 26. Parties/candidates publish transparent financial accounts 27. Rich people buy elections 28. Some states resources were improperly used for campaigning
Election day	8. When voting	29. Some voters were threatened with violence at the polls 30. Some fraudulent votes were cast 31. The process of voting was easy 32. Voters were offered a genuine choice at the ballot box 33. Postal ballots were available 34. Special voting facilities were available for the disabled 35. National citizens living abroad could vote 36. Some form of internet voting was available
Post-election	9. After the polls closed	37. Ballot boxes were secure 38. The results were announced without undue delay 39. Votes were counted fairly 40. International election monitors were restricted 41. Domestic election monitors were restricted

TABLE 4.1 (*continued*)

Period	Sections	Questions
	10. Official results announced	42. Parties/candidates challenged the results 43. The election led to peaceful protests 44. The election triggered violent protests 45. Any disputes were resolved through legal channels
	11. Electoral authorities administering elections	46. The election authorities were impartial 47. The authorities distributed information to citizens 48. The authorities allowed public scrutiny of their performance 49. The election authorities performed well

Source: Pippa Norris, Ferran Martinez i Coma, Alessandro Nai and Max Groemping. *The expert survey of Perceptions of Electoral Integrity*. (PEI-4.5). Available at www.electoralintegrityproject.com.

month after the announcement of the official results in each country, so PEI aims to capture contemporary evaluations while memories of each contest remain fresh, rather than seeking to recall detailed evaluations from previous contests, which can be easily colored by recent events.

One of the chief questions when trying to gauge electoral integrity is where to draw the boundaries when it comes to deciding which items are most relevant? To reflect the conceptualization used in this book, it is important to go beyond polling day and the vote count to include the broad determinants of electoral integrity throughout the electoral cycle. Hence many aspects of elections are monitored in PEI well before or immediately after polling day. Close attention is paid to each step in the electoral cycle. As with all survey work, experts are not cued by the questionnaire about the meaning of these items; instead they are asked to make their own judgments based on their own perceptions. One of the advantages of the PEI dataset is that the disaggregated score is available for each of the items, allowing analysts to pinpoint the issues which are of most concern. Issues include the fairness of the EMB, the process of campaigning, the aftermath of the results, and facilitating the process of aggregating the data flexibly so that analysts can fit alternative theoretical concepts.

To operationalize the core notion, the electoral cycle is employed where elections are understood as a sequential process broken down into eleven stages, ranging from the election laws, electoral procedures, and boundary delimitation to the voting process, vote count, and declaration of results. Like complex links in a chain, violating international standards in any one of the sequential steps undermines principles of electoral integrity.[14] Thus concern about electoral fraud often focuses on acts such as multiple voting, stuffing ballot boxes, or putting a thumb on the scales of the vote count, all of which clearly damage the people's choice. But the concept of electoral integrity emphasizes that many other problems can also undermine international standards, such as the use of electoral laws, ballot access requirements, and district electoral boundaries stacked to favor incumbents. Trumped up criminal charges can be used to disqualify opposition candidates well before the campaign starts. Harassment and intimidation of political activists is commonly threatened to discourage opponents. During the campaign, imbalanced access to media and money provides incumbents with major advantages.[15] Electors can find their names missing from outdated or inaccurate voter registers. Once the results are announced, lack of impartial and timely judicial processes for resolving electoral disputes can trigger protests and violence. Many of these sorts of problems are often suspected of arising from strategic manipulation by the regime, but, like any complex logistical operation, shortcomings may also arise from happenstance, lack of capacity, and sheer incompetence.

Another tricky issue arising from any cross-national survey concerns how to gauge the responses if respondents from different cultures, countries, or groups employ different standards, or if they understand the meaning of questions in divergent ways. Cultural biases are only to be expected; for example, experts living in long-established democracies that have held a long series of high-quality elections may prove more critical of any cases of voter fraud or minor inaccuracies in electoral registers that come to light than those living in states with little historical experience of these contests. The dataset was tested to see whether evaluations of electoral integrity varied systematically based on an expert's social and demographic background (age, education, and sex), country of birth, their length of time living in the country of the election, and their ideological views on a left–right scale.[16] The analysis shows that the length of experience in living in the country of an election proved important; longer-time residents were more positive in their evaluations. Familiarity, it appears, may breed content. Equally importantly and perhaps surprisingly, nationality and citizenship were not significant for electoral evaluations, suggesting that international and domestic experts shared largely similar assessments. Political ideology, age, and education (across the left-right scale) also proved unimportant in predicting judgments.

Individual responses to items in the expert survey were recoded in a consistently positive direction and scored on an ordinal scale, with 0 representing the most negative evaluations and 5 the most positive. Individual scores were also averaged for the election and the country as a whole. Where the standard deviation of the mean in any contest or country proved higher than average, the individual scores were further scrutinized and checked. The responses across all items were then summed and standardized to 100 points to generate the Perceptions of Electoral Integrity Index. Using similar procedures for more accurate and detailed diagnosis, standardized 100-point indices were also generated for each of the eleven subdimensions in the electoral cycle. The main advantages of the PEI dataset, therefore, are that the evidence generates a multidimensional assessment of electoral integrity reflecting the core concept developed in this book, which can be broken down into its component parts. The results display a considerable degree of external and internal validity.

The fourth release of the study covers independent nation-states around the world that hold direct (popular) elections for the national parliament or presidential elections, with the exclusions noted earlier. The PEI-4.5 dataset used in this book covers 87 percent of all the independent nation-states around the world meeting our criteria (153 out of 175 countries), including those that held national presidential or parliamentary elections from mid-2012 to mid-2016. This includes diverse types of societies and types of regimes, ranging from the United States, Japan, and the Netherlands on the one hand, to Burkina Faso, Sierra Leone, and Belarus on the other. Because of the rolling design of the survey, the data in PEI-4.5 provides a random cross-section of all contemporary elections in every country worldwide, with the exclusion of microstates. A comparison of the countries which are and are not included in this release of the dataset against several standard indicators showed no significant differences except in mean population size. Thus, the generalizations emerging from the study can be extrapolated to elections elsewhere in the world with a fair degree of confidence.

Tests of Validity, Reliability and Legitimacy

Can assessments by election experts be trusted? The PEI data has been demonstrated to show a high degree of internal reliability (consistency among experts), external reliability (when compared with equivalent independent indicators), and legitimacy (when expert judgments are compared with public assessments).[17]

One way to check the estimates is to compare the overall summary PEI Index with other comparable national assessments created by independent scholarly and think-tank research projects. In particular, the PEI index and its subdimensions can be compared at the national level with many equivalent independent macrolevel measures of the quality of elections.[18] Correlations are not expected to be perfect due to the use of different concepts, measures, and time periods in each study. Nevertheless, the comparisons consistently

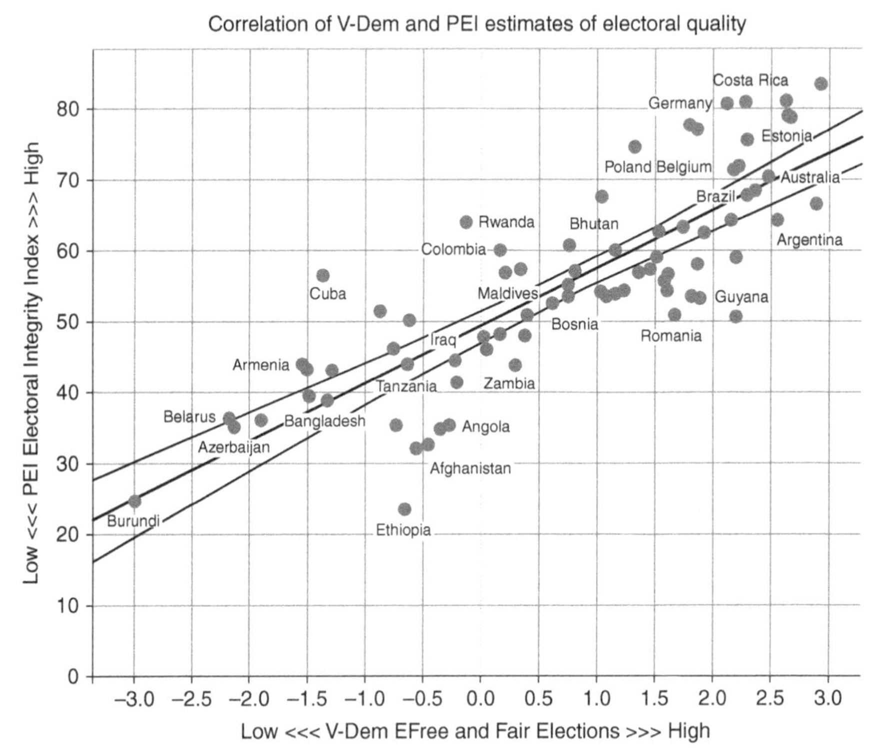

FIGURE 4.1. Electoral integrity measured by PEI and V-Dem.
Note: Varieties of democracy (V-Dem) estimates of Free and Fair Elections compared with the PEI Index.
Source: Pippa Norris, Ferran Martinez i Coma, Alessandro Nai and Max Groemping. *The expert survey of Perceptions of Electoral Integrity.* (PEI-4.5). Available at www .electoralintegrityproject.com; Varieties of democracy project www.v-dem.net.

demonstrate strong relationships at the national level, lending confidence in the *external* reliability of our data, and thus on the validity of the PEI measure of the concept of electoral integrity. This includes the combined Freedom House/ imputed Polity measure of democratization (R = .762** N. 151), and the Varieties of Democracy measure of electoral democracy (polyarchy) (R = .824**, N.140).[19] Figure 4.1 illustrates the comparison of the PEI-4.5 Index with assessments of the quality of electoral democracy, measured by the Varieties of Democracy project (V-Dem).[20] There are clearly some cases where each study arrived at different assessments, which is hardly surprising given differences in the methods, concepts, and measurement used by each. Nevertheless, overall the comparisons display a remarkably strong and significant correlation between the results of two independent studies. The Perceptions of Electoral Integrity Index were also correlated with many other alternative indices.[21] In addition, tests published elsewhere confirm the *internal* validity of our methods and the consistency of expert assessments.[22]

Therefore, the summary PEI Index is comparable with many other measures of the quality of free and fair contests. Unlike many of these, however, the PEI results can also be broken down into far more granular detail, which is essential to pinpoint specific weaknesses and strengthens in each contest. Hence the PEI data can be used to compare how elections rate across eleven stages of the electoral cycle, and across 49 indicators, such as in the processes of district gerrymandering, the opportunities that contests provide for women and minority candidates, the provision of equitable access to political finance, the fairness of electoral officials, and the occurrence of peaceful and violent protests after the announcement of the results, and so on. This is critical for the accurate diagnosis of any underlying problems and prescribing the most appropriate types of reforms and electoral assistance programs that are most likely to strengthen integrity in any contest.

DIAGNOSING STRENGTHS AND WEAKNESSES

On this basis. which global regions, countries, and stages of the electoral cycle are most problematic? What are the risks and opportunities that electoral assistance programs should address? To summarize the evidence, Figure 4.2 illustrates the contrasts in the overall 100-point PEI index for all the countries covered in the survey since 2012, divided into global regions for comparison. The ranking and map (Figure 4.3) provide a worldwide overview.

Established Democracies in Scandinavia and Western Europe

The comparisons highlight that countries located in Scandinavia and Western Europe are rated most highly in their overall levels of electoral integrity, not surprisingly given the long tradition of liberal democracy in these regions. The worldwide rankings in the PEI index are led by several Scandinavian states – Denmark, Finland, Norway, and Sweden – all of which also usually perform exceptionally well in most other standard indices of the quality of democratic governance. At the same time, however, significant contrasts can be observed in PEI-4.5 scores even among relatively similar European Union member states and affluent postindustrial societies; for example, experts assess states in Mediterranean Europe as usually having lower quality elections compared with Northern Europe.

Denmark 2015

Denmark exemplifies a smaller Scandinavian welfare state and power-sharing or consensus democracy with a long history of free and fair elections. It ranks 1st among all 153 countries compared in PEI-4.5. The country uses an open-list PR electoral system that generates highly proportional results and the inclusion

Africa	PEI	Asia-Pacific	PEI	C&E Europe	PEI	Middle East	PEI	Americas	PEI	N.&W.Europe	PEI
Cape Verde*	71	New Zealand	76	Estonia	79	Israel	74	Costa Rica	81	Denmark	86
Benin*	69	Republic of Korea*	74	Lithuania	77	Tunisia	67	Uruguay	75	Finland	86
Mauritius	64	Taiwan*	73	Slovenia	77	Oman	60	Canada	75	Norway	83
Rwanda	64	Australia	70	Czech Republic	76	Kuwait	55	Brazil	67	Iceland*	82
South Africa	63	Japan	68	Slovak Republic	75	Iran*	50	Chile	66	Sweden	81
Lesotho	63	Mongolia*	64	Poland	74	Turkey	48	Grenada	66	Netherlands	79
Namibia	60	Vanuatu*	63	Latvia	72	Jordan	46	Jamaica*	66	Switzerland	78
Ivory Coast	59	Micronesia	61	Croatia	67	Iraq	44	Argentina	64	Austria	77
Sao Tome & Principe	58	Bhutan	61	Georgia	59	Egypt	42	Barbados	63	Portugal*	75
Botswana	58	India	59	Moldova	57	Bahrain	38	United States	63	Belgium	71
Ghana	57	Samoa*	57	Bulgaria	56	Afghanistan	32	Peru*	63	Ireland*	71
Sierra Leone	57	Solomon Islands	57	Hungary	56	Syria*	25	Panama	60	Cyprus*	70
Guinea-Bissau	54	Maldives	57	Albania	54			Colombia	60	Spain*	69
Nigeria	53	Indonesia	57	Kyrgyzstan	54			Mexico	57	Italy	67
Burkina Faso	53	Myanmar	54	Bosnia	52			Cuba	56	Greece	66
Mali	52	Nepal	54	Serbia*	52			Bolivia	55	Malta	65
Central African Rep*	52	Fiji	53	Ukraine	51			Ecuador	55	United Kingdom	65
Niger*	52	Singapore	53	Romania	51			Paraguay	55		
Malawi	48	Philippines*	52	Macedonia	48			El Salvador	54		
Cameroon	46	Sri Lanka	52	Kazakhstan*	45			Belize	53		
Swaziland	45	Thailand	51	Armenia	44			Guyana	53		
Comoros*	45	Pakistan	50	Uzbekistan	39			Suriname	50		
Zambia	44	Laos*	48	Turkmenistan	38			Guatemala	48		
Mauritania	44	Bangladesh	39	Belarus	36			Venezuela	45		
Tanzania	44	Malaysia	35	Tajikistan	36			Honduras	45		
Sudan	43	Vietnam*	34	Azerbaijan	35			Dominican Rep*	44		
Algeria	43	Cambodia	32					Haiti	28		
Guinea	42										
Kenya	41										
Madagascar	39										
Togo	38										
Uganda*	37										
Zimbabwe	35										
Angola	35										
Mozambique	35										
Chad*	31										
Djibouti*	29										
Congo, Rep.*	27										
Equatorial Guinea*	25										
Burundi	24										
Ethiopia	23										
Total	47	Total	56	Total	56	Total	48	Total	57	Total	75

FIGURE 4.2. Electoral integrity by global regions.
Source: Pippa Norris, Ferran Martinez i Coma, Alessandro Nai and Max Groemping. *The Expert Survey of Perceptions of Electoral Integrity*. (PEI-4.5). Available at www.electoralintegrityproject.com.

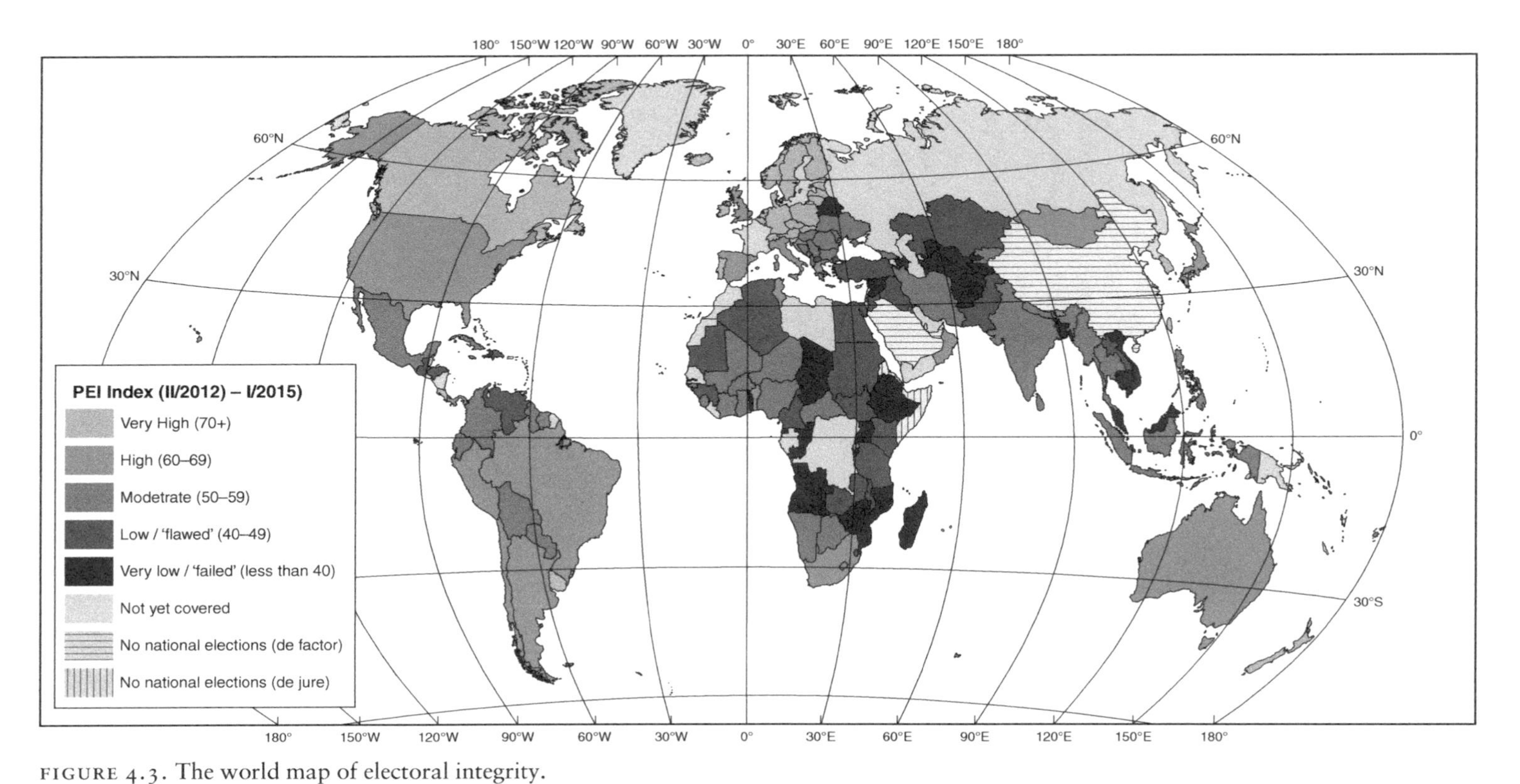

FIGURE 4.3. The world map of electoral integrity.
Source: Pippa Norris, Ferran Martinez i Coma, Alessandro Nai and Max Groemping. *The expert survey of Perceptions of Electoral Integrity*. (PEI-4.5). Available at www.electoralintegrityproject.com.

of multiple parties in parliament. The contest for the Folketing on June 18, 2015 was narrowly won with 90 seats going to the "blue" opposition alliance led by Venstre, headed by Prime Minister Lars Rasmussen, which took power replacing the "red" Social Democratic-led government. The Danish People's Party, a populist-authoritarian anti-immigration party, also won 21.1 percent of the vote, however, making it the second largest party in parliament, while the Denmark Liberal Party came third on 19.5 percent of the vote. Turnout was 85.9 percent.

UK 2015

By contrast, among European societies the United Kingdom scores exceptionally poorly, with a PEI Index around 20 points less than the top ranking Scandinavian states. In the United Kingdom, the May 7, 2015 general election was assessed by experts as the worst of all Western European states, ranking only 43rd worldwide.

Despite considerable debate over electoral reform in recent decades, the electoral system for Westminster continues to use the plurality "first-past-the-post" formula with 650 single-member constituencies. The system systematically penalizes geographically dispersed minor parties, with a mechanical "winner's bonus" for the seats allocated to the party in first place. In general, majoritarian electoral systems usually score less well in the PEI index than proportional representation systems.[23] Polling day in the United Kingdom generated several technical problems. Despite expectations of a close result and hung parliament, in fact the 2015 general election returned a Conservative government with a comfortable parliamentary majority, led by Prime Minister David Cameron. The Liberal Democrats and the Labour party performed poorly, while there were significant gains for the Scottish National Party. Since the election, the government subsequently implemented individual voter register, replacing a household-based system. The reform has been justified by ministers as a more secure system guarding against alleged voter fraud, although critics charge that this may discourage participation by several sectors of the electorate including students and ethnic minorities.[24]

North America

U.S. 2016

In North America, Canada and the United States show striking contrasts across the shared border despite many cultural similarities. Overall, American elections rank 52nd worldwide out of all 153 nations under comparison, based on US elections since 2012, the lowest score for any Western democracy.

One reason is that ever since Florida in 2000, the Republicans and Democrats have become increasingly divided over processes of electoral registration and balloting.[25] The GOP have emphasized the desirability of photo identification and verification checks on the electoral register to prevent the risks of voter impersonation, while the Democrats have highlighted the risks which this process poses to restricting voter's rights and advocated the expansion of convenience voting facilities, such as extended hours and postal and advance voting to boost turnout. These partisan disagreements have intensified with a series of new laws passed in state houses and challenged in the courts.[26] While many of the more restrictive attempts have been struck down by judges as discriminatory, the process has politicized the electoral process and fueled public mistrust. These problems have been further exacerbated by Donald Trump's repeated claims of massive fraud where he asserts that 3–5 million illegal votes were cast and the election in several battleground states was "rigged," a serious charge without any evidence, going far beyond previous Republican claims of fraud. These bogus claims serve to delegitimize the outcome and they may lay the basis for further attempts by Republican state legislators to restrict voting rights.

Like its predecessors, the 2016 US presidential campaign also saw concern about many other issues in American elections. During the campaign, problems focused on the prevalence of negative reporting, disinformation campaigns, and fake news. The outcome also saw widespread debate about the way that President Trump's victory in the Electoral College failed to reflect Hillary's Clinton's 2.8 million vote lead in the popular vote.[27] The aftermath of the election saw further questions about foreign interference in the elections, raising concern about issues of cybersecurity, disinformation campaigns, and the vulnerability of computer servers to hacking. Chiefs of seventeen agencies in the intelligence services, including the FBI and the National Security Agency, warned that Russian-based hackers were behind the break into the emails of the Democratic National Committee, with the results fed to the media during the campaign.[28] The agencies also documented failed attempts to break into two state registration databases. One incident included stealing information in Illinois from roughly 200,000 voting records. In another attempt, in Arizona, cyber criminals used malware to try and breach voting records, forcing state officials to disable online voting registration for nine days as they investigated the unsuccessful hacking.[29] Neither succeeded but the lack of sophisticated security used to protect computerized state records and the age of many US electronic voting machines make these particularly vulnerable to attack. At the same time, the Obama administration pointed out that the decentralized nature of US electoral administration provides at least a partial protection against wholesale efforts at vote rigging. The risks remain real, however, because even relatively minor security breaches in a couple of states could potentially reduce the credibility of the overall electoral process and throw doubts upon the legitimacy of the eventual outcome.

Even before these events came to light, in the series of US PEI surveys conducted at both national and state levels since 2012, experts have consistently rated American elections poorly compared with other Western democracies, with most concern expressed about the quality of the electoral laws, voter registration, the process of drawing district boundaries, and regulation of campaign finance. Voter registration, in particular, has become increasingly polarized and litigious in the United States ever since the 2000 Florida debacle, generating growing controversy in state houses and the courts.[30] State regulations on voter registration were revised in many states.[31] America also suffers from exceptionally partisan and decentralized arrangements for electoral administration – problems that were addressed by the blue-ribbon bipartisan 2014 Presidential Commission on Electoral Administration.[32] The role of money in American politics is a persistent issue of concern, especially following major decisions by the Supreme Court deregulating campaign funding and the weakness of the Federal Election Commission tasked with this job.[33] In addition, experts highlighted endemic problems of gerrymandering in the processes used to draw voting district boundaries. The United States has the second-worst score out of all countries on redistricting (Malaysia was the worst). The United States is also the only country worldwide where redistricting decisions in most states are determined by state lawmakers, with the partisan conflict of interest which this arrangement entails.[34] In these circumstances, it is hardly surprising that Gallup found that during the campaign only six in ten Americans were very or fairly confident that their vote would be accurately cast and counted in the US election, down from around three quarters of all Americans a decade earlier.[35] Among Republicans, the proportion who were confident dropped to around half, the lowest that the Gallup poll has ever recorded on this question when asked in a series of surveys. At a time of persistently low confidence in American institutions, this deepening erosion of faith in elections is cause for serious concern.

Canada 2015

By contrast to the United States, in PEI-4.5 the October 2015 Canadian federal election was ranked relatively well (17th best worldwide), following the decisive parliamentary victory for the Liberal Party under the leadership of Justin Trudeau. Some previous disputes had occurred in the 2011 Canadian federal election surrounded the misuse of "robocalls." The Conservative government of Stephen Harper had also passed the controversial Fair Elections Act, a measure which sought to strengthen voter identification requirements, despite heated opposition claims that this would lead to voter suppression.[36] The 2015 elections proved to be largely free of any major glitches, despite some room for minor improvements according to international observers and news reports: "The 2015 parliamentary elections demonstrated the credibility of the election process in Canada ... All OSCE/ODIHR EAM interlocutors expressed trust and confidence in the election administration's professional performance, impartiality and transparency ... The competitive and vibrant campaign was conducted with respect for the fundamental freedoms of expression, association and assembly."[37] After the 2015 election, the Trudeau administration pledged to replace the traditional Canadian majoritarian "first-past-the-post" electoral system inherited from Westminster. The Parliamentary Committee charged with considering alternative systems generated little consensus about the pros and cons of alternative reforms, however, and a large-scale public consultation exercise undertaken by the government found little appetite for change, with most Canadians expressing satisfactions with the existing electoral system.[38]

Central and Eastern Europe

Several post-Communist states in Central Eurasia remain the home of repressive authoritarian states, which hold multiparty elections to legitimate ruling parties, exemplified by the performance of elections in Azerbaijan, Tajikistan, and Belarus. By contrast, however, in the Baltics and Central and Eastern Europe, several states score well in the quality of their elections today, notably Estonia, Lithuania, and Slovenia, all power-sharing democracies, smaller welfare states, and mid-level income economies.

Belarus 2015

Belarus, for example, ranked 136th worst among 153 countries in PEI-4.5. The October 2015 presidential elections saw the return of President Lukashenko, with 84 percent of the vote, winning his fifth successive term of office. One of the most repressive states in the world, numerous malpractices undermined political rights and civil liberties. The president exerts absolute control, with appointment powers over all branches of government. International and domestic election observers were highly critical of the conduct of the elections, with the United Nations Special Rapporteur on human rights in Belarus, Miklós Haraszti, stating: "The election process was orchestrated, and the result was pre-ordained. It could not be otherwise, given the 20 years of continuous suppression of the rights to freedom of expression, assembly, and association, which are the preconditions for any credible competition."[39] Over successive contests, Belarus consistently scored poorly in failing to meet international standards of electoral integrity.

Estonia 2015

In the Baltics, by contrast to Belarus, Estonia was ranked 8th highest among all 153 countries in PEI-4.5. In 2015, parliamentary contests returned the Estonian Reform Party as the largest party. Like neighboring third-wave democracies and smaller welfare states in the Baltics, Estonia has conducted well-ranked elections. Starting in 2005, it is notable that Estonia was also the first state worldwide to offer all eligible voters the possibility to vote via the internet in all national and municipal elections. In these elections, almost one-third of all ballots (30.5 percent) were cast via the internet. Estonia has pioneered a series of procedures designed to protect the security of internet voting and despite some potential vulnerabilities, the OSCE observers expressed a high degree of trust in the overall reliability and security of this process.[40] Poland also performed well, according to experts, ranking 20th out of 153 countries in PEI-4.5. After a tight race, the presidential election was won on 10th May 2015 by Andrezej Duda for the far-right Law and Justice party. As the observers concluded: "The elections were competitive and pluralistic, conducted with respect of fundamental principles for democratic elections in an atmosphere of freedom to campaign and on the basis of equal and fair treatment of contestants."[41]

Latin America

Latin America saw important gains in the consolidation of democratic procedures during the third wave era, when a history of military coup d'états, one-party states, and dictators was replaced by recruitment through relatively peaceful and orderly multiparty contests, constitutional systems of checks and balances, and respect for civil and political rights. Nevertheless, although little nostalgia persists for the authoritarian past, the contemporary quality of democracy varies across Latin America.[42] Many states grapple with challenges of corruption and inequality, partisan gridlock arising from the combination of presidential executives with proportional representation electoral systems and fragmented party systems in Congress, and political instability, exemplified by impeachment proceedings against President Dilma Rousseff in Brazil, violent protests in Venezuela, and corruption scandals triggering plummeting support for Michele Bachelet in Chile.[43] The varied performance of democracy in the region is reinforced by the considerable disparities observed in electoral integrity, as illustrated by the contrasting cases of Costa Rica and Uruguay, all well-rated by PEI experts, compared with the poor scores for Guatemala, Venezuela, Honduras, and Haiti.

Haiti 2015

In Haiti, the poorest country of the Western Hemisphere, the country held the first round of presidential elections and the second round of legislative contests on October 25, 2015. The elections were ranked worst in the Americas among all the countries in PEI-4.5. Elections had been delayed for more than three years, the country had not conducted a presidential election since 2010, and the president, Michel Martelly had disbanded parliament in January 2015 and begun governing by executive order.[44] The former Prime Minister, Laurent Lamothe, resigned after the elections were not held as scheduled. For the first round of parliamentary elections in August 9, 2015, violence and intimidation were widespread before and during Election Day. Men armed with rocks and bottles attacked voters at polling stations in Port-au-Prince and about two dozen voting centers were forced to close.[45] There were complaints that hundreds of thousands of party agents were permitted to vote in any polling station, without adequate accreditation checks against fraud, allowing duplicate voting. A government commission assigned to review the election examined a sample of the tally sheets and found that only 8 percent were free of errors. Thirty percent showed voters who did not appear on voter lists, and nearly half the sheets featured voters who presented an incorrect voter ID number.[46] For the second-round legislative elections, turnout dropped to only 18 percent.[47] The aftermath saw widespread claims of fraud and mass demonstrations. On January 18, 2016, the second-place presidential candidate, Jude Celestin, formally announced that he would not run, and opposition parties called for a boycott. The second round for the presidential contest, originally scheduled for December, was postponed in a leadership crisis, threatening political stability and violence. USAID has invested over $1.5 billion in Haiti since the 2010 earthquake, including over $33 m on the first-round elections.[48]

Asia-Pacific

Elsewhere around the world, similar wide disparities can be observed for elections in Asia-Pacific, with the affluent postindustrial societies of Australia, South Korea, New Zealand, and Japan heading the ratings, as well as Mongolia, which has made rapid progress in abandoning its Soviet past. Yet other countries in the region perform far worse in the PEI Index, notably Cambodia, Malaysia, and Bangladesh.[49]

Myanmar 2015

One example of important gains comes from Myanmar, where historic parliamentary contests on November 8, 2015 signaled significant progress to end of military rule, following genuine competition, substantial seat gains for Aung San Suu Kyi's National League for Democracy (NLD), and important steps towards the liberalization of the country.[50] Nevertheless as a transitional contest, experts rated the elections fairly high despite major challenges which remain, notably in the treatment of the rights of ethnic minorities, and there are many steps needed on the long pathway to reform and civilian control of the military. The election process could also be made more transparent. The 2015 contest illustrates the way that where rulers are committed to reform, elections respecting international standards of integrity can provide an effective and relatively peaceful first step in the transition from authoritarianism. As the EU observer mission concluded: "The poll was well organized and voters had a real choice between different candidates. In the future, constitutional, legal and procedural improvements will be required for truly genuine elections."[51] Overall the PEI evaluations echoed these sentiments, with Myanmar rated 83rd out of 153 elections in PEI-4.5.

Middle East and North Africa

Tunisia 2014

In the Middle East and North Africa, Tunisia also stands out as holding the most promising prospects for democracy, despite continued political instability and a poor economic performance. Following the 2011 uprisings, the country held its transitional parliamentary election on October 26, 2014 followed in the next two months by two rounds of presidential elections on November 23 and December 21. The elections were widely regarded as a test for Tunisia's reform process. Turnout for the 217-seat Assembly of the Representatives of the People election was estimated at 66 percent, with the secularist Nidaa Tounes gaining 86 seats (37.6 percent), and the moderate Islamic Ennahda Movement achieving 69 seats (27.9 percent).[52] Both international and domestic monitors observed the polls. The National Democratic Institute concluded that electoral authorities at national and local levels exhibited professionalism during the balloting and counting. Security forces maintained a largely calm and peaceful atmosphere and some isolated irregularities and incidents were not serious enough to damage the integrity of the election.[53] The legal framework – worked out during the country's constitution-building process – was inclusive, transparent, and participatory.

At the subsequent presidential election held under the majoritarian second ballot system, in the first round, Béji Caïd Essebsi of Nidaa and Moncef Marzouki of the Congress for the Republic (CPR) each gained roughly a third of votes. This triggered the second round between the top two candidates, where Essebsi won with 55.7 percent of the vote.[54] EU observers reported that presidential polls were held in a fairly calm and peaceful atmosphere, and the electoral management body handled the process and the transparency of results professionally.[55] The Carter Center observers largely concurred with this positive assessment but they noted low turnout among young voters.[56] An estimated 29,000 citizen observers, and close to 59,000 party agents, were accredited to scrutinize the polls. Both Tunisian the Assembly and presidential elections performed well according to the PEI index; experts evaluated voting procedures and counting as the best parts of the process, although they were more critical of the voter registration process in the legislative contests and the role of the news media in the presidential election.

Afghanistan 2014

In contrast to Tunisia, several other states in the MENA region (exemplified by Bahrain, Afghanistan and Syria) were rated as having exceptionally poor elections. Among the worst-rated contests in 2014, the Afghan elections were undermined by massive fraud, vote-buying, and corrupt practices, with the vote count suspended in favor of a brokered power-sharing deal. Afghanistan held presidential elections on April 5, 2014. The third poll since the fall of the Taliban, this election was open because the incumbent, President Hamid Karzai, had reached his constitutional term limit and could not stand again. The majoritarian 2nd ballot election was held in two rounds. Eleven candidates contested the first round of the election, down from the original twenty-seven nominated by the October 6, 2013 deadline.

Campaign polls suggested that Abdullah Abdullah, former Foreign Minister and leader of the National Coalition, and Ashraf Ghani Ahmadzai, former finance minister and World Bank official who ran as an independent, were leading the race, followed by the president's older brother, Qayoum Karzai.[57] Several major problems occurred in this election, notably violence from insurgents. Security threats initially forced 24 out of the 414 polling centers to be closed, but the government subsequently declared them open.[58] The registration process proved problematic, as the voter identification cards in circulation exceeding the number of eligible voters, and the cards could be easily transferred. Due to cultural sensitivities, women were not required to carry photos to vote, which further compounded the problem. Reports suggest that electoral fraud, bribery, and vote-buying were all potential flaws.[59] NDI observers noted multiple malpractices during the 2010 Afghan contests: the endemic threat of violence, widespread mistrust of electoral institutions, voting irregularities, barriers to women's participation, and the existence of massive numbers of false voter identification cards.[60]

During the count for the second round, one leading candidate, Abdullah Abdullah, alleged fraud "on an industrial scale," and the UN-led observers intervened to coordinate the mammoth task of auditing all eight million votes cast. This process failed to determine a legitimate winner and only a US-brokered backroom deal produced a compromise for power-sharing accepted by the two leading contenders. Ashraf Ghani Ahmadzai became president, while Abdullah Abdullah agreed to serve in the government. The final disputed vote share was not released by the Electoral Commission. Given these issues, PEI experts scored the Afghan election very poorly in the PEI Index, 144th worldwide, around the same rating as Mozambique and Cambodia. Electoral procedures, voter registration, campaign finance, and the declaration of results were all ranked as problematic by experts.

Iran 2016

Iranian elections for the 290-seat bicameral parliament, known as the Islamic Consultative Assembly (also called Iranian Majlis, or People's House), provide another illustrative case of flawed contests from the region. Members are directly elected to this body for four-year terms in single- and multiseat constituencies by a two-round plurality vote electoral system where winners need at least 25 percent of the vote. There are also reserved seats for several minority communities. The Ministry of Interior, including the Central Executive Elections Board and the Election District Executive Committees, administers all election-related activities. The main cleavage is between moderate reformists and fundamentalist conservatives.

Simultaneous elections were also held on February 26, 2016 for the Assembly of Experts for Leadership, the 88-member body with the authority to appoint the Islamic Republic's Supreme Leader.[61] All members are Islamic scholars and jurists. Districts are divided among 31 provinces based on population size. Members are elected using a single round plurality electoral system, with no minimum threshold.[62]

Problems over the restrictive ballot access led to the exclusion of many potential candidates in both contests.[63] The Guardian Council (a 12-member panel of Islamic jurists) vetted and disqualified all but around 4,700 out of more than 12,000 potential parliamentary candidates.[64] They also approved only 166 of the 801 candidates who applied to run for the 88-member Assembly of Experts, excluding all 16 women.[65] Indeed, no woman has never been elected to the Assembly of Experts. In 2012, the vetoing of candidates led to a parliamentary election boycott by reformist parties, but this tactic was not used for the 2016 elections.[66]

The election was seen by some commentators as a referendum on the future direction of the revolution.[67] The win by moderates gave President Hassan Rouhani more scope to push through reforms, such as the codification of political crimes and a prohibition on the policing of religious adherence, which had been blocked by his more conservative political opponents.[68] Rouhani has achieved a lot since wresting the presidency away from hardliner Mahmoud Ahmadinejad, including securing a groundbreaking nuclear deal with world powers.[69] The agreement sought to improve Iran's economic situation through the lifting of crippling international sanctions.[70] In the wake of the nuclear deal, Rouhani toured Europe to sign multimillion dollar trade deals and met with the Pope, a sign of increasing international engagement.[71]

The result of the elections saw a historical victory for the moderates led by President Hassan Rouhani and Akbar Hashemi Rafsanjani, along with their allies, who secured 59 percent of the seats in the assembly, up from 20 seats before. Turnout was officially declared at 62 percent, out of 55 million eligible voters. In the PEI 4.5 study, experts scored the Iranian elections on the standardized PEI Index as 50 out of 100, ranking Iran 104th out of 153 countries. Experts rated the most problematic stages in the Iranian electoral process as the electoral laws, candidate access to the ballot, and campaign finance.

Syria 2016

Syria exemplifies elections used as a fig leaf of legitimacy for repressive regimes. Estimates suggest that more than 270,000 people have died in almost five years of civil war armed conflict.[72] Conflict has destabilized the Middle East and has forced more than 11 million Syrians away from their homes, fueling the refugee crisis in Europe.[73] The conflict, which began as an antigovernment protest in 2011, has also facilitated the rise of the Islamic State (IS) in the region.

Three elections have been held since the initial uprising against Assad; in 2012 and 2016 for Syrian People's Council (Majlis al-Sha'ab) and in 2014 for the presidency. The latter saw Bashar al-Assad win by a landslide victory with 88.7 percent of the vote,[74] allowing him to rule until 2021. Opponents of the regime regard the contest as fraudulent, as voting did not take place in areas controlled by the opposition, effectively excluding millions of citizens.[75] In October 2015, Assad stated that he was willing to hold early presidential and parliamentary elections, as well as discuss constitutional changes, but only if terrorist groups were defeated beforehand.[76]

The parliamentary election to the Syrian People's Council on April 13, 2016 was the second held in the midst of the civil war. The 250 members of parliament were elected by plurality vote from 15 multimember districts. Several seats are assigned to each constituency. Under the block voting electoral system (also known as plurality at large), each citizen has as many votes as seats are available. Candidates with the most votes in each district (but not necessarily a majority) are returned to office.[77] This gives an advantage to the more developed and established parties – in Syria's case, the Ba'ath party. The block vote system works against the opposition if it is fragmented, as in this country. It gives the party that has even a slight lead in the popular vote an overwhelming number of seats.[78] About 3,500 candidates ran for office and non-Ba'athist candidates were eligible, although all went through a careful screening process. Half of Syria's parliamentary seats are reserved for laborers and farmers who have no party affiliation. Various committees, whose members are appointed by either Assad himself or provincial governors, determine who is a nonaffiliated farmer or laborer. There were 7,300 polling centers established in government-controlled areas of the country, but large parts of the country controlled by insurgent groups did not participate. State employees were warned that they must show up to vote, with fears of retaliation and punishment if they failed to comply.[79] The Ba'ath Party-led National Progressive Front coalition, including Syria's ruling Baath party and its allies, won 200 of the 250 seats (80 percent), for an increase of 32 members. The Syrian electoral commission announced that 50 other candidates were elected but did not announce the underlying share of the vote. The media widely reported the number of seats but gave no indication of the vote share. The major opposition coalition inside and outside the country boycotted the elections. In total, 33 women were elected (13.2 percent).[80] Voter turnout was estimated at 57.6 percent (up from 51.2 percent for the previous 2012 elections).

The results were widely denounced by opposition forces as illegitimate and sham political theatre. The UN and Western powers also condemned the elections, including official spokespersons from the United States, the United Kingdom, France, and Germany, since it was impossible to hold free, fair, and transparent contests meeting international standards across the whole country in the context of the ongoing civil war.[81] The Council is also largely a symbolic and powerless body. On the PEI study, experts scored the Syrian election as 25 out of 100 points on the standardized PEI index, ranking Syria 151st out of 153 countries in the dataset. The fraudulent contests were a façade serving to prop up the Assad regime, rather than providing a genuine choice allowing all Syrians to exercise their voice over the future of the country. No international observers were allowed to monitor the contests, with Assed claiming that foreign interference would undermine Syrian sovereignty.[82]

These were followed by the Syria presidential elections, held on June 3, 2014, despite the fact that the country was in the midst of a bloody civil war and a deep humanitarian crisis that started in 2011. The contests illustrate a fake election, violating human rights to cloak the incumbent with the appearance of a popular mandate. President Bashar Hafez al-Assad from the Arab Socialist Ba'ath Party was reelected overwhelmingly for another seven-year term with a reported 89 percent of the vote. Assad's main rivals standing as independents, Hassan Abdullah al-Nouri and Maher Abdul-Hafiz Hajjar, each got less than 5 percent of the vote. Yet the election was deeply problematic because several areas of the country were not under government control, and polling did not take place in the regions where the insurgents were strongest. The National Coalition – the main Western-backed opposition group – boycotted the contest. In addition, an estimated 9 million Syrians had fled their homes since the conflict began in 2011, including 2.5 million refugees and 6.5 million internally displaced persons. Those refugees who crossed through government-controlled "official" border crossings with an exit stamp were eligible to vote abroad, but most refugees did not have an official stamp. The Gulf Cooperation Council, the European Union, and the United States all criticized the election as illegitimate, although the contest was defended by spokespersons for the Russian and Iranian governments. PEI ranked Syria as the third worst record out of all countries under comparison, with an exceptionally poor performance across the board.

Sub-Saharan Africa

In sub-Saharan Africa, more than half the states included in the survey had poor integrity ratings, with Burundi, Equatorial Guinea, and Ethiopia all at the bottom of the subcontinent – and with some of the lowest ratings around the globe. Nevertheless, there are some bright spots on the continent, and Africa also saw positive scores for electoral integrity in Benin, Mauritius, Lesotho, and South Africa, as well as gains in Nigeria.[83]

Ethiopia 2015

The Ethiopian parliamentary election on May 24, 2015 proved the *worst* ranked election in PEI-4.5. Ethiopia's repressive ruling party, the People's Revolutionary Democratic Front (EPRDF), has governed Ethiopia for more than two decades. The party and its allies were declared by the government-controlled national election board to have won every single parliamentary seat in May's elections. Article 19, an international nongovernmental organization focusing on the right to freedom of expression, reports that there are major restrictions on freedom of the press – Ethiopia is the second biggest jailer of journalists after its neighbor, Eritrea. Its broadcasting and telecommunications sectors are dominated by the state, and the minimal private media sector is heavily regulated and frequently censored.[84] Opposition parties that wanted to organize peaceful protests and rallies were arrested and harassed, their equipment confiscated, and permits denied.[85] The opposition movement remains fragmented and weak, unable to forge a common platform. No invitation to the Carter Center or to European Union observer missions were sent. The EU noted that "previous reports of Election Observer Missions have not been accepted by Ethiopia, which calls into question the value of a further EOM this year."[86] The African Union appraised the electoral process and gave a more positive assessment, however, concluding that the parliamentary elections "were calm, peaceful, and credible as it provided an opportunity for the Ethiopian people to express their choices at the polls."[87] The international community has also not pressed strongly on electoral rights due to security concerns in the region arising from the Somalia-based terrorist group al-Shabaab.[88] As a result, far from using any aid conditionality, Ethiopia continues to receive more than $3 billion a year from the Organisation for Economic Cooperation and Development. Two months after the elections, on July 27, President Obama rewarded the country with the first-ever state visit to Ethiopia by a sitting US president.

Burundi 2015

Burundi ranked the second worst of all 153 countries worldwide according to experts in the PEI-4.5. The presidential election on July 21, 2015 was marred by weeks of violent protests against President Pierre Nkurunziza's attempt to win a third term in office, despite controversy over whether he was eligible to run again under the constitutional peace-settlement. Disputes reportedly triggered mass demonstrations and hundreds of deaths. On May 13, a coup attempt was launched by elements in the military opposed to Nkurunziza's third term bid, but loyalist soldiers reasserted control by the next day. The night before polling day, there were reported sporadic blasts and gunshots. The election was boycotted by seventeen opposition parties and condemned by the international community as lacking the conditions to ensure it was fair.[89] The European Union suspended its mission because of concerns about the credibility of the electoral process.[90] The African Union refused to send electoral observers for the first time in the organization's history. The Catholic Church also stood down their election observer missions before Election Day. The US State Department concluded that the election lacked credibility since the legitimacy of the process "has been tainted by the government's harassment of opposition and civil society members, closing down of media outlets and political space, and intimidation of voters."[91] The Burundi legislative elections on June 29, 2015 were almost as badly rated, ranked 5th worst ever in PEI-4.5.

Benin 2015

By contrast, Benin, one of the poorest societies on the poorest continent in the world, ranked 30th highest out of 153 countries in PEI-4.5, despite turbulent instability among neighboring states in Francophone West Africa. As a result, the 2016 elections mark a further peaceful milestone in Benin's democratic consolidation, a process that started with the introduction of the new constitution and the introduction of multiparty elections in 1991.[92] For more than a quarter century, despite widespread poverty, Benin has experienced a series of legislative and presidential elections that domestic and international observers have reported as free, peaceful, and fair, including transitions bringing the opposition party into power. Today Benin is widely regarded as a successful African democracy with constitutional checks and balances, multiple parties, a high degree of judicial independence and respect for human rights, and a lively partisan press that is often critical of the government. The country is categorized as "free" by the 2016 Freedom House index, comparable to Argentina, Mexico, and Romania in its record of civil liberties and political rights.[93] Nevertheless, Benin faces endemic poverty (with a GDP per capita of $800) and many problems of governance common in African states, including corruption in the public sector. Alleged coup attempts occurred in 2012 and 2013 and in 2013 local elections were delayed, triggering mass protests.

In 2016, when President Thomas Boni Yayi had completed his second presidential term, he was constitutionally barred from running again.[94] In many African states, incumbent leaders have sought to extend constitutional term limits, and President Yayi repeatedly attempt to follow suit, but he was defeated in parliament and he subsequently stood down at the election. Like many Francophone African states, Benin uses a two-round (second ballot) electoral system for the presidency where the winning candidate needs 50 percent (plus one) of the valid votes cast. If no candidate obtains more than 50 percent in the first round, a runoff election is held between the two candidates with the highest number of votes. The candidate who obtains the highest number of votes in the second round is the winner.[95] The first round of the Benin presidential was held on March 6, 2016, followed by a runoff on March 20.

Over thirty candidates entered the first round of the contest, including leading contenders from diverse backgrounds, such as technocrats and successful businesspersons from the private sector. The campaign was largely peaceful and the leading candidates focused on the economy, presenting detailed programs for reducing unemployment and stimulating agriculture.[96] For the first time in Benin, a presidential debate was telecast live, allowing candidates to reach out to the electorate.[97] Candidates had free access to the media and they campaigned across the country. The diaspora living abroad were also allowed to vote.

In the first round, the leading candidates were prime minister Lionel Zinsou, leader of the Cowry Forces for an Emerging Benin, who placed first with 28.4 percent of the vote; and Patrice Talon, an independent candidate and Beninese cotton entrepreneur, with 24.8 percent. In the second round, however, Talon won the election with 65.7 percent of the vote and his opponent quickly conceded defeat. The elections saw a fall in turnout (66 percent) compared with the previous contest.[98] International observers reported that candidates complied with provisions of the Constitution and the legal framework governing the electoral process, as well as making every effort to preserve the social peace and national cohesion.[99] Overall the presidential election in Benin was rated 69 in the 100-point PEI Index, scoring equivalent or marginally better than several West European contests.

Nigeria 2015

Other positive news on the continent comes from the Nigerian elections on March 28, 2015. The most populous state in Africa, Nigeria remains a hybrid regime, which has a checked history of veering erratically between autocracy and democracy, currently ranked in 2015 as "partly free" by Freedom House.[100] Many contests have been marred by outbreaks of violent conflict, catalyzed by ongoing tensions between the Muslim north and Christian south. There were technical flaws but nevertheless the 2015 elections were celebrated as a relatively violence-free handover of power via the ballot box, following victory for President Muhammadu Buhari. EU observers considered the overall outcome of the elections as "peaceful and orderly ... despite frustration and challenges caused by often late opening of polling sites, failing biometric voter verification, some regrettable violent incidents, and repolling on Sunday."[101] Despite marked improvements, problems remain in the quality of Nigerian elections, rated 88th out of 153 countries in PEI-4.5.

Stages in the Electoral Cycle

Which stage of the election cycle is commonly the most problematic? It is often assumed that the voting process and the count are potentially most problematic, certainly when it comes to cases of fraud, ballot-stuffing, and vote-buying. Yet, according to experts, the most common flaws emerging from the eleven stages in the electoral cycle, illustrated in Figure 4.4, are related to political finance and campaign media. By contrast, the best dimensions of cycle concern voting procedures and the count. Subsequent chapters discuss several thematic topics in more detail and programs designed to overcome these issues, including reforms to poor-quality electoral laws, quota policies designed to make parliaments more socially inclusive of women, challenges of regulating campaign finance, the role of the news media, and ways to improve voter registration processes.

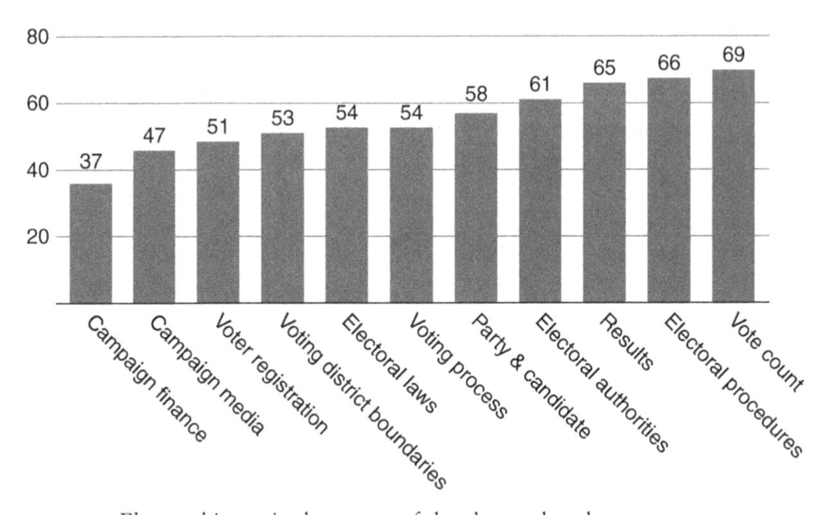

FIGURE 4.4. Electoral integrity by stages of the electoral cycle.
Source: Pippa Norris, Ferran Martinez i Coma, Alessandro Nai and Max Groemping. *The Expert Survey of Perceptions of Electoral Integrity.* (PEI-4.5). Available at www.electoralintegrityproject.com.

THE THREATS AND OPPORTUNITIES FACING ELECTORAL ASSISTANCE PROGRAMS

No single factor that can explain why countries perform well or badly when it comes to electoral integrity. Instead the previous book in this trilogy documented how the drivers lie in a combination of three types of conditions – structural constraints, international forces, and institutional designs – each of which provides certain threats and opportunities facing international agencies seeking to support programs of electoral assistance.[102]

- ***Structural constraints:*** Electoral integrity is more challenging in societies with widespread poverty and illiteracy (Afghanistan), a legacy of deep-rooted conflict (Burundi), battling the "curse" of natural resources and state capture (Equatorial Guinea), and the confronted with a historical legacy inherited from previous regimes and elections within each country;
- ***International leverage and linkage:*** The quality of elections is also shaped by how far societies are open to the spread of international norms and standards through cosmopolitan communications and membership of regional organizations (such as within the OAS and OSCE), the positive or negative impact of neighboring regional powers, such as South Africa and Russia, and through the provision of international development aid and technical assistance; and
- ***Institutional arrangements:*** Electoral integrity also rests upon the power-sharing design of constitutional arrangements, electoral systems, and

procedures, providing transparent, fair, inclusive, and legitimate rules, as well as the powers, capacity, and ethos of the electoral authorities when managing elections.

Evidence from the PEI index can be compared with many national-level indicators compiled in the Quality of Government and the Varieties of Democracy cross-national datasets,[103] and with classifications of types of power-sharing constitutions and electoral regulatory agencies from cross-national sources, including International IDEA and the ACE Project.[104]

The Structural Constraints of Poverty, Lack of Economic Development, and Natural Resources

In general, the cross-national comparison with levels of economic development suggest that the riskiest elections occur in many of the worlds' low-income developing societies, for example, Haiti, Afghanistan, Bangladesh, and Burundi. The reasons can be found in theories of developmental studies, political economy, and political sociology, exemplified by the long tradition established by Seymour Martin Lipset in the mid-twentieth century.[105] The so-called "Lipset thesis" argues that democracies (and, by extension, levels of electoral integrity) flourish best in industrialized and postindustrial societies characterized by conditions of widespread literacy and education, with a substantial affluent professional middle class and a pluralistic range of civic associations serving as a buffer between citizens and the state.[106] The original claim by Lipset specified most simply that: "The more well-to-do a nation, the greater the chances that it will sustain democracy."[107] Development consolidates democracy, Lipset theorized, by expanding access to information derived from literacy, schooling, and the mass media, broadening the size of the middle classes, reducing the extremes of rural poverty, facilitating intermediary organizations such as labor unions, professional associations, and voluntary organizations, and promoting the cultural values of legitimacy, moderation, and social tolerance. Poor societies also typically lack the resources and public sector capacity to manage peaceful and stable contests. Following in Lipset's footsteps, in subsequent decades the relationship between wealth and democracy has been subject to rigorous empirical inquiry. For more than half a century the association has withstood repeated empirical tests under a variety of different conditions, using cross-sectional and time-series data with a large sample of countries and years, and with increasingly sophisticated econometric models, as well as in many historical accounts of political developments occurring within particular nation states. Many studies have reported that wealth is associated with the standard indicators of democratization, although the precise estimates of effects are sensitive to each study's choice of time period, the selection of control variables specified in causal models, and the basic measurement of both democracy and economic growth.[108]

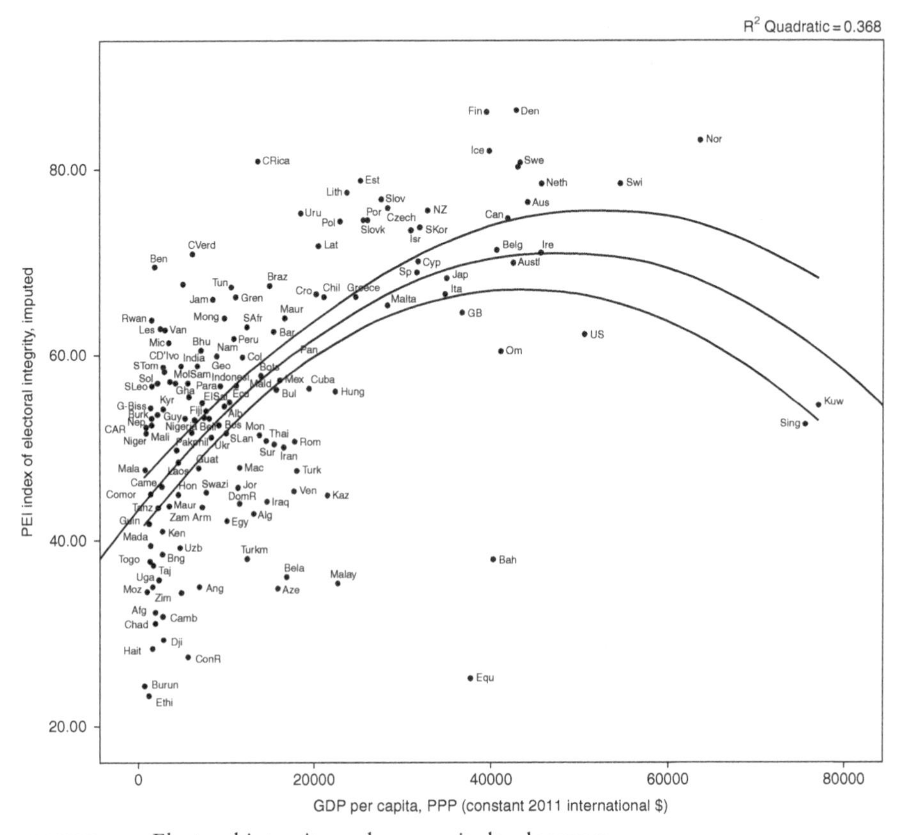

FIGURE 4.5. Electoral integrity and economic development.
Note: The Perception of Electoral Integrity Index (PEI-4.5); GDP per capita (in purchasing parity power) World Bank Development Indicators.
Source: Pippa Norris, Ferran Martinez i Coma, Alessandro Nai and Max Groemping. *The Expert Survey of Perceptions of Electoral Integrity*. (PEI-4.5). Available at www .electoralintegrityproject.com.

There is also convincing evidence for the modernization theory as an explanation of the observed cross-national variations in the quality of elections; as Figure 4.5 illustrates, a significant correlation links level of economic development (measured by per capita GDP in purchasing power parity) and the PEI levels of electoral integrity (R = .54***, N147). Yet it is also obvious that among the poorest countries, several cases – such as Benin, Lesotho and Micronesia – perform relatively well in the global comparison, according to the PEI Index. By contrast, as already discussed, several other low-income economies perform poorly in this regard – notably Ethiopia, Burundi, and Haiti. Moreover, we have already shown that among affluent postindustrial societies and Western democracies, elections in the United States and the United

Kingdom are relatively poorly rated. In addition, one of the world's most affluent societies, Singapore, is a clear outlier, scoring only moderately in the PEI Index.[109]

The well-known "resource curse" is another related structural explanation, suggesting that countries with GDP highly dependent upon abundant reserves of nonrenewable mineral resources, such as Kuwaiti oil, DRC gold, or Sierra Leone diamonds, usually produce less diversified and less competitive economies, more income inequality with less investment in social policies building human capital, and heightened danger of state capture and rent-seeking by ruling elites.[110] Lootable natural resources that can be smuggled across borders, such as diamonds, rare minerals, ivory, and the ingredients needed to produce cocaine and heroin make countries particularly vulnerable to criminal cartels, civil war, insurgency, and rebellion.[111] Natural resource-rich states are therefore commonly found to have worse problems of corruption and state-capture. Assessing the degree to which an economy is dependent upon natural resources is not easy, however, especially the black-market trade in illicit goods. The previous book measured the distribution of natural resources using the World Bank's measure of total natural resources rents, 2012 (% of GDP), where these rents are the sum of oil, natural gas, coal, minerals, and forest. "Rents" are estimated as the difference between the value of production of these resources at world prices and the total costs of production. "Rentier states" are those like Saudi Arabia which derive all or a substantial portion of their national revenues from the rent of indigenous resources to external clients. The evidence presented in the earlier volume suggests a strong and consistent correlation between the distribution of natural resources and the level of electoral integrity in any country, even after controlling for per capita GDP.

Therefore, although levels of economic development and resource-dependent economies are usually significantly associated with the quality of free and fair contests, and the threats are highest in the world's poorest societies and oil-rich states, the relationship should not be regarded as deterministic. For agencies offering electoral assistance, this suggests that the risks of failure arising from environmental conditions are usually likely to be greatest in the combination of low-income developing societies and in resource-dependent/oil-rich economies, such as Libya and Equatorial Guinea.

International Leverage and Linkage

The broadest international process thought to effect electoral integrity arises from globalization and cosmopolitan communications. Theories of globalization suggest that cultural values are flowing at an increasing rate across national borders, so that cosmopolitan societies are learning from each other, positively or negatively, due to the expansion of international markets and the flow of capital, labor and goods, patterns of human migration, and technological developments in transportation and networked communications.[112] The diffusion of norms is thought to be particularly influential among neighboring states sharing similar historical cultures, languages, and religions, media sources, strategic alliances, trade, financial, and labor markets, peoples, and diplomatic links within each cultural region.[113] Cultural diffusion effects can be understood to occur in an active way, for example where states seek to use mass communications to spread democratic values, or where trade agreements and economic sanctions, or membership of regional organizations are conditional upon member states' adherence to certain international standards. Or the effects may be expected to arise in a largely passive domino fashion, where information flows over national borders through processes of global communications, so that similar events occur successively through contagion and emulation within a cultural region. The "Color Revolutions" in post-Communist countries are often cited as examples of the diffusion processes, including the November 2003 people-power Rose Revolution that deposed veteran president Eduard Shevardnadze in Georgia, which is thought to have influenced events in Ukraine culminating in the Orange Revolution the following year.[114] Counteracting negative phenomenon include the role of President Putin in his attempts to reassert Russia's influence on the global stage, exemplified by Crimea's secession from Ukraine, which tightened Russia's economic and military pressures on neighboring states. Similarly, during the Arab uprisings the chain of events following the Tunisian overthrow of President Ben Ali strongly suggests a regional contagion effect in Libya, Egypt, Bahrain, Syria, Mali, Nigeria, and Iraq, with divergent influences on protest movements and contentious politics, state stability, regime change, and processes of democratization.[115] One reason why Tunisia seems to have moved more successfully towards democracy than many other states in the region may be close relations with France and Italy, as well as through economic cooperation with the European Union.

In addition to the information flows arising from access to global information flows, regional effects are also expected to be important in the diffusion of norms of electoral integrity that are actively reinforced by the soft-power influence of hegemonic states and by membership of regional intergovernmental organizations.[116] As observed in the previous chapter, regional intergovernmental organizations have played an active role in promoting international principals of electoral integrity within their sphere of influence, including the European Union, the Organization of American States in Latin America, the Organization for Economic Cooperation in Europe (OSCE), and, to a lesser extent, the African Union after member states endorsed the *African Charter on Democracy, Elections, and Governance.*[117] The impact of regional organizations is exemplified through the enlargement of membership of the European Union to eight Central and Eastern European countries in 2004, including Poland, Lithuania, and the Czech Republic, followed by expansion to

Romania and Bulgaria in 2007.[118] States seeking EU membership are required to respect the "principles of liberty, democracy, respect for human rights and fundamental freedoms, and the rule of law" and the Copenhagen European Council set out the specific conditions which applicant states need to meet to qualify for membership. States seeking economic cooperation and trade with the EU have a strong incentive to introduce political reforms to meet these conditions, including improving the quality of electoral processes, although this mechanism weakens once states become members. The evidence from my previous book confirmed that both cosmopolitan communications and membership of regional organizations were significantly associated with higher levels of electoral integrity, even after controlling for structural constraints.[119] This suggests that international agencies face more strategic opportunities for effective electoral assistance support in countries that are open to global information flows across national borders and which are already (or aspiring) members of regional intergovernmental organizations sharing democratic norms. By contrast, the threat of failure for any attempted programs of electoral assistance is likely to be greatest in isolated societies with neighboring authoritarian states, such as in Central Eurasian states buttressing Russia or in South East Asian countries close to China.

Political Institutions

Finally, the institutional arrangements in any state, including the adoption of power-sharing political institutions and the role of the Election Management Body, also help to explain why some elections have greater integrity compared with others held in similar types of society within global regions. Power-sharing constitutions, with strong parliaments, multilevel governance, and independent judiciaries, provide important checks and balances. This usually prevents the abuse of power by the executive, including the temptation to put a thumb on the scales by amending the rules, by attempting to run for an unconstitutional third term, or by stacking the electoral management body. Power-sharing also builds greater trust in the electoral process amongst multiple stakeholders, including among election losers, avoiding the temptation to boycott the election, or mobilize massive protests. By contrast, majoritarian constitutions that concentrate power in the hands of the executive are often associated with worse levels of electoral integrity.

The design of the electoral rules is particularly important.[120] The evidence can be illustrated by comparing the PEI scores by the type of electoral system. In general, countries using List Proportional Representation for the lower house of the national legislature scored 60 out of 100 on the PEI index, 11 points higher than countries using majoritarian electoral systems. The reasons for this contrast are that proportional representation (PR) electoral systems lower the threshold for minor parties to enter parliaments, and deprive the largest party of an absolute parliamentary majority, thereby typically generating coalition governments. This arrangement produces institutional check and balances that maximize the number of institutional veto-players in the policy process and thereby avoid the potential risks of electoral rules being manipulated in favor of any single party in government, especially ruling parties controlling the legislature and executive. Therefore, power-sharing arrangements limit the capacity of governing parties to rig the rules of the electoral game in future contests. These rules build trust in the system – even among losers. By contrast, the risks of majoritarian elections are particularly strong if used in autocratic states where the governing party holds an absolute majority in the legislature, and in presidential republics where "rubber stamp" assemblies have weak legislative powers and autonomy, as opposition parties may then be unable to counterbalance and check any abuse of powers and manipulation of electoral rules by the executive.

The explanations for flawed and failed contests considered so far emphasize the wider constitutional environment far removed from managing any specific elections. An additional critical factor concerns the structure, capacity, and ethos of the electoral authorities charged with administering elections. These are the frontline agencies embedded within the broader societal, international, and constitutional settings for electoral governance. Ideally for contests to meet global norms, electoral officials should ensure that they deliver public services meeting international standards.[121] Unfortunately, too often contests appear to fall foul of simple human errors, technical malfunctions, and logistical failures. Problems occur where polling stations run out of paper ballots. Poorly trained poll workers are unfamiliar with procedures. Dead people are listed on voter registers. Other legitimate citizens are turned away. Electronic voting machines break. Indelible ink washes off fingers. Ballot boxes have broken seals. Officials fail to check voter identification. Long lines delay closure. Electoral legitimacy can be damaged by accidental maladministration and indeed official incompetence may facilitate intentional acts of partisan fraud and manipulation. Moreover, if administrative flaws arise on polling day, there are often minimal opportunities to correct them in a timely fashion, potentially damaging confidence in the electoral process and authorities. In particular, the previous book established that two factors about EMBs were consistently associated with better electoral integrity, according to the PEI index.[122] One concerns functional effectiveness and how far the public sector has the skills, experience, powers, and resources to manage the delivery of public goods and services, including, by extension, how far electoral authorities have sufficient technical expertise, trained and competent officials, consistent procedural guidelines and rules, sufficient planning time, and adequate budgets. In addition, elections are more likely to meet international standards where an impartial and professional *administrative ethos* predominates among officials within the public sector, setting expectations about what is acceptable within the organization, with norms of impartial service in the public interest predominating over a culture corrupted by patronage politics, partisanship, and clientalistic practices.

CONCLUSIONS

The PEI dataset provides systematic evidence for the threats and opportunities that programs of electoral assistance face. Several consistent patterns can be observed; the chances of electoral malpractices rise in the world's poorest societies, as has been repeatedly found in the body of research on transitions from autocracy and processes of democratic consolidation. Oil-rich economies also heighten the odds of failure, by encouraging corruption, patronage politics, and practices and cultures tolerant of vote-buying and bribery. The challenges of effective elections rise in states that are cut off from the diffusion of global norms, lacking access to cosmopolitan communications, as well as where regional intergovernmental organizations have not yet strongly endorsed democratic norms. Finally, the constitutional structures of power-sharing and the capacity and ethos of electoral management bodies are also important for the probability of strengthening electoral integrity. On this basis, we need to consider in more detail what types of programs are commonly used in the sector of electoral assistance, the strengths and weaknesses of each, and what interventions have generally proved most effective. It is to these issues that the next section of the book turns.

PART III

THE STRENGTHS AND WEAKNESSES OF ELECTORAL ASSISTANCE PROGRAMS

5

Reforming Electoral Laws

In many countries, attempts to strengthen electoral integrity involve establishing or reforming the basic framework of electoral laws and administrative regulations. A wealth of research has documented the significant consequences that flow from the choice and design of electoral laws, including patterns of party competition, the social basis of political representation, patterns of electoral turnout, issues of governability and political stability, policy performance, and levels of electoral integrity.[1] What is less well-understood concerns the agenda-setting and policymaking processes leading towards the adoption and revision of electoral institutions. One major barrier to reform is that legislators are the main actors responsible for revising the rules, yet they are also the beneficiaries of the status quo and thus have strong incentives to block change.[2] Many stakeholders within each country can help to break the logjam of incumbent self-interest, including public disaffection, protests channeled through civil society and election reform NGOs, the mobilization of opposition forces, and the use of popular referenda.[3] The reform agenda may also be influenced by the international community when intergovernmental agencies like the Organization of American States or the European Union highlight electoral malpractices in a contest, share knowledge about best practices, provide technical advice for draft legislation, advocate electoral procedures reflecting international standards, and support the reform process through funding and organizing expert roundtables, discussion workshops, and public consultation events. External actors are independent of partisan interests within a country and they may therefore help to overcome institutional inertia and resistance to implementing electoral reforms from governing parties, legislative incumbents, and special interests.

But are external actors effective in catalyzing electoral reforms? This addresses the question: Does electoral assistance work? Whether recommendations by agencies in the international community are adopted and implemented can be theorized to be influenced both by the threats and opportunities that elections face within the societal context and also by the types of recommendations that agencies propose. On the one hand, at the macrolevel, technical advice and electoral assistance from regional organizations such as the OSCE, EU, and OAS can be expected to prove most influential among member states where international linkages are strong, among countries where communication, trade, and migration are closely networked through global ties, in poorer developing societies most dependent upon the international community for Official Development Aid, as well as in more democratic states sharing norms of electoral integrity. In addition, the type of recommendations may also be important. For example, procedural legal and administrative reforms may be easier to implement than those requiring additional financial or human resources, while general policy recommendations from external agencies may be more acceptable to states rather than those specifying detailed guidelines.

To consider these issues, the first section of this chapter lays out the theoretical and conceptual framework and then briefly reviews what is known from the previous literature about the multiple roles of regional organization as watchdogs, human rights advocates, and policy advisers. In particular, to establish new evidence about the latter role, the chapter examines the implementation rate for the series of recommendations contained in election observer reports published by the Organization of American States, which suggest reforms to electoral laws and procedures in member states in Latin America and the Caribbean. The study addresses several unanswered questions: What is the overall implementation rate of the range of electoral reforms that regional organizations recommend in their observer reports? Which specific types of policy recommendations are most often adopted? And in what types of states are regional organizations most effective as agenda-setters, catalyzing or reinforcing domestic processes of electoral reform? To answer these questions, the second section establishes the data and methods used to examine the impact of regional organizations when they offer technical policy recommendations for electoral reform. The study focuses upon Latin America and the Caribbean, a region where electoral laws vary in quality, but where societies share many similar cultural traditions, political experiences, and socioeconomic characteristics. Evidence draws upon an original dataset on Democratic Diffusion, developed by the Electoral Integrity Project in cooperation with the Organization of American States.[4] Data is derived from systematic content analysis of the recommendations contained in around 140 observer mission reports published from 1999 to 2015 by the Organization of American States in 28 Latin American and Caribbean states. These reports contained over 1,000 recommendations in total. The key dependent variable is measured by the implementation rate of the OAS recommendations. Section 3 describes the results of the analysis using hierarchical logistic models (HLM): Level 1 concerns the recommendations and Level 2 concerns the societal context. The concluding fourth section highlights three key findings.

Firstly, regional organizations are perhaps surprisingly effective as policy advisers; despite many incumbents resistant to change, roughly half of all electoral reform recommendations contained in mission reports are implemented by member states, either partially or fully, before the subsequent contest. This can be regarded as a classic case of the cup half full or half empty, but given widespread skepticism about the general impact of electoral assistance, and the lack of enforcement and systematic follow up mechanisms by observer missions, this can also be interpreted as a considerable success. This association should not be understood to imply that the OAS alone catalyzed the reforms, since the observer reports may well pick up and amplify suggestions for changes arising from discussions with domestic stakeholders. Electoral reforms engage a coalition of multiple actors within the state and civil society. It does seem safe to conclude that proposals published in the OAS mission reports provide an impartial and legitimate source reinforcing the domestic agenda-setting stage of electoral reform process within a country. Secondly, the type of recommendations was also found to matter: the implementation rate was highest for proposals seeking to improve civic education, electoral laws, voter registration, and electoral procedures, all activities occurring during the long-term preelection stage of the electoral cycle. These are often the areas where the electoral authorities have primary responsibility so the OAS can work with these bodies. By contrast, two areas that are often the responsibility of other specialized regulatory agencies and are commonly problematic in many elections – campaign media and political finance – proved more intractable to OAS reform proposals. Procedural legal reforms (not requiring resources) and those recommending general principles and standards (rather than specific proposals) were also most likely to be enacted. Finally, confirming the importance of international linkages, Latin American and Caribbean societies that are politically integrated with the international community in general were also the ones that implemented OAS recommendations most often. This suggests that political globalization and linkages matter for voluntary compliance by states with international standards of electoral integrity. By contrast, many other institutional and structural factors, including levels of economic development and democratization, were not significant impediments to the adoption of reform proposals. The overall conclusions from the analysis, therefore, suggests that in addition to their watchdog and human rights advocacy work, the policy advisor role of regional organizations makes a valuable contribution towards strengthening electoral integrity through sharing best practices, advocating improvements, and catalyzing the domestic electoral reform agenda within member states.

THE ROLES OF REGIONAL ORGANIZATIONS IN ELECTORAL ASSISTANCE

Regional intergovernmental organizations have played a leading role in supporting elections, as exemplified by the assistance provided by the Organization of American States, the European Union, and the Organization for Security and Cooperation in Europe.[5] Three main functions have become common in this sector; as *watchdogs*, regional organizations dispatch teams of electoral observers to monitor contests, with the goal of expanding transparency and deterring malpractices; as *human rights advocates*, they seek to foster consensus among member states about the appropriate standards and norms which should governing electoral conduct; and as *policy advisers*, they aim to share knowledge about best practices, build technical expertise, identify alternative policy options, and catalyze legal and administrative reforms in member states. All these activities can be understood as forms of soft power or linkage designed to strengthen electoral institutions, laws, and administrative procedures among diverse local stakeholders, especially the electoral authorities, political parties, and civil society organizations within each country.

Election as Watchdogs

The first role of regional organizations in electoral assistance concerns their watchdog work as electoral observers. International election missions typically seek to observe the quality of elections, highlight malpractices, and thereby deter the potential abuse of power. The roots of electoral monitoring started with the founding of the United Nations in 1945 when the agency supervised and monitored elections in several dependent territories, although this was mainly done informally through sending small teams of top-level UN diplomats and high-ranking officials. The Organization of American States started observing elections in 1962 and a few years later the Commonwealth Secretariat undertook some similar missions as part of the decolonization process. In later decades, the UN subsequently withdrew from this arena, due to a potential conflict of interest with their other work in providing electoral assistance.

Since the end of the Cold War era, however, a diverse range of organizations have become engaged in electoral observation. The approach of the leading international agencies has become increasingly professionalized with trained teams and more systematic guidelines, tools, and techniques.[6] The focus shifted over time from more ad hoc methods to standardized procedures, from focusing upon a discrete event to long-term cooperation and institution-building, and from countering fraud on election day to scrutinizing the quality of the process throughout the electoral cycle. As shown in Figure 5.1, according to V-Dem data, the third wave of democratization witnessed the start of the dramatic rise

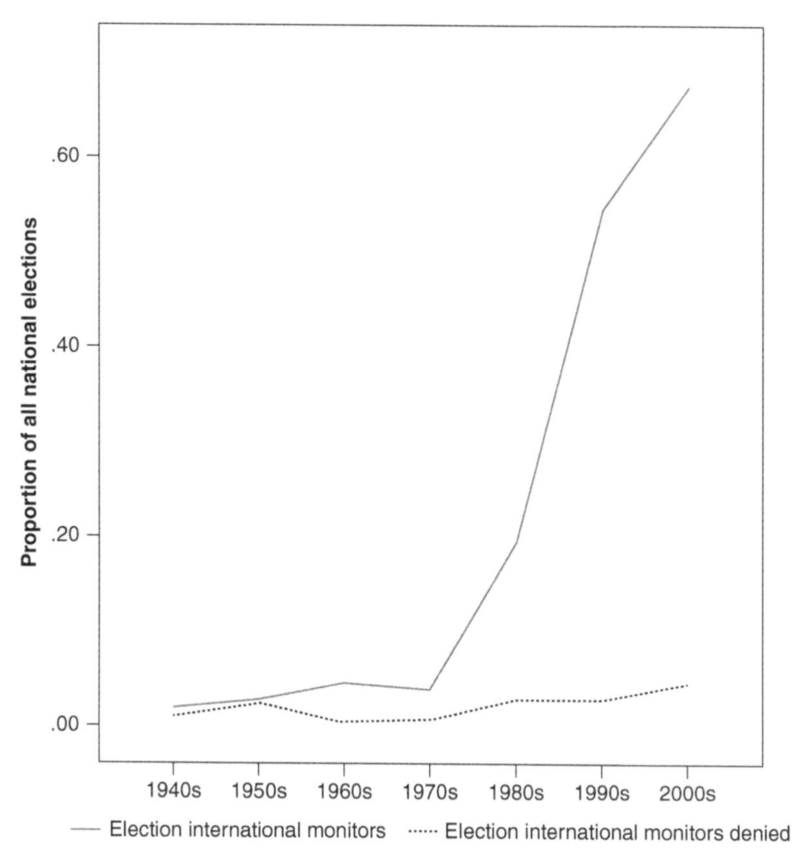

FIGURE 5.1. The rise in the proportion of elections with international monitors.
Note: (v2elintmon) "In this national election, were international election monitors present?" Yes = 1. (v2elmonden) "In this national election, were some international monitors denied opportunities to be present by the government holding the election?"
Source: V-Dem Varieties of Democracy Codebook Version 6 – Mar 2016.

in this phenomenon. In the 292 national elections held during the 1980s, just under one-fifth of all elections (54) were observed by international monitors. The trickle gradually became a flood; in the 590 national elections held during the millennial decade, two-thirds (360) had international monitors present.

Regional intergovernmental organizations played a major part in this expansion, for example, since 1962, the Department for Electoral Cooperation and Observation of the Organization for American States (OAS) has monitored over 200 elections in more than 30 countries, deploying more than 5,000 international observers. The first efforts were largely symbolic but recent missions have become far more rigorous and systematic, with manuals, methods, and tools adding topics well beyond any irregularities on election day, such as media observation, campaign finance, the use of election technologies, and gender equality in elected office.[7] OAS has observed legislative and presidential contests as well as referendum, constituent assemblies, municipal, and local elections. Contributions expanding their observer methods have come primarily from the United States, Canada, and Spain.[8] Similarly, since the mid-1990s the Office for Democratic Institutions and Human Rights (ODIHR/OSCE), has conducted over 300 missions in Central and Eastern Europe and published over 700 mission reports, working with partners such as the Parliamentary Assembly of the Council of Europe, the European Parliament, the NATO Parliamentary Assembly, and the Congress of Local and Regional Authorities for the Council of Europe.[9] Electoral observer missions by these agencies seek to evaluate how far parliamentary, presidential and referendum elections meet international standards of electoral integrity. Typically following an initial needs assessment mission, if further action is determined to be worthwhile a smaller number of long-term observers, gathering contextual information, often begin work around two months before polling day. Their numbers typically swell substantially through teams of short-term observers deployed during the campaign, election day, and immediate aftermath. An interim report may be published. The final conclusions and recommendations of the mission are published in reports presented in press conferences following the announcements of the official results.

Similar programs have been offered elsewhere by the Council of Europe, the African Union (AU), the Electoral Institute of Southern Africa (EISA), the Commonwealth Secretariat, and the European Union (EU). Several bilateral developmental agencies and nongovernmental organizations (NGOs) have also played a leading role in this work, including in the United States by the National Democratic Institute for International Affairs, the International Republican Institute, the International Foundation of Electoral Systems (IFES), and the Carter Center. Most organizations focus on national parliamentary and presidential elections and occasional referenda and plebiscites. The Congress of the Council of Europe also monitors local and regional contests. During the last decade the work of leading agencies has become increasingly professionalized and standardized, including through the 2005 UN Declaration of Principles for International Election Observation, which established a common code of conduct and norms protecting observers, endorsed by almost 50 agencies.[10] Similar methods and techniques have evolved across the leading organizations and these have been codified into training manuals, guidelines, and handbooks, for example concerning how observers can monitor campaign media, gender equality and minority representation, the electoral rights of the disabled, and political finance.

At the same time, recent years have seen growing political diversity in the monitoring organizations active in this subfield, with the Association of South East Asian Nations (ASEAN) delegating this function to civil society organizations linked together by the Asian Network for Free Elections

(ANFREL). To counter OSCE criticisms, the former Soviet republics have organized missions through the Commonwealth of Independent States. The League of Arab States and the Organization of Islamic Cooperation have also recently entered the fray.[11]

Many countries have also seen the rise of domestic observers organized in nonpartisan NGOs since the mid-1980s.[12] The Global Network of Domestic Election Monitors, founded in 2009, covers 175 organizations based in over seventy countries, including in Africa, Latin America, and Asia.[13] Regional associations encourage cooperation and knowledge sharing; for example, over twenty civic organizations cooperate under the umbrella of the European Network of Election Monitoring Organizations (ENEMO), covering countries in the former Soviet Union.[14] There are similar networks in West Africa, Southern Africa, East Africa, the Arab states, and Latin America. The NDI has supported the participation of local civil society group in over 80 countries, including by providing resources, capacity-building guidance, and practical handbooks concerning issues such as organizational development and planning, external relations and advocacy, and best practices for monitors during the preelection, campaign and postelection periods.[15] The United Nations *Declaration of Global Principles for Nonpartisan Election Observation and Monitoring*, launched by the UN Secretariat and endorsed by over 260 domestic monitoring groups, seeks to establish the normative framework governing the work of domestic monitors.[16]

Where there are large organizations, domestic observers live in all parts of the country. They can observe political developments throughout the long inter-election period. These observers are familiar with local customs, languages, and practices among diverse communities, rather than parachuted in for the campaign and its aftermath. As a sustainable form of political participation by ordinary citizens that builds local election watch groups in civil society, this is also worthwhile in itself. One potential disadvantage, however, is that domestic observers may be regarded by electoral authorities as less impartial and more partisan in their assessments, as well as being less skilled and trained in international standards of electoral integrity. The reports may also carry less weight and authority than those published by regional organizations.[17] Compared with international actors, domestic observers are thought to have more local knowledge about conditions, while at the same time being more vulnerable to intimidation, banning, or obstruction by legal requirements, as well as possibly being more partisan.[18]

External monitoring is theorized to raise the costs of cheating in polling places where observers are deployed, thereby deterring fraudulent and illegal acts, such as ballot-stuffing, impersonation, dishonest counts, and voter coercion. As a result, problems in the balloting and the vote count process are expected to become less common in local areas where polling stations are being monitored by observers. This literature is built in large part on the logic that observers provide information about the extent of any election fraud or malpractices to international and domestic audiences. For democratic reform movements and human rights NGOs, the work of international observers expands transparency, provides independent evidence that publicizes abuses, and legitimizes criticisms of the quality of elections. The publication of negative reports increase the likelihood of mass protests and thus also raise the domestic costs of cheating.[19] With regards to international audiences, this information can also trigger diplomatic pressures and lead to the withdrawal of "democracy-contingent" benefits, such as development aid.[20] Transparency can thereby potentially deter actors from manipulating the electoral rules or the outcome and reduce potential malpractices.

Is there good evidence of these sorts of consequences? A substantial literature has examined the empirical evidence for any short-term deterrence effect of international monitoring on electoral malpractices. The body of research generally suggests that under certain circumstances, international monitors deployed by many of the leading regional organizations have usually exerted a positive impact in strengthening free and fair elections.[21] A series of observational, experimental, and quasi-experimental studies has documented the impact arising from the deployment of monitors to polling station on deterring incidents of local fraud.[22] Where any such effects occur, however, these are limited in certain important regards.

Critics continue to question the effectiveness and impartiality of the observers, including whether regional organizations are willing to publish critical reports in fragile states like Haiti and Kenya, where doubts about the legitimacy and fairness of the outcome can trigger renewed conflict and political instability.[23] Moreover Western monitors now face growing challenges from the proliferation of rival organizations in this sector, both international and domestic, generating muddy messages through press conferences and the publication of reports providing divergent assessments of the outcome.[24] Government leaders aiming to blunt the edge of Western critics will invite observers to visit from friendly monitoring organizations.

Most research focuses on the effects of international observers in detecting and deterring fraud during the balloting process as electors go to the polls and then at the vote count stage when ballots are tabulated. Yet evidence from the PEI survey suggests that malpractices in these stages are, in fact, relatively rare.[25] The PEI data indicates that many other problems commonly occur earlier during the electoral cycle, exemplified by gerrymandering and malapportionment in the redistricting stage, limited ballot access for parties or candidates who fail to quality, or inadequate, incomplete, or inaccurate registration procedures preventing citizens from casting a ballot. Structural problems and technical irregularities that undermine electoral integrity often occur far earlier during the electoral cycle, such as through the disproportionate allocation of broadcast news to benefit ruling parties, the lax regulation of political finance, or the way that majoritarian electoral systems, excessively high legal electoral thresholds and/or boundary districts discriminate disproportionately against smaller political parties.[26] The diffuse effects of the works of the long-term observers is less clearly established.

In addition, even where there are effects on fraud at local level, research by Ichino and Schundein detected displacements effects; given limited resources and staff, not all polling areas can be monitored, especially in physically vast terrains with poor transportation, such as in Afghanistan or the Democratic Republic of Congo. As a result, any malpractices on election day, such as voter impersonation or ballot stuffing, can simply move to other polling areas (or indeed to earlier stages of the contest) where observers are not deployed.[27] Those intent on manipulating the results can learn from the work of observers and simply shift the location of their activities – out of sight, out of mind. Finally, Donno argues that monitoring is most effective not in isolation but when it is undertaken in combination with diplomatic pressures.[28] In particular, her research suggests that conditionality is important for compliance, so that states are threatened by bilateral donors with penalties such as reductions in ODA contributions or trade deals, or where they are offered incentives in return for improving electoral conduct, such as member states applying to belong to the European Union.

All these qualifications suggest that the outcome of the monitoring missions is more complicated than is often assumed in popular media accounts.[29] Research suggests that there are often some beneficial consequences, but the impact of monitoring remains more contingent and conditional, rather than being a blanket solution to all types of electoral malpractices. In general, the move towards electoral monitoring can be seen as part of the resurgent interest in the potential capacity of transparency – the public availability of information – to improve democratic governance. Timely, accurate, granular, and freely available information is generally regarded as intrinsically valuable, as well as having many instrumental benefits. In development, transparency and accountability is thought to help plug the leaky pipes of corruption and inefficiency, channel public spending more efficiently, and produce better services.[30] In the field of electoral governance, openness about the rules and procedures, outcomes, and decisions processes used by electoral authorities is widely assumed to build public trust, improve policy-making, and facilitate accountability.[31] By contrast, in the words of the Open Society Institute: "Silence and secrecy are two of the most powerful tools that governments can employ to mute critics and cloak their actions from public scrutiny."[32] Advocacy groups such as the Open Election Data Initiative seek to expand public information about basic matters such as the provision of an accurate and comprehensive list of all polling stations, the electoral register, voting laws and rights, and the campaign expenditure of political parties and candidates.[33] Even if unable to generate positive benefits, there is still a presumption in favor of open governance since, by contrast: "The absence of transparency in electoral processes invariably leads to the suspicion that fraudulent activities are taking place."[34]

In practice, however, the instrumental consequences of electoral transparency are less clear-cut than many proponents claim and it remains naïve to assume that greater information *alone* strengthens the accountability of governments to their own citizens, the quality of elections, or the compliance of election management agencies with international norms and standards. In general, like other policy reforms replying upon transparency, the power of information needs ideally to be combined with effective mechanisms for accountability and redress of wrongdoing. If the press is muted and corrupt, the legislature and judiciary dominated by the executive branch, electoral officials in the pocket of the ruling party, civil society and opposition movements weakly organized, and the public ill-informed or indifferent, and if the international community is disengaged or reluctant to exert diplomatic leverage, then no amount of critical reports published by regional organizations seem likely by themselves to generate sufficient pressures on the regime so that officials have an incentive to improve electoral laws and minimize malpractices.

Regional Organizations as Human Rights Advocates

In addition to monitoring, the literature on democratization has long emphasized the important role of regional intergovernmental organizations in securing agreement about human rights conventions, treaties, and standards, and thereby reinforcing norms of conduct among member states.[35] This work involves debating issues and endorsing agreements about human rights among representatives in regional intergovernmental forums. Regional organizations seek to foster awareness and share information about best practices and political rights through their work conducting regional studies, disseminating guidelines, handbooks, and reports, and supporting local training workshops and outreach activities. The OAS, for example, has published reports on diverse challenges facing elections in Latin America and the Caribbean, such as monitoring standards and training observers, strengthening electoral participation, using ICTs in electoral administration, respecting the voting rights of disabled citizens, ways to improve gender equality in elected office, deterring bias in the campaign media, and regulating political party finance.[36] Similarly organizations such as International IDEA, the Inter-Parliamentary Union, the OSCE/ODIHR, the Council of Europe, and IFES have disseminated a wealth of publications offering general guidance on electoral laws and processes. The ACE Electoral Knowledge Network – supported by EISA, Elections Canada, the Mexican INES, the Carter Center, UNDP, UNEAD, IFES, and International IDEA – provides a wealth of practical guidance and an encyclopedia pooling information and best practices on everything from drawing electoral district boundaries to voter and party registration, the representation of women and minorities, and electoral dispute resolution mechanisms.[37]

Relatively little work has scrutinized the systematic impact of regional organizations when they seek to establish a consensus among member states about appropriate normative standards and principles governing the conduct of elections. Nevertheless a broader literature has emphasized their general effectiveness as human rights advocates, especially where international agencies reinforce the work of domestic networks of reformers and civil society social movements.[38] Through this process, regional organizations are thought to strengthen the impact of "neighborhood effects" among member states, where regimes in each country gradually come to resemble others within their region. This is a general process of democratization but in the sector of electoral integrity as well, evidence from experts suggests that the quality of elections in any country is significantly related to other states within their global region. The effect can operate both positively, to reinforce democratic norms and values, such as in Latin America and the Southern Cone of Africa, and negatively to undermine these practices, in spheres of influence dominated by hegemonic autocracies such as Russia, Saudi Arabia, Iran, and China.[39]

The underlying mechanisms to explain exactly how this regional contagion process works, however, are not well established. The diffusion of democracy among member states within global regions such as Europe and Latin America could occur as a result of a passive emulation effect, as cosmopolitan communications flowing across neighboring borders serve to spread international norms and standards among neighboring states located in shared cultural regions of the world.[40] In this regard, more open societies with permeable boundaries, free media, and cultural and linguistic ties are thought most likely to learn democratic values and elections standards from other states around them. Alternatively, however, it could be due to the "carrots and sticks" that intergovernmental organizations provide to members. The entry of new post-Communist member states into the European Union exemplifies this process, with improvements in human rights and democratization required as a condition to gain the substantial economic and trade benefits associated with membership.[41] Incentives represent the prospect for states receiving development aid, inwards investment, and economic rewards, such as access to markets and the lifting of visa requirements for travel. By contrast, regional organizations can also wield pressures, including through the use of trade embargoes, or the deployment of peacekeeping troops.

There is certainly evidence that the quality of electoral integrity is shared among neighboring states within regions. Unfortunately, it is more difficult to pin down the specific use of regional reports, guidelines, and handbooks among local actors in member states, and thus to determine the overall impact of these in decision-making processes. At the same time, the role of regional organizations in this regard can be expected in general to disseminate information about shared norms and practices for elections. Process-tracing can also provide insights into specific cases about the trickle-down effects of these activities, such as the way that international advisors and legal experts helped to inform choices about the design of electoral system and the use of reserved seats for women in particular countries that revised their national constitutions.[42] Therefore in regional organizations such as the European Union and Latin America, where the majority of member states adhere strongly today to the principles of democratic governance, the role of regional organizations in strengthening human rights is likely to facilitate the adoption of a common normative framework and standard of conduct that govern electoral practices in member states.

Regional Organizations as Policy Analysts Catalyzing and Reinforcing Reforms

Regional organizations are watchdogs. They seek to prevent manipulation and maladministration. They are human rights advocates reinforcing international laws. Regional organizations also seek to identify policy reforms to legal and administrative frameworks that could strengthen electoral institutions, processes, and practices among member states. As part of this function, the final observer mission reports provide advice and suggestions for improvements designed to spur reforms and strengthen electoral integrity in each country. The publication of international monitoring reports is intended both to highlight problems, where elections fall short of international standards, and to identify positive policy reforms designed to prevent the repetition of malpractices in subsequent contests. These recommendations are directed towards several actors, especially electoral management bodies and official related regulatory agencies, such as independent media commissions, parliamentary oversight bodies, and judicial appeals courts, as well as civil society NGOs, political parties, and the media. The mission reports typically list a series of proposals designed to overcome particular electoral malpractices and shortfalls which have been observed. This includes suggesting major and minor policy reforms concerning electoral laws and procedures throughout all stages of the electoral cycle, whether those governing the process of redistricting, voter, candidate, and party registration, campaign media and political finance, or the capacity of the electoral authorities. The observer reports may also be followed by technical cooperation projects designed to help implement reforms in practice. In this regard, the Organization of American States specifies the goals of this their electoral observation activities as twofold:

> 5. To highlight the substantive contribution made by the Organization of American States (OAS) to the strengthening and development of electoral processes and systems in the member states, through OAS electoral observation missions, electoral advice, and technical cooperation, upon the request of a member state and consistent with the Declaration of Principles for International Election Observation.
>
> 6. To request the General Secretariat to provide assistance to member states that so request in the implementation of recommendations contained in the reports of OAS electoral observation mission.[43]

Similarly, the OSCE-ODIHR also provides a list of recommendations in its final reports published following each election observation mission and then follows up with support for the authorities in their efforts to improve electoral processes.[44] The OSCE-ODIHR reviews election-related legislation, trains members of election commissions, and provides technical expertise on issues such as voter's registries, transparent financing of political parties, the role of the security forces in electoral processes, and the conduct of electoral campaigns.

In some cases, regional organizations follow up on observer missions by offering technical cooperation projects, such as by sending teams of lawyers to provide advice about revising the constitutional and legal framework and to review draft legislation, organizing expert workshops and civil society roundtables, briefing parliaments and legislative committees, encouraging public consultation, and dispatching technical experts and providing financial resources to assist EMBs with the procurement and implementation of new technologies, such as the purchase and use of biometric voter registration or electronic balloting machines.[45] Reflecting international principles of state sovereignty and national ownership, the electoral authorities in each country and related political institutions such as government departments, parliamentary bodies, and official regulatory agencies, are responsible for deciding whether to adopt or disregard any external recommendations. Many actors may be involved, such as political parties, the media, and NGOs in civil society, as well as state agencies. Observer reports can be understood to serve as a classic form of "soft" power, designed to encourage member states to implement domestic reforms, but regional intergovernmental organizations like the OAS are hesitant to deploy strong enforcement powers, such as using restrictions on political cooperation, development assistance, or sanctions among their own members.[46] Regional organizations have usually also lacked systematic monitoring mechanisms to review and determine whether the recommendations in the reports are implemented by the time of subsequent missions, although this situation is starting to change with the OSCE developing more systematic follow-up efforts.[47]

As discussed in the previous chapter, reform of the legal framework is important not necessarily because it is the most problematic stage of the electoral cycle, but because it sets the formal rules-of-the-game that govern much everything else in how contests work, as well as being potentially open to legislative and administrative amendment. Both informal cultural practices and formal legal institutions can be expected to influence the quality of elections. Indeed, unwritten codes of conduct and entrenched social norms can be expected to be especially influential in states with weak rule of law where official regulations are widely flouted, where public officials are embedded in cultures of corruption, or where partisan officials prevail over impartial procedures. In these contexts, cultural norms may override legal compliance. But formal statutes, bureaucratic rules, and written regulations are policy-relevant, since they are open to change through parliamentary legislation, executive decisions, and judicial rulings.

Proposed reforms to the legal framework can involve both minor and major types of changes.[48] The exact dividing line between these categories is open to interpretation. In general, the concept of electoral reform has traditionally been understood to refer to wholesale changes altering the basic type of electoral system used for national legislative and presidential contests. This is exemplified by New Zealand's replacement of a majoritarian system for parliament (first-past-the-post or simple plurality) when they adopted a Mixed Member Proportional system in 1993, or Japan's shift the following year from Single Non-Transferable Vote for the House of Representatives to a mixed system.[49] Lijphart reflects this conventional view when he defines electoral reform as a significant change (20 percent or more) in the proportionality of the electoral system that affects the seat shares of parties in the lower house of national parliament, including reforms that substantially affect the electoral formula, district magnitude, the electoral threshold, and/or the assembly size.[50] This provides a precise definition, setting boundaries for the topic, but one problem is its conservative scope. If strictly applied, few major electoral reforms have ever occurred in established democracies.[51] Any cutoff point is also inevitably arbitrary (why not a change of 15 percent or 35 percent?). In practice, major upheavals are infrequent. Many states have experienced a succession of incremental legal amendments with significant consequences, such as expanding the franchise, regulating campaign finance, or enacting legal gender quotas.

Minor electoral reforms are understood in contemporary usage to encompass a comprehensive range of legal and technical changes to legal and administrative regulations governing the process of elections.[52] These are exemplified by the series of more than thirty new laws passed in US states to alter voter registration and balloting processes, such as photo identification requirements, with implications for electoral security and inclusive voting rights (see Chapter 10). In the United Kingdom, as well, the basic electoral system for the House of Commons remains first-past-the-post, but reforms have been implemented at all other levels, adding the Additional Member electoral systems used for the Scottish Parliament and Welsh Assembly, the Supplementary Vote for the London Mayor, the Single Transferable Vote for the Northern Ireland Assembly, and regional closed Party List PR for European parliamentary contests.[53] Other reforms implemented in many countries involve altering the balloting process from paper-and-pencil to electronic machines or using biometric technology for the electoral register, as well as introducing legal gender quotas (discussed in the next chapter). Each of these steps can obviously have important consequences for the body politic and democratic governance, as well as for patterns of party competition, the choice of candidates, and voting behavior in the electorate. For example, the implementation of directly elected assemblies in Scotland and Wales and the choice of proportional electoral systems for these bodies has expanded opportunities for the geographically concentrated Scottish Nationalist Party to gain representative office and thus provided a broader platform for their political agenda of devolution and independence, with serious consequences for the unity of the UK as a state.

How widespread are problems of electoral laws? Figure 5.2 provides a global map illustrating the quality of electoral laws as assessed by experts in the PEI survey. Three items tapped into whether electoral laws were regarded as unfair to smaller parties, whether election laws favored the governing party or parties, and whether election laws restricted citizens' rights. All these dimensions are clearly important for ensuring political rights and that the rules produce equitable party competition and a level playing field fair to all contestants. Since these three items were closely intercorrelated (R = .78 or above), they were used to construct a 100-point scale monitoring the integrity of electoral laws in each country. This was then categorized into five bands, were countries with scores below 50 classified as "flawed," while those below 40 were classified as "failed" electoral laws. The results of the comparison in Figure 5.1 shows that the quality of electoral laws were most commonly seen as problematic in Eurasia, East Africa, the Middle East, and North Africa. This reflects the familiar map of trouble spots in broader indicators of democracy and human rights. But at the same time, there are also some other notable contrasts, notably that both the United Kingdom and United States score only moderately well on the quality of their electoral laws. More systematic investigation suggests that the type of electoral system plays a major role here; in particular, both countries use majoritarian electoral systems for the lower house of the national parliament (with single member plurality or "first-past-the-post" systems). This type of electoral system is systematically associated with lower scores on the overall PEI electoral integrity index, as well as the quality of electoral laws, even after controlling for many other structural and institutional factors.[54]

The Impact of Recommendations

Are the observer mission reform recommendations adopted and, if so, are they successful in reducing malpractices in elections? This topic has been neglected by researchers.[55] It remains to be determined whether 1. the policy suggestions proposed in the final reports by intergovernmental observer organizations are subsequently implemented by member states by the time of the next contest or 2. the suggestions and advice are largely disregarded by the authorities.

In this regard, as policy advisors, regional organizations can be understood to function as external actors in the agenda-setting stage of the domestic public policymaking process. Ever since the seminal work by Maxwell McCombs and Donald Shaw (1972), agenda-setting theory has suggested that in democratic states, multiple domestic actors seek to influence which issues get onto the

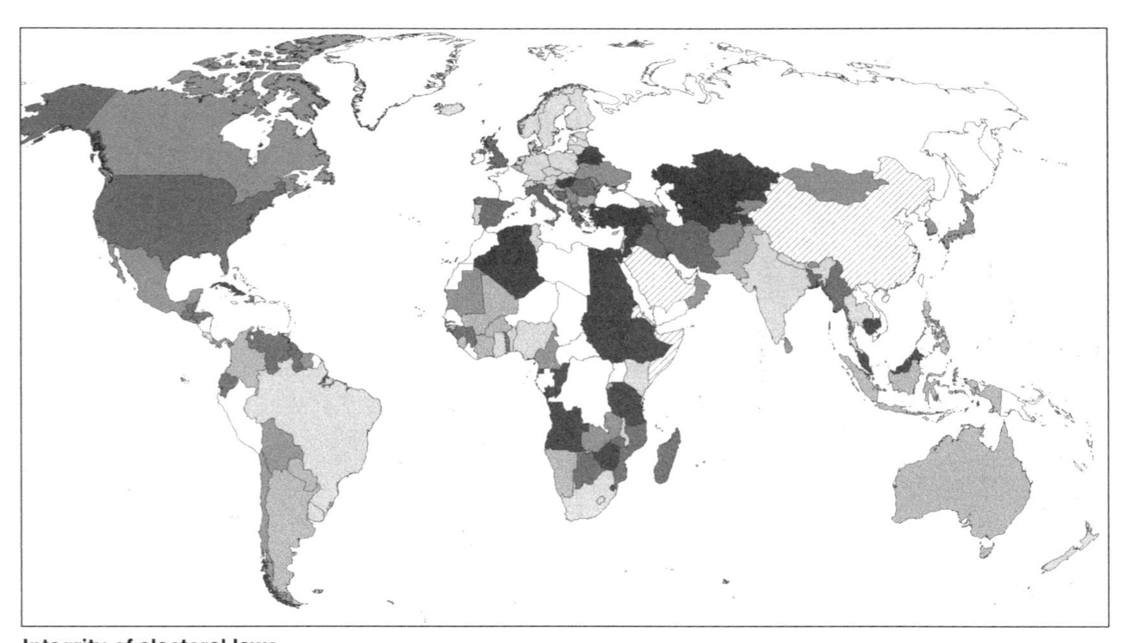

FIGURE 5.2. The integrity of electoral laws.
Source: Pippa Norris, Ferran Martinez i Coma, Alessandro Nai, and Max Gromping. *The Perceptions of Electoral Integrity rolling expert survey* (PEI-4.5). www.electoralintegrityproject.com.

policy agenda, including those issues which are of greatest concern to public opinion, party leadership elites, the news media, and organized interest groups.[56] In democratic regimes, mass perceptions of problems in public opinion are often understood as setting the broad context, and studies have examined the empirical links between issue concerns expressed by the general public and the responsiveness of elected officials.[57] In turn, public concern is mobilized by political parties, the news media, and interest groups, and thereby channeled into the policymaking priorities of the legislature and executive. During the last 40 years an extensive literature has examined the links between the agendas of the public, the media, and legislation.[58]

Most work examining Western democracies has conventionally regarded the agenda-setting, decision-making, and implementation stages of the policy process as largely determined by domestic actors and institutions. The most common approach to understanding the choice of types of electoral rules in this context draws upon theories of rational choice institutionalism. This account emphasizes the rational self-interested calculations of vote-seeking office-holders (parties and legislators) when seeking to maximize prospects for reelection through the adoption and revision of legal rules.[59] Yet the idea that partisan interests alone drive the process of electoral reform has been subject to extensive critique as providing too narrow a perspective. There are many reasons why these theories fails to predict the outcome, including cases where reforms arise from external pressures on nation-states; members of the winning coalition are divided; politicians miscalculate the unforeseen consequences of new rules; parties value long-term change over short-term electoral advantage; and parties trade electoral benefits for other goals and ideological values.

The process is also complicated because any legal and procedural policy reforms passed by the legislature are subsequently subject to interpretation by the courts and judiciary (who may block new laws), and implemented by public sector agencies at national and local levels. Electoral reforms that are successfully implemented subsequently feed back into public perceptions of problems, functioning as a continuous loop in the agenda-setting cycle from one contest to the next. Regional organizations and international agencies can function as one of the catalysts (but only one actor out of many) encouraging the adoption of reforms to electoral institutions, laws, and administrative procedures in member states.

During the last decade, a growing literature has examined the national drivers of electoral reform, both long-term, such as changing patterns of party competition in the electorate and legislature, and catalytic contingent factors, such as scandal-induced political crisis. By contrast, however, the role of the international community in influencing the electoral reform process is not clearly established. Much of the literature on agenda-setting in established Western democracies assumes that reforms occur due to domestic politics and actors within each country. Elsewhere, cases can be cited of constitution-building following dramatic regime transitions, such as Afghanistan in 2004, where developmental agencies within the international community appear to have played a major role in the choice and adoption of electoral systems, through providing technical assistance and legal advice to local stakeholders.[60] The international community can also be expected to play a vital role as part of state-building initiatives, following deep-rooted civil war (such as the DRC or Nepal), external military intervention (such as Iraq and Afghanistan), or with newly independent states (such as Timor-Leste and South Sudan). In these types of contexts, both domestic and international elites can be observed to play a role in constitution-writing processes. In many cases, new electoral systems are forged by extraparliamentary processes prior to the consolidation of party systems, such as constitutional drafting bodies and public referendums. The outcome is likely to be strongly influenced by external forces in the international community. The impact of international norm diffusion on specific reforms within countries, for example the adoption of gender quotas around the world, has also been examined in depth.[61] Another recent study compared states in postwar Europe to understand the diffusion of two mechanisms designed to restrict party fragmentation in PR systems – low district magnitudes and high electoral thresholds.[62]

Norms may diffuse globally through multiple mechanisms and actors. One channel concerns the recommendations for major and minor electoral reform, broadly defined, provided in a series of routine monitoring reports published by international agencies and regional intergovernmental organizations. Judith Kelley compared 15 selected cases since the early 1990s with a series of monitoring reports, 23 monitoring missions by different agencies (such as Georgia) while others had only ten missions (Kenya). Kelley concluded that a mixed pattern of adoption could be observed, with some countries (and some types of recommendations) more commonly implemented compared with others. Several factors were associated with the outcome of reform efforts, including the type of electoral system, with majoritarian systems proving an obstacle to reform; self-censorship by monitors, where observer criticisms were toned down; international forces, where powerful neighboring countries like Russia restrict the effectiveness of reforms recommended in monitoring reports; capacity problems, where EMBs lack the basic infrastructure and resources to implement reforms; the use of political conditionality, as a "carrot" where a country wanted to cooperate with the West; domestic pressures, where local actors seek to undertake meaningful reforms; and consistent long-term engagement, following repeated visits by monitoring organizations. Each of these observations may generate further insights but with only 15 selected cases observed in the study, it remains difficult to know how far these patterns reflect valid generalizations if the evidence were examined from a broader and more diverse sample of countries, alternative types of policy recommendations, and different international observer organizations. Moreover, the suggested propositions remain a "shopping list," arising inductively from observing the cases, and thereby lacking a systematic and integrated theoretical framework and rationale.

Theory of Strategic Threats and Opportunities

This leads to the core questions framing the impact of observer missions on reform agenda at the heart of this chapter. Three issues are addressed.

1. How often are reforms recommended in the reports published by international monitoring organizations in one election, subsequently implemented by the time of the next or subsequent contest?
2. If adopted, what types of recommendations are most commonly implemented?
3. And, under what macrolevel conditions does this process work or fail to work, in terms of the social structural and institutional characteristics of societies with the highest implementation rates?

The types of recommendations could well be expected to play a role in their subsequent adoption. In particular, those requiring procedural reforms, such as constitutional amendments and legislation, may prove easier to implement than those policy proposals requiring substantial additional resources, such as the addition of more poll workers to reduce long queues, the expensive purchase and maintenance of biometric technologies used to register and verify electors, or training programs to expand the skills and capacity of thousands of poll workers. Recommendations also vary in whether they address the preelection period of the electoral cycle, the campaign, or polling day and its aftermath, although it is unclear theoretically which of these are most likely to be adopted. In addition, OAS recommendations may highlight general principles and global standards (such as the need for authorities to strengthen women's empowerment and gender equality in elected office, to encourage participation among young people and minorities, or to ensure an equitable distribution and level playing field in public resources used for political finance or party funding). Alternatively, OAS mission reports may propose specific actions and suggest detailed types of reforms. In general, it is expected to be easier for states to meet general principles and global standards, which can be implemented in many different ways within each country.

The context at the macrolevel should also be important. In particular, the theory of strategic threats and opportunities, outlined in the previous chapters, emphasizes that elections are generally most likely to meet international standards of integrity under certain conditions. The main factors include *social structure* (levels of development and natural resourced-based economies, along with the population and physical size of countries), *international linkages* (through networks and ties of political globalization, and the provision of Official Development Aid in the sector of democratic participation), and political institutions (the level of democratization, the type of electoral system, and the independence and ethos of the electoral authorities). Where all these conditions are in place, then in general this has been found to reduce the most common risks of electoral malpractice. In particular, wealthier countries have more resources that can be invested in public sector administration. Natural resource-based economies are commonly plagued by problems of corruption and state capture, both of which can undermine electoral integrity through patronage politics and vote-buying. Societies with larger populations and more physically dispersed terrains can also be expected to exacerbate the task of managing the complex logistics needed for running elections. Ties of globalization are expected to be important for the diffusion of global norms and standards, with cosmopolitan societies more open to the flow of information across national borders compared to more parochial societies. Countries that are integrated globally into political networks can also be expected to be more open to global norms and closely linked with regional intergovernmental organizations, including the OAS. In addition, countries that are more democratic, with a free press and proportional representation electoral systems have also been found usually to have higher levels of electoral integrity.[63] Building on these propositions, states with these conditions are also expected to be more willing to adopt the reform recommendations contained in regional observer reports.

DATA, EVIDENCE, AND RESEARCH DESIGN

Comparative Framework

To gather evidence suitable for testing the core theoretical propositions, this study focused on whether technical recommendations issued in a long series of monitoring reports by a long-standing international observer regional agency, the Organization of American States, was associated with subsequent electoral reforms implemented in a range of Latin American and Caribbean member states. The advantages of focusing upon a single region is that this process rules out several confounding conditions by comparing countries that are relatively similar in their cultural traditions, geographic proximity, levels of economic development, types of regime institutions, and stages of democratization. At the same time, there is diversity among member states. Latin America includes many moderate-income economies such as Panama and Mexico, as well as several low-income economies, notably in impoverished Haiti as well as in Honduras (with per capita GDP in ppp below US$5,000). The types of states under comparison includes regimes classified by Freedom House as "free" or democratic, such as Costa Rica and Panama, as well as hybrid regimes, exemplified by Venezuela and Guatemala. Scholars suggest that previous authoritarian governments have been largely discredited in the region, so that democracy has survived even severe economic downturns and political shockwaves that might have destabilized it in the past.[64] At the same time, several indicators suggest major cause for concern about the contemporary quality of democracy in the region, exemplified by the crisis generated by the suspension of President Dilma Rousseff of Brazil, the deterioration of democracy and erosion of human rights under Presidents Hugo Chavez and Nicolas Maduro in Venezuela, the effects of narcotics-related organized crime, corruption, and violence in Mexico, and political instability and government chaos in Haiti, the poorest state in the region. The varied colonial heritage among member states may also be important, including the Spanish, British, and French legacies in the region.

Assessing the Contents of the Recommendations

To gather evidence about the recommendations included in the OAS reports, as the primary independent variable, this study content analyzed those contained in the Department of Electoral Cooperation and Observation *Electoral Observation Mission Database*. This resource compiles information from each of the missions the OAS has deployed in Latin America missions since 1962 and provides in-depth information on those deployed from 2010 onwards. The database was used as a starting point to conduct a systematic and comprehensive content analysis review of OAS recommendations published in the series of observer mission reports in Latin America. The research focuses upon classifying 142 OAS electoral mission reports for national presidential and parliamentary elections held in 25 member states from 1999 to 2015. The content analysis developed a coding scheme used to classify the original report texts into analytical categories, such as the type of recommendations, the stages of the electoral cycle the recommendations addressed, and the type of changes proposed. In recent years, the OAS has standardized and professionalized its methods for observer missions, especially following publication of its 2005 manual. The OAS conducts a needs-assessment to evaluate whether an observer mission would be a worthwhile use of limited resources. Only one mission was conducted in a few countries during this period (such as in Argentina, Bahamas, Belize), although elsewhere up to a dozen missions were deployed (such as in Bolivia and Ecuador). For consistent comparisons, the OAS reports that are analyzed cover national presidential and legislative contests, excluding observer reports for primary and referendum campaigns, as well as contests at regional, local, and municipal levels.

To examine the empirical evidence, comprehensive and fully specified models seeking to understand the adoption of policy reforms need to incorporate a series of measures. The multilevel hierarchical logistic models (HLM) used in this chapter treat the specific recommendations as Level 1 and the societal context as Level 2. Models include the following factors:

1. ***Types of policy recommendations***, coded by whether the EMB was the main agency primarily responsible for implementing the proposals, whether these proposals were mainly formal/legal or whether they required additional resources, the stage of the electoral cycle which they

concerned, and whether they involved general principles or detailed guidelines and suggestions;
2. ***Institutional arrangements***, including the type of electoral system for the lower house of the national parliament (from International IDEA), annual levels of democratization (from the Freedom House/Polity IV combined measure), the type of EMB (coded as governmental, mixed and independent, from International IDEA), and annual levels of media freedom (from Reporters without Borders);
3. ***Structural constraints***, including annual levels of economic development (measured in per capita GDP in purchasing power parity in constant prices), natural resources (oil/gas rents as a proportion of GDP), and the physical and population size of the state (from the World Bank); and
4. ***International linkages***, including levels of political globalization (measured by the KOF index), and the provision of Official Development Aid spent in this sector (annual spending on ODA for democratic participation, from AidData); and,

The HLM models use restricted maximum likelihood techniques (REML) to estimate effects. Specific recommendations are thus grouped within states. As is customary in these types of models, all variables are first centered by subtracting the grand mean. The standardized variables have a standard deviation of 1.0. The strength of the beta coefficients in the regression model can be interpreted intuitively as how much change in the implementation rate can be generated by a 1 percent change in the independent variables. Details on how the core factors are measured and operationalized and the data sources are given in the book's Technical Appendix.

To monitor whether recommendations were subsequently adopted as the key dependent variable, researchers classified gathered formal amendments to constitutional and legal electoral instruments from several sources, such as Lexis-Nexis, the ACE website, the websites of the relevant electoral management body, and Google. The implementation rate was estimated based on the number of recommendations contained in the OAS reports that were subsequently determined to have been implemented in laws or administrative procedures.

RESULTS AND ANALYSIS

First, what does the OAS most commonly recommend and how far are these proposals implemented in member states? Figure 5.3 describes the proportion of OAS recommendations addressing each stage in the electoral cycle. Proposed reforms to electoral procedures and voting processes are most commonly made by the missions, followed by recommendations concerning the vote count and voter registration process. Clearly, observer missions are not just concerned with problems occurring on election day and its immediate aftermath; instead recommendations range across all stage of the electoral cycle.

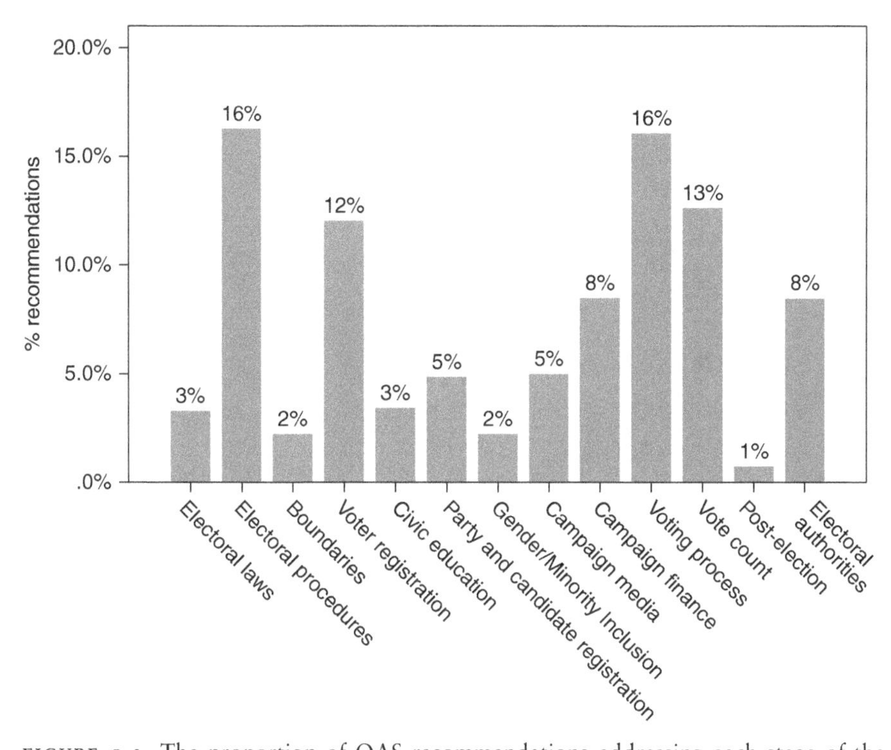

FIGURE 5.3. The proportion of OAS recommendations addressing each stage of the electoral cycle.
Source: EIP-Democratic Diffusion Project. www.electoralintegrityproject.com.

But are the proposals subsequently adopted? There are plausible reasons for skepticism after all, as Kelley noted:

> When organizations return to countries they have previously monitored, they should review their previous recommendations and systematically recount the actions – or lack thereof – taken in response. Oftentimes this does not happen at all. Monitors make long lists of recommendations in their reports but never follow up. Attention to these recommendations in the next round will enable them to exert greater leverage on the local actors, and it will also give them greater credibility from one election to the next.[65]

Nevertheless, the results of the analysis suggest that, despite reasons for doubt about effectiveness, in fact *around half of all proposals were subsequently implemented before the next election.* Figure 5.4 shows that the rate rises even higher in proposals concerning civic education, voter registration, electoral laws, and electoral procedures, all in the long-term period before the start of the campaign stage of the electoral cycle. Issues of gender equality and minority inclusion, and improvements to EMBs, were also

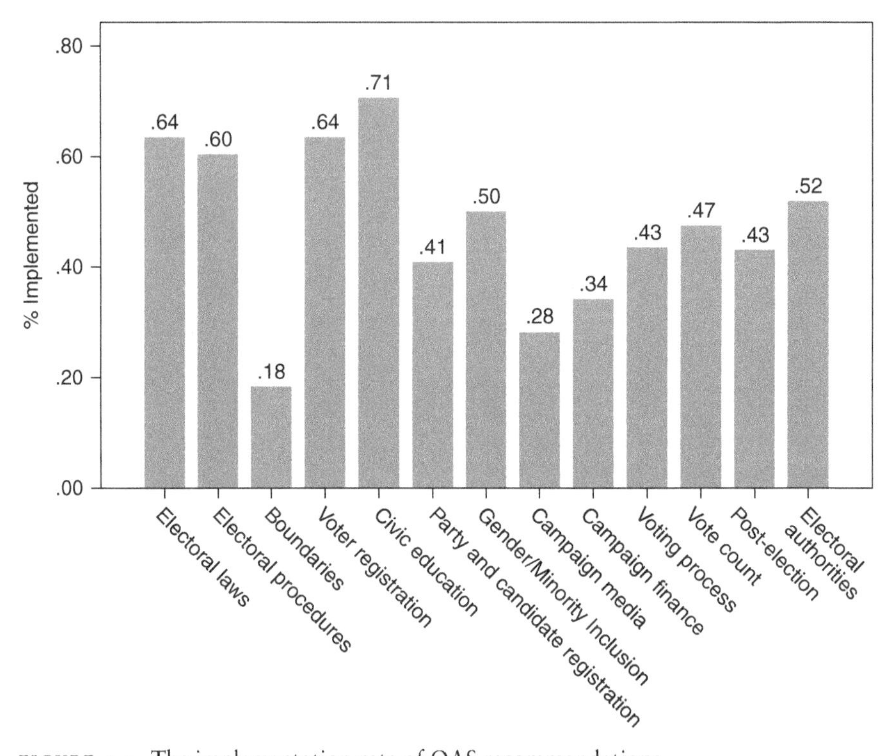

FIGURE 5.4. The implementation rate of OAS recommendations.
Note: The implementation rate is calculated as the proportion of recommendations contained in OAS observer mission reports which are implemented before the subsequent election.
Source: EIP-Democratic Diffusion Project. www.electoralintegrityproject.com.

relatively widely implemented. By contrast, suggestions for improving the regulation of campaign media and political finance during the middle stage of the electoral cycle were least often adopted. These are also some of the most intractable issues in many elections – and with less clear international regulatory standards than many other aspects of electoral integrity.[66]

The implementation rate also varies substantially by country. As shown in Figure 5.4, the rate is highest in Latin American states such as Ecuador, Columbia, and El Salvador, where two-thirds or more of all OAS suggestions were subsequently adopted. By contrast, the implementation rate is below 20 percent of all recommendations in the Caribbean island states of Dominica, Bahamas, St. Kitts and Nevis, and Antigua and Barbuda. What explains this variation? The argument presented in this study suggests that whether states respond to external recommendations (measured by their implementation rate), is partly dependent upon the strategic threats and opportunities facing elections from the macrolevel external environment and

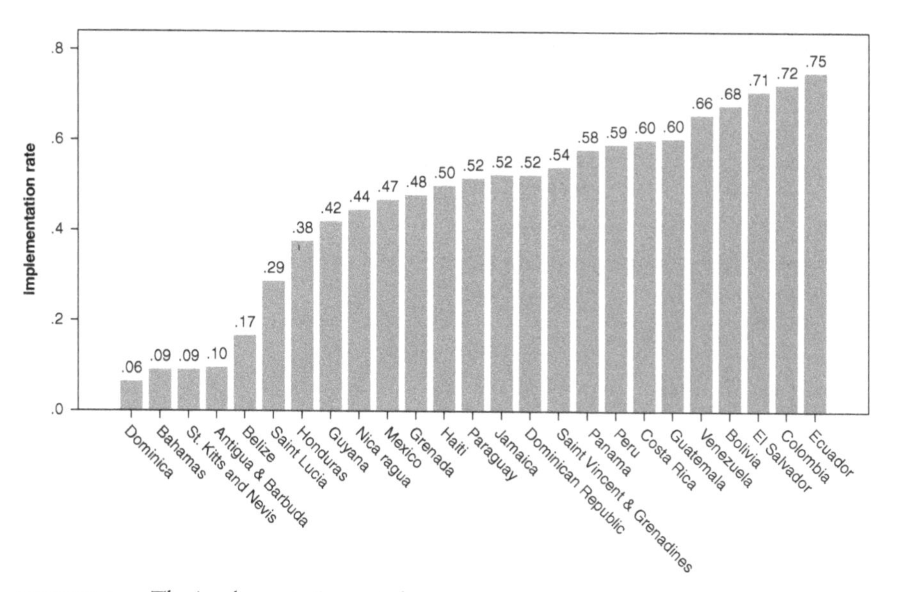

FIGURE 5.5. The implementation rate by country.
Note: The mean implementation rate is calculated as the proportion of OAS recommendations which were enacted before the subsequent election.
Source: EIP-Democratic Diffusion Project. www.electoralintegrityproject.com.

the strength of interstate linkages with the international community, as discussed in the previous chapter.

In particular, the evidence of the HLM models in Table 5.1 suggests that the rate of implementation can indeed be explained in part by the degree of political globalization, indicating that the general degree of interconnections among member states within the international community helps to predict whether states respond positively to OAS recommendations. Political globalization is measured by KOF as a continuous index for each state in terms of the number of embassies in a country, membership in international organizations, participation in UN Security Council Missions, and endorsements of international treaties.[67] Figure 5.6 illustrates this relationship in more detail, showing that the states with the highest implementation rates were also the most connected through political globalization networks. It is striking that the more that cosmopolitan societies are integrated with other states through these mechanisms of global governance and the shared norms arising through these networks, the more effective the recommendations of OAS missions. The highest implementation rates for OAS recommendations occurred among long-standing charter member states in Latin America that joined when the organization was founded in 1948, where multilateral ties may be expected to have become most entrenched. They also share common Hispanic colonial legacies and shared cultural traditions. By contrast, the Caribbean states,

TABLE 5.1 *The Implementation Rate of Electoral Reform Recommendations*

	Model 1		
	B	S.E.	Sig
TYPE OF POLICY RECOMMENDATIONS			
EMB is the main implementing agency	.020	.018	.290
Recommendation requires constitutional, legal or procedural reform (1) or additional human, financial or technical resources (0)	**−.040**	**.017**	**.026**
Overall assessment of electoral integrity (1 = low, 5 = high)	−.006	.025	.797
Recommend preelection reforms (1/0)	**.040**	**.018**	**.030**
Recommend postelection reforms (1/0)	−.002	.018	.896
Recommend general principles (1) or detailed guidelines (0)	**.064**	**.017**	**.000**
INSTITUTIONAL CONTEXT			
PR type of electoral system for lower house (IDEA)	−.011	.055	.842
Majoritarian type of electoral system for lower house (IDEA)	−.009	.158	.954
Annual level of Press Freedom (Reporters without Borders)	−.027	.042	.534
Annual level of democratization (Freedom House/Polity IV)	−.008	.040	.841
Type of EMB (Governmental, Mixed, Independent, IDEA)	.054	.138	.714
INTERNATIONAL LINKAGE			
Annual index of political globalization (KOF)	**.114**	**.038**	**.035**
Annual level of ODA spending on democratic participation	−.012	.021	.545
STRUCTURAL SOCIAL CONTEXT			
Economic development (Per capita GDP ppp in current $)	.056	.034	.155
Natural resources (Rents as% GDP) (World Bank)	.027	.042	.549
Population size (millions) (World Bank)	−.008	.043	.857
Physical area size (Sq. acres) (World Bank)	−.011	.065	.873
Constant	.522	.056	.003
Schwartz's Bayesian Criterion	1212		
N. recommendations	1006		
N. countries	28		

Notes: HLM binary logistic regression analysis where the implementation rate of OAS recommendations is the dependent variable in OAS member states. The implementation rate is calculated as the proportion of recommendations contained in OAS observer mission reports which are implemented before the subsequent election. Beta (B) and Standard errors (SE). All models used tolerance tests to check that they were free of problems of multicollinearity. See the technical appendix for more details about all the selected indices.

Sources: Pippa Norris, Ferran Martinez I Coma, Alessandro Nai, and Max Gromping. *The Democratic Diffusion project.* www.electoralintegrityproject.com; Other indices from specified sources and the Quality of Government Cross-national Dataset www.qog.pol.gu.se/data/.

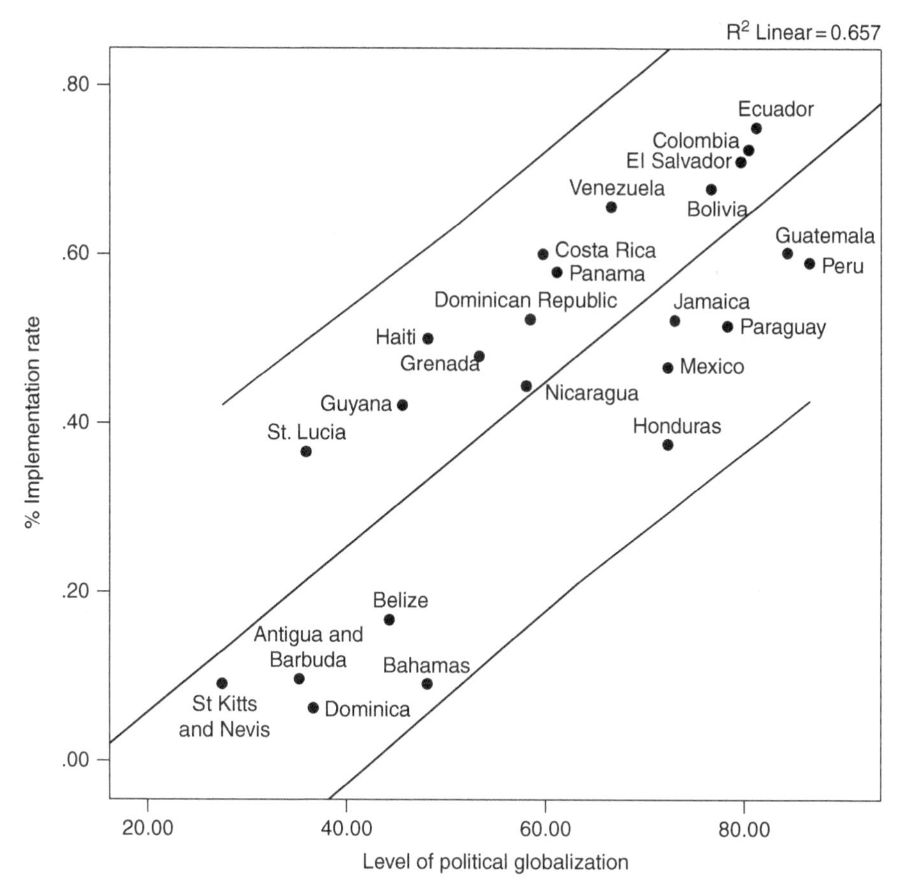

FIGURE 5.6. The implementation rate rises with political globalization.
Note: The implementation rate is calculated as the proportion of recommendations contained in OAS observer mission reports that are implemented before the subsequent election. The level of political globalization is measured by KOF by the political integration of states within the international community.
Source: EIP-Democratic Diffusion Project. www.electoralintegrityproject.com.

where implementation rate lagged, joined the OAS later, usually during the early 1980s.

By contrast, however, other structural macrolevel factors contained in Table 5.1 were not significant predictors of the implementation rate, including the population, area size, and the dependency of the economy on natural resources (oil and gas). This suggests that these are not insuperable barriers to the adoption of reform proposals. Contrary to expectations, other factors which were also not significant in the model include the provision of international commitment (ODA spending in this sector) as well as the political institutions in any state (the type of electoral system, the degree of democratization, the type of EMB, and the level of press freedom). The lack of any association between aid spending and the adoption of recommendations can be explained in several ways; although aid-dependent societies should be more open to pressure from the international community, in fact levels of aid spending are poor proxies for electoral assistance.

The recommendations in the final reports published by international monitors are therefore predicted as most likely to be bear fruit and be adopted in more cosmopolitan societies with the most favorable conditions. The techniques of soft power used by regional organizations in programs of electoral assistance thereby fortify societies integrated through strong ties with the international community.

In addition, the specific types of recommendations that regional organizations publish are also important predictors of the implementation rate. As Table 5.1 shows, contrary to expectations, recommendations that require additional resources (human, financial, or technical) are significantly more likely to be adopted rather than those requiring constitutional, legal, or procedural reforms. Recommendations during the early stage of the electoral cycle are also the most likely to be adopted, as observed earlier. And finally, recommendations involving general principles and standards are more likely to be implemented rather than those giving detailed guidance about specific types of reform. This suggests that regional organizations should emphasize broad principles, such as the desirability of introducing policies achieving gender equality and women's empowerment, rather than suggesting specific steps that states should take to achieve these goals, such as endorsing the use of legal gender quota policies or recommending equal opportunity strategies in candidate training.

CONCLUSIONS

Is electoral assistance effective? This chapter focuses on the role of regional organizations in strengthening electoral integrity, including, human rights advocates and policy advisors as watchdogs. The impact of their first two roles has been most heavily scrutinized by scholars. In addition, as policy advisers, it has become standard practice for the final reports issued by election observer mission to identify areas for improvement and to publish a series of concrete recommendations that are designed to encourage states to strengthen their electoral institutions, laws, and procedures in line with international treaties. Through this process, regional organizations function as part of the agenda-setting stage of the policymaking process, seeking to highlight the electoral standards, obligations and commitments that states should fulfill. Little is known with any certainty, however, about the consequences when regional organizations propose alternative steps that could be taken to improve electoral integrity in member states. Previous research has not established whether and how domestic stakeholders respond to these suggestions – including government and opposition parties, electoral officials, parliaments, the courts, and civil society organizations. Many domestic obstacles may prevent the implementation of the recommendations, arising from lack of financial resources and professional capacity, technical limitations and lack of time, challenging conditions such as outbreaks of instability and conflict, and political forces resistant to reform, where incumbents block change. Recommendations may be seen by domestic actors as inappropriate, unconvincing, or ineffective. Thus suggestions may well fall on deaf ears, in which case any shortcomings are likely to persist, and may even worsen.

The chapter presents new evidence suggesting several key findings. First, the agenda-setting stage of the policymaking process is indeed strongly influenced by the recommendations issued by regional organizational monitoring missions. Around half of the recommendations published in monitor reports are subsequently implemented by member states, fully or partially. Given the many obstacles littering the pathway to any reform, this level suggests the effectiveness of electoral assistance programs. Of course the changes could have arisen without the intervention of the monitoring agency, since they may echo and reflect dissatisfaction within each society among diverse stakeholders, such as opposition parties and civil society organizations. Nevertheless, by highlighting salient problems and suggesting possible policy solutions, regional organizations seem likely to add momentum to the reform agenda-setting process. Secondly, the type of recommendations also mattered: the implementation rate was highest for proposals seeking to improve civic education, electoral laws, voter registration and electoral procedures, all activities occurring during the preelection stage of the electoral cycle. By contrast, policy advice concerning ways of overcoming problems of campaign media and political finance were less likely to be adopted. Procedural reforms and those recommending general principles and standards were also more likely to be enacted. This helps to identify important opportunities for international agencies seeking to encourage electoral reforms – and the limits of these proposals. Finally, confirming the international linkage theory, cosmopolitan societies with high levels of political engagement with the institutions of global governance implemented OAS recommendations most often. By contrast, many other institutional and structural factors, including levels of economic development and democratization, were neither significant advantages nor disadvantaged for reform. The overall conclusions, therefore, are that the policy advisor role of regional organizations, sharing best practices, advocating improvements, and catalyzing the electoral reform agenda within member states, can make a significant contribution towards the implementation of legal and procedural electoral reforms.

Several qualifications to these conclusions are also important to note. First, this only examines the middle part of the "chain-of-results" framework outlined in Chapter 3, and therefore it still remains an open question whether the implemented reforms actually achieve their broader objectives and thereby help to strengthen electoral integrity. An extensive research literature has examined the consequences of electoral systems, and analyzed the impact of major reforms, on diverse issues such as levels of vote to seat disproportionality, party competition, voter turnout, political representation, and so on.[68] All of these can be seen as contributing towards the ultimate objective of electoral integrity, although it remains difficult to establish the connections across the whole chain-of-results framework. Secondly, it is also important to expand the comparative framework by considering whether similar patterns can be observed in the role and impact of regional intergovernmental organizations elsewhere, since the African Union, OSCE, ASEAN, the EU, and League of Arab States differ in the level of their engagement with democracy promotion, human rights, and the provision of electoral assistance.[69] Studies also need to compare multilateral organizations with international NGOs that conduct electoral observer missions, such as Democracy International, IFES, and the Carter Center. Such research would expand generalizations about the overall impact of electoral observer work of the international community, providing evidence-based evaluation research, as well as deepening insights into the policy effectiveness of electoral assistance. Finally, to go further, we need to explore not just whether proposed reform recommendations are adopted (the middle step linking program activities with program outcomes in the chain-of-results framework), but also the next step, whether they also achieve certain agreed global norms concerning electoral integrity. To do this, the next chapter explores the role of gender quotas as mechanisms designed to strengthen gender equality (the number of women and men in elected office) – with the ultimate and more diffuse goal of improving women's empowerment.

6

Strengthening Women's Representation

For the last two decades, international organizations and national governments around the world have repeatedly endorsed the aim of strengthening women's empowerment and gender equality in elected and appointed public office. The world community met in Beijing in 1995 and agreed on the target that women should be one-third of elected officials. This goal was recognized by the UN general assembly in the 2000 Millennium Development Goals and reiterated in the subsequent 2015 Sustainable Development Goals. There has been progress towards this target during the last two decades; the proportion of women in the lower house of national legislatures has doubled from around 10 percent in 1995 to 23 percent by mid-2016. This represents a substantial gain over twenty years, although remaining far from parity.[1] Progress remains patchy – 46 countries have achieved the Beijing target of 30 percent women members in at least one chamber of the national parliament. Most countries have fallen short of the Beijing target. This is not simply a problem confined to women in elected office nor one that will gradually be overcome through the process of human development expanding opportunities for women in literacy, education, and the paid workforce. Within the 28 European Union member states (all relatively affluent postindustrial societies), on average women are below the 30 percent mark for most decision-making posts. Thus in EU states, women constitute on average 29 percent of members of parliament (MPs), 27 percent of senior government ministers, 19 percent of major party leaders, and 19 percent of judges in the European courts.[2]

Understanding the barriers and opportunities facing women in decision-making positions and the effectiveness of policies designed to achieve gender parity is important for human rights and for public policy. A growing body of research suggests that the implementation of effective and well-designed quota policies has usually served to increase the number of women members in elected assemblies.[3] These laws encourage descriptive representation where the composition of parliamentary bodies comes to resemble the population in society at large, an important objective in its own right. This development expands the pool of women in the pipeline gaining valuable experience and qualifications for the pursuit of higher executive office. It is often argued that descriptive and substantive representation are linked if women leaders bring distinctive policy priorities, legislative behaviors, and political concerns into the public arena.[4] Through this process, rising numbers of women in decision-making positions may contribute towards women's empowerment. In particular, gender quotas may potentially influence the kinds of women who are elected, the policy-making agenda for gendered issues, the way that ordinary citizens view women as political leaders, and patterns of civic engagement for women and men in the electorate, such as levels of political interest, voting turnout, and campaign donations.[5] Systematic evidence on all these issues, as well as the pros and cons of alternative measures designed to strengthen gender equality in leadership roles, continue to be debated by both advocates and critics.

Many factors have contributed towards the rising number of women in elected office. One of the most common electoral reforms has been the implementation of gender quotas in many countries and regions across the world. This includes three basic types of policies, each with many variants: (i) constitutional and legal provisions of *reserved seats* determining the overall composition of the membership of elected or appointed bodies; (ii) the constitutional or legal provision of quotas regulating the composition of each's party's list of candidates nominated for elected office by certain specified criteria (legal quotas); and (iii) candidate quotas implemented through particular party constitutions and rule books (voluntary quotas). Quotas can specify requirement by gender, ethnicity, or other criteria, such as for workers. These policies are designed to encourage socially diverse and inclusive parliaments that reflect the composition of the societies from which they are drawn in several important regards.[6] They are an extension of the use of single-member districts, which are traditionally designed to ensure geographic representation from all constituencies and regions. Figure 6.1 illustrates the remarkable rise during recent decades in the number of countries worldwide implementing either legal gender quotas for parliamentary candidates (governing the nomination process) or else reserved seats for women (governing the gendered composition of parliaments).

In the light of these developments, this chapter focuses upon two issues. What has driven the worldwide adoption of legal gender quota policies and, in particular, what has been the role of international forces and multilateral organizations in the diffusion process? And, equally importantly, have these policies proven effective by strengthening gender equality in representative bodies, which is a core dimension of women's rights and electoral integrity?

The previous chapter discussed how international agencies highlight malpractices and advocate reforms to the constitutional, legal, and procedural framework governing the electoral process. The adoption and implementation

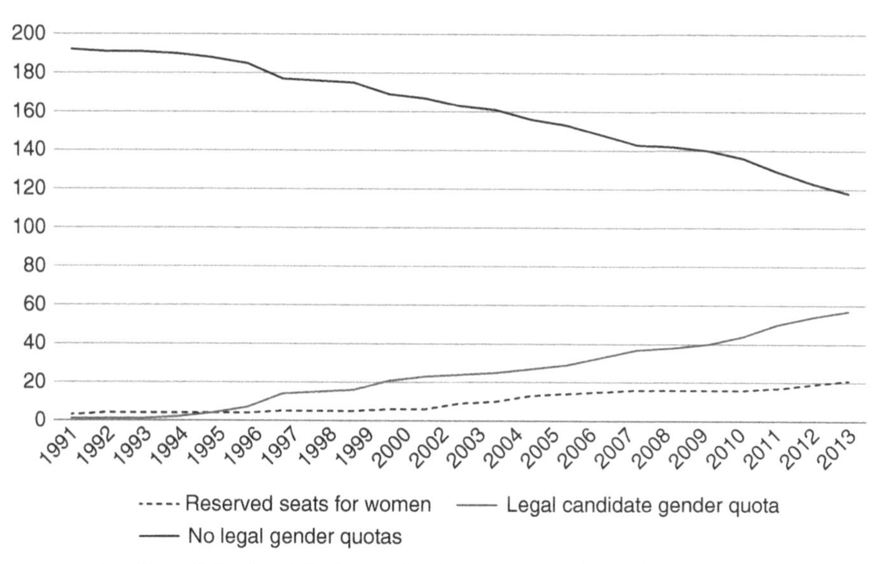

FIGURE 6.1. Trends in the global spread of gender quota laws since 1990.
Note: Number of independent nation-states using each policy for lower- or single house of national parliaments since 1990.
Source: The Quota Project. www.quotaproject.org.

of legal gender quotas exemplify how this process works. The first section describes how a wide range of international agencies have advocated women's empowerment and gender equality in elected office during recent decades, exemplified by the role of UN Women and UNDP, intergovernmental bodies like International IDEA, and the Inter-Parliamentary Union, and regional organizations like the Council of Europe, OSCE, and OAS, and bilateral donors, especially among Nordic states. Agencies deploy several common soft-power strategies to highlight inequalities, to expand awareness about how different quota systems function, and to share best practices across national borders. Typical activities involve integrating policies designed to strengthen gender equality across all mainstream program activities; supporting knowledge-sharing networks such as I-KNOW politics[7]; providing rosters of election experts available to provide legal advice on draft legislation and party regulations; publishing technical handbooks and practical guidelines synthesizing the state of scholarly and applied research on gender equality; funding training programs, conferences, and leadership workshops for party officials and legislative candidates; and encouraging data collection and monitoring of the proportion of women and men in decision-making roles by official statistical agencies and equal opportunity bodies, NGOs in civil society, parliaments and local elected assemblies, women's organizations, and political parties. In this regard, international organizations interact with local stakeholders to encourage the implementation of policies designed to strengthen the proportion of women and gender equality in elected and appointed office.

But are these efforts effective? As with many aspects of soft power, the impact of several strategies are not easy to pin down. The second section describes the evidence testing this claim, drawing upon the *Gender Quota Database* (GQD), a comprehensive cross-national time-series dataset classifying the initial adoption and the subsequent amendment to quota policies used worldwide from 1990 to 2014.[8] The dataset classifies the main types of gender quotas that have been implemented around the world and identifies trends over time (waves) during this period in the adoption and amendment of quotas.

The analysis of this evidence, in the second section, demonstrates several main findings. To address the first question, the data suggests that international forces do play a significant role in the initial adoption of gender quota policies. In particular, the regional diffusion of legal quotas matters; states are influenced, for better or worse, by linkages with their neighbors. This echoes and consistently reinforces the findings presented in the previous chapter, where OAS membership and strong linkages with the international community were demonstrated to strengthen other types of electoral reforms in Latin America. The regional effects of gender quotas remain robust even after controlling for other long-term societal conditions commonly thought to influence gender equality in public life, including socioeconomic development, levels of democratization, cultural religious traditions, and the strength of domestic advocacy women's movements. Thus in the case of gender quotas, common types of policies have often been implemented within global regions, even in states with conditions that seem less than ideal. At the same time, several other ways that international forces may be expected to influence the adoption of gender quotas were found not to be significant once further controls were introduced, including levels of globalization, the amount of aid spending on democratic participation, and international advocacy. Moreover, the role of regional effects should not be exaggerated since the adoption of quota policies was also influenced by the local advocacy efforts of women in political parties and women's movements in civil society in each state.

Turning to the effect of these policies, the second issue under scrutiny, the evidence also provides further confirmation that quota policies also work by strengthening the number of women elected to national office; most (although not all) states experienced a subsequent increase in women's representation in the national elections after the first quota law was implemented. The degree of change varied, however, and several detailed factors in the design of quota laws matter for their degree of effectiveness, including the use and strength of any penalties for noncompliance, the level of any target, and whether there is "zippering" (rank ordering) for allocating quota positions within party lists. Yet the broader question of whether the increased *number* of women in elected office in turn affects women's empowerment and substantive representation, such as by altering the policy agenda, parliamentary behavior, or attitudes among the mass electorate, remains an open question. The conclusion summarizes the key findings and discusses their broader implications. The evidence throws light on broader theoretical questions about descriptive representation, as well as providing general insights into the overall effectiveness of international assistance for electoral integrity.

THEORETICAL FRAMEWORK

Attempts to strengthen gender equality in elected office have generated an extensive research literature during recent decades. This can be subdivided into three categories using the analogy of the political marketplace. Some of this work has focused upon the supply side of the recruitment process, influencing whether candidates come forward to pursue elected office, exemplified by social psychological theories suggesting that women lack political ambition, confidence, and interest in seeking political careers.[9] Attempts to encourage more women to become candidates have often used initiatives such as awareness-raising programs, training and capacity building workshops, and funding initiatives.[10] By contrast another related body of literature has emphasized the demand side of recruitment, or the factors that deter or encourage women who come forward from being nominated for office, and the pivotal role of political parties and related elites as the main gatekeepers to elected positions. Finally, the alternative institutional perspective focuses upon the rules of the game or market regulations that determine who is nominated and elected. This includes the role of electoral systems, the impact of gender quota policies, and regulations determining candidate recruitment, such as ballot access and campaign finance laws. To understand the adoption and effectiveness of gender quota policies, this chapter first outlines the central argument concerning the role of the international community and then considers alternative theories about important drivers for the diffusion of these rules. The study then examines the evidence using data comparing countries worldwide.

The Role of International Organizations

Why have gender quotas been adopted? One common explanation emphasizes the role of the international community when establishing conventions, treaties, and agreements attempting to shape global norms, including strengthening the principles of gender equality and women's rights.[11] A range of international actors – including UN agencies and bureaus, regional organizations and transnational feminist organizations, as well as bilateral donors – advocate appropriate models and standards of legitimate action, both worldwide and within regions. Intergovernmental regional organizations, commonly promote human rights within their area. The principles of gender equality have been recognized in a long series of conventions, protocols, guidelines, and targets adopted by the international community. These include the seminal Universal Declaration of Human Rights, adopted in 1948, which enshrines "the equal rights of men and women," including the right to participate in government. A series of other documents signed by United Nations (UN) member states over the years – including the World Plan of Action in Mexico City in 1975, the Convention on the Elimination of All Forms of Discrimination Against Women in 1979, CEDAW and the Nairobi Forward- looking Strategies in 1985 – resulted in a landmark commitment in the 1995 Beijing Platform for Action, signed by all member states at the UN's Fourth World Conference on Women.

The Beijing declaration represented new aims and strategies. Based on a power perspective on women's underrepresentation, the declaration not only talks of "discriminatory attitudes and practices," but also of "unequal power relations," thus opening up for affirmative action, even if the controversial word "quotas" was not mentioned. Pointing to the fact that the specific target of 30 percent women in decision-making positions by 1995 (which was recommended by UN Economic and Social Council (ECOSOC) in 1990) had not been met, the Beijing declaration sets the goal as "equitable distribution of power and decision-making at all levels."[7] The world's governments endorsed gender equality and women's empowerment as the third of the eight Millennium Development Goals (MDGs) at the 2000 UN Summit, however in rather vague terms when it comes to political representation. Similar principles underlie the Sustainable Development Goals that are due to replace the MDGs in 2015. The engagement of countries in the world community can be monitored through their endorsement of international conventions and treaties, especially ratification of CEDAW and state participation with official delegations sent to UN conferences, as well as through the growing number of transnational feminist movements.[12] The availability of international comparisons through comparative research and by the global ranking list of women's parliamentary representation,[13] and the global web site on quota provisions country by country,[14] have increased competition among states seeking to look modern by demonstrating a relatively high representation of women in their national parliaments compared with neighboring states in their region.

Reflecting these agreements, a wide range of multilateral organizations are engaged today in technical assistance promoting women's rights and gender equality in elected office, including UN Women, the United Nations Development Program (UNDP), the Inter-Parliamentary Union (IPU), the International Federation of Electoral Systems (IFES), the Organization for Security and Cooperation in Europe (OSCE), the European Union, the Commonwealth, the Organization for American States (OAS), the African Union, International IDEA, and bilateral donors such as USAID, SIDA, NORAD, and CIDA. The role of these bodies is particularly important in peace-building and state-building processes after sustained conflict and in the constitutional arrangements for newly independent states, such as in Rwanda, South Sudan, and Timor-Leste, as transitional regimes look to their neighbors for legal models.

How this process works remains poorly understood, however, as little is known with any certainty about the more complex impact of technical assistance and aid spending on institutional capacity building initiatives. As discussed earlier, continued heated debate continues about the general question of whether electoral aid and assistance works, including by strengthening women's rights.[15] International forces could flow through several different channels. One involves the diffusion of global norms through the free exchange of information and the spread of cosmopolitan communications across national borders. More open societies, such as those with a free press and unrestricted internet access, can be expected to facilitate transnational NGO-communications and public awareness of international treaties and conventions. Globalization through cosmopolitan communications, open trade barriers, the free flow of information, and membership of regional and transnational organizations, may thus be predicted to facilitate the general diffusion of international norms about gender equality in public life within societies.[16] In addition, the distribution of official development aid and technical assistance can also be expected to play a role. Although program effectiveness is only loosely related to levels of aid spending, the more development aid spent in general on democratic participation, the more this may be expected to open opportunities for women's empowerment and gender equality in political life. International organizations and bilateral donors often endorse the principles of gender equality, but this can involve many types of policies such as ensuring equal opportunities for women and men in capacity building and funding initiatives. If agencies go further so that they are also active advocates for gender quota policies, this may also prove important for advancing these types of laws. Finally, regional proximity may also contribute towards the adoption of gender quotas within neighboring states, with the types of policies adopted in each society expected to spread across national borders most easily among countries linked by similar languages, cultures, and religious traditions, trade relations and media markets, and colonial legacies.[17]

Controlling for Local Conditions

The evidence for the impact of the international community on the adoption and revision of gender quota policies has not been systematically demonstrated worldwide. Fully specified models analyzing the evidence need to control for several potentially confounding local conditions.

Domestic mobilization by women activists

While authorizing international conventions and norms of gender equality in elected office, the international community and multilateral regional organizations by themselves are unable to generate sustainable and effective legal reforms in sovereign member states unless domestic stakeholders, NGO policy advocates, governments, and grassroots advocacy movements are mobilized within each society. Despite the growth of global governance, the United Nations continues to respect the principle that nations have the right to considerable autonomy over their own domestic affairs and UN agencies as well as international organizations providing democratic assistance such as IPU and International IDEA provide assistance only at the invitation of member states. Thus the adoption of gender quota policies is likely to come about through the international community working closely with local partners in government, such as official state equality agencies, and with activist NGOs in civic society, political parties (including women's organized sections within parties), and feminist social movements.

For example, the Organization for Security and Cooperation within Europe has worked with government agencies, political parties, and women's NGOs in post-Communist states to implement gender quotas and other measures designed to strengthen the proportion of women in elected office.[18] UNDP has provided technical assistance and encouraged the development of national strategic action plans for gender equality in Asia and the Pacific.[19] Demands for gender equality in elected office can be expected to be influenced in each society by the strength of the women's movement and women's activism in NGOs, as well as by the presence of women's sections within political parties.[20] Accounts have emphasized how voluntary party quotas were adopted in specific Western European political parties, especially by left-wing and Green parties, following pressure from the independent women's movement and from women's sections within political parties, for example in the Nordic countries, and in the case of the use of all-women shortlists in the UK Labor party.[21] Women's groups may therefore be critical advocates in quota promotion through participating in transnational movements, bringing the new international norms of gender equality into national policy discussions and pointing to best practice policy measures in neighboring countries.

The exact role of international and domestic forces continues to be debated. Some accounts suggest that gender quota policies implemented in state-building initiatives in Afghanistan, South Sudan, and Iraq were driven by the priorities of the world community, by foreign constitutional technical consultants, and by strings attached to external development aid, more than by genuine demands made by local politicians, local women's groups or grassroots activists.[22] In traditional societies such as Iraq and Afghanistan, or Bhutan and Tunisia, international technical assistance from the world community may either override or else supplement demands for strengthening gender equality in politics mobilized by local women activists.[23] Consequently alongside the role of the international community, the strength of the women's mobilization around quotas needs to be tested.

Socioeconomic conditions

Modernization theories common in developmental political sociology emphasize the need to control for fixed socioeconomic conditions and levels of development. These accounts emerged in the mid-twentieth century, exemplified by the long tradition established by Seymour Martin Lipset.[24] Over the last six decades, an extensive literature has linked theories of societal modernization with growing female participation in the workforce and public sphere and the breakdown of traditional sex-role stereotypes. Simultaneous patterns of development, economic growth, industrialization, urbanization, demographic trends and changes in fertility, the spread of communications, and wider access to education, are theorized from this perspective as the standard "usual suspects" to drive gender equality and cultural change, as well as transitions from authoritarian regimes and processes of democratization.

These theories suggest that as economies develop from those based largely upon agricultural production towards industrial and postindustrial societies, changes in the labor force and society (typified by the entry of more educated women into administration, management, and the professions) facilitate the growing mobilization of women and fuels opportunities for female careers in elected office. Supply-side theories of political recruitment emphasize that aspirants need the skills, networks, and resources to succeed in elected office and hence women gaining educational qualifications and relevant professional employment provides advantages in public life. The structural viewpoint has become less common today although it has not died away. Some contemporary studies continue to emphasize the impact of residual gender gaps in literacy, educational qualifications, family responsibilities, work-based professional networks, or political ambitions on women's entry into political elites. All of these factors are regarded as limiting the resources, experience, and capacities that women bring both to civic engagement at mass level, and well as to the pursuit of elected and appointed office for legislative, executive, and judicial elites.[25] Hence Michael Ross has claimed that in the Arab region, the well-known "resource curse" (oil, gas), has led directly to inequality of men and women's participation in the paid labor force and this, in turn, indirectly limits female opportunities to run for elected office in these states.[26] Several other empirical studies suggest that women's participation in the workforce is an important predictor of the proportion of women in parliament.[27]

Levels of democratization

Among political conditions, there are reasons to expect that the adoption of legal quotas would also be affected by the level of democratization in a country. By expanding opportunities for women to mobilize and strengthening government responsiveness to public concern, gender quotas may be more likely to be adopted in democratic states. More competitive multiparty elections could also potentially strengthen opportunities for women's representation, as nomination processes are no longer in the hands of a single party elite. In fact, however, several cases cast doubt on this argument. For example, some of the world's oldest democracies, including New Zealand (the first state to extend the suffrage to women in 1893) and the United States (birthplace of the 1848 Seneca Falls Convention women's movement), have no legal quotas in use today. The Nordic countries with their high political representation of women already from the 1970s never adopted quotas by law for popular elections. Many Nordic parties use of voluntary party quotas, as do many other countries in Western Europe.[28] By contrast, legal quotas have been established in some of the world's newest independent nation states, including South Sudan and Timor-Leste.

Cultural and religious values

Finally, fully specified models also need to control for the potential mediating role of cultural values, including predominant religious legacies. Previous work by Inglehart and Norris presented extensive evidence that linked the spread of more egalitarian attitudes towards sex roles with women's representation in national parliaments.[29] Others have also found cultural values to be an important predictor of women's success in gaining elected office and one which outweighs institutions.[30] In addition, Norris and Inglehart theorized that the main type of religious faith in any society will continue to leave an enduring imprint on cultural values towards sex roles, even in places where secularization has taken hold.[31] The predominate type of religion is predicted to be associated with the passage of laws governing gender quotas, with Muslim predominant societies more conservative in attitudes towards traditional sex roles than Protestant and Catholic societies.[32] If religious cultures influence public policies, then the predominant type of faith should predict the adoption of gender equality policies. On the other hand, gender quotas for parliament is a widespread practice in many contemporary states in the Middle East and North Africa, partly as a symbol of being modern.[33]

RESEARCH DESIGN

What evidence would throw new light on the core propositions? Single-nation studies have traditionally used historical process-tracing to account for the passage of quota reforms in specific countries and to assess their effects over time. Event history analysis techniques have examined the factors leading towards the adoption of voluntary gender quotas by political parties in Western Europe.[34] Research has also compared cross-national patterns across global regions and by type of regime,[35] as well as comparing both developing and affluent societies.[36] Building upon this foundation, this chapter seeks to compare legal gender quota policies adopted and revised for the lower or single house of national parliaments in all independent nation-states around the globe during the period from 1990 to 2014. Models test the effects of the potential international forces behind the adoption and revision of electoral gender quotas worldwide, controlling for rival domestic factors. In particular, this study examines cross-national evidence testing whether the adoption of gender quota laws can be attributed to the role of the international community, while controlling for domestic feminist mobilization, socioeconomic conditions, levels of democratization, and cultural religious legacies.

Typology of Gender Quota Policies

While the use of gender quotas for elected office is widely debated, the core notion and classification is often poorly understood and conceptualized, and the ways in which these policies operate vary widely in many detailed aspects.[37] To clarify our terms, therefore, in this chapter, *quotas* are defined as regulatory policies designed to achieve descriptive representation through *rules entailing that the composition of a candidate list or a body must contain a certain minimum number or proportion of a specified category of people.* Quotas can be applied to the representation of communal groups and minorities in plural societies, such as in elected bodies in Lebanon, Macedonia, India, and New Zealand, and the relevant groups can be defined by indigenous heritage, language, race, caste, and ethnicity, nationality, region, or religious affiliation.[38] *Gender* quotas are defined by sex. Beyond representative assemblies, quota provisions can apply to diverse institutions in the public, nonprofit and private sectors, including party conference delegates, internal party offices, regulatory bodies, official commissions, judicial appointments, access to education, and most recently the membership of company boards.[39]

Gender quotas for representative assemblies therefore specify that a certain minimum number or proportion of women (women-specific) or of women and men (gender neutral) should be included at specific stages of the recruitment process. Like a game of musical chairs the "funnel of recruitment" progressively narrows the stages leading towards legislative office.[40] Consequently, a further distinction is made between *aspirant quotas, candidate quotas (legal or voluntary), and reserved seats:*

1. *Aspirant gender quota* policies govern *the pool seeking nomination.* Constitutional provisions, laws, or party rules regulate the composition of nomination shortlists (for example, for the Scottish parliament), or who can run in primary elections (such as in Panama).
2. *Candidate quota policies* regulate the gender composition of lists officially nominated by political parties or other nominating bodies for election or appointment to representative bodies. These fall into two main subcategories:
   - *Legal candidate quotas* are legally binding requirements applying to *all* political parties nominating candidates in an election in any state. These regulations may be specified in party laws, election laws, party finance

laws, or national constitutions. These measures are an extension of other common legal requirements for eligibility to become a candidate, such as age, citizenship, and residency requirements. Sanctions for noncompliance of legal gender quotas are usually determined in the law and implemented by election management bodies and electoral courts.

- By contrast, so-called *"voluntary" candidate quota* are specified in specific political parties through internal party rulebooks, selection procedures, and party constitutions. These requirements within particular party organizations are usually internally enforced by recruitment rules and procedures set up by the party.

3. Finally, *reserved seats for women* target the membership of elected or appointed assemblies, exemplified by seats reserved for women (and scheduled castes) on Indian village councils. These principles are often specified in national constitutions and implemented through electoral laws. Reserved seats are constructed in various forms, but are increasingly based on direct elections among only women candidates.

Gender quotas for political office may apply to elected or appointed assemblies at subnational, national, or supranational levels, including those running for local councils, regional assemblies, national parliaments, or continental parliaments, including the European parliament and the Assembly of the African Union. Appointed members of parliament, be they women or men, tend to be especially dependent upon party leaders and they may therefore simply serve as compliant supporters for rulers seeking to stack assemblies. By contrast, women (and men) competing as candidates for election have incentives to develop a grassroots support base in order to win legitimate contests, allowing more independence in office. It has proved important that the elected women have a constituency basis of their own, in contrast to added seats such as in Bangladesh (local) and Morocco (national).[41]

Country Coverage and Time Period

This section focuses upon understanding the adoption and reform of gender quotas designed to regulate the nomination or election of women for the lower- or single house of federal or national parliaments. We cover 196 independent nation-states from 1990 until 2014. The Global Database of Quotas for Women has gathered data providing comprehensive estimates for the number of independent nation-states using these policies.[42] Based on this database and supplemented with additional information, this chapter draws upon *The Gender Quota Database (GQD)*. The cross-national comparisons include all contemporary nation-states around the world dichotomized into those with/ without any legal quota (whether a law specifying candidate quotas or reserved seats) used for the lower/single house of the federal or national legislature in

2014. The sources and operationalization of all measures are described more fully in Technical Appendix 6A.

Measures and Indicators

The role of international organizations is tested using several indicators. The role of globalization, especially access to cosmopolitan communications, may be important to strengthen the diffusion of international norms, since this process exposes countries to cultural norms and standards beyond national boundaries, helping to network transnational and national women activists. How far countries are either largely isolated from this process, or else bound tightly with transnational ties of trade, communications, technology, labor, cooperation, and migrant flows of peoples, can be monitored empirically through the KOF Globalization Index, combining social, economic, and political indices.[43] In addition to worldwide diffusion, how far countries learn from policies adopted in bordering societies (or regional contagion effects) can be compared by estimating the mean adoption of legal gender quotas as a norm among neighboring states within each global region. Based on the Quota Project, coders identified states where international organizations advocated passing gender quota laws. The provision of development aid and technical assistance can be examined through AidData, including ten year averages estimating levels of Official Development Aid spending on democratic participation and civil society (which includes support for gender equality groups in civic society).[44] All things being equal, if international forces are important, then the adoption of legal gender quotas should be higher in more cosmopolitan states, in regions where these policies have been widely adopted, in states where international organizations or donors have advocated passing gender quota laws, and in countries where the international community has provided long-term development assistance supporting inclusive and participatory forms of democratic governance.

Models control for several potentially confounding factors. *Activism by domestic advocacy groups* is measured through coding information from the Quota Project and from supplementary search procedures for whether women's organizations mobilized in the passage of the first gender quota law. Agencies were also subdivided and classified as domestic women's or feminist NGOs, women in some political parties, and woman's commissions or other official state equality policy agency. *Socioeconomic conditions* were monitored through including several macrolevel factors in models (see Technical Appendix 6A), including the role of economic development (logged per capita GDP), the ratio of women in the labor force, the ratio of girls to boys in schools, and the distribution of natural resources (logged per capita resource rents as a proportion of GDP). To control for the impact of *political conditions*, models also include the state's contemporary level of democratization (measured by the combined Freedom House and Polity IV estimates). Finally, *cultural factors* are monitored through identifying the predominant religion and whether societies were classified as Muslim or Orthodox.

THE GLOBAL SPREAD OF GENDER QUOTAS

Contemporary patterns and trends in the adoption and revision of gender quotas observed around the world can be described before looking at the multivariate evidence for the core propositions already discussed.

The typology developed earlier helps to classify contemporary policies in use around the world. Figure 6.2 suggests that almost two decades after Beijing, by May 2014 the majority of countries worldwide (56 percent) used gender quota policies for election or appointment to the lower or single house of the federal or national parliament. By May 2014, out of 196 independent nation-states

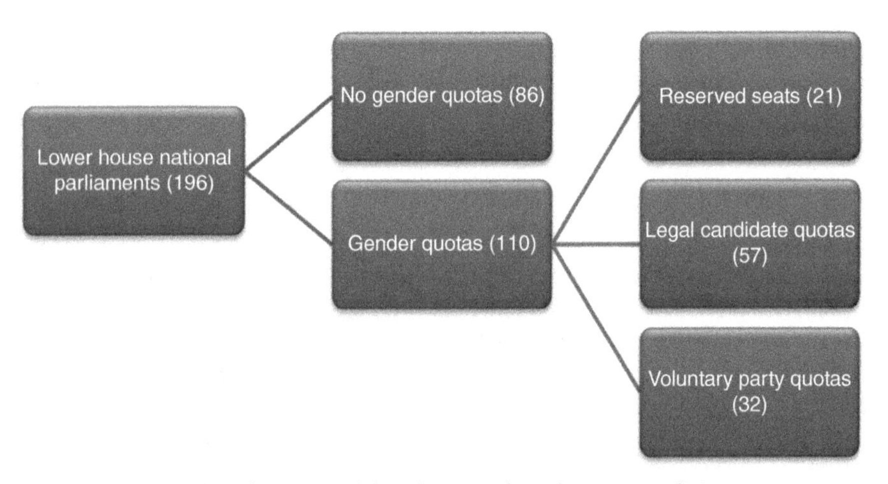

FIGURE 6.2. The classification and distribution of gender quota policies.
Note: The use of gender quota policies for the lower- or single house of the federal or national parliament in 196 contemporary independent nation-states (incl. Palestine, Taiwan, and Kosovo). May 2014. Countries are categorized into reserved seats for women members in the lower house of the national parliament; legal candidate gender quotas (applying to all lists of party nominees); voluntary candidate gender quotas (applying to some lists of party nominees); and no gender quotas. Six countries have both reserved seats and candidate quotas and are listed according to the strongest provision, the reserved seats (Algeria, Iraq, Kenya, Kosovo, Mauritania, and Rwanda). A country is listed as having voluntary party quotas if at least one of the three biggest parties represented in parliament has opted for gender quotas. Only countries without legal quotas (reserved seats or candidate quotas) are listed as having voluntary party quotas. Since Venezuela and Italy have abandoned their quota laws, they are omitted in Figures 6.2 and 6.3, which show the current use of gender quotas.
Source: The Gender Quota Database (GQD). Release 1.0 2014. Stockholm: University of Stockholm.

worldwide, 57 (29 percent) have legal candidate quotas regulating the gender composition of the nominated candidates, while 21 (11 percent) have reserved seats for women.[45] An additional 32 countries (16 percent) without legal provisions have adopted voluntary gender quotas in the internal rule-book used by at least one of the three largest individual political parties represented in parliament. Gender quotas in politics have therefore become a global phenomenon.

Waves of Gender Quota Law Adoption and Revision

Several successive periods of reforms can be identified over time.

The *First Wave* consists of various types of gender quotas used in many Communist states. Under state socialism, the Communist Party mobilized separate women's organizations, which in some countries, for instance in the FDR, were secured a certain number of seats alongside with trade unions and youth organizations. Also, efforts were made to ensure that legislative bodies contained women through the use of loose quotas or guidelines for candidate selection. Nevertheless, real power remained in the upper ranks of the party, such as the Central Committee or Politburo, where far fewer women held office.[46] Reserved seats were also used in a few other countries, including in Pakistan since 1956, Bangladesh since 1972, and Egypt 1979–84. Further, during the 1970–80s, several Nordic political parties starting using voluntary gender quotas for their own internal organizations and their electoral lists of candidates, contributing to the relatively high level of political representation of women in Scandinavia.

The *Second Wave* of gender quota adoption occurred after 1990. This started with the Argentinian "Ley de Cupo Feminino" from 1991, which required that 30 percent of the candidates of the electoral lists of all parties should be women. In some of the countries, especially in Western Europe, the quota law was preceded by voluntary party quotas adopted by one or more political parties, but in other cases gender quotas for election started by an act of legislation passed in parliament and binding for all parties.

A *Third Wave* can also be identified reflecting recent amendments of quota laws. Thus in all the 80 countries that had adopted legal gender quota in 2000, almost half (37) subsequently amended their law, often within a relatively short span of time.[11] Revisions have often occurred where previous measures have failed to meet expectations. Overwhelmingly, most amendments have usually strengthened the quota provisions, for instance by raising the percentage level, changing rank order rules on the candidate lists, and raising sanctions for noncompliance. To give some examples: In *Belgium*, the 2002 law requires that the two top positions cannot have candidates of the same sex, and the whole list shall have 50–50 of each sex, while the first quota law only demanded a minimum of one-third of each sex. In *Armenia*, a quota rule in 1999 required 5 percent women among the candidates for the PR part of the election to be increased to 15 percent in 2007, from 2012 with stronger rank order rules. In

Uganda, women on reserved seats were prior to 2006 elected indirectly, but from 2006 in direct elections of 112 district seats reserved for women candidates. In *Morocco*, following the first introduction of reserved seat quotas in 2002, the number of seats reserved for women was raised from 30 to 60 in 2011 and the provisions in general made more sustainable.[47] In a few exceptional cases, however, amendments have weakened or even abandoned gender quota policies, including in Egypt, where the regime for the 2011 election exchanged the reserved seats for a minimalistic demand of just one woman on each list, as well as Venezuela and Italy, which abandoned their quota laws.

WHY ARE QUOTAS FIRST ADOPTED?

So what factors have driven the adoption of legal gender quotas since 1990? Table 6.1 presents the results of a series of multivariate logistical regression models.

International Forces

The results in Model A support the core proposition that international forces have played a significant role in the diffusion of gender quotas.[48] External factors which are important for the adoption of legal quotas, without other controls, include the overall level of Official Development Aid invested in democratic participation within a country. Developing countries seeking to attract inward investment and bilateral donor aid have a strong incentive to comply with international norms and standards, especially in transitional regimes writing new constitutions as part of state-building and peace-building processes. Moreover, the provision of resources and technical assistance for democratic participation can assist local actors to implement gender equality policies designed to meet the goals and targets set by the UN's Millennial Development Goals. International organizations encourage the adoption of effective gender quota policies through sharing knowledge about international standards and best practices, encouraging south-south cooperation, organizing capacity-building workshops, highlighting countries lagging behind the MDG target in women's representation, and providing technical reports, handbooks, guidelines, and expert advice. Through conventions, treaties, and agreements such as the MDGs and SDGs (Sustainable Development Goals), the international community strengthens norms to ensure gender balance and women's rights in public life, including through many equal opportunity and positive action measures.

In Table 6.1 Model A, the regional adoption of use of legal gender quotas also proves significant; this suggests a contagion effect of policy learning flowing across national borders, especially among neighboring states sharing cultural, linguistic, colonial, and economic ties. The clearest

TABLE 6.1 *Explaining the Adoption of Legal Quotas*

	Model A: INTERNATIONAL		Model B: DOMESTIC		Model C: ALL	
	Beta	Sig	Beta	Sig	Beta	Sig
INTERNATIONAL FORCES						
Globalization index	.039	.068	−.025	.523	.063	.354
Aid spent on democratic participation, 10 year average	**.000**	**.043**	.000	.439	.000	.717
International advocacy	22.30	.999	22.6	.998	23.9	.998
Regional adoption of legal quotas	**9.09**	**.000**	**13.4**	**.010**	**17.8**	**.024**
DOMESTIC ADVOCACY						
Women's Commission advocated quota			24.1	.998	27.8	.997
Women in political parties advocated quota			3.09	.071	**6.65**	**.048**
Women's movement advocated quota			**4.06**	**.001**	**3.73**	**.003**
CONTROLS						
Log per capita GDP					.000	.109
Ratio of women in the labor force					−.113	.964
Gender ratio in schools					.054	.396
Log natural resources					.194	.509
Predominant Muslim society					1.99	.151
Predominant Orthodox society					−.989	.846
Levels of democratization					−.057	.828
Constant	−7.12		−7.01		−18.7	
Nagelkerke R2	.410		.839		.872	
% predicted correctly	75.2		93.4		91.7	
N countries	121		121		121	

Note: The models use logistic regression with cross-national data where the dependent variable is whether the country has adopted "legal gender candidate quotas for all party lists of nominees or reserved seats" (0/1). See the Technical appendix for details of all the variables. Significant coefficients are highlighted in bold.**Sources:** The Gender Quota Database (GQD). Release 1.0 2014. Stockholm: University of Stockholm; Quality of Government standard dataset (Dec 2013). www.qog.pol.gu.se/.

examples include the rapid diffusion of gender quotas in the form of legal candidate quotas in Latin America following their adoption by in Argentina in 1991.[49] Similarly, the use of reserved seats in Afghanistan was probably influenced by policies in neighboring Pakistan and Bangladesh. Another widely cited example is the 73rd and 74th amendments to the Indian constitution in 1993. Through the reservation of 33 percent of seats for women, 1,000,000 slots were created for women in local self-government institutions. The effective ANC-party quota, which raised women's representation to over 30 percent and later to over 40 percent in the South African parliament, are also commonly cited in discussions about Africa. The French parity law influenced debates for quota adoption in Morocco, Tunisia, and in other Francophone African countries. It inspired other Western European countries such as Spain, Portugal, and Belgium to move from voluntary party quotas, usually initiated by left-wing and Green parties, to gender quotas by law. The countries in the former Yugoslavia adopted legal candidate quotas one after the other. Experience in Uganda influenced the adoption of reserved seats in Rwanda, the country which was later to obtain the first parliament in the world with a female majority. Regional diffusion is not always positive for women, however, as shown by the abandonment of all quotas that had been used in Communist party recruitment in Central and Eastern Europe. This led to a sharp decline in women's representation in the early 1990s following the fall of the Berlin Wall, before the eventual re-adoption of some quotas in more recent years.[50]

To examine this further, Figure 6.3 maps the geographic distribution of gender quota policies in use today. Regional patterns can be observed, including the popularity of reserved seats in the Middle East and North Africa, South Asia, parts of East Asia, and in many countries with single-member plurality electoral systems and often with more authoritarian regimes. By contrast, legal statutory gender quota policies have diffused throughout Central and South America, and these policies are also popular in Central Africa and parts of Francophone Africa. Europe was never in the forefront in adoption of quotas by law, but today legal quotas are also found in some established democracies in Western Europe, including Belgium, France, Portugal, Spain, and in a few of the new democracies in Eastern and Central Europe, including Slovenia and Poland. Yet, quota policies are uncommon today in many states in post-Communist Eastern Europe, where the legacy of the Soviet-era continues to make these policies unpopular, although legal quotas now have been implemented in Albania, Armenia, Kyrgyzstan, Uzbekistan, and most of the countries in the former Yugoslavia.[51] Voluntary gender quotas have been adopted by specific political party rules in countries in the Southern Cone of Africa, as well as in many Anglo-American democracies (with the exception of the United States) and in many (although not all) states in the Nordic region.

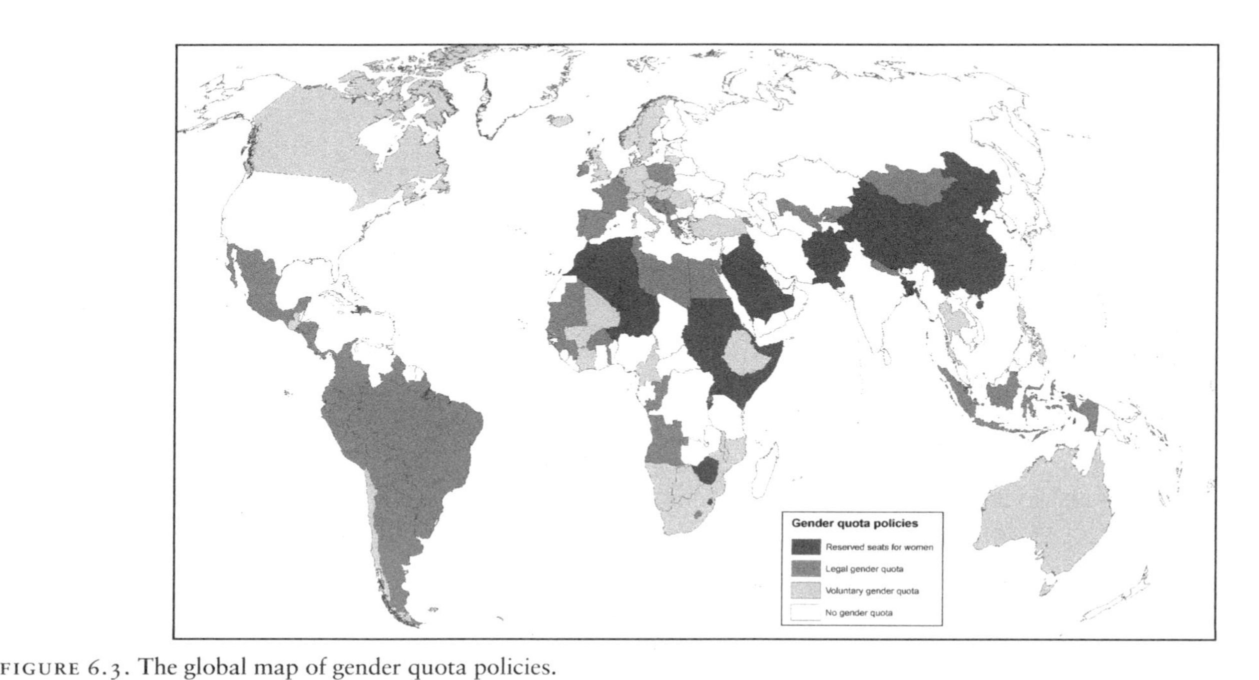

FIGURE 6.3. The global map of gender quota policies.
Note: The global distribution of gender quota policies for the lower or single house of the national parliament, 196 countries, May 2014. Countries are categorized into reserved seats for women members in the lower house of the national parliament; legal candidate gender quotas (applying to all lists of party nominees); voluntary candidate gender quotas (applying to some lists of party nominees); and no gender quotas.
Source: The Gender Quota Database (GQD). Release 1.0 2014. Stockholm: University of Stockholm.

Adding Controls for Local Conditions

Do these relationships persist once additional factors reflecting local conditions are added to the models? Table 6.1 Model B adds measures for domestic advocacy. This evidence suggests that quotas are not simply imposed on countries as a result of external pressures by Western donors or regional organizations; the initial adoption of legal gender quotas are also influenced by advocacy within each country by the women's movement and women in political parties. Where activists press policy-makers to strengthen opportunities for women's representation through the adoption of positive action reforms, this appears to have a significant impact on the successful passage of these laws. This suggests that a combination of international factors (advocacy, technical assistance, and the role models of neighboring countries which have passed gender quota laws) combined with the strength of women's advocacy groups, facilitates the adoption of these measures.

Table 6.1 Model C incorporates successive structural, political and cultural controls into the analysis. The results of the full model confirm that the adoption of legal gender quotas was significantly correlated with the factors already identified, although it was unaffected by levels of economic development or societies where girls and boys have had relatively equal educational opportunities. The ratio of women to men in the labor force, an indicator of women's growing entry into the economic marketplace, also does not explain the adoption of these measures, even though others have found this to be associated with the success of women in elected office.[52] Ross argues that the "resource curse" appear to hold back women's engagement in the paid workforce and also opportunities in public life, as well as having many other negative consequences for corruption and patronage politics.[53] Nevertheless, the use of gender quota policies does not seem to be affected today by whether Middle East and North African societies are oil rich (such as Iraq) or relatively oil-poor (such as Tunisia). Cultural explanations suggest that more women will succeed in elected office where traditional social mores and norms about the appropriate division of sex roles in the home, family, and public sphere have become more egalitarian. Yet the predominant type of religious faith in a society, where Muslim societies might be expected to prove both more culturally conservative and also against the use of quotas, remain insignificant. Societies with an Orthodox tradition may also be expected to be more negative towards these policies, which are widely associated as part of the Communist legacy of earlier decades. Nevertheless, the main type of religious culture does not prove to be a significant predictors of the adoption of gender quotas. As shown by the cases of Bangladesh and Pakistan, some Muslim societies have in fact been some of the earliest adopters of reserved seats. Legal quotas have today been adopted by many other Muslim societies, such as Afghanistan, Iraq, Morocco, Tunisia, and Indonesia. In the final model the initial adoption of gender quota policies seems shaped most strongly by regional norms and practices, combined with women advocates who support these policies in political parties and in the women's movement.

DO GENDER QUOTA POLICIES SUCCEED?

What is the evidence that gender quotas are effective in meeting their goals and international targets? Comparisons can be drawn between the proportion of women who were elected to national parliaments in contests immediately before and after the implementation of the gender quota laws. In several countries, quota rules can be seen as very effective, generating dramatic leaps in the proportion of women in elected office, gains exemplified by Rwanda in 2003 (more than doubling from 26 percent to 56 percent of women), Costa Rica in 2002 (from 19 percent to 35 percent), Senegal in 2012 (from 23 percent to 43 percent), Algeria in 2012 (from 8 percent to 32 percent) and Bolivia in 2014 (from 25 percent to 53 percent). Yet by contrast elsewhere, reforms have often failed to achieve their full objectives and gains have proved more modest.

Table 6.2 estimates the short-term effects of the adoption of the first quota laws. The impact is measured by percentage point change, no matter the level, from the election just prior to the quota implementation to the election immediately afterwards. Table 6.2 shows that 83 percent of all countries experienced an increased proportion of women in parliament after the quota provision took effect. The degree of short-term change varied, but the overall pattern was clear. Only one country had no change in this regard although another 16 percent experienced a fall in women's representation. Countries with reserved seats saw more substantial increases than the countries with legal candidate quotas.

What explains these variations? The impact of legal gender quota policies on women's representation varies substantially due to several factors associated with their detailed design.[54] The evidence suggests that in general, they are most effective in establishing gender equality in elected office when:

(1) These laws require a relatively *high proportion* of female candidates to be nominated by political parties;
(2) These laws have *placement mandates* (also known as "double quotas") which regulate the alternative rank order of women and men candidates on party lists ("zippering");
(3) These laws include *penalties for noncompliance* which strictly bind the behavior of political parties through financial sanctions or the rejection of nomination lists which do not comply with the law, or, alternatively, which create positive incentives for parties to nominate more women; and,
(4) *Compliance is monitored* by independent bodies, including electoral commissions, the courts, NGOs and women groups, using legal and political means if necessary, to ensure that parties implement these policies to their fullest degree.

TABLE 6.2 *The Effects of Quotas on Women's Representation*

Change in the Percent of Women in Elected Office	Countries with Reserved Seats		Countries with Legal Candidate Quotas		Total Countries		Proportion of Countries
	N	%	N	%	N	%	%
Decrease	3	14.3	7	16.7	10	15.9	15.9
No change		0.0	1	2.4	1	1.6	1.6
Increase < 5%	6	28.6	17	40.5	23	36.5	82.5
Increase 5–9.99%	2	9.5	7	16.7	9	14.3	
Increase 10–19.99%	7	33.3	7	16.7	14	22.2	
Increase >20%	3	14.3	3	7.1	6	9.5	
N=	*21*	*100*	*42*	100.0	*63*	*100.0*	*100.0*

Notes: The effect of quota policies is estimated by comparing the change in the proportion of women in the lower or single house of parliament in elections held immediately before and after the implementation of gender quota laws. The estimate excludes 3 cases with no prior election for comparison and 10 cases where elections with quotas have not yet been held. Significant coefficients are highlighted in bold.
Source: The Gender Quota Database (GQD). Release 1.0 2014. Stockholm: University of Stockholm.

Two post-Communist states – Albania and Kyrgyzstan – provide contrasting cases illustrating the importance of quota design. Both countries introduced legal quotas in 2008 and 2007, respectively. In Albania, the quota law specifies that 30 percent of candidates should be women, with a financial penalty for noncompliance. The absence of a placement mandate and a mixed electoral system, however, meant that the policy's overall effect was limited, and in 2010 only 16 percent women were elected to Albanian parliament. The opposite situation can be observed in Kyrgyzstan, where the 30 percent quota law includes the requirement that no more than three positions separate male and female candidates. Combined with a PR electoral system, this policy resulted in an overnight shift in women's representation: the proportion of women in parliament jumped from zero percent to one quarter of all members after the 2007 elections. Such outcomes suggest that legal quotas can serve as an effective measure for electing greater numbers of women to political office, especially when they are well-specified in terms of their requirements, if they are combined with the PR (proportional representation) electoral system, and if compliance is carefully enforced.

CONCLUSIONS

The worldwide spread of gender quota policies in recent decades has been a remarkable development; these statutes are more radical than many other alternative policies that are designed to strengthen equal opportunities in elected office such as investing in training and capacity development for candidates or providing public funding for women. This chapter emphasizes the role of international organizations and domestic political activists in this process and the relative level of women's representation prior to the adoption and revision of gender quota policies. Models control for the role of structural conditions and mass cultural values.

The results underline the importance of international diffusion as well as domestic advocates for the initial adoption of gender quotas. This reflects the process of norm diffusion in international human rights. The international community adopted the issue of gender equality in elected office. The radical Beijing declaration from 1995 changed the 30 percent target, even if the controversial word "quotas" was not mentioned. The push for gender equality in elected office was reinforced by the 2000–2015 MDGs and their replacement by the SDGs. Insights into the causes of women's low political representation have gradually shifted from emphasizing supply-side factors (women's alleged lack of political interest, ambition, and competence) to blaming demand-side factors (including political parties and parliaments). Following international declarations, initiatives designed to strengthen women's participation agencies have been advocated by agencies such as UN Women, multilateral organizations such as the OSCE, International IDEA, IPU and OAS, and northern bilateral donors such as NORAD and SIDA. Consequently, many countries have adopted gender quotas, and today such measures are in use in a broad selection of political regimes, more often in democratic and authoritarian regime, less often in hybrid regimes. The successful example of gender quotas in several countries encouraged neighboring states with cultural ties to follow suit, exemplified by the influence of South Africa on other countries in the southern cone of Africa and the impact of Argentina on Latin American states. Women activists working in human rights NGOs, and within political parties have been able to use global norms, technical assistance, and development aid to amplify demands that countries should take action to meet international standards. Comparative analyses have fostered an international competition between states to have a higher level of women's representation in parliament than at least their neighboring countries.

Finally, it would be wrong to call the wave of quota adoption (1990–2014) merely symbolic, since almost half of the countries with quota laws experienced a substantive increase in women's numerical representation in the first election after the adoption, an important achievement in its own right. However, during the recent wave of quota amendments, many countries with only weak results from quota regulation have strengthened their provisions, for example by introducing or tightening penalties for noncompliance, rank-order rules, or raising levels. Strengthening has also taken place in countries with more effective policies, probably as a result of experiences learned, including those of neighboring countries. It has also raised expectations. Only two countries have abandoned their quota law, and only one has weakened it, indicating that electoral gender quota as a measure to change women's historical underrepresentation has won widespread acceptance in spite of controversies around their adoption. In conclusion, the previous chapter suggested that the reports published by regional organizations such as the OAS played an important role in encouraging electoral reforms to be subsequently implemented. The broader evidence scrutinized here further confirms the patterns, with the important proviso that electoral assistance from the international community works best in conjunction with local stakeholders, combining to strengthen women's rights and inclusive electoral processes. Are similar patterns evident when we look at electoral management bodies? The next chapter considers this issue.

7

Supporting Independent Media

Recent years have seen major threats to freedom of information and the independent media. Reporters Without Borders' annual review reports that in recent years a climate of fear has spurred growing government attacks on journalistic independence and a clampdown on the media:

> The many reasons for this decline in freedom of information include the increasingly authoritarian tendencies of governments in countries such as Turkey and Egypt, tighter government control of state-owned media, even in some European countries such as Poland, and security situations that have become more and more fraught, in Libya and Burundi, for example, or that are completely disastrous, as in Yemen.[1]

The Committee to Protect Journalists documents approximately 80 to 90 media workers killed annually during the last decade in connection with their work, with hundreds more imprisoned or exiled.[2] Similarly the annual report by Freedom House reports that press freedom declined to its lowest point in 12 years in 2015, as political, criminal, and terrorist forces sought to co-opt or silence the media in their broader struggle for power: "Fewer than one in seven people live in countries where coverage of political news is robust, the safety of journalists is guaranteed, state intrusion in media affairs is minimal, and the press is not subject to onerous legal or economic pressures."[3] Reflecting general restrictions of freedom of expression and independent journalism documented by these organizations, the quality of the election coverage provided by the traditional news media is also of major concern. The Perceptions of Electoral Integrity assessment estimates that of all eleven stages throughout the electoral cycle, campaign media are the second weakest stage worldwide, with only campaign finance achieving worst scores.[4] Given all these problems, it is important to learn what international media assistance programs and agencies can do most effectively to improve the quality of free, fair, and balanced journalism during election campaigns and their immediate aftermath. This contributes more broadly towards democratic governance, since independent media are widely considered essential as a component of an open, inclusive, and well-governed society.

Although with roots during earlier eras, media assistance emerged as a significant aspect of development work in the late-1980s and the 1990s following the end of the Cold War and the dissolution of the former Soviet Union. After the tragic events in Rwanda and the former Yugoslavia, which showed how hate speech in broadcasts could play a role in instigating and directing violence, the international community began supporting media projects in countries torn apart by civil war. In recent years, support for independent media has gained added prominence in the context of the emerging governance transparency and anticorruption agenda.[5] Media aid has evolved from relatively modest programs with minor donations of equipment and training tours for journalists to long-term, multifaceted projects with multimillion dollar budgets.[6] Media assistance programs employ a varied toolkit, including strengthening the legal and regulatory framework, building journalistic training and capacity, developing oversight agencies, and monitoring media performance.

This chapter focuses upon the impact of programs of formal educational providing training for news workers as one of the most common types of activities by international organizations and domestic stakeholders. Journalism education is seen as improving the quality of the news media by improving journalistic practices.[7]

The chapter scrutinizes evidence for two pervasive assumptions underlying these programs. The first proposition concerns the *causes* of role perceptions, in particular that *formal education and journalism training has the capacity to mold the role orientations held by journalists and their perceptions about the functions of the news media*. In particular, reflecting liberal conceptions of the free press, education, and professional journalism training is expected to encourage news workers to prioritize roles as neutral reporters and as mobilizing watchdogs checking the abuse of power and encouraging civic engagement, rather than roles serving as unofficial spokespersons supporting the authorities. The second concerns the *consequences* of role perceptions, in particular that *media cultures prioritizing journalistic roles as neutral reporters and mobilizing watchdogs are assumed, in turn, to improve the quality of campaign coverage, electoral integrity and liberal democracy*. If journalism works well in this regard, it is commonly believed that during elections, rational citizens will have opportunities to decide how to cast their ballot based on information which is fair, balanced, pluralistic, critical, and independent. With fuller information, public preferences should more accurately match voting choices, strengthening electoral accountability and liberal democracy. The sequential logic is illustrated in Figure 7.1.

To explore these propositions, the second section summarizes the research design and cross-national empirical evidence. This chapter uses the 65-nation

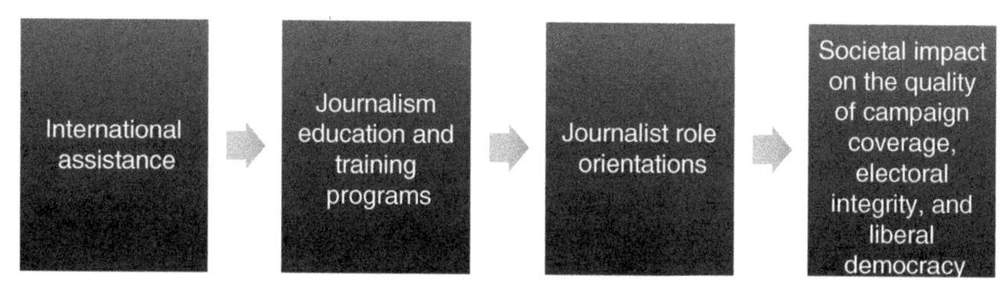

FIGURE 7.1. The chain-of-results framework for media assistance programs.

World of Journalism survey conducted among news workers in 2012–15, aggregated to country level, to identify the predominant role orientations and media culture within each society.[8] Factor analysis of the survey data identifies three distinct role journalistic orientations – as neutral reporters, engaged watchdogs, and official spokespersons. In the first step, the analysis explores whether college education and professional journalism education influence the predominant roles endorsed in each media culture. Education is measured by the percentage of journalists in each country holding a college or university degree in general, and professional journalism training is measured by the proportion holding a degree in journalism, media studies, or mass communications. In the second step in the sequence, the study also analyzes whether the type of journalistic roles adopted in each media culture influences the quality of campaign communications, electoral integrity, and liberal democracy. Models controlled for several standard factors, such as levels of development (per capita GDP in purchasing power parity). The third section summarizes the results and considers their implications for effective international programs of media assistance.

PROGRAMS OF MEDIA ASSISTANCE

Support for the media in transitional democracies and developing countries has become a mainstream area of work among international agencies, regional organizations, development ministries, NGOs, and local stakeholders. Official Development aid and assistance supporting the media is used for several purposes, which are commonly conflated.

- *Communication for development initiatives* seek to use media channels as a means to heighten awareness about development issues. Examples include disseminating public health information about preventing the Zika virus in Brazilian ads, the promotion of conflict-sensitive journalism and laws banning hate speech in fragile states, and online crowdsourcing platforms designed to locate victims of natural and humanitarian disasters.[9]
- *Public diplomacy* focuses on how governments use mass media strategically as a form of soft power to influence public opinion in other countries and

thereby promote their interests and cultural values abroad.[10] This is exemplified by US government-funded Voice of America broadcasts and by European Union cultural exchange and study abroad programs.
- *Infrastructure investments* are also common in this sector. This includes foreign loans and grants designed to build telecommunications networks, expanded access to digital technologies, and equipping community radio stations in low-income African states.
- By contrast, *media assistance programs* – the focus of this chapter – seek to strengthen the quality, sustainability, and/or independence of the news media. This subsector is usually part of general efforts to bolster electoral integrity, government transparency, and democratic accountability. The distinctive emphasis of these programs is how to improve the quality of the news media per se according to values such as independence, diversity, freedom of expression, and pluralism. Other initiatives typically support the media mainly as an intermediary mechanism to achieve other important development goals, like health care, security, or access to communications.

Many agencies are engaged in all these activities and the subsector of media assistance. Within the United Nations, UNESCO's has a specific mandate to promote "the free flow of ideas by word and image."[11] The agency seeks to foster media that is free, independent, and pluralistic in print, broadcast, and online. It does so through advocacy and awareness-raising, capacity-building, monitoring, fostering the safety of journalists, supporting media law, and fostering enabling regulatory frameworks. Other UN agencies and bureaus also active is this area include UNDP, the UN Democracy Fund, the UN Peacekeeping Fund, the International Telecommunications Union, and UNHDCR. Within the World Bank, the Communications for Governance & Accountability Programme serves this function. Regional intergovernmental organizations and regional NGOs also maintain many active programs promoting transparency, freedom of expression, and diversity in the media landscape, exemplified by the European Union's Article 11 of the Charter of Fundamental Rights.[12] Numerous other intergovernmental and nonprofit advocacy organizations also promote media freedom in Europe, especially in post-Communist states, including the Council of Europe, the OSCE, the European Center for Press and Media Freedom, the Open Society Foundation, the Index on Censorship, Amnesty International Human Rights Watch, and the European Broadcasters Union.

Worldwide, many bilateral donors offer media support, although differing in their aims and priorities.[13] In 2012, the biggest providers of development aid for media support were Germany, the United States, Japan, Sweden, and the EU institutions, providing 80 percent of ODA for this sector.[14] But two-thirds of German funds (67 percent) are dedicated to public diplomacy, while 90 percent of the funds from Japan are loans allocated to building media infrastructure. If we focus only upon support for the subsector of media assistance, then the

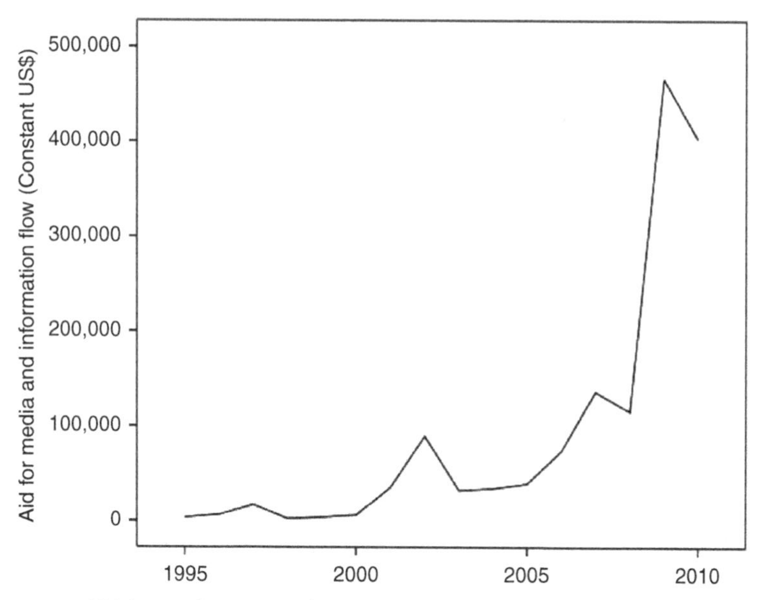

FIGURE 7.2. ODA spending on media assistance.
Source: AidData 3.0.

U.S. leads (providing 39 percent of total funds in this subsector), followed by Germany (14 percent) and then Sweden (12 percent). A wide range of foundations and philanthropic organizations also provide media assistance including the Konrad Adenauer Foundation, the Friedrich Ebert Foundation, the Ford Foundation, the Independent Journalism Foundation, the John S. & James L. Knight Foundation, the Thomson Reuters Foundation, the BBC Media Action (formerly the World Service Trust), the MacArthur Foundation, the Markle Foundation, the Friedrich Naumann Foundation, the Rockefeller Foundation, and the Open Society Foundations.

Estimates about the total amount of Official Development Aid (ODA) expenditures in this subsection need to be treated with caution, as media support programs can be classified and coded under several different categories (e.g., aid for public information campaigns about the risks of HIV-AIDS could be coded under heath care or media support). Figures also differ across official sources. Nevertheless, AidData estimates of annual spending upon media assistance programs (defined as those on "media and the free flow of information" categorized as 15153), illustrated in Figure 7.2, suggest that levels of Official Development Aid annual expenditures were fairly steady until the last decade, when spending rose substantially to around a half-billion US dollars in 2010. This represents only a small proportion out of the total US$27 billion ODA spent on Government and Civil Society in 2010.[15] At the same time, these figures should be put into perspective since, in comparison with other sectors such as poverty-alleviation, healthcare, and schools, the total invested in media assistance is only a miniscule fraction of overall development spending.[16] Among the recipients, many disbursements for media assistance are channeled through national and international NGOs with expertise in this sector. Major organizations such as the National Endowment for Democracy (NED), Internews, International Media Support, and IREX together receive around one-third of the total disbursements.[17] Activities in this subsector are usually managed by these international agencies working with local partners, government departments, and networks of civil society NGOs.

International media assistance, like other types of electoral support illustrated in Chapter 2, involves diverse programs and projects.[18] This includes, among other activities:

- **Legal regulation** – advocating policy and regulatory reforms, and providing technical advice on draft legislation to constitutional assemblies, parliamentary committees, government ministries, election management bodies, and judicial bodies, such as those concerning the laws governing broadcasting regulations, freedom of expression, and rights to information.
- **Capacity building, education and training** – building the capacity of independent journalists and other media workers in print, broadcast, and social news media; supporting independent media, media-watch NGOs, and media literacy in civil society; expanding access and use of information and communication technologies, especially community radio and social media among women, minorities, young people and the disabled in developing countries; strengthening professional associations and local networks; promoting civil society organizations, citizen voices, civic engagement through communication channels, and media literacy; and providing material infrastructure and technical equipment, such as community radio stations and social media blog networks.
- **Strengthening press accountability and oversight agencies** – such as supporting the work of independent Broadcasting Authorities, industry Press Councils, complaints commissions, ombudsmen, voluntary codes of professional conduct, human rights NGOs, and media watch organizations.[19]
- **Monitoring** – including generating official media statistics, household surveys of media use, media sector audits, and cross-national ranking indices of freedom of the press, internet censorship, media sustainability, open and transparent governance, access to ICTs, and rights to information.

Among bilateral donors, USAID illustrates this subsector of work, since it has supported independent media since the 1980s, as part of its promotion of democracy and civil societies.[20] Early programs focused on Latin America, training journalists, and assisting independent media outlets. In the 1990s, USAID launched a major effort to strengthen independent media in Eastern Europe and Eurasia. Case studies suggest that these efforts have sought to establish viable (if not always profitable) independent media outlets; improve professional journalistic standards; reform media laws and regulation; and promote media organizations committed to democracy and a free press. Recent efforts have increasingly focused upon digital media, supplementing traditional outlets. The agency recognizes that the threats and opportunities facing media assistance vary in different contexts, including in authoritarian, hybrid, and democratic states in developing and middle-income countries, as well as in postconflict societies.[21] Spending by USAID for 46 media freedom and freedom of information programs was around $76.3 million in 2012, with the largest investment in Africa and Europe/Eurasia, as well as hotspots in Iraq and Afghanistan.

Another example comes from International Media Support, a leading nonprofit organization working to support local media in countries affected by armed conflict, human insecurity, and political transition.[22] Established in Denmark in 2001 and funded by Nordic and international donors, the organization has an annual budget of around $US19 m. Their mission statement specifies their aims to promote press freedom, strengthen professional journalism, and ensure that media can operate in challenging circumstances. In practice, the organization's work involves providing protection for journalists, advocating media rights, promoting fair media laws, developing media business skills, supporting media unions and associations, providing training in digital platforms and technologies, and professionalizing reporting through media monitoring and specialized training, especially in investigative and conflict-sensitive journalism. In the Arab world, IMS has trained and supported media monitoring of elections in Egypt, Tunisia, Lebanon, and Bahrain in cooperation with a network of Arab human rights organizations. Programs have been implemented in war zones and failed states (such as Syria), in postconflict transitions (such as Afghanistan), in hybrid regimes and countries emerging from authoritarianism (such as Somalia and Niger), and in authoritarian states with major restrictions on press freedom (such as Azerbaijan).

Journalism Education and Training Programs

Among all these activities, one of the most common forms of international media assistance programming is supporting colleges with the provision of education and professional journalism training. These programs are designed for those who go on to become news workers employed in the print, broadcasting, and digital media sectors, as well as independent bloggers and online activists, as well as developing communication and media management skills for broader stakeholders in the public, nonprofit, and private sectors, such as public relations, market researchers, campaign communication specialists, and press officers.

Media assistance programs typically support long-term college programs in mass communications, journalism, and media studies, as well as short-term training workshops by NGOs and journalism educators seeking to strengthen specific types of professional knowledge and communication skills, such as photojournalism, investigative journalism, or business management. Media assistance may also be targeted towards expanding educational opportunities for particular groups and sectors who are underrepresented in newsrooms, like women, young people, and ethnic minorities. Fellowship programs also seek to build professional capacity by supporting midcareer journalists seeking to study in communication and media studies departments and centers abroad.[23] Online journalism training courses for distance learning (MOOCs) are increasingly available. For example, UNESCO has published extensive guides for journalists on a range of topics from conflict-sensitive reporting to investigative reporting and produced online curricula, including a model curricula for journalism education. Online media and information literacy courses are offered by the Centre for International Media Assistance, the European Journalism Centre, the International Center for Journalists, the Knight Center for Journalism in the Americas, Poynter Online, and others.

Resources are also invested in deepening national educational networks in developing countries, designed to strengthen teaching curricula and research opportunities in professional journalism and communication programs in colleges and universities. During the last twenty years, thousands of university departments and educational programs in journalism, mass communications, public relations, advertising, and media studies have been established in all regions around the world. Reviews have identified more than 2,300 journalism education programs, with rapid growth in places such as China and India.[24] These are connected through global networks such as the World Journalism Education Council, the International Communications Association, and the Association for Education in Journalism and Mass Communications, as well as by regional organizations like the European Journalism Training Association and the Asian Media Information Center, national associations, and professional meetings.[25]

The types of education content can be roughly divided into two categories. One focuses on *how* to be a journalist. Vocationally oriented educational programs in journalism, mass communications, and media studies aim to improve practical and technical skills, where journalism is regarded as a craft, such as in the use of digital platforms, techniques of data mining, editing and production, business management, market research, and specialist training on specific policy issues such as economics, international relations, or environmental studies. Short-term training courses are also offered in countries transitioning from autocracy to expand knowledge about politics, campaigns, and elections, such as awareness of election laws and regulations, registration and voting procedures, and the use of opinion polls.

Beyond these areas, educational and training programs also seek to influence more general news practices, ethical standards, values, and role orientations, or *what* exactly journalists do. If they succeed in this regard, programs may have a more profound effect on media cultures by shaping how the next generation of news workers come to see their core professional roles, duties, and responsibilities, expectations for professional conduct, work practices, and behavioral norms. What is taught in the curricula about the values and norms of journalism remains diverse in countries around the world, even across within Western Europe, rather than conforming to a single ideal model of objective and neutral professional journalism that is common in the United States.[26] Some argue that in the past it was commonly assumed that training programs for journalists in the developing world should follow a particular Western/American model, but this tendency has now faded, so that today education more commonly reflects local norms, practices, and customs.[27] Others suggest that, compared with twenty years ago, the quality of journalism education programs has made considerable improvement in the acquisition of technical craft skills, such as the use of new communication platforms and digital technologies, but that the overall quality remains more uneven worldwide in terms of teaching journalism ethics, values, roles, and professional standards.[28]

The Concept of Journalistic Roles

Journalist roles are understood as a set of expectations governing the behavior of individuals and institutions holding a particular function in society.[29] By defining how persons and institutions should and do work, roles have both normative and empirical dimensions. Journalistic roles are expected to be acquired from many sources, including from personal background and experiences, formal education, one-the-job training, observation of media routines and practices, guidance from employers and coworkers, formal codes and standards of professional conduct, practical job experience, organizational structures, and the incentives in the workplace.[30]

Many standards can be used to evaluate the performance of media assistance programs. Assessment depends upon notions of how journalists are expected to function both in general and within the context of election campaigns.[31] These are contentious matters for genuine debate. Traditional values are also under challenge from technological and economic developments and the multiplicity of communication channels. The role of unpaid citizen bloggers and freelance commentators on social media platforms muddies traditional boundaries of professional journalism who used to be employees or freelancers working for news organizations. For example, should journalists see their role as advocates for social change or more neutral observers of events? Committed partisans or evenhanded and open-minded critics of all sides? Opinion commentators or investigative reporters? Providers of popular infotainment or public educators on civics and current affairs? This chapter focuses on identifying how journalists see their roles in a wide range of countries, including as investigative watchdogs, neutral reporters, and unofficial spokespersons. The types of roles that journalists believe are appropriate are expected to influence the informal rules and routine practices in newsrooms and the predominant media culture in any society, as well as the quality of political communications, electoral integrity, and the independent media.

Some scholars suggests that journalists around the world have gradually come to converge in their values and norms, where the ideals of objectivity and impartiality dominate newsrooms across the globe, and one can find many similarities in professional routines, editorial procedures, and socialization processes in diverse countries.[32] Yet others caution that there is far less consensus. For example, Weaver compared surveys of journalists conducted in 21 countries and he concluded: "There are strong national differences that override any universal professional norms or values of journalism around the world."[33] Conversely, a number of other comparative studies have documented cross-national contrasts in role orientations and media cultures, even within relatively similar Europe societies, which are attributed to the national context rather than individual factors.[34] Even where there is a broad consensus about ideal role orientations, moreover, these may not reflect newsroom practices, given barriers arising from constraints by the state, the market, and the profession.[35]

Neutral Reporters

Perhaps the most common ideal is one where, as *neutral reporters*, the role of journalists is to serve as strictly impartial actors, providing factual reporting corroborated by credible sources of evidence, without expression of partisan preferences, personal judgments, or political leanings.[36] In this view, journalists should strive to be unbiased and nonpartisan recorders of events, prioritizing principles such as objectivity, neutrality, fairness, accuracy, detachment, and impartiality. This approach is particularly common in the United States, and it can also be observed among European public broadcasters. This conception sees journalists as seeking to report competing sides in controversial debates, functioning as evenhanded gatekeepers bringing together a plurality of diverse interests, political parties, viewpoints, arguments, and social sectors to comment about issues of public concern, but not advocating or favoring any particular perspective.[37] The notion of balance is sometimes taken to mean that all sides in any debate should be given equivalent length of coverage (using principles such as stopwatch television news) and/or equivalent positive-negative directional tone. This idea is particularly important for generating a level field in election campaign communications where all parties and candidates are given similar coverage. Beyond elections, the notion of balance has been widely used to describe the general process of news selection, whether arising from the individual editorial decisions about the choice of headline topics, images, or specific stories, or the broader balance of voices, parties, and interests that are represented as sources, authoritative spokespersons, or leaders in news coverage. Based on these ideas, media watch organizations and international observers routinely monitor media reporting during election campaigns to document how much broadcasting time and print coverage was devoted to incumbents and challengers, whether journalists faced any obstacles or censorship, and whether any media outlets faced interference from authorities.[38]

Engaged Watchdogs

As *watchdogs*, liberal theories suggest that the independent news media should probe issues deeply to uncover new facts and reveal problems, investigate abuses of power, and thereby provide a check and balance on powerful sectors of society, including leaders within the public and private domains.[39] This represents the classic notion of the news media as the fourth estate, counterbalancing the power of the executive, legislative, and judiciary branches. According to this notion, investigative journalists should keep a skeptical eye on the powerful, guarding the public interest and protecting it from incompetence, corruption, and misinformation. The watchdog role for reporters is sufficiently broad, fluid, and open to encompass both a more neutral function – as an evenhanded disseminator of information about public affairs that were previously hidden from public attention (such as the scandal of child sexual abuse within the Catholic church) – and a more active role as an investigator of the behavior of decision-makers or even as an adversary of the powerful (exemplified by the events of Watergate). The Nieman Foundation for Journalism at Harvard University, specified the role as follows:

> The premise of watchdog journalism is that the press is a surrogate for the public, asking probing, penetrating questions at every level, from the town council to the state house to the White House, as well as in corporate and professional offices, in union halls, on university campuses and in religious organizations that seek to influence governmental actions. The goal of watchdog journalism is to see that people in power provide information the public should have.[40]

Engaged watchdogs are also concerned to mobilize public concern about issues.

The defining feature of watchdog journalism is not the political stance of the reporter, story, or media outlet, but rather the task of asking hard or probing questions of powerful interests to maximize transparency and serve the public interest. Watchdogs may also seek to champion causes and advocate social change based on underlying problems revealed in their investigations. On a routine basis, timely and accurate information provided by news coverage of elections and public affairs should help citizens evaluate the performance of political leaders and parties during election campaigns, for example, the government record in improving economic growth, health care, or schools. Investigative reporting in elections commonly highlights failures, especially those arising from cases of bribery, fraud, corruption, and malfeasance; from abuse of power by electoral authorities or repressive governments; or from incompetent management of public service delivery, such as the delivery of ballot papers or the accuracy of the vote tally. Through this process, journalists should help to facilitate informed choice by citizens during elections. Ideally reporters investigate claims made by public officials and scrutinize the action of public and corporate elites, irrespective of the party in power, economic advantage, or personal biases, to advance the broader public interest. The media can give whistleblowers a voice, spearhead the downfall of powerful politicians, and expose widespread corruption. Public disclosure and transparency, though not sufficient by itself to stamp out these problems, is regarded as the sunshine that can act as a disinfectant to eradicate cases of malfeasance, to bring official misconduct to the attention of the electorate and the courts, and to deter others from similar behaviors. The liberal notion of reporters as watchdogs is one widely subscribed to by journalists in many democratic states, as confirmed by surveys of journalists in Sweden, the United States, and Britain.[41] At the same time, it is also challenged by those who believe that too much exposé journalism undermines faith and trust in elections, reducing legitimacy, fueling conflict and instability, and thereby undermining fragile states.

Unofficial Spokesmen for the Authorities

Finally, journalists may see themselves alternatively as serving mainly as loyal unofficial spokesmen to those in authority. In this regard, journalists regard their primary job as providing a channel conveying positive news about the government and their policies, informing the public about the activities and speeches of party leaders, official press releases, and ministerial statements. This form of journalism positions itself as consensual and nonadversarial, supporting established authorities, and expressing loyalty to those in power, as well as possibly guiding public opinion. As Hanitzsch describes this role: "These journalists pay disproportionately high attention to the authorities and rarely question the official version of the story. Instead, they accept information provided by government sources as authoritative, credible, and trustworthy, and they often become public relations channels for the transmission of government messages to the public."[42] This role perception may be particularly strong in non-Western countries, in postconflict settings, in newly independent countries, and in deeply divided fragile states, where regimes are seeking to build their legitimacy and authority against conflict, instability, and active security threats. It may also be seen as the traditional role of journalists, editors, and producers in practice where they are employed in state-owned media in the world's most repressive states, such as in Egypt under Sisi and Syria under Bashar al-Assad, where journalists openly critical of the regime face the threat of imprisonment, exile, or even death.[43]

The Causes of Role Orientations

Given these distinctions, do education and professional journalism training in colleges have the capacity to shape journalistic role orientations, as often assumed by programs of media assistance, especially by strengthening the norms and values of impartial reporting and investigative watchdog journalism? Unfortunately, previous evidence on this issue remains inconclusive.[44] In particular, despite the popularity of training and educational initiatives, and their potential value in providing technical and vocational skills, there is little systematic evidence whether these have the capacity to alter the predominant values and practices embedded in media cultures. A recent review concluded that most previous project evaluations of media assistance training programs have involved simple assessments of short-term activities.[45] For example, a series of media workshops are typically assessed in results-based management reports by counting the number and type of journalist who attended, or by consultants using a simple standard survey checklist to measure satisfaction among participants after these events. The results are commonly used to report activities to donors and executive bodies, and to satisfy the agencies' standard accountability systems for program managers. But it is unclear whether the formal audit of particular programs achieves rigorous evidence or in-depth insights or broader lessons which could determine assistance priorities and improve future activities in this subsector.

In addition, the effectiveness of educational initiatives for journalists is open to measurement by many alternative criteria and metrics. Media curriculum may be designed to foster specific practical, vocational, and technical skills, such as the use of digital platforms, multimedia reporting, and broadcasting production techniques. Classes may be designed to deepen ethical standards, alter engrained cultural attitudes and values, and change newsroom practices. A review for USAID media projects by Krishna Kumar highlighted many limitations with their impact. Much international media assistance has been driven by the donor agencies, he argues, rather than reflecting genuine local demands. It has also focused on short-term training workshops and fellowships to study abroad, rather than creating sustainable domestic educational institutions, such as supporting local colleges, schools, and departments of communications that gradually build media capacity over time.[46] In developing countries, government-funded communication programs have grown in universities and colleges, but many of these face tough challenges in the standards they offer, due to a lack of sufficient funding, practical experience, competent faculty, IT access, affordable textbooks, and up-to-date curricula.[47] International training may also seek to foster Western perspectives about journalistic norms of behavior and ethical values that may confront traditional notions about the appropriate role of journalists within a media culture. International media assistance may also be viewed with suspicion and rejected by governments as attempts at foreign interference. As Kumar concluded:

While their overall contribution has been both positive and significant, many training projects initiated (by USAID) in the 1990s in the Balkans, Eastern Europe, and Eurasia suffered from limitations. Sometimes training was undertaken without a systematic needs assessment. Little effort was made to ascertain specific needs of the local journalists that could be addressed through training. Much of the training in the early 1990s was conducted by expatriates, who had neither proficiency in the local language nor sufficient understanding of the environment in which the trainees worked. The selection of the participants has been problematic in many cases. Because of the time pressure and limited dissemination of information about the training facilities, journalists from small media outlets or from remote areas were often underrepresented. Short-term training courses of a day or two proved of limited value, and in Eastern Europe and Eurasia, USAID and other international donors made quite limited investment in long-term training. Many international NGOs preferred to provide direct training or to establish their own institutes rather than work with local universities and other institutions.[48]

Similarly a review of investigative journalisms programs by Kaplan concluded that unfortunately much media training is ad hoc, short-term, individualistic, episodic, and unsustainable, ignoring the structural constraints on the quality of journalism, such as pressures on reporters from powerful elites, advertisers, and owners, state restrictions on the independent media and freedom of expression, and cultures of corruption.[49] Echoing these concerns, Price call for initiatives focusing on the enabling environment of the news media, rather than short-term training.[50] Buckley and coauthors also maintain that it is not sufficient for reform efforts to focus on policies to train journalists or extend access to information without addressing issues of media independence, pluralism, accessibility, and capacity.[51]

The Consequences of Role Orientation

Turning to the second step, a cross-national review of previous research has demonstrated the general link between the strength of the free press in any country and levels of electoral integrity and democratization.[52] Hence Birch and van Ham argue that effective oversight institutions are both necessary and sufficient to scrutinize the electoral process, to deter potential malpractices like vote rigging, and to strengthen transparency. Evidence from their comparative study suggests that the risks of electoral malpractices can be reduced by either an active and independent judiciary and/or an active and independent media.[53] They suggest that by exposing fraud, coercion, and the manipulation of elections, the independent media can provide one of the main safeguards on the potential abuse of executive power. My previous book in this trilogy also compared cross-national evidence and established that freedom of the press (measured by Reporters Without Borders and Freedom House) generally serves as an important safeguard of the electoral process, restricting malfeasance (measured by the PEI index). This relationship was observed after controlling for different types of horizontal institutional checks and balances, such as proportional representation electoral systems, strong parliaments, and structural conditions providing threats and opportunities for electoral assistance.[54] Case studies illustrate the underlying processes and suggest that in countries such as the Philippines, Mexico, and Russia, independent media have served as a powerful watchdog and agenda-setter safeguarding against electoral malpractices, informing the public about abuses of power, and mobilizing pressures for reform, through highlighting acts such as ballot rigging, voter fraud, and campaign finance scandals.[55] The news media can also serve a positive function for the quality of elections where reports strengthen the transparency of the electoral process, revealing malpractices like fraud or vote-rigging. By contrast, lack of an independent media silences the voices of potential critics and makes it difficult or dangerous for reporters to highlight abuses of power by the ruling elites, for example in countries such as Syria, Turkmenistan, North Korea, and Eritrea, ranked lowest out of 180 countries worldwide in the Reporters without Borders 2016 *World Press Freedom Index* and where broadcasters remain under the thumb of the state.[56]

Nevertheless, the underlying processes that are driving this relationship remain unclear, and it still needs to be established whether it is a consequences of journalistic role orientations and practice, or it is arising from other factors, such as the legal framework or the structure of newspaper and television ownership and distribution. Here we test the assumption that media cultures where reporters see their roles as either impartial reporters or as investigative watchdogs are likely to strengthen the quality of campaign communications, electoral integrity, and liberal democracy (as positive societal impacts). Conversely, in media cultures where journalists see their roles as functioning as unofficial spokespersons for the regime authorities, these outcomes are predicted to be less likely to be achieved.

EVIDENCE

To examine the evidence, this chapter builds upon an extensive research literature seeking to understand the role orientations of journalists as an important indicator of national media cultures.[57] Previous studies have gathered data derived from surveys of representative samples of news workers, including monitoring professional routines, editorial procedures, and socialization processes, as well as work expectations and satisfaction. These data help to study particular sectors to contrast the roles of print versus broadcast reporters or to compare national media cultures.[58] Early studies compared media cultures in the United States with several other established democracies, including Germany, Great Britain, and Italy.[59] This approach has subsequently been extended globally to cover many low- and middle-income countries with diverse regimes, such as Brazil, Indonesia, Russia, China, Egypt, Bangladesh, Nepal, and Tanzania.[60]

For the most extensive comparison, we examine the Worlds of Journalism Survey (WJS), conducted among 27,000 journalists in 65 countries from 2012 to 2015.[61] This survey uses a common instrument to monitor how journalists prioritize the importance of a wide range of activities in their job, as well as collecting information about their reporting practices, ethical norms and standards, degree of editorial autonomy, and background sociodemographic characteristics and educational qualifications.[62] To understand the predominant media culture within each society, the survey results are analyzed at the national level.

Role orientations were analyzed using 11 items in the survey. Journalists were asked about the importance of a range of roles in their work using five-point Lickert-type scales. Factor analysis was used to identify clusters of items. As shown in Table 7.2, three roles emerged: that of being neutral reporters, engaged watchdogs, and unofficial spokespersons. The data in the table items were summed and used to construct 100-point standardized scales measuring the importance of each role in each media culture.

TABLE 7.1 *Journalist Role Orientations*

	Neutral Reporters	Mobilizing Watchdogs	Unofficial Spokespersons
Report things as they are	.826		
Provide analysis of current affairs	.815		
Set the political agenda		.598	
Monitor and scrutinize political leaders		.945	
Monitor and scrutinize business		.855	
Provide information people need to make political decisions		.848	
Motivate people to participate in political activity		.645	
Support government policy			.890
Provide the kind of news that attracts the largest audience			.854
Convey a positive image of political leadership			.849
Influence public opinion			.775
% variance	10.8	21.7	46.5

Notes: Question: Please tell me how important each of these things is in your work. Scale: 5 = extremely important; 4 = very important; 3 = somewhat important; 2 = little important; 1 = unimportant. Extraction Method using Principal Component Factor Analysis with Varimax rotation and Kaiser Normalization.
Source: Worlds of Journalism survey 2012–14.

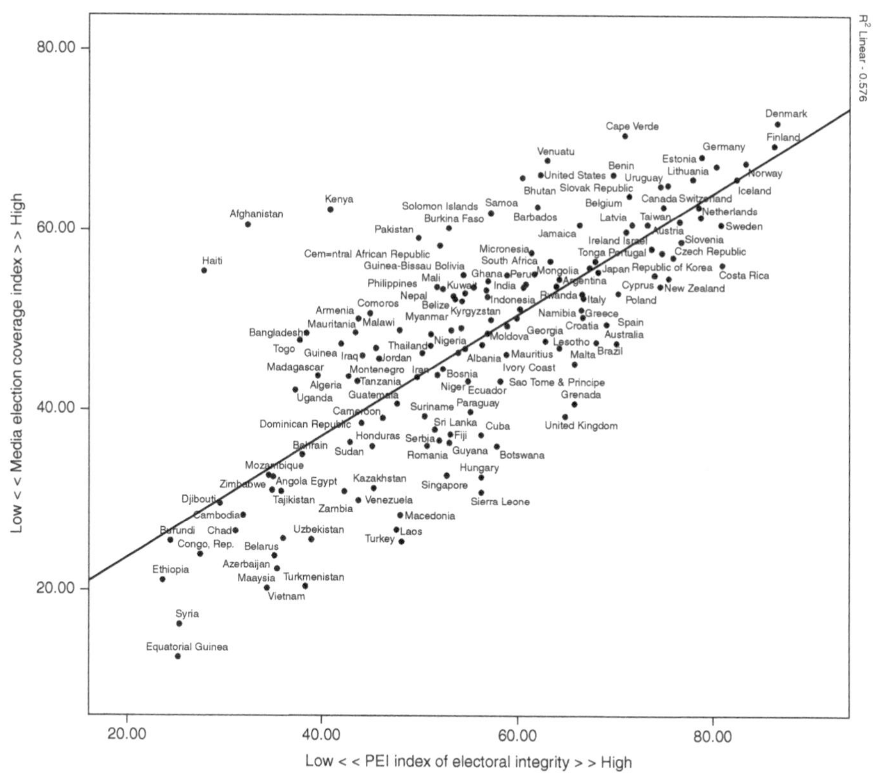

FIGURE 7.3. The quality of media campaign coverage and levels of electoral integrity. Source: Perceptions of Electoral Integrity, PEI-4.5.

To monitor their consequences and provide an independent and reliable assessment of the quality of the media campaign and overall levels of electoral integrity in each country, data is derived from the PEI-4.5 cross-national expert assessments. PEI data was matched with the WJS survey to cover national parliamentary and presidential elections held in the same countries and during the same years (see Chapter 4 for details). The PEI-4.5 dataset covers 213 national parliamentary and presidential contests held from July 1, 2012 to June 31, 2016 in 153 countries worldwide. In total, this we compare 59 countries contained in both the WJS and PEI surveys. Standard measures assessing levels of media independence and press freedom were used (from Freedom House's Freedom of the Press annual indices) and for levels of democratizations (using the combined Freedom House/Polity measure). In addition, the multivariate models controlled for several factors, which previous research suggests is likely to influence electoral integrity and democratization, such as levels of economic development.

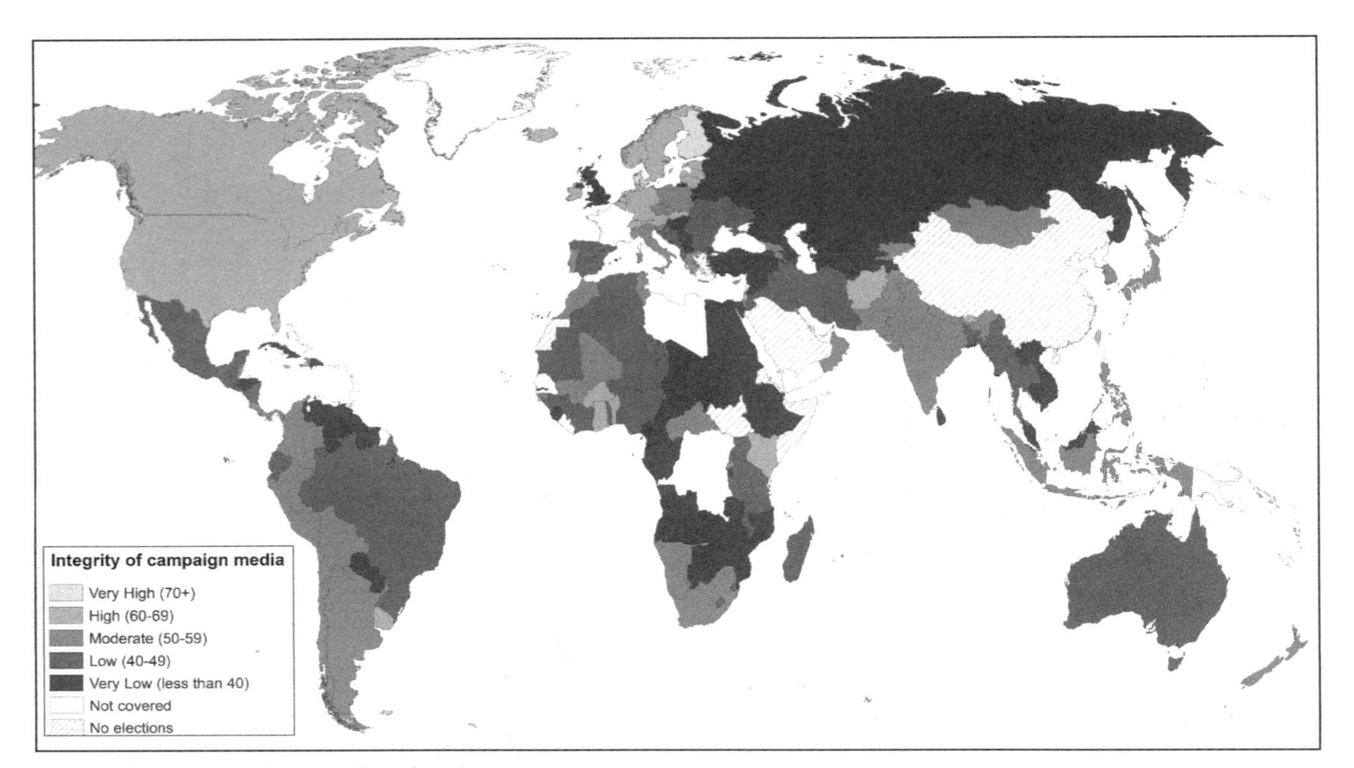

FIGURE 7.4. Global map of the quality of media campaign coverage.
Source: Perceptions of Electoral Integrity, PEI-4.5.

To illustrate the problems observed worldwide using some of these indices, Figure 7.3 illustrates the expert assessments about the quality of campaign communications in each country (on the vertical axis) compared with the overall PEI Index of electoral Integrity in each country (depicted on the horizontal axis). As previous research has emphasized, not surprisingly, these two indices are strongly correlated (R = .759***). The results demonstrate that the freer, more fair, and more balanced the media coverage, – such as in Denmark, Finland, and Estonia – the higher the overall level of electoral integrity. By contrast, suppression of independent journalism in countries such as Syria, Ethiopia, and Equatorial Guinea is associated with worse quality elections. There are a few outliers, however, where countries like Kenya and Afghanistan score more highly in media campaign coverage than in the overall PEI index, probably due to other serious problems of violence and corruption that occur at later stage in these contests. To make sense of the global picture, Figure 7.4 maps the quality of campaign media around the world and indicates that the worst ratings of campaign media are common in sub-Saharan Africa and Central Asia, as well as a showing patchy performance in South America.

RESULTS

The Impact of Education on Journalistic Role Orientations

The first issue to analyze is whether role perceptions are shaped by formal educational experiences, especially training through journalism, communication, and media studies degrees, as widely assumed by media assistance programs. Table 7.2 presents the results of multivariate OLS regression models testing the effects at a macrolevel of college education (the proportion of journalists holding a university or college degree), and the impact of professional journalism training (the smaller proportion of journalists holding a degree in journalism, mass communications, or media studies) on the three role orientations, with controls.

The results demonstrate that (contrary to popular wisdom) according to this evidence, *the predominant role perceptions in each society are not significantly linked with the proportion of journalists with formal college education nor the proportion with formal college journalism training*. The main factors which seem to influence these roles are levels of freedom of the press and economic development. In particular, the conception of journalists functioning as neutral and impartial reporters is most common in more affluent postindustrial societies and those with independent media. By contrast, the idea that journalists should function as unofficial spokespersons or press officers for the regime authorities is most common in repressive autocracies lacking freedom of the press and in developing societies. Finally, the idea of journalists as engaged watchdogs presents a more mixed profile, as this is significantly more popular in

TABLE 7.2 *The Societal Impacts of Journalist Role Orientations*

	Model 1 PEI Campaign Media Index			Model 2 PEI Electoral Integrity Index			Model 3 FH Freedom of the Press			Model 4 Level of Democratization		
	B	s.e.	Sig	B	s.e.	Sig	B	s.e.	Sig	B	s.e.	Sig
JOURNALIST ROLE ORIENTATIONS												
Neutral reporters (WJS)	.361	.285	N/s	**.498**	**.211**	*	**.679**	**.254**	**	**.133**	**.032**	***
Engaged watchdogs (WJS)	.039	.175	N/s	.025	.129	N/s	.103	.156	N/s	−.011	.020	N/s
Unofficial spokesperson (WJS)	−.302	.173	N/s	**−.444**	**.128**	***	**−.748**	**.154**	***	**−.072**	**.020**	***
JOURNALIST EDUCATION												
% of journalists holding a university degree (WJS)	14.2	12.4	N/s	−6.85	9.21	N/s	7.96	11.0	N/s	−.317	1.40	N/s
% of journalists with a journalism/ communication degree (WJS)	.122	7.62	N/s	−1.57	5.65	N/s	7.62	6.8	N/s	.953	.860	N/s
CONTROLS												
Economic development (per capita GDP ppp in current $) World Bank	.000	.000	N/s				.001	.001	**	.001	.001	N/s
Constant	22.3			50.0			52.1			2.10		
Adjusted R^2	.289			.689			.767			.653		
N. countries	56			56			56			56		

Notes: The coefficients represent the unstandardized beta (B), the standard errors (s.e.) and their significance. * = .05, ** = .01, *** = .001 N/s Not significant. Figures in bold are statistically significant. The Campaign Media index and the Electoral Integrity index are from PEI-4.5. The Freedom House measure is the mean Press Freedom score 1993–2014. The level of democratization score is the combined Freedom House/Imputed Polity. The role orientations and background are from the World of Journalism Survey (WJS) 2012–2014.
Sources: See above note.

developed societies but there is no significant link to freedom of the press. Further analysis using alternative controls did not alter the interpretations of the results. The notion that news workers should be unofficial spokespersons for the regime was particularly common in Africa, the Middle East and Asia, but endorsed far less by reporters in Western societies.

The overall results suggest that formal education in schools and departments of journalism and communications may develop professional technical skills about *how* to communicate in the digital age, building vocational skills, but this does not mean that the experience will necessarily convey common values in the priorities for *what* journalists should do. The implication is that media assistance programs can support the proliferation of new journalism education schools in states such as China, but the values and norms of trained graduates who enter the news media is likely to reinforce, rather than challenge, long-established practices within this media culture.[63]

Examining the Consequences of Journalistic Roles for Electoral Integrity

Turning to the second stage, the consequences of journalistic roles and media cultures can be assessed against four indices. The Perception of Electoral Integrity expert survey (PEI-4.5) is used to measure the severity of the challenges arising throughout all eleven sequential stages in the electoral cycle, as discussed in Chapter 4. All stages are aggregated for the Perception of Electoral Integrity Index. The Campaign Media index is composed of five items within the PEI survey: whether newspapers provided balanced coverage, whether television news favored the governing party, whether parties/candidates had fair access to political broadcasts and advertising, whether journalists provided fair election coverage, and whether social media were used to expose electoral fraud. These items are aggregated to generate the standardized 100-point Campaign Media index. Each of these items was selected as an important part of the communications environment during election campaigns, engaging different actors. As shown earlier in Figure 4.4 assessing the most common problems of electoral integrity in contests around the globe, the campaign media index has the second worst rating for any stage of the whole electoral cycle, with only campaign finance evaluated more poorly (an issue discussed in the next chapter). Finally, models also tested the effects of role orientations on the annual indexes on freedom of the press generated by Freedom House,[64] and also on general levels of democratization as measured by the combined Freedom House/Polity index.[65]

To assess the impact of role orientations upon these indices, Table 7.3 presents the regression analysis models after controlling for economic development. The results in Model 1 show that none of the roles had a significant impact upon the expert assessments of the campaign media. At the same time, however, Models 2–4 demonstrate that after controlling for development, countries where the media culture prioritized the roles of

TABLE 7.3 *Professional Education and Role Orientations*

	Model 1 Neutral Reporters			Model 2 Engaged watchdogs			Model 3 Unofficial Spokesperson		
	B	s.e.	Sig.	B	s.e.	Sig.	B	s.e.	Sig.
JOURNALIST EDUCATION									
% of journalists holding a university degree (WJS)	–.10.6	5.97	N/s	13.4	10.3	N/s	5.3	8.5	N/s
% of journalists with a journalism/ communication degree (WJS)	.010	3.73	N/s	.927	6.46	N/s	1.83	5.30	N/s
CONTROLS									
Freedom of the press (FH 1993–2014)	.174	.045	***	–.107	.079	N/s	–.567	.064	***
Economic development (per capita GDP ppp in current $) World Bank	.001	.001	***	.000	.000	*	.001	.001	**
Constant	.110			70.8			110		
Adjusted R^2	.293			.214			.785		
N. countries	55			55			55		

Notes: The coefficients represent the unstandardized beta (B), the standard errors (s.e.) and their significance. * =.05, ** =.01, ***=.001 N/s Not significant. The Press Freedom score is the mean Freedom House index 1993–2014. The level of economic development is per capita GDP in purchasing Power Parity in current US$ from the World Bank indicators. The role orientations and background are from the World of Journalism Survey (WJS) 2012–2014.
Sources: See above note.

journalists as neutral reporters showed higher levels of electoral integrity, freedom of the press, and levels of democratization. Conversely, the opposite picture was evident in countries where journalists often saw their function as unofficial spokespersons for the regime, where there were lower levels of electoral integrity, freedom of the press, and levels of democratization. The levels of formal college education and training in journalism were not significantly associated with the indices. Robustness tests using alternative measures of independent media generated similar results.[66]

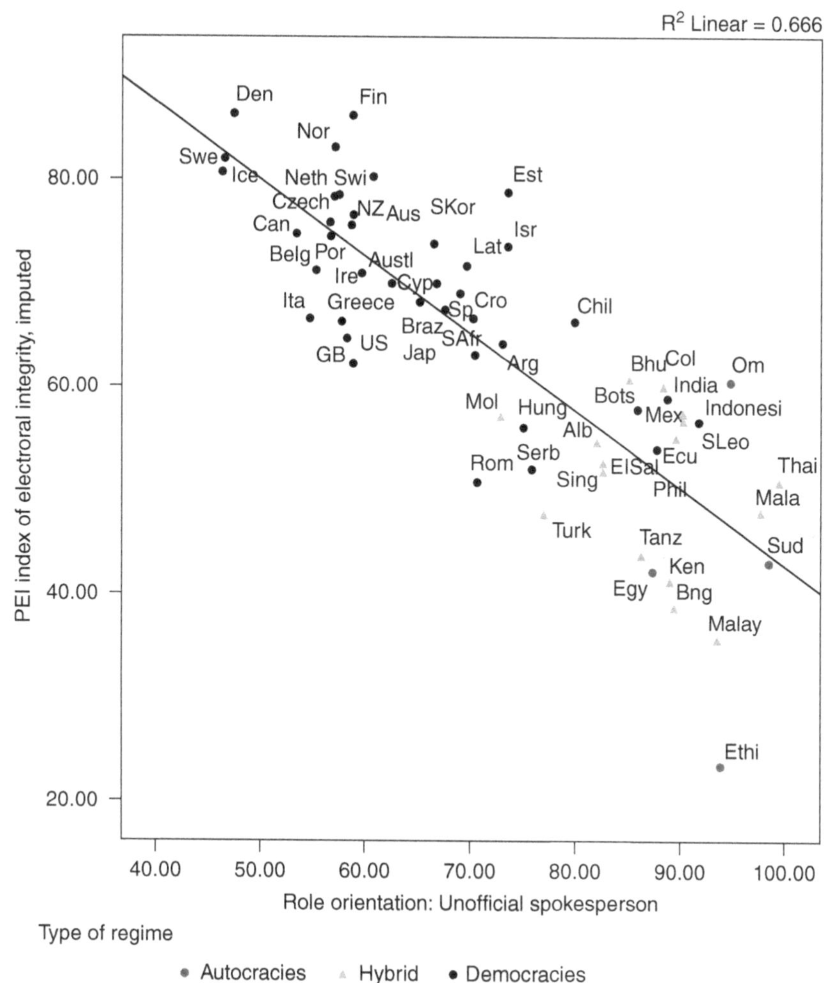

FIGURE 7.5. Journalist roles and electoral integrity.
Notes: See Chapter 4 for the construction of the standardized PEI Index. See Table 8.1 for the survey items in the WJS role orientation standardized scales.
Sources: Perceptions of Electoral Integrity survey PEI-4.5 2012–2016; Worlds of Journalism survey 2012–2014.

To examine the patterns more closely, Figure 7.5 illustrates the strong correlations between the priority given to the roles of serving as unofficial spokespersons for the regime in each society (measured by the WJS survey) and levels of electoral integrity (measured by PEI). Thus in countries like Ethiopia, Bangladesh, and Sudan, the deferential and consensual media culture allows problems of electoral malpractice to be downplayed in the public sphere. By contrast, in states such as Denmark, Sweden, and the Czech Republic, there is strong rejection of this passive role, so that any flaws and failures that arise in election campaigns and their aftermath are more likely to be reported critically by the press. This helps to account for the strong relationship observed in previous cross-national research linking freedom of the press and electoral integrity.[67]

CONCLUSIONS

Interventions designed to strengthen electoral coverage by the independent media typically include advocating strengthening rights to freedom of information, expression, and publication in law; supporting the deregulation of state ownership of broadcasting to facilitate a plurality of independent channels; investing in the infrastructure supporting diverse community radio stations, newspapers, and websites; and reforming professional journalistic training and accreditation bodies. It is also very common to assist with the provision of education and training programs that seek to foster the professional skills of news workers. Programs focused upon strengthening the capacity of journalists, through college departments of journalism and communications, and through more specialized short-term training workshops, are supported by many multilateral agencies, governments, donors, professional journalism bodies, and nongovernmental organizations (NGOs). The question addressed by this chapter is whether professional education strengthens the roles of the independent media and whether these roles contribute towards electoral integrity, the free press, and democratization processes.

Work roles can be conceptualized in many ways. Ideally as *neutral reporters*, journalists seek to reflect a balanced plurality of viewpoints and persuasions from all parties and sectors of society, thereby maximizing the diversity of arguments heard in political debates, informing electoral choices, and enriching the public sphere. As *engaged watchdogs*, journalists help to guard the public interest during campaigns by fact-checking statements by candidates and leaders and by warning about problems in the past performance and record of those seeking elected office, especially highlighting any cases of corruption or maladministration, thereby ensuring that accurate information is available for citizens to judge the record and experiences of candidates seeking their support.[68] They can also raise awareness of pervasive problems and advocate reforms, thereby mobilizing public concern about issues. By contrast, as *unofficial spokespersons* for the regime authorities, reporters are deferential towards the ruling party and leadership elites, providing positive coverage of official news bulletins, speeches, and events, but failing to provide critical commentary, independent assessment of their record, and balanced coverage of the government and opposition parties.

This analysis of the evidence suggests two key findings: First, as theorized, *the predominant role orientations in national media cultures* (monitored through the surveys) *are significantly associated with indicators of overall levels of electoral integrity in each country* (both measured by PEI), *freedom of the press, and levels of democratization*. In particular, where journalists regard their role as unofficial spokespersons for the regime authorities (like ministerial press officers, providing positive images of political leaders and supporting government policies), this damages the quality of levels of electoral integrity, press freedom, and processes of democratization.

Second, *it remains unclear from the evidence considered in this chapter whether formal college education and journalistic training programs have the capacity to alter the predominant way that journalists see their work*. Role orientations seem to be deeply embedded within national media cultures and the product of levels of economic development and freedom of the press rather than the product of formal college education. At the same time, this study looked broadly at macrolevel patterns. We lack individual-level evidence monitoring the effects of specific training projects. But if the experience of studying journalism in college for three or four years does not influence the predominant work roles in media cultures, then the effects of any short-term training workshops supported by development agencies are expected to have even less impact upon shaping role orientations, journalistic values, and media cultures. Nevertheless, the evidence for this claim deserves to be examined more closely in future evaluations using program and project-level data with other types of research, such as through pre/post randomized experimental designs and/or surveys of workshop participants.

In conclusion, therefore, training and capacity building programs for journalists are likely to continue to be one common form of media assistance offered by development agencies and domestic stakeholders, but these types of activities can be expected to strengthen useful technical skills for news workers, improving *how* they do their work, more than altering their underlying ethical standards and values, and *what* they do. Many alternative types of policy interventions are available to supplement training and strengthen the quality of news coverage by independent media during election campaigns. This includes through working with local NGOs advocating legal reforms of the regulatory framework (such as lobbying for Freedom of Information laws and protecting journalists), expanding investment in the digital infrastructure in poorer countries and fighting internet censorship in repressive states (to widen public access to pluralistic communication platforms), and building the domestic capacity for systematic media monitoring (to highlight problems in election coverage). The next chapter goes on to consider whether there are similar lessons for attempts to improve the regulation of money in politics, another major problem occurring in many countries, both rich and poor, during elections.

8

Regulating Political Finance

Political finance raises some of the most common problems of electoral integrity around the world. The Recruit scandal in Japan, the misuse of Westminster expenses in Britain, and Watergate in the United States exemplify long-established democracies rocked by major problems of financial malfeasance. In the United States, a series of Supreme Court decisions, including Citizens United v. the Federal Election Commission (2010) and McCutcheon v. FEC (2014), has dramatically expanded the ability of wealthy individuals, corporations, and groups to spend as much as they like to influence elections.[1] The Center for Responsive Politics estimated that $6 billion would be spent in the 2016 US elections by campaigns, political parties, and corporations hoping to propel their candidates into the White House and what Mark Twain once called the "best Congress money can buy."[2] In Europe, a review by Transparency International reports that party political finance is inadequately regulated and at high risks for corruption, parliaments are not living up to ethical standards, lobbying remains veiled in mystery, and access to financial information is limited, all fueling growing concern among the general public that corruption is on the rise in the region.[3] In the Mediterranean region, in particular, political corruption has damaged governments in Greece, Italy, and Spain.[4] Brazil has been rocked by the Petrobras scandal, resulting in the removal of President Dilma Rousseff from office, in which politicians are reported to have taken kickbacks in exchange for awarding public contracts. In the developing world, graft, malfeasance, and cronyism plague public affairs, delegitimize governments, and heighten conflict in countries such as Iraq, Afghanistan, Libya, Haiti, and Venezuela, all states rated poorly by Transparency International's 2015 Corruption Perception Index.[5] The World Bank estimates that about $1 trillion is paid each year in bribes around the world, and the total economic loss from corruption is estimated to be many times that number, harming prosperity, worsening crime, and hurting development, since the poor pay the highest share of bribes.[6]

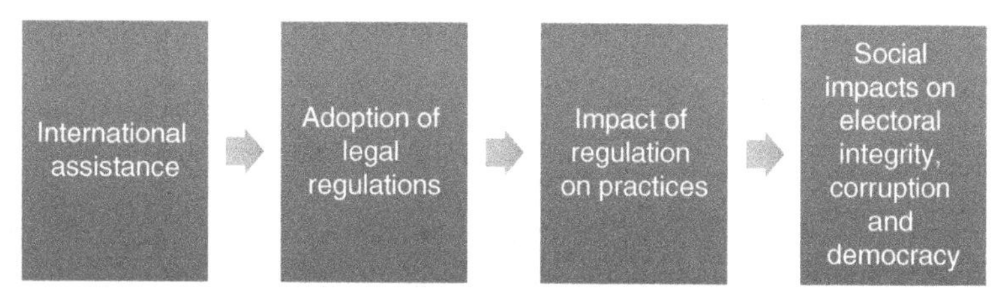

FIGURE 8.1. The chain-of-results framework for political finance reforms.

What policies are used in attempts to regulate political finance? And do these legal regulations work in practice by strengthening electoral integrity, reducing corruption, and improving democratic governance? There have been many case studies, but little recent systematic comparative research, and no established consensus about which public policies have proved most effective in regulating political and campaign finance – and which have largely failed to meet their objectives.[7] To consider these issues, the first section describes some of the key international actors engaged in this field of electoral assistance and classifies several types of policies designed to regulate the role of money in electoral politics. These range from light touch regulatory frameworks emphasizing transparency to more interventionist strategies involving direct public funding of political parties.

The second section identifies the potential effects of these policies upon short-term policy outputs. Figure 8.1 lays out the chair-of-results logic. As always, it is easiest to observe concrete program activities, such as the number of participants in civil society watchdog training groups, or how many tools, handbooks, and guidelines on political finance are published by international organizations engaged in this sector, such as Transparency International, International IDEA, or IFES. It is far more difficult to pin down with any certainty how far programs of electoral assistance in this subsector have contributed towards specific outcomes, such as whether technical advice and project support from the international community helped local stakeholders to establish new legal and administrative rules designed to regulate political finance spending and fundraising. Evidence in this study seeks to analyze whether the legal framework governing money in politics is actually implemented in practice. It even more challenging to establish any plausible evidence in the chain-of-results framework connecting legal reforms with more diffuse long-term societal and political objectives, such as the impact of laws upon electoral integrity, corruption, and democratic governance. The third section examines systematic cross-national evidence to see whether particular types of political finance regulations are plausibly associated with indicators of better elections. The conclusion in the fourth section considers the lessons learned and the implications for future campaign finance reforms.

TYPES OF REGULATORY POLICIES

During the last two decades, concern about corruption in general, especially in the public sector, has grown substantially among international agencies, national governments, and NGOs. Signs of change appeared following the fall of the Berlin Wall: in 1993, Transparency International was established in Germany and three years later this issue was championed at the World Bank in a seminal speech by James D. Wolfensohn attacking "the cancer of corruption" for its effects on the poor.[8] A decade later, the UN Convention against Corruption (UNCAC) came into force, the first legally binding international instrument designed to stamp out domestic and foreign bribery, embezzlement, money laundering, and influence peddling, endorsed by 178 governments.[9] Following this agreement, multilateral agencies expanded efforts to assist countries in meeting their international obligations under this convention, spearheaded by the United Nations Office of Drugs and Crime. Under their agenda on good governance, the World Bank has supported around 900 anticorruption projects across all sectors, spending around US$324 million on these initiatives in 2017.[10] In a recent report, they continue to emphasize the role of citizen engagement and transparency on effective development.[11] Initiatives by intergovernmental organizations are exemplified by International IDEA's series of political finance handbooks, reports, and online global database,[12] and a similar program on regulating money in politics by IFES.[13] Among regional organizations, the European Union has proposed reforms to standardize standards in party funding across member states,[14] while the OAS has issued guidelines for electoral observers when monitoring election fundraising and spending.[15] Numerous anticorruption reforms have been championed by national commissions, NGOs, and civil society networks of activists, notably by local branches of Transparency International, the Open Society Foundation, the Freedom of Information network, and many others.[16]

Several strategies are common in programs advocating political finance reforms to those used more generally to provide electoral assistance on in other subsectors, although organizations vary in their strategies according to their mission and resources. This includes monitoring general problems of integrity in the public sector through indices and ranking countries around the world; sharing technical and legal advice, toolkits, voluntary codes of conduct, and guidelines about best practices; capacity building and training enforcement authorities, electoral management bodies, official audit agencies and anticorruption commissions, including working with the police, judiciary, and watchdog groups in civil society; and supporting other local initiatives designed to strengthen transparency, expand accountability, and thereby improve standards of integrity in public life. As discussed in the previous chapter, strengthening the roles of the news and social media, especially watchdog journalism following the money spent in election campaigns, is an important part of these initiatives.

The issue of political finance has been at the heart of concern about problems of corruption, transparency, and accountability in the public sector, including electoral practices such as illicit acts, influence peddling, vote-buying, and the distribution of patronage. There is widespread endorsement within the international community that integrity should lie at the heart of any attempts to regulate political finance. For example, the UN handbook states that "The national electoral law must also protect the political process from corruption, official malfeasance, obstruction, undue influence, personating, bribery, treating, intimidation and all other forms of illegal and corrupt practice."[17] States need to stamp out illegal acts such as bribery, vote-buying, corruption, extortion, kickbacks, cronyism, graft, embezzlement, malfeasance, and outright criminality. These are common problems in several developing countries. In India, for example, reforms to the system of political financing have led unfortunately to unintended consequences through encouraging increasing numbers of candidates with criminal records to run for office.[18] In recent Mexican elections, criminal violence, intimidation, and corruption from drug cartels have also had a major impact upon.[19], The role of money in autocratic regimes in the worst cases has facilitated rentier states, oligarchies, and kleptocracies.

Problems of money in politics are also often far subtler, such as lack of a level playing field in campaign resources or failure to disclose all sources of party income in public records, and indeed flaws may well reflect practices that are perfectly legal and regarded as above board. The broadest concept of political finance defines this as "money for electioneering," including resources spent by candidates for public office, by political parties, and by other individuals/organized groups.[20] This includes party funds, as it remains difficult to draw a precise line between the resources used for routine political activities, such as building local party organizations, conducting polls, paying staff, or contacting supporters, and those used for electioneering during the official campaign period. Moreover, the topic includes the financial value of in-kind subsidies, such as free party political broadcasts in Europe, as well as voluntary services and expenditures by affiliated groups, such as trade unions, corporations, or advocacy political action committees. International IDEA reflects this broader understanding by defining political finance as the "legal and illegal financing of ongoing political party activities and electoral campaigns (in particular campaigns by candidates and political parties, but also by third parties)."[21] It also makes little sense for comparative studies to focus upon income and expenditures only during the official campaign period, since this may extend for more than a year in some countries using primaries and general elections, including the United States (thus sharply increasing costs), while involving just three or four weeks in some other countries. The international community has also moved away from understanding elections as a specific event around polling day to adopting the broader notion of an election cycle.[22] Building upon these considerations, therefore, this chapter focuses upon *political* finance regulations covering the use of financial resources by political actors throughout the whole electoral cycle, including during the precampaign phase, the campaign, polling day, and its aftermath.

Classifying Types of Public Policies

Four main categories of political finance regulation can be distinguished – each of which can be employed singly or in combination – including disclosure requirements, contribution limits, spending caps, and public subsidies. These are the main ideal types of policies commonly used to control the abuse of money in politics, although the de facto operation of these regulations depends upon multiple details, including the design and scope of these policies, the effectiveness of oversight by administrative, audit, and judicial bodies, and the strength of informal cultural norms and social sanctions. These categories can also be understood as part of an underlying continuum scale concerning the *degree* of regulation. From this perspective, political finance laws can be regarded as equivalent to many other regulatory policies, such as laws on economic markets, environmental protection, food safety, or telecommunications.[23] Thus, depending upon the degree of government intervention, political finance rules can be understood to range from laissez-faire or free market policies at one pole to state management policies at the other (see Figure 8.2).

Thus a light regulatory touch emphasizing disclosure and transparency is recommended where it is believed that market forces should generally prevail in elections and a more active role for the state poses serious risks for the potential abuse of power. Extraparliamentary political party organizations are traditionally treated in this approach as voluntary associations located in civil society with a right to determine their own internal affairs, operational rules, and funding arrangements largely free of external interference and public scrutiny. By contrast, more interventionist policies, such as those providing public funding of political parties, seek to have greater impact by ensuring greater equality of outcomes for candidates and parties competing for elected office.

Disclosure Requirements

The first category concerns rules requiring financial reporting and transparency through stipulating requirements for the disclosure of donor identities,

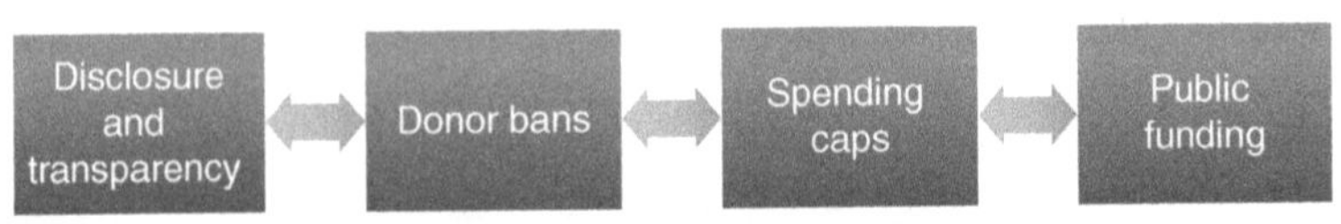

FIGURE 8.2A. Types of political finance regulations, from market to state intervention. Source: Pippa Norris and Andrea Abel van Es. 2016. *Checkbook Elections? Political Finance in Comparative Perspective*. New York: Oxford University Press.

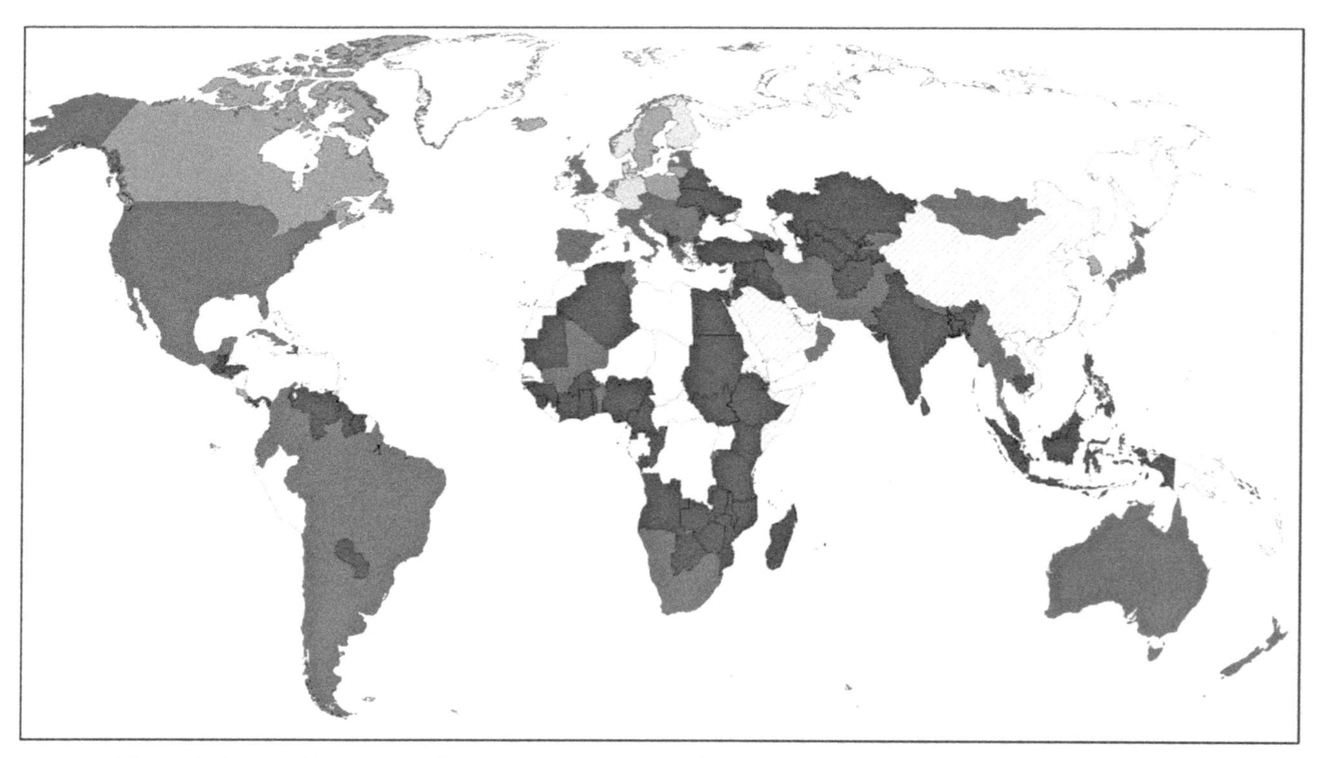

FIGURE 8.2B. The global map of integrity in the Campaign Finance Index.
Source: The Campaign Finance Index from the Perceptions of Electoral Integrity database (PEI-4.5).

donation amounts, and/or spending accounts. These policies aim to expand transparency, to reduce the anonymity of "dark money," and to strengthen the accountability of political actors. In development, transparency and accountability are generally thought to help plug the leaky pipes of corruption and inefficiency, channel public spending more efficiently, and produce better services.[24] Article 7(3) of the UNCAC obligates signatory states to make good faith efforts to improve transparency in candidate and political party financing, for example, through submitting timely and regular public reports to an independent supervisory body with monitoring and auditing powers, including appropriate and reasonable sanctions for noncompliance. Proponents of transparency argue that other direct forms of state intervention may prove deeply problematic and risky, for example by either limiting free speech or by generating rules favoring incumbent parties and candidates.[25] As a result, by default, it is preferable to encourage civic society monitoring agencies and the news media to convey full information about campaign funding to citizens, thereby deterring potential abuses and strengthening electoral accountability. In India, for example, reforms since 2003 have attempted to increase transparency in politics. The Right to Information movement, which has made considerable headway in India, contributed to passage of the 2005 Right to Information Act (RTI).[26] Candidates have been compelled to disclose any criminal, educational, and financial details at the time of nomination. Legislation has provided tax incentives associated with disclosure for company political donations. Moreover, under this law, political parties have been compelled to release their income and expenditure records, expanding public information on political finance.[27] This is part of the worldwide movement; by 2011, it is estimated that 89 countries had adopted Rights to Information laws.[28]

Transparency is widely endorsed as a desirable guiding principle for political finance regulations. For example, the Inter-American Democratic Charter of the Organization of American States endorses the principle: "The strengthening of political parties and other political organizations is a priority for democracy. Special attention will be paid to the problems associated with the high cost of election campaigns and the establishment of a balanced and transparent system for their financing."[29] Similarly, the Council of Europe states that: "Party funding must comply with the principles of transparency and accountability."[30] The UNCAC, adopted by the General Assembly in 2003, provides the strongest international agreement about the need for financial disclosure. Article 7(3) states that "Each State Party shall also consider taking appropriate legislative and administrative measures, consistent with the objectives of this Convention and in accordance with the fundamental principles of its domestic law, to enhance transparency in the funding of candidatures for elected public office and, where applicable, the funding of political parties."[31] Although the procedures to implement this remain unspecified, the Convention strongly endorses the principle of disclosure, and subsequent clauses emphasize the need to limit undue influence, bribery, and illicit enrichment in the public sector, including among elected officials.

Traditionally political parties used to be treated by the state as private organizations within civil society, bound by their own rulebooks, internal procedures, and forms of governance. Proponents of disclosure requirements, however, regard party campaign funds as public records which can serve to limit the potential abuse of political funding, analogous to the publication of annual financial accounts by corporations and nonprofit organizations. Transparency rules typically require that political parties, candidates, and/or contributors disclose financial contributions and/or expenditures to the electoral authorities, such as the US Federal Election Commission or the UK Election Commission, to state audit offices in Eastern Europe, or to judicial tribunals and parliamentary bodies. Through becoming a matter of public record, advocates argue that this expands opportunities to scrutinize the role of money in politics and its potential abuse by parliamentary and judicial oversight bodies, investigative journalists, and civil society watchdog organizations. For example, the Center for Responsive Politics in the United States uses the FEC data to publish the size of major contributions by lobbying groups, where the money goes, how much money candidates raise and spend, and similar information for Congressional and Presidential races.[32] By monitoring this information, citizens can potentially make more rational voting decisions and candidates can be deterred from abusing political funds.

Critics suggest, however, that several weaknesses may undermine this approach.[33] Firstly, if transparency is not accompanied by accountability, disclosure remains a weak tool by itself.[34] For example, if cases of malfeasance are highlighted without any sanctions, then potentially this can erode public trust and confidence in the electoral process, undermining legitimacy, with risky consequences in fragile democracies.[35] A general overview of the evidence for the effects of transparency on the quality of public services concluded that policies can fail because of the difficulties in mobilizing collective action, obstacles arising from political resistance, and long chains of implementing authorities.[36] Thus even if disclosure reveals problems, such as the widespread abuse of state resources in an election, grossly inflated levels of spending, or unequal access to party funding, there may be no will or capacity to address these problems. Moreover, loopholes in transparency requirements may allow dark money to flow through alternative channels; hence US Congressional candidates need to report financial donations to the FEC in considerable detail, but money has instead increasingly poured into political action committees (PACs) exempt from this requirement. Moreover, dark money is thought to have fueled ideologically extreme issues and candidates, contributing towards party polarization in America.[37] Finally, levels of spending reported in the formal disclosure requirements may diverge sharply from actual practices, particularly in countries with weak rule of law, ineffective audit agencies, and inadequate penalties for nondisclosure.

Contribution Limits

The second type of policy seeks to restrict financial contributions. Donations can be banned outright from particular entities, such as foreign donors, trade unions, and corporations. Or donations may be capped at an individual level – how much any individual can contribute overall, or how much can be given to a particular candidate, group, or party. The primary goal of this form of regulation is to mitigate the risks of undue influence arising from substantial campaign contributions from particular interests, preventing backdoor cronyism, favors for sale, peddling access to lobbyists, and other corrupt and illicit practices. At the same time, the use of contribution limits may simultaneously restrict free speech, an important channel of civic participation, and the capacity of political parties and candidates to mobilize their potential support.

In the United States, for example, in 1974 the Federal Election Campaign Act (FECA) was amended to limit individual contributions to candidates and political committees, as well as creating an administrative agency, the Federal Election Commission, to enforce the restrictions. Watergate had highlighted the way that large contributions ("fat cats") had been linked to government policies. The Justice Department also revealed that large campaign donors had also been rewarded with ambassadorial appointments. Under the new law, individual candidates and elected officials had to fundraise from a wide range of smaller donors, although to sidestep these restrictions the law also sanctioned the use of PACs by corporations, unions, and professional groups; political parties could also raise money and channel support to candidates.

Contribution limits can be understood as located in the middle of the regulatory spectrum. Compared with transparency requirements alone, these types of rules intervene more directly to provide more equitable party competition and to limit the risks of corruption. Contribution limits usually require that parties and candidates have to raise funds from multiple smaller donors, rather than just a few large contributors. At the same time, compared with public funding, donor caps are essentially designed to generate equality of opportunity, rather than equality of outcomes. To be implemented effectively, these policies also depend upon public disclosure requirements, so they also need transparency rules.

Spending Limits

The third category of policies involve restrictions on campaign spending. These policies can also be seen to fall roughly in the middle of the regulatory spectrum. Countries usually outlaw explicit acts of vote-buying and the abuse of state resources for private gain. Laws can also restrict the total levels of routine campaign expenditure by political parties, groups, and candidates for elected office. Regulations generally focus upon spending during the official campaign periods, but they may also apply at other times throughout the electoral cycle. The core aim of these policies is to curb the general role of money in politics and, in particular, to level the playing field so that those with the largest bankroll do not automatically convert financial advantages into votes. Like donor restrictions, however, spending caps can also be regarded as violating the principles of free speech and limiting the capacity of candidates and parties to mobilize support and campaign effectively. In practice, the exact levels of any spending limits may also be inappropriate. If too generous, then in practice candidates and parties are unlikely to reach the nominal ceiling. If too restrictive, then candidates and parties may be unable to campaign effectively and reach supporters, and rules may well be flouted in practice.

In Britain, for example, the 1883 Corrupt and Illegal Practices (Prevention) Act established election spending ceilings at constituency level where local campaigns are fought, and this policy continues to be used today. Candidates for elected office have to declare expenditures to their local returning officer within a month after the election and this record is then compiled and published by the Electoral Commission. Violators face criminal sanctions. Candidate spending includes any expenses incurred, whether on goods, services, property, or facilities, for the purposes of the candidate's election during the regulated period. This includes local advertising, staff, and transportation costs. The ceilings are calculated for the long (12 month) and short campaign periods. The limit is set from a base plus variable amount calculated from the number of registered electors in a constituency. In the 2015 general election, the fixed maximum amount of spending for both periods was set at £39,400 (US$63,475) plus a modest variable amount for different types of constituencies.[38] For the average-sized constituency, the ceiling allows each parliamentary candidate to spend around £1 per elector (US$1.61) in a general election. Since no paid broadcasting advertising can be purchased by candidates or parties, the costs are largely used for printing local leaflets and posters. In practice, candidates often spend far less than the ceiling. In the 2010 general election, for example, on average across all parties, candidates spent only 15 percent of the total regulated expenditure, with the greatest amount spent by Labour candidates (25 percent) and Conservative candidates (38 percent).[39] The Electoral Commission reports widespread compliance with the spending limits, and few candidates face criminal investigations or prosecutions. At the same time, political parties faced few, if any, disclosure requirements or spending limits, and it was only recently that national party spending levels were capped for the first time by the Political Parties, Elections and Referendums Act 2000.

Both contribution and spending limits are often justified by the principle of seeking to provide a fair and level playing field in party and candidate competition. The desirability of genuine political competition is articulated in Article 21 of the Universal Declaration of Human Rights and many subsequent international agreements. For example, the Southern African Development Community (SADC) declares that "In the interest of creating conditions for a level playing field for all political parties and promoting the integrity of the electoral process, parties should not misuse public funds in the electoral process. The electoral law should prohibit the government to aid or abet any party gaining unfair advantage."[40] Similarly the European Commission's Handbook for EU Election Observers states that: "Reasonable limitations on campaign expenditure may be justified to ensure that the free choice of voters is not undermined or the democratic process distorted by disproportionate campaigning on behalf of any candidate or party."[41]

In this sense, the regulation of political finance is often justified by the principle of equality of opportunities rather than equality of outcomes. Bans on the misuse of public funds or campaign expenditures are important, it is argued, to ensure that candidates or parties contesting elections do not gain an unfair advantage through their ability to get out their message to citizens, to mobilize supporters, or, even buy votes, because of inherent differences in either private wealth or their ability and willingness and ability to fundraise. Particular concern is raised where the level playing field is imbalanced and governing parties and incumbent politicians enjoy substantial advantages in access to resources used to mobilize electoral support, whether through access to the mass media, abuse of state resources by public officials, or access to donor contributions.[42]

Direct or Indirect Public Subsidies

The final type of regulation concerns the provision of public funding through direct financial assistance for candidates or parties from the public purse, or indirect assistance through mechanisms such as free or subsidized access to media or tax breaks.[43] This is more interventionist than the other types of policies. These laws may specify that parties and candidates have to use any public resources for particular purposes, such as for civic education, youth mobilization, and campaign communications, or uses may be unrestricted. Moreover, the level of subsidies may be tied to the share of either the proportion of parliamentary seats or votes won in previous elections, providing an incumbency advantage, or it may be equally divided among all parties and candidates registered in an election. Subsidies may also be directed towards specific levels of party organizations, such as central headquarters or regional offices, or they may be left unspecified. The recent introduction or expansion of party subsidies has been one of the most common reforms in countries as diverse Japan, South Africa, Britain, Russia, and Indonesia, but there are some exceptions. For example, the role of public funding has simultaneously weakened over time for presidential elections in the United States.

Sweden illustrates the use of these types of policies.[44] Since the 1960s, Swedish parties have been generously funded from the public purse. Central government support goes to political party organizations and secretarial

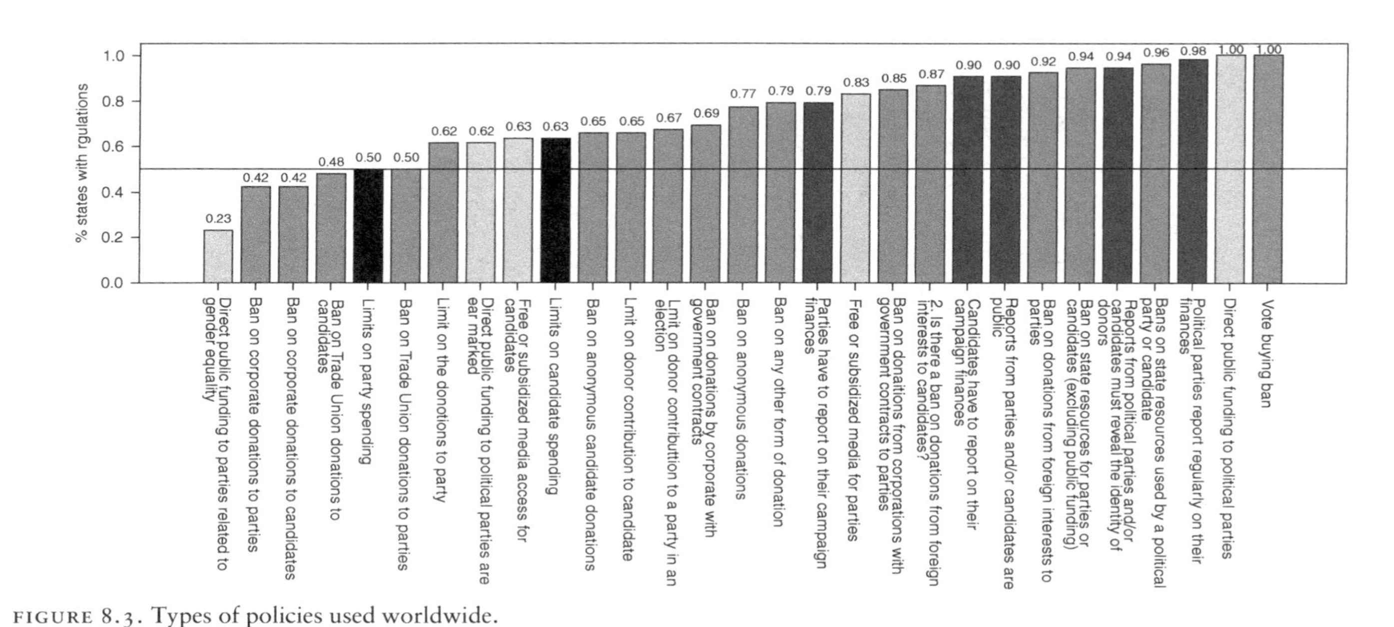

FIGURE 8.3. Types of policies used worldwide.
Note: Disclosure requirements (■), donor bans (■), spending caps (■), and public funding provisions (□).
Source: International IDEA. 2016. *Political Finance Database*. Stockholm: IDEA. www.idea.int/political-finance/index.cfm.

support that reach a minimum threshold of nationwide vote (2.5 percent). Financial resources are also provided to political party groups in parliament and this is allocated proportionally to the share of seats won in the previous two elections. Parliamentary parties have become highly dependent upon this subsidy, generating roughly two-thirds of their funds in recent years. Local governments also contribute towards the revenues of local and regional party organizations. At the same time, there are no restrictions upon the use of public funds and, even more strikingly, until recently there were no legal requirements for disclosure and financial reporting in Sweden, although informal practices and cultural norms favored transparency.

How common are each of these types of policies? Figure 8.3 shows the proportion of states in the International IDEA database on Political Finance in 2016 with legal regulations relating to the 29 specific indicators in 153 countries.[45] Thus, the right-hand side of the chart shows that some policies are widely employed according to this database, including legal bans on vote-buying and misuse of state resources by parties or candidates, requirements on party financial reports, and bans on foreign donations. By contrast, the left-hand side shows that some types of regulations remain relatively rare, including direct party funding related to gender equality for candidates (such as under the Parity Law in France)), limits on party spending, and bans on corporate donations to parties and candidates.

EVALUATING PROGRAM OUTCOMES

What is the impact of all these types of policies? As with evaluations of other forms of electoral assistance, the benchmarks are not self-evident and, beyond obvious measures banning illicit and corrupt acts such as vote-buying and the abuse of state resources, debate continues about the ideal standards that regulations should meet and the priority among several trade-off values. For example, what is the importance of transparency versus privacy? Should we value equality of opportunity or seek to generate equality of outcomes? What is the desirability of providing public subsidies versus relying upon the political marketplace? These controversies cut across country, partisan, and ideological cleavages, and responses are likely to vary among countries with different cultural traditions, economic conditions, and political contexts.[46]

To start to evaluate effectiveness, like other sectors of electoral assistance considered in this book, the impact of regulations on campaign finance can be analyzed based on program *outcomes*, that is so say, whether practices in each society are observed to reflect the formal legal rules. The de jure statutes regulating campaign finance may diverge sharply from the de facto practices, especially in states characterized by weak rule of law, widespread tolerance of malfeasance and corruption, and ineffective implementing agencies. Anticorruption laws may be passed as a façade in response to international pressures, to please donors and to attract development aid and inward

TABLE 8.1 *Correlations Between Political Finance Laws and Practices*

In law and in practice ...	R	Significance
Is there direct public funding for election campaigns?	.854	**
Is there a transparent and equitable mechanism to determine direct public funding for election campaign?	.255	N/s
Is the use of state resources for or against political parties and individuals prohibited?	-.076	N/s
Do political parties and candidates have free or subsidized access to equitable air time for electoral campaigns?	.510	**
Political parties and candidates are requires to report their financial information on a monthly basis during election campaigns.	.486	**
Third-party actors such as foundations, think tanks, and political action committees report itemized reports contributions received and expenditures to an oversight authority.	.699	**
High level appointments to the oversight authority are based on merit.	.600	**
The independence of high-level appointees is guaranteed.	.474	**

Note: The coefficients are the simple Pearson correlation (R) between the expert assessments of the law and practice and its significance. The items asked experts to assess each item in each country in law and then in practice. Responses were coded No (0), Partially (0.5) and Yes (1). N = 54 countries.
Source: Global Integrity. *Money, Transparency and Politics database, 2015*. For more details, see http://moneypoliticstransparency.org.

investment, but with little political will to follow through by implementing policies that hurt the interest of governing elites. Or administrative agencies responsible for regulating political finance may try to implement new laws, but they may lack the technical capacity, resources, or authority to do so effectively. Thus laws and regulations may be observed to be unenforced in practice. The implementation gap is examined in this chapter by drawing upon indicators from expert surveys monitoring the de jure regulations and de facto practices governing political finance in a wide range of 54 countries worldwide, ranging from Albania, Argentina, and Australia to the United States, Uruguay, and Venezuela.[47]

Table 8.1 looks at the simple correlations between how experts first assessed the legal regulation on eight different aspects of political finance, such as whether public funding was available for elections, whether there were bans on the abuse of state resources, and whether parties and candidates were required to report their finances on a monthly basis and how they also assessed the actual practice operating in each country. The results demonstrate that according to country experts, there was a strong and significant correlation between the legal de jure regulations governing money in politics and the actual de facto practices on six of the eight items. For example, the independence- and merit-based appointment to the political finance oversight authorities were correlated. The main exceptions concerned whether there were transparent and equitable mechanisms to determine public funding and also bans on the use of state resources by parties and candidates, both areas where practices diverged from the law. Overall the Global Integrity data suggests that the legal framework is not simply symbolic, but on many matters experts suggest that how political finances work during campaigns does seem to reflect the law.

EVALUATING SOCIETAL IMPACTS

Thus we have established some comparative evidence that the statutory framework seems to affect how campaign finance works in practice (according to expert perceptions). This helps to illuminate the intermediary step in the chain-of results model, where laws are implemented and not merely symbolic. But what are the longer-term consequences and ultimate goals of political finance regulation? There are multiple reasons why campaign finance reforms may fail to achieve their stated objectives, such as faulty design of any remedies and lack of technical capacity. There are also the constraints of fixed conditions such as deeply rooted informal norms and cultural attitudes tolerant of corruption in public affairs and widespread mistrust of politicians. Policies may fail to work for multiple reasons, including poorly designed regulations, inadequate public sector capacity and resources to implement new rules, limited technical expertise, weak sanctions for noncompliance, and/or lack of political will. Expectations may also be inflated; previous research comparing policies in many countries concluded that when judged against the grandiose rhetorical promises of proponents, limited or no effects could usually be observed to arise from attempts at campaign finance reform.[48] Even if practices closely follow laws, this does not mean that the regulatory framework necessarily generates outcomes serving the public interest. The laws may well be designed to benefit ruling parties or legislative incumbents, such as the cartel-like distribution of any public funding to parties in parliament, excluding access for new challengers.[49] Effective political finance regulation can be expected to improve several desirable goals in electoral integrity, including the strengthening of equitable access to political subsidies and donations, freedom of information and transparency, as well as reducing or eliminating abuse of state resources in election campaigns. Using the chain-of-results framework, the type of regulations may also be expected to generate several longer-term and more diffuse societal-level impacts on citizens, regimes, and societies, including, for example, whether the type of regulations are observed to be associated with electoral integrity, perceptions of corruption, and levels of democratization.

Evidence from case studies suggests a somewhat mixed picture.[50] In some circumstances, for example, democratic political practices have been subverted by political finance laws. For example, in India a relatively hands-free system of political financing has meant that large sums of money are required to run for candidacy within a political party, favoring many candidates tied to the criminal underworld. Indonesia, shows however that increasing state regulation does not necessarily solve these problems – parties in this country are becoming increasingly dominated by oligarchs with the resources to fund their political careers and political parties. Meanwhile, Russia suggests that the legal framework has led to the manipulation of access to and control over financial resources, thereby entrenching electoral authoritarianism. In other circumstances, however, increased levels of state intervention have strengthened governance and democracy. Japan illustrates how increased state interventionism has cut the cost of elections and also increased political competition through alternation of the political parties in power. Brazil also exemplified how increased state intervention via direct and indirect public subsidies has led to enhanced political competition. One possible explanation for these sorts of observed outcomes is that alternative ways to regulate the flow of money into politics have trade-offs. For example, a ban on particular forms of donation may help to promote fairness and integrity in elections, but also simultaneously limit individual freedom and civic participation. Which combination of regulatory policies is most suitable for any state depends upon the importance placed on rival normative principles. Thus, while caps on expenditures may help to ensure fairness of political competition, these also curtail party and candidate autonomy.

The mixed results reported in the case studies mean that systematic comparisons are needed for more reliable generalizations. For cross-national evidence, we can turn to macrolevel indicators to see whether the type and degree of regulations used in different countries are associated with several significant societal impacts. Legal regulations are drawn from International IDEA's Political Finance Database, as this provides the most comprehensive and up-to-date classification worldwide.

Two key measures can be constructed from this source. The first concerns the *type* of de jure policies governing political finance, divided into the categories of donation bans and limits, public subsidies, spending limits, and transparency and disclosure rules. The International IDEA dataset allows us to calculate summary scales showing how far each country has legal regulations falling into each of these four categories.[51]

The second monitors the overall *degree of regulation* of political finance, ranging from laissez faire to highly interventionist regimes. This is measured using the Political Finance Regulation Index, a continuous 100-point measure derived from all the 29 items in the International IDEA database irrespective of the type.

The impact of these factors can be examined using four societal-level indices, including the PEI Campaign finance index, the PEI Electoral

Integrity index, Transparency International's Corruption Perceptions Index, and the level of democratization measured by the combined Freedom House/Polity IV index. The first indicator is drawn from the Perceptions of Electoral Integrity expert survey.[52] The Campaign Finance index within PEI is composed of five items: 1. parties/candidates had equitable access to public political subsidies; 2. parties/candidates had equitable access to political donations; 3. parties/candidates publish transparent financial accounts; 4. rich people buy elections; and, 5. some state resources were improperly used for campaigning. Each of these items asks experts to evaluate what occurs in practice in each election under comparison. The campaign finance index score is calculated based on an additive summing (equally weighted) or each of these five indicators, standardized to a 100-point scale. The higher the country score, the better the level of integrity. The global map of the quality of Campaign Finance Index, based on this data, is illustrated in Figure 8.3. It can be observed that there are problems in many parts of the world, as noted earlier in Chapter 4. These are particularly evident, according to these expert assessments, in many parts of the African continent, as well as in Eurasia, South Asia and South-East Asia, and parts of the Americas, including the United States. Only Northern Europe, Scandinavia, Canada, and Australia get a better bill of health on these issues.

For further robustness checks, the type and degree of regulation is also expected to shape the overall quality of any contest (measured by the PEI Electoral Integrity Index), levels of democratization (using the combined Freedom House/Polity IV measure), and perceptions of corruption (measured by the 2015 Corruption Perceptions Index, compiled by Transparency International.)[53] Where similar results are observed consistently across separate measures, this increases confidence in their general reliability and robustness.

Any well-specified models also need to consider suitable controls.[54] Like other issues leading to electoral flaws and failures, the models control for levels of development (measured by per capita GDP in purchasing power parity), which is widely linked with the strength of democratic governance. Models also control for the distribution of natural resources (which is closely related to levels of corruption in any society) measured by the rents derived from oil and gas as a percentage of GDP. The geographic size of the country and the population size are also added as controls, since these factors are commonly associated with state capacity and levels of democratization (larger and more populous countries are commonly regarded as more difficult to govern than smaller states). A succession of linear regression models presented in Table 8.2 tests the relationships observed between each of the types of political finance regulation and the four societal-level indices, with controls. The models suggest three key findings.

Firstly, contrary to expectation, after controlling for economic development and resource based economies, *the regulations for public funding, spending caps, and donor limits were not significantly related to the societal impact indicators*. This may disappoint the hopes of advocates, if it is assumed that these types of regulations alone have the capacity to improve the quality of campaign finance, as well as strengthening electoral integrity, weakening perceptions of corruption, and improving levels of democratization. Nevertheless, campaign finance is only one component that may contribute towards these outcomes. Many other institutions need to work effectively, such as the independent judiciary and courts, competent audit authorities, and the free press, for regulations to have a substantial impact on these diffuse goods.

Secondly, however, the results of the models demonstrated that contrary to other types, the *laws regulating the transparency of political finance were significantly associated with positive outcomes*. As Table 8.2 shows, the four societal-level indices were all predicted by levels of economic development; not surprisingly, more affluent postindustrial nations had better levels of campaign finances, electoral integrity, and stronger democracies (although they also had more, rather than less, less corruption perceptions). Natural-resource-based economies were consistently negatively associated with the indices; as previous research has commonly demonstrated, the concentration of economies on oil and gas is closely linked with state-capture, corruption, and concentration of power in the hands of elites. After controlling for these factors, stronger disclosure laws for campaign finance were linked with better-quality campaign finance and levels of electoral integrity (according to PEI experts) as well as levels of democratization.

Finally, what about the degree of regulation? All types of regulations can be aggregated into a regulatory scale using the 29 indicators in the IDEA database. The analysis in Table 8.3 shows that the degree of regulation is also significantly correlated with the PEI Campaign Finance Index, overall levels of Electoral Integrity, and levels of democratization, controlling for other factors. On balance, *the more that a state intervenes in its system of political financing by enacting regulations around contributions, spending, disclosure, and public subsidies, the higher the quality of its political finances and elections (according to the PEI Index)*. Among the other control variables, again economic development had a consistently positive effect, while resource-based economies were negatively related to the indices.

At the same time, there should be caution about interpreting these patterns before making any causal claims. Any cross-national analysis quickly encounters issues of endogeneity: for example, scandals over graft and malfeasance in public life can be expected to encourage reforms attempts to introduce more stringent legal constraints on the abuse of money in politics, such as strengthening the powers of oversight agencies. Moreover, any new reforms may also take many years to strengthen standards of public life in deeply rooted cultures of corruption. Thus process-tracing and time-series data is needed to untangle the complex interactive processes.

TABLE 8.2 *Political Finance Disclosure Regulations and Societal Impacts*

	Model 1 PEI Campaign Finance Index			Model 2 PEI Electoral Integrity Index			Model 3 Perceptions of Corruption			Model 4 Level of Democratization		
	B	s.e.	Sig	B	s.e.	Sig	B	s.e.	Sig	B	s.e.	Sig
POLITICAL FINANCE LEGAL REGULATIONS												
Disclosure requirement	.077	.040	*	.074	.038	*	-.025	.039	N/s	.018	.007	*
CONTROLS												
Economic development (per capita GDP ppp in current $) World Bank	.001	.000	***	.001	.000	***	.001	.000	***	.001	.000	***
Natural resources (rents as% of GDP)	-.318	.094	***	-.374	.089	***	-.288	.093	**	-.084	.017	***
Population size	-.001	.000	N/s	-.001	.000	N/s	-.001	.000	N/s	.000	.000	N/s
Area size	-.001	.000	N/a	-.001	.000	N/s	-.001	.000	N/s	.001	.000	N/s
Constant	25.1			46.6			32.6			5.46		
Adjusted R^2	.555			.498			.689			.440		
N. countries	119			119			119			119		

Notes: The coefficients represent the unstandardized beta (B), the standard errors (s.e.) and their significance. * = .05, ** = .01, *** = .001 N/s Not significant. The coefficients in bold are statistically significant. The Campaign Finance index and the Electoral Integrity index are from PEI-4.5. Corruption Perception index is from Transparency International. The level of democratization score is the combined Freedom House/Imputed Polity. The types of political finance disclosure regulations are classified from the International IDEA database. Sources: See above.

TABLE 8.3 *The Strength of Political Finance Regulations and Societal Impacts*

	Model 1 PEI Campaign finance Index			Model 2 PEI Electoral Integrity Index			Model 3 Perceptions of Corruption			Model 4 Level of Democratization		
	B	s.e.	Sig	B	s.e.	Sig	B	s.e.	Sig	B	s.e.	Sig
POLITICAL FINANCE LEGAL REGULATIONS												
The strength of all types of regulations	**.212**	**.080**	**	**.214**	**.079**	**	−.036	.090	N/s	**.039**	**.014**	**
CONTROLS												
Economic development (per capita GDP ppp in current $) World Bank	.001	.000	***	.001	.001	***	.001	.000	***	.001	.000	***
Natural resources (rents as% of GDP)	−.171	.143	N/s	−.323	.139	*	−.308	.159	*	−.084	.024	***
Population size	.001	.000	N/s	.001	.001	N/s	.001	.000	N/s	.001	.000	N/s
Area size	.001	.000	N/s	.001	.001	N/s	.001	.000	N/s	.001	.000	N/s
Constant	12.1			33.4			32.7			3.53		
Adjusted R^2	.641			.579			.695			.565		
N. countries	49			49			49			49		

Notes: The coefficients represent the unstandardized beta (B), the standard errors (s.e.) and their significance. * = .05, ** = .01, *** = .001 N/s Not significant. The coefficients in bold are statistically significant. The Campaign Finance index and the Electoral Integrity index are from PEI-4.5. Corruption Perception index is from Transparency International. The level of democratization score is the combined Freedom House/Imputed Polity. The strength of political finance regulations are a combined index from all types of regulations contained in the International IDEA database. Sources: See above.

CONCLUSIONS

Among all the policy instruments, the last decade has seen landmark revisions in many countries that often seek to strengthen disclosure requirements and thus boost transparency, countering the risks of corruption. The expansion of disclosure requirements in political finance reflect broader changes in democratic governance, following the expansion in transparency policies and open government, as exemplified by the worldwide movement spreading Freedom of Information Acts.[55] Many countries also increasingly provide public funding and subsidies to parliamentary parties to deal with rising campaign costs at a time of falling membership dues and voluntary fundraising by local activists. Parties need sufficient resources to mobilize voters without relying solely on private sector donors. The adoption of public funding is also in line with the broader regulation of many other political party activities, understood as a shift from mass membership to cartel party organizations.[56] Although several countries have adopted either spending limits or donor caps, these policies tend to be less commonly used. The net effect of the era since the mid-1990s has been to abandon a pure laissez-faire model where political finance was traditionally treated as a private matter governed largely by internal rules and informal norms within each political party, to moving towards greater state regulation. Yet the pace and degree of change differs across states, with some countries remaining today far less strongly regulated than others.

When it comes to the question of what works, there is no single "right" mix of policies regulating political finance that fit countries with diverse institutional, cultural, and economic parameters. Instead, the decision to intervene in the flow of money into politics and the consequences of this intervention are affected by numerous contingent factors, some of which may be controlled and some of which lie beyond the control of policymakers and politicians. Some heavily regulated countries, exemplified by Russia, continue to be plagued by endemic corruption and imbalanced party competition, while others which are lightly regulated by statute, notably Sweden, perform well against all the standard indicators of democratic governance. In this regard, there are grounds to remain cautiously agnostic about any specific policy recommendations. Elsewhere, case studies suggests that a balanced mix of regulatory policies are most effective to control political finance, so that regulations blend a combination of disclosure and transparency requirements, limits on spending and contributions, and public subsidies to political parties.[57] No single policy instrument is sufficient by itself to control money in politics. Unfortunately, even well-designed policies that try to incorporate each of these elements in a comprehensive package of reforms sometimes become unbalanced due to judicial rulings, implementation failures, or prevalent cultural norms.

Judgments about what works in terms of the political finance regime depends inherently on the normative goals the regime is set up to achieve. Where laws and rules are designed to provide a distinct advantage for an incumbent party or politician, a system of one-party rule or electoral authoritarianism is able to exist behind a façade of legality. This seems especially true in relation to systems of public funding, which can be designed to exclude any potential opposition or new parties from their share of the spoils, rather than on an egalitarian basis. There are also inherent trade-offs to be made when thinking about the design and reform of a system of political financing.

Nevertheless, the evidence presented in this chapter suggests three positive findings. First, practices in each country often do reflect the legal framework, so that regulations are not merely a façade of window dressing to attract aid and investment. Laws matter. Second, there are many variations among all the types of campaign finance regulations, and the devil is often in the details when it comes down to the legal requirements and forms of implementation. Nevertheless, the regulations emphasizing public disclosure, which are one of the most popular reforms in recent years, also seem to generate the most positive impacts on the quality of campaign finance, electoral integrity, and democracy. Finally, no single form of regulation exists in most countries. These rules are used in combination, for example emphasizing the importance of transparency as a quid pro quo for the introduction of public funding for political parties. The analysis also shows that although there are some well-known exceptions, in general more heavily regulated systems of campaign finance also tend to be associated with better societal outcomes. As with other areas of electoral assistance offered by the international community, the findings provide further positive support buttressing the pragmatic argument.

9

Improving Voter Registration

The practical and technical challenges of implementing effective, comprehensive, and accurate processes of voter registration and balloting should not be underestimated, as problems can arise even in long-established democracies. These issues can be illustrated by the case of the United States. The 2014 report of the bipartisan US Presidential Commission on Election Administration documented a long series of vulnerabilities in US elections.[1] These have been under close scrutiny ever since the notoriously flawed ballot design in Florida in 2000. Since then, reports of wait times in excess of six hours to cast a ballot in Ohio, inaccurate state and local voter registers, insufficiently trained local poll workers, and the breakdown of voting machines in New York have continued to put the quality of US elections in the headlines.[2] Standards remain uneven across the country; the Pew Center's 2012 Election Performance Index suggests that states such as North Dakota, Minnesota, and Wisconsin performed relatively well against a range of quality indicators combing voting convenience and electoral integrity, but others, including California, Oklahoma, and Mississippi demonstrated noticeable shortfalls.[3]

It was no different during the 2014 midterm elections. The media reported a range of problems on election day, some trivial, others more serious, though it remains to be determined whether these were arising from accidental maladministration or intentional dirty tricks. At least 18 state election websites were reported to have experienced disruptions on election day, preventing voters from using the sites to locate polling places and ballot information.[4] In Hartford, Connecticut, voters were turned away from polling places that did not open on time due to late arriving voter registration lists.[5] The Chicago Board of Election Commissioners reported that more than 2,000 election judges did not turn up at their polling stations after receiving erroneous information from "robocalls."[6] In Virginia, a State Department of Elections spokesman said that 32 electronic voting machines at 25 polling places experienced problems. In both Virginia and North Carolina, there were also claims that electronic polling machines recorded a vote for the Democratic candidate when the screen was touched to cast a vote for the Republican.[7] The statewide voter registration system crashed in Texas, forcing many to complete provisional ballots when poll workers were unable to confirm voter eligibility.[8] Meanwhile, new state laws requiring electors to present photo identification were reported to cause confusion in several states, including Texas, Georgia, and North Carolina.[9]

Several problems continued, and even intensified, in the bitterly divided 2016 presidential elections, with Donald Trump claiming during the campaign that, if he lost, the election would have been "rigged" by practices of voter impersonation and multiple voting. Flaws include the drawing of district boundaries to favor incumbents, the long-standing problem of gerrymandering (which has worsened since 2004). In these districts, US elections are determined by politicians choosing voters, rather than the reverse.[10] A comprehensive global study found only two cases (the US and France) with single-member districts which give partisan legislators the dominant say in determining boundaries, rather than using independent commissions.[11] Since 2000, and particularly since 2010, many Republican-controlled state houses have implemented laws designed to make it harder to vote, such as requiring strict voter IDs and cutting early polling days or hours.[12] Another problem in the 2016 campaign was the flood of disinformation, propaganda, hoaxes, and fake news spread via social media, some attributed by the intelligence community to Russian sources and others homegrown, which overwhelmed attempts by fact checkers in mainstream journalism to counteract the flow. The overwhelmingly negative tone, lack of serious policy discussion in the mainstream news media, and false equivalencies were also problematic for media coverage.[13]

What explains procedural problems occurring in US elections? In particular, how far are reforms to registration and voting procedures used in US states associated with the risks of either voter suppression or voter fraud? Debate about electoral laws has become increasingly polarized along party lines in the US, with policy reforms generating a complex patchwork quilt of registration and voting procedures across the United States. It is commonly claimed in popular debate that stricter registration and voting procedures safeguard the security of the ballot but at the risk of raising the logistical costs of participation and thereby suppressing voting rights. In counterpoint, it is also claimed that more lenient electoral procedures with lower barriers may prove more socially inclusive, but at the risk of increasing voter fraud. Is there good evidence supporting these rival claims and counterclaims?

It is important to understand this issue for several reasons. First, public awareness of electoral malpractices matters for civic engagement, by eroding confidence in elected institutions, such as parties, parliaments, and governments, as well as dampening turnout and sparking protest activism.[14] Therefore flawed contests are not simply an abstract technical issue of concern for liberal elites; these have important implications for civic engagement and the quality of democratic governance. Second, a flourishing literature and new sources of empirical evidence have developed during the last decade studying the quality of electoral administration in the United States and abroad.[15] Many of these studies have focused on specific types of laws, such as mail ballots or identification requirements, either within specific states or across the United States. Yet previous studies have not generally compared a comprehensive range of registration and voting state laws nor judged these against expert evaluations of electoral performance in US states. Expert evaluations are a common technique employed for many other topics which are difficult to measure directly through official statistics or mass surveys, such as comparative studies estimating corruption (by Transparency International), good governance (by the World Bank Institute), and the quality of democracy (by the Variety of Democracies project).[16] It is an appropriate technique that can throw new light on the electoral performance of US states. Finally, from a policy perspective, it is critical to identify legitimate concerns about the workings of US elections in order to identify appropriate remedies and thereby encourage inclusive, accountable, and responsive government.

To understand the impact of US state registration and balloting procedures, this chapter first sets out the conceptual and theoretical framework. This study focuses upon the effects of institutional variations across US states. In particular, the chapter theorizes that the logistical costs of registration and voting determined by state-level laws will influence the quality of state electoral performance, as monitored through expert judgments. The chain-of-results logic is illustrated in Figure 9.1.

As more fully discussed later, within-country comparisons provide an opportunity to hold the general levels of economic development and international forces constant, in order to best analyze variance in institutional procedures among US states. The second part describes the research design, which takes advantage of new data to assess the performance of US state elections, as the core dependent variable. PEI-US-2014 is based on an expert survey of Perceptions of Electoral Integrity conducted in 21 states immediately after the 2014 US Congressional elections. States were selected to be representative using a structured random sample. Experts were asked to evaluate how multiple dimensions of electoral integrity performed in their

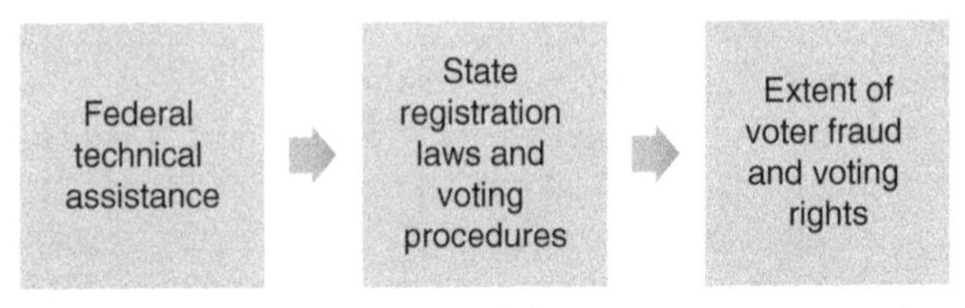

FIGURE 9.1. The chain-of-results framework for voter registration reforms.

state of residence using a detailed survey instrument covering all eleven stages in the electoral cycle, the same questionnaire described earlier for cross-national comparisons in Chapter 4. This chapter explores the relationship between this measure of election quality and institutional variance between states, namely state voting and registration laws. The standardized Convenience Election Law (CEL) Index is used to estimate variations in the leniency of state regulations for registering and voting, the primary independent variable. Multilevel (HLM) analysis examines the impact of a CEL index of state-level laws compared with expert estimates of electoral performance, derived from PEI-US 2014. The models control for many conditions expected to influence expert perceptions of the electoral integrity of registration and voting processes, including Level I social and partisan characteristics of the respondents and Level II political characteristics of the states under comparison.

The evidence demonstrates that *more lenient convenience election laws are related to higher levels of electoral integrity*. The findings are contrary to assertions that more lenient procedures open the door to fraud and thereby undermine the honesty of elections. The chapter concludes that institutional variants in registration and balloting procedures among states cannot account for the overall quality of US elections, and comprehensive explanations need to take account of the earlier stages of the whole electoral cycle, including electoral administration, redistricting, political finance, and campaign media. The implications of the US case are more general, however, and the findings are likely to hold important lessons for many other countries seeking to improve voter registration processes.

THE CONCEPTUAL AND THEORETICAL FRAMEWORK

To address the contemporary popular debate in US politics, this chapter focuses on the registration and voting processes where problems of voter suppression and electoral fraud are claimed to arise. One of the most striking observations arising from the results of the Perceptions of Electoral Integrity expert survey concerns the United States; out of 127 contests worldwide, the 2012 US presidential election ranked 42nd and the 2014 US Congressional elections ranked 45th. The combined US score represents the worst national performance among all established democracies in the comparison, rating well below many newer democracies such as Lithuania, Costa Rica, the Czech Republic, and Uruguay (see Figure 4.2). The fact that both these US contests were poorly ranked, coupled with the finding that PEI is strongly correlated with equivalent independent cross-national indices measuring the quality of elections,[17] suggests that this is not simply an anomaly or measurement error. Among all mature democracies, the nuts and bolts of US elections seem particularly vulnerable to incompetence, malpractices, and simple human errors, as well as structural flaws. In particular, the PEI survey suggests that in the 2012 and 2014 US contests, experts consistently identified the stages of district boundaries, electoral laws, voter registration, and campaign finance as the most severe problems arising in US elections, in that order.[18] Similar patterns can be observed at state levels as well, as discussed later. Not surprisingly, concern about these types of issues have also been the focus of heated debate in state houses and within the Beltway. In general, systematic cross-national evidence suggests that compared with equivalent societies, recent US elections are regarded by experts as exceptional – and exceptionally bad.

Do Electoral Laws Explain Variance in Electoral Integrity?

From the mid-1960s onward, and especially since the 2000 Bush *v.* Gore presidential election and the unfortunate events in Florida, many US state houses have sought to amend their registration and voting laws. However, these attempts have typically encountered contentious partisan debate and litigious appeals in the courts.[19] Like many other disputes in contemporary US politics, there is no agreement about what further types of reforms to state laws should be prioritized to address issues of electoral integrity in the United States. Debate surrounds whether integrity is hurt more by *overly strict* procedures (which are thought to cause low turnout, political inequality, and lack of inclusive voting rights by all sectors of society), or by *overly lenient* requirements (which are believed to increase the risks of voter impersonation and thus fraud at the ballot box, invalidating legitimate results and damaging public trust). Electoral laws can therefore either reduce or raise the logistical barriers (time, effort, and possibly money) that citizens face when seeking to register and/or cast a ballot.[20] These logistical costs reflect one part of the turnout calculus made by rational voters, alongside informational costs and calculations of the anticipated benefits arising from participation.[21]

Those arguing for the loosening of registration procedures contend that electoral laws may point to convenience electoral facilities as a way of strengthening electoral integrity by reducing logistical costs facing citizens seeking to register and cast a ballot and thereby promoting full and equal participation. These varied procedures are exemplified worldwide by online registration, automatic registration, election day registration, prequalifying age registration, and rolling registers. In the United States, registration via the internet has become widely available, with 20 states allowing online registration applications in the 2014 elections, although making up only 7 percent of registration submissions.[22]

Other convenience facilities allow for varied methods of casting ballots, such as advance voting, assisted voting, overseas voting, absentee balloting, postal voting, extended hours/days, and weekend polling, internet voting, proxy voting, special facilities for the disabled, the production of multilanguage informational materials, and the deployment of mobile polling stations.[23] As a result, voting in person at a local polling station on election day has become less and less common. According to the 2014 Electoral Administration and

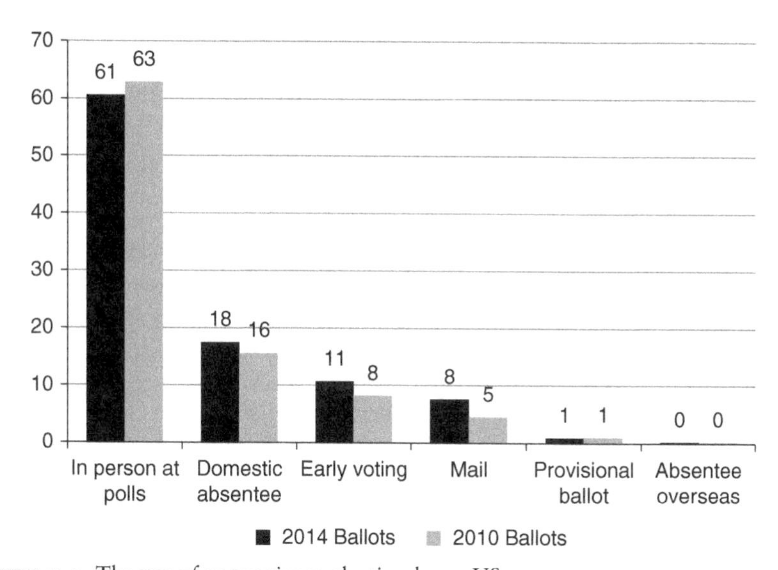

FIGURE 9.2. The use of convenience election laws, US 2012–2014.
Note: The proportion of ballots cast through different procedures.
Source: Electoral Assistance Commission. 215. *The 2014 EAC Election Administration and Voting Survey Comprehensive Report*. www.eac.gov/research/election_administration_and_voting_survey.aspx.

Voting Survey, for example, almost one in four US electors cast their ballot before election day. Figure 9.2 shows the changes in the use of alternative voting measures from 2010 to 2014.[24] But the rules surrounding various convenience voting facilities vary across states.

Of course, participating through these facilities is a necessity rather than a 'convenience' for several types of citizens – those with physical disabilities or illnesses, those responsible for the care of dependents, populations living in remote areas, care homes such hospitals or retiree communities, the military and expatriates based abroad, those whose religious commitments prevent them attending polling places on election day, and so on. Governments have, however, increasingly relaxed the rules to allow any qualified citizen to make use of early and remote voting, without any need to provide a reason such as immobility or travel. In this sense, the "convenience voting" label seems accurate.

Most research about the effects of convenience voting on turnout has been conducted in the United States, including studies focusing upon the impact of introducing different types of reforms in particular states (such as postal voting in Oregon) or across the US, with some work in several other established democracies, such as the United Kingdom and Switzerland.[25] It remains difficult to establish conclusively the effects of any single type of electoral law on participation, however, not least because multiple individual and macrolevel factors affect turnout.[26] In one of the seminal early studies on convenience voting, Rosenstone and Wolfinger concluded that US states that used the most relaxed registration processes had higher turnout, and they suggested that similar effects would follow by lowering the costs of registration elsewhere in the country.[27] Similarly, Piven and Cloward have argued that legal-institutional factors, including registration procedures, are the most important barriers to voting participation for disadvantaged groups in the United States.[28] Burden et al. find that while election-day registration has a positive effect on participation, another convenience measure, early voting, actually tended to depress turnout.[29] So while most empirical studies find that stricter registration and balloting rules do correlate with lower turnout, at the same time, reforms designed to ease the process do not necessarily boost participation substantially. Thus in practice the effects of adopting convenience electoral facilities have often fallen well short of the claims of proponents, generating only limited or even null effects on mobilizing overall levels of voter turnout.[30] One reason, Hanmer argues, is that US states like Minnesota with strong participatory cultures are most likely to adopt lenient registration laws, such as election day registration. As a result, it is misleading to extrapolate from these contexts to assume that similar effects would arise from exporting lenient registration facilities to other states with more restrictive traditions of voter rights.[31] Another reason is that these facilities are often most likely to be used by engaged citizens, reinforcing their propensity to vote, but this may exacerbate any social gaps in turnout arising from age, socioeconomic status, education, ethnicity, or sex.[32]

Additionally, critics claim that well-meaning procedural reforms making legal requirements for the registration and voting process more lenient may also have unintended consequences, such as through heightening security risks, undermining the secrecy of the ballot, increasing administrative costs and complexities, producing inconsistent and unequal voting rights across the United States, and thereby possibly ultimately damaging public confidence in electoral integrity.[33] In other words, the desire for inclusive participation needs to be counterbalanced by the need to protect security of the ballot.[34] In particular, many on the right argue that overly lax registration and balloting requirements in the United States have heighted risks of voter impersonation, allowing noncitizens to vote, and other forms of electoral fraud.[35] There is nothing novel about the specter of voter fraud, a rhetorical claim used for more than a century in attempts to limit minority voting rights. Nevertheless, US debate became more heated after the 2000 election. In fact, only 14 US states required some sort of identification to vote in 2000, with the number accelerating to 32 by 2014.[36] These changes are designed to minimize the risks of voter impersonation, but they also arguably raise the logistical costs of casting a ballot, depending upon the time, effort, and financial costs of fulfilling the identification requirements for eligible citizens. Critics such as Schaffer charge that in practice, even good faith efforts to clean up electoral rolls may suppress participation.[37] Several marginalized groups of citizens, for example, the elderly, students, transient populations, and the poor, are more likely to lack access to the polls where balloting depends upon presentation of a government-issued photo identification card. As a result, it is believed that stricter qualifications may disadvantage these groups at the polls, although the empirical evidence remains mixed.[38,39]

In attempts to detect the effects of procedures on incidence of voter fraud in the US, recent work has scrutinized the evidence available from legal records and federal prosecutions of electoral crimes in the registration, balloting, and counting processes.[40] Incident reports reported by poll workers and legal records of prosecutions and convictions have also been used in the United States to monitor the frequency of criminal charges of voter impersonation (implying voting more than once).[41] Scholars have also deployed techniques of electoral forensics, pouring over precinct returns to detect anomalies, although there is no consensus about the most appropriate statistical tests.[42] Other scholars have examined the impact of state electoral laws on public confidence and trust in the electoral process, reporting that any effects are cued by partisan leanings, winner-loser effects, and use of the news media.[43] Therefore, although popular debates claim that registration and balloting laws will influence many aspects of electoral integrity, for good or ill, and anecdotes are often quoted by proponents on either side of the aisle, systematic observational evidence remains largely indeterminate.

RESEARCH DESIGN

Given this conceptual framework, how can the performance of US state elections be assessed? More specifically, what evidence is available to assess the impact of restrictive or lenient legal regulations on the integrity of registration and balloting processes? Studies have utilized several techniques and sources of data to monitor electoral integrity, each with certain strengths and weaknesses, including content analysis of observer reports, randomized controlled experiments, forensic autopsies of polling results, indices constructed for related proxy concepts, event analysis derived from the contents of news media reports, and analysis of public opinion polls.[44] Measures in the United States have relied upon multiple sources of data, including the US Census Bureau's Voting and Registration Supplement of the Current Population Survey (CPS), the Election Administration and Voting Survey (EAVS) conducted by the Election Administration Commission, state and local election board records, and also public opinion surveys.[45] These resources provide invaluable evidence, although data remains of uneven quality.[46] For example, the EAVS depends upon the quality of information provided voluntarily by local election officials, and inconsistent concepts are used to describe the same electoral procedures in different places. Evidence from the CPS, the EAVS, and from local officials typically provides information on matters such as the proportion of registered citizens, voting turnout, and reasons for not voting. But this sort of data, while useful as indicators, is not directly evaluative. Any interpretation of the performance of US elections requires a consensus about the appropriate normative criteria which can form the basis of any judgment. Thus available evidence is unable resolve more fundamental disagreements about optimizing preferences involving trade-off values, such as the priority which should be given to administrative efficiency, citizen convenience, equal nondiscriminatory voting rights, and inclusive participation, or accurate, reliable, transparent, honest, and secure registration processes.

Other evidence about public perceptions of elections and reported behaviors are available from opinion polls such as the World Values Survey, the Pew Center postelection surveys, and the American National Election Survey.[47] But this source of data is also limited. Firstly, many cross-national surveys are limited to asking about only one or two types of electoral malpractices, such as experience of incidents of vote-buying or electoral intimidation. Other surveys use indirect measures, such as trust in electoral authorities, rather than monitoring perceptions about multiple problems that can occur throughout the electoral cycle. In addition, while mass survey data is useful to gauge citizen evaluations, the public may well be unaware of more technical problems arising in electoral administration, especially illegal and clandestine acts not highlighted by election watchdogs and the press. Finally, in countries where there is strong partisan debate about these matters, including the United States, mass attitudes are often heavily filtered through partisan cues framed by party leaders and the news media, and also biased by the winners-losers effect.[48]

To provide alternative evidence, the Electoral Integrity Project has gathered expert evaluations to monitor the performance of both nationwide and state elections in the United States. PEI-US 2014 used a structured random sampling procedure to select 21 US states.[49] The survey monitored expert perceptions of the integrity of registration and balloting processes in these states. We also classified several features of state laws for registration and balloting used for the 2014 midterm Congressional elections. These procedures are then compared against evidence derived from the PEI-US 2014 survey. Multilevel models (HLM) are used for the cross-sectional analysis.

The Perception of Electoral Integrity Expert Survey (PEI-US)

This study builds on the techniques and methods that the Electoral Integrity Project established when developing the cross-national Perceptions of Electoral Integrity rolling survey, as discussed earlier in Chapter 4.[50] The standard PEI questionnaire includes 49 items monitoring the quality of elections within each country, and this approach was replicated by asking respondents to evaluate the quality of elections within US states.

PEI-US 2014 selected a sample of 21 US states, chosen through a simple random walk. We sought to identify 40–50 expert respondents per state through membership lists from the American Political Science Association (APSA) and university political science department listings. Preference was given to academic faculty who had published in related fields. The survey was distributed one month after the end of the 2014 midterm contests. Respondents were asked to assess the quality of the 2014 Congressional election in the specified state where they were resident. They were instructed not to report their own direct experience of elections or to provide information about legal or factual technical matters in each state (such as the proportion of the eligible electorate registered to vote, for example, which can be gathered more accurately from alternative sources, including electoral laws and official statistics). We received 195 completed replies, representing a response rate of 22 percent. The state-level sample can also be compared with the results of the "standard" nationwide expert surveys conducted separately in the 2012 and 2014 US elections, providing a cross-check on the representativeness of the sample. In the analytical models, several variables are included to control for the social and demographic characteristics of experts which could color their judgments, including their age, sex, as well as their self-reported left-right ideological position, and their partisan preferences. Given the polarization of issues of voter integrity in the United States, it seems important to make sure that any expert judgments of the quality of state elections are not simply attributable to partisan leanings.

Classifying and Measuring State Laws on Registration and Balloting

State laws governing the registration and balloting process were also classified and coded from several sources. First, the National Conference of State Legislatures (NCSL) Election Laws database contains information on recent changes to election laws and procedures passed in state legislatures.[51] It outlines legislation in all 50 states ranging from voter identification requirements to methods of disseminating voter information. Data was also derived from the Election Administration and Voting Survey (EAV), which has been administered by the United States Election Assistance Commission (EAC) for every election since 2004. The EAC has surveyed local county and townships election officials biennially to gather statistics on issues such as: the number and types of registrations, the number of ballots accepted and rejected using each voting procedure (in-person, absentee ballots etc.), the characteristics of poll workers, and the use of voting technologies.[52] These types of statistical indices help to monitor the technical efficiency of electoral administration. They reflect the mandate and legal framework for the EAC, established following the 2002 Help America Vote Act, including the National Voter Registration Act (NVRA), and the Uniformed and Overseas Citizens Absentee Voting Act (UOCAVA). For the 2014 Congressional elections, the surveys were completed by electoral officials in 4,611 local jurisdictions, and these responses were aggregated at state level.

Based on data contained in the EAV and NCSL, the legal framework used by states in the 2014 elections for the US House of Representatives was classified. State laws regulating common registration and balloting procedures were coded from the most restrictive conditions (coded low) to most lenient requirements (coded high). Table B in the Technical Appendix provides our classificatory schema and coding. In particular, states were classified in the restrictions or leniency of laws governing the following electoral procedures:

i. Election-day registration;
ii. Online registration;
iii. Pre-registration (prior to attaining the age of 18);
iv. Voter identification requirements to cast a ballot;
v. Voting rights for felons;
vi. Absentee ballots;
vii. Mail ballots;
viii. Early ballots;
ix. Provisional ballots;
x. Publication of voter leaflets;
xi. Publication and distribution of sample ballots.

The Convenience Elections Laws Index (CEL) was created by summing these criteria and standardizing the score to 100 points for ease of interpretation, where a high score reflects the more lenient procedures for registration and voting in the United States. The reliability of the scale was analyzed and the items generated a moderately strong score (Cronbach's Alpha = .53).

To test the external validity of our measure, the constructed index was compared with the EVAS measure of the proportion of traditional in-person ballots cast on election day at a polling place in each state. The two indices were negatively correlated (R = –.332, P.21), as illustrated in Figure 9.3. That is to say, as expected the more convenience voting facilities are available in each state, then the fewer the proportion of citizens waiting until election day to go to the polls. This observed relationship increases confidence in the external validity of our preferred measures. The CEL was also significantly negatively correlated with the proportion of Republican votes for the US House in the 2014 elections (R = –.279, P.49); also as expected, more Republican-leaning states had more stringent registration and balloting procedures while by contrast Democratic-leaning states tended to have more lenient procedures. Several other social, demographic and economic characteristics of states, such as population size and density, race and ethnicity, mean educational attainment, and even party control of statehouses were tested and excluded from models as these failed to be associated with Convenience Electoral Laws. The main exception was that more affluent states (measured by median household income) were significantly more likely to have lenient procedures (R = .275, P = .51, N.15). The

TABLE 9.1 *Convenience Election Laws in US States, 2014*

State	Convenience Election Law Index standardized	% In person voting in polling place 2014 (EAVS)	No need for voter ID	Can vote absentee with no excuse	Can vote by mail	Can vote early	Election Day Registration allowed (NCSL)	Online Registration allowed (NCSL)	Felon voting most lenient	Can cast provisional ballot if not on register	Can register under 18	Voting info pamphlets issued	Sample Ballots issued
California	99	35	✓	✓	✓	✓		✓		✓	✓	✓	
Maine	95	78	✓	✓		✓	✓		✓	✓	✓		
Nebraska	95	76	✓	✓	✓	✓				✓	✓	✓	✓
Oregon	95		✓	✓	✓(Only)			✓		✓	✓	✓	
Washington, DC	86	6	✓	✓		✓	✓			✓	✓		
Nevada	86	44	✓	✓	✓	✓		✓		✓	✓		
Vermont	86	83	✓	✓	✓	✓			✓	✓			
Wyoming	86	79	✓	✓		✓	✓			✓	✓	✓	
Illinois	82		✓	✓		✓	✓	✓		✓			
North Carolina	82	6	✓	✓		✓				✓		✓	
Colorado	77	4		✓	✓(Only)	✓	✓	✓		✓	✓	✓	
New Jersey	77	92	✓	✓		✓				✓			✓
New Mexico	77	47	✓	✓	✓	✓				✓			
West Virginia	77	78	✓			✓				✓	✓		
New York	65		✓					✓		✓			
Utah	65	56		✓	✓	✓		✓		✓		✓	
Arizona	56	19		✓	✓	✓		✓		✓		✓	
Total	54	68		✓		✓				✓			
Arkansas	47	54			✓	✓				✓			

TABLE 9.1 *(continued)*

State	Convenience Election Law Index standardized	% In person voting in polling place 2014 (EAVS)	No need for voter ID	Can vote absentee with no excuse	Can vote by mail	Can vote early	Election Day Registration allowed (NCSL)	Online Registration allowed (NCSL)	Felon voting most lenient	Can cast provisional ballot if not on register	Can register under 18	Voting info pamphlets issued	Sample Ballots issued
Georgia	47	63		✓		✓		✓	✓	✓	✓		
Montana	47	4		✓		✓	✓			✓		✓	
Florida	43	47		✓	✓	✓				✓	✓		
Texas	43	44			✓	✓				✓	✓		✓
Kansas	39	73		✓		✓		✓		✓	✓		
Ohio	39	71		✓		✓				✓			
Oklahoma	39	91		✓		✓				✓			✓
Alabama	34					✓			✓	✓			✓
Delaware	34	97				✓		✓			✓		
Hawaii	34	39		✓	✓	✓					✓		
Idaho	34	71		✓	✓	✓	✓					✓	
Louisiana	34	84			✓	✓		✓			✓		
New Hampshire	34	93					✓			✓		✓	✓
Wisconsin	34	85		✓		✓	✓			✓			
Connecticut	26	95					✓	✓					
North Dakota	26	61		✓		✓							
Tennessee	26	56				✓				✓			
Virginia	26	94				✓		✓		✓			
Mississippi	22	79			✓					✓		✓	
South Dakota	22	8		✓		✓							
Kentucky	17	96											✓

Iowa	9	59	✓	✓		✓	✓			✓	✓		✓
Maryland	9	77	✓	✓		✓		✓		✓	✓		✓
Minnesota	9	88	✓	✓	✓	✓	✓	✓		✓	✓		
Alaska	6	69		✓					✓	✓	✓	✓	
Massachusetts	6	95	✓							✓		✓	
Pennsylvania	6	97	✓							✓			
Washington	6			✓	✓(Only)	✓		✓		✓		✓	
Michigan	4	74											
Indiana	3	84				✓		✓		✓			
Missouri	3	95						✓			✓		
Rhode Island	3	95								✓	✓	✓	
South Carolina	3	87						✓		✓			
All 50 states +DC			19	31	18	38	12	20	5	41	22	16	9

✓State balloting and registration facility available in the 2014 elections.

Sources: National Conference of State Legislative (NCSL) Election Law Database (www.ncsl.org/research/elections-and-campaigns/2011-2013-elections-legislation-database.aspx) and the 2014 Election Administration and Voting Survey (EAVS) Statutory Overview Report (www.eac.gov/assets/1/Page/2014_Statutory_Overview_Final-2015-03-09.pdf).

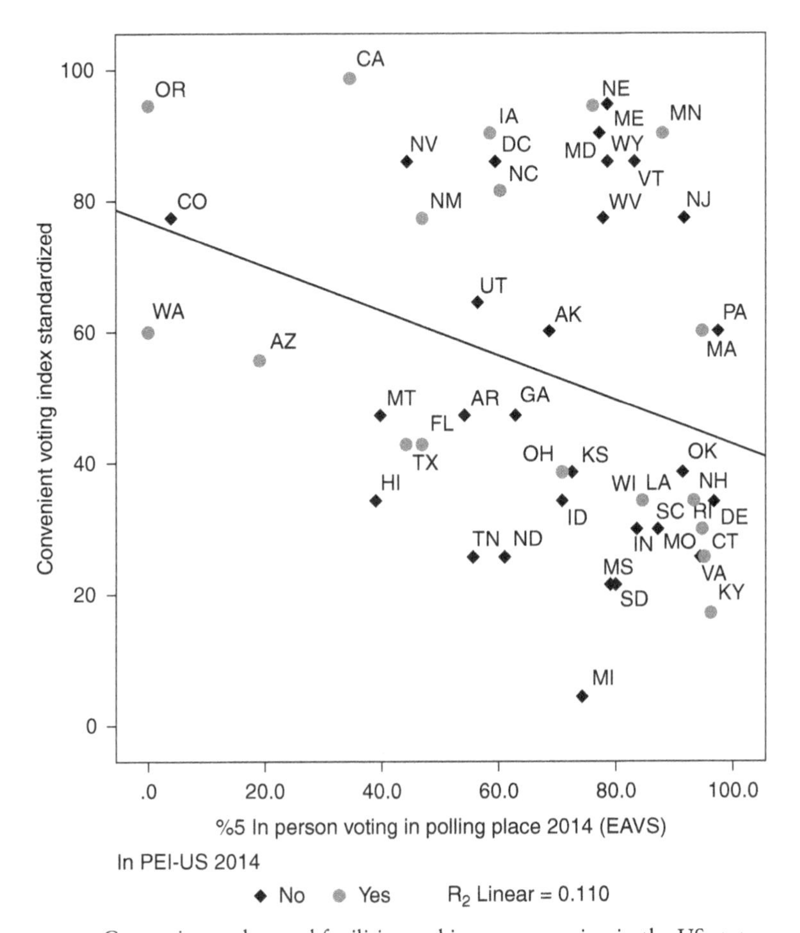

FIGURE 9.3. Convenience electoral facilities and in-person voting in the US states, 2014.

multivariate models therefore controlled for the partisan leanings of states (% GOP vote 2014) and median household income.

EXPERT PERCEPTIONS OF ELECTORAL INTEGRITY AND US STATE LAWS

In the light of these procedures, how did experts perceive the quality of elections in each state, especially regarding the registration and voting processes? And is there a significant relationship between CEL and how experts evaluated electoral integrity in the 2014 Congressional elections?

Table 9.2 presents the perceptions of electoral integrity index and scores on each of the eleven sub-dimensions across the states under comparison. The results illustrate the considerable variance in the overall PEI index, ranging

TABLE 9.2 *Perceptions of Electoral Integrity in Selected US states, 2014*

State	PEI index	Electoral laws	Electoral procedures	District boundaries	Voter registration	Party and candidate registration	Media coverage	Campaign finance	Voting process	Vote count	Results	Electoral authorities
Connecticut	80	55	84	60	66	88	77	75	83	95	94	84
Iowa	78	61	84	81	64	80	73	68	77	90	85	84
Nebraska	76	47	91	52	78	88	68	56	79	90	85	81
Oregon	75	61	97	47	80	82	57	54	81	91	80	88
New Hampshire	75	64	76	70	57	87	67	68	74	87	92	75
Minnesota	74	62	87	58	69	88	62	57	78	85	84	79
Kentucky	73	50	84	32	62	87	67	70	77	75	97	82
Florida	73	51	84	35	65	88	73	65	77	82	79	80
Illinois	72	64	85	39	57	79	61	56	75	90	88	82
California	72	48	86	53	64	80	63	50	75	84	88	85
New Mexico	71	45	79	44	59	83	53	77	73	85	79	79
Rhode Island	70	43	75	39	70	85	63	50	72	91	86	82
Massachusetts	70	57	83	33	68	74	63	57	74	83	85	81
Texas	70	58	79	37	57	83	63	58	72	83	86	77
Missouri	69	49	76	42	56	85	62	59	70	87	81	76
Washington	69	54	80	45	53	78	66	51	74	80	80	78
North Carolina	69	47	76	29	64	78	68	53	73	85	81	79

TABLE 9.2 *(continued)*

State	PEI index	Electoral laws	Electoral procedures	District boundaries	Voter registration	Party and candidate registration	Media coverage	Campaign finance	Voting process	Vote count	Results	Electoral authorities
Alabama	68	46	80	37	54	77	61	61	67	83	86	72
Arizona	66	44	74	42	58	75	64	42	73	83	81	75
Ohio	65	36	79	22	60	77	55	53	72	83	85	70
Wisconsin	64	39	74	27	56	74	55	41	74	82	85	71
Total	71	51	81	42	62	80	64	56	74	85	85	79

Source: Electoral Integrity Project sub-national expert survey of Perceptions of Electoral Integrity (PEI-US 2014) in 21 US States, ranked by the overall 1-point PEI index.

from the best overall performance in Connecticut and Iowa compared with the worst in Ohio and Wisconsin. A glance at the rankings of the PEI index suggests that there is no clear regional pattern; thus overall Massachusetts is ranked as similar to Texas, while Alabama and Arizona are equivalent. The average score in the 100-point PEI Index across the states under comparison (71) is strikingly similar to that found nationwide in the 2014 Congressional elections (69), suggesting that this selection of states is indeed representative of the whole country.

Moreover, the contrasting evaluation of the 100-point standardized measures for each of the eleven stages of the electoral cycle in the PEI-US 2014 are also very similar to those recorded in the nation-wide PEI survey. The worst performing stages across most states were those involving whether *district boundaries* discriminated against some parties, favored incumbents, and failed to be impartial (with a mean score of 42), whether *electoral laws* were unfair to smaller parties, favored the governing party, or restricted voter's rights (51), *campaign finance* (such as whether parties/candidates had equitable access to public subsidies and political donations), and *voter registration* (including whether some citizens were not listed on the register, whether the register was accurate, and whether some ineligible electors were registered). Yet it is worth nothing that *voting processes* were rated more favorably (including whether any fraudulent votes were cast, whether the voting process was easy, whether voters were offered a genuine choice at the ballot box), along with the *vote count* (85) and *postelection results* (85).

But were expert evaluations of the performance of elections more positive in those states with more lenient registration and balloting procedures? Given the use of multilevel data, hierarchical linear models (HLM) are most appropriate for analysis.[53] The models in this study use restricted maximum likelihood techniques (REML) to estimate direct- and cross-level effects for hierarchical data. Individual expert respondents are thus grouped into states. Each state has a different set of parameters for the random factors, allowing intercepts and slopes to vary by nation.[54] All the coefficients were first standardized (Z-scores). The models controlled in Level 1 for several characteristics of the individual experts that might influence their judgments, including age, sex, political views on a ten-point left-right ideological self-placement scale, and their partisan preferences (a five point scale from Democrat to Republican).[55] In addition, models controlled in Level 2 for the partisan characteristics of states, measured by the percentage GOP vote in the 2014 contests, as well as median household income. The treatment of missing data is also important. Mean substitution replaced missing data for individual-level judgments where any items were omitted in the expert survey. Models were tested with and without these treatments to check that they did not have a substantial effect on the interpretation of the results. The multilevel regression models used in this study usually generate small differences in the size of the slope coefficient (b) compared with the results of OLS models, but the average standard errors for

TABLE 9.3 *Models Explaining Expert Perceptions of Electoral Integrity*

	Model A Voter Registration Index			Model B Electoral Integrity index		
	b	SE	Sig.	b	SE	Sig.
INDIVIDUAL-LEVEL						
Demographic characteristics						
Age (years)	**-3.01**	**1.50**	**.049**	-.697	.712	.330
Sex (male=1)	-.800	1.40	.573	**-1.36**	**.653**	**.039**
Self-reported ideological L-R placement	1.73	2.24	.445	**1.97**	**1.00**	**.053**
Partisan preferences	-1.91	1.81	.294	-.038	.869	.965
STATE-LEVEL						
% Vote GOP 2010	-.263	2.30	.912	.797	1.81	.667
Median household income (US$)	.001	.000	.654	.000	.000	.203
Convenience Election Law (CEL) Index	**4.31**	**1.62**	**.045**	1.17	1.32	.393
Constant	60.6			54.1		
Goodness of fit: Schwarz's BIC	754			741		
N. respondents	193			193		
N. states	21			21		

Note: All independent variables have been standardized using mean centering (Z-scores). *Model A* presents the results of the REML multilevel regression models. The PEI-US 2014 expert evaluations for Voter Registration and Electoral Integrity 100-point scales were the dependent variables. Models report the unstandardized beta coefficients (b), the standard errors, and their significance. The models were checked by tolerance tests to be free of any multi-collinearity problems. See Technical Appendix A for details about the measurement, coding, and construction of all variables. Significant coefficients are highlighted in **bold**.

level 2 variables often tend to be slightly larger. The process is thus more rigorous and conservative, avoiding Type I errors (false positives, concluding that a statistically significant difference exists when, in truth, there is no statistical difference). The goodness-of-fit statistic in OLS is the adjusted R^2, where models with a higher coefficient indicate that it accounts for more of the variance. In the REML model, by contrast, Schwarz's Bayesian Criterion (BIC) is used, where the model with the *lower* value is the best fitting.

Table 9.3 presents the results of the models. The first model examines the effects of the independent variables on the PEI-US Voter registration Index. This includes expert assessments (agreed or disagreed on a 5-point scale) as to whether following statements applied to their state elections:

- Some citizens were not listed in the register
- The electoral register was inaccurate
- Some ineligible electors were registered.

The items were therefore deigned to catch many concerns about the quality of the voter registration process, including whether it included all eligible citizens, was correct, and was free of fraud. The items were recoded in a positive direction to generate the scale. The results of the regression models in Table 9.3 show that only two factors predicted expert's judgments: individual-level age (with older experts more critical) and the state-level Convenience Election Law Index. Thus this suggests that *where state laws are more lenient towards registration and balloting, the performance of the voter register is perceived to be of significantly better quality*. Convenience laws are regarded positively by experts. Among the other control factors in the model, the ideological position and party preferences of the experts did not significantly affect their evaluations of voter registration processes. Age was also a significant predictor, with older respondents more negative, for reasons which are not self-evident.

The second model in Table 9.3 examines similar models but using the Electoral Integrity Index, which covers multiple dimensions of performance throughout the electoral cycle from electoral laws, campaign media, and political finance to the vote count and electoral management agency. The results of the second model *did not detect a significant link between the Convenience Elections Law Index and overall levels of electoral integrity*. In many ways this is not surprising since many other laws govern each of these dimensions of elections, such as state laws and procedures for redistricting, political finance, and the role of state and local officials in administering contests. The only factors that emerged as significant in this second model were sex (where women have more negative views of electoral integrity than men, a consistent but still puzzling finding for reasons that currently remain unclear) and the left-right ideological scale, where those on the left have more positive evaluations of electoral integrity in the United States than those on the right. Given the claims of the right about fraud, this is not surprising. Future research needs to explore whether other types of laws, beyond those governing the registration and balloting process, could be help to explain additional linkages. In exploring the data, however, we were unable to detect any further significant relationships between the Convenience Elections Law index and other performance indicators in PEI, including measures about the incidence of fraud, the fairness of election officials, or the impartiality of electoral authorities, all of which raise important questions for further research.

CONCLUSIONS

This study sought to test whether the logistical costs of registration and voting determined by state-level laws influence the perceived quality of US elections. A long series of studies in the previous research literature has sought to determine the impact of registration and balloting laws on voter turnout, as well as whether laws affect public trust and confidence in the electoral process. By contrast, we sought to look more directly at the impact of the legal frameworks on measures of the performance of US state elections, as monitored through expert judgments.

Controversies about electoral reforms have become deeply mired in bitter arguments along party lines in the US, with Republicans arguing that overly lax registration procedures have heightened the risks of significant ballot fraud "stealing elections" in close contests, while Democrats counterclaim that overly zealous voter identification laws are enacted where claims of fraud are used as a smoke screen disguising new attempts at voter suppression of the poor and minorities. Trump's claims have deepened controversy by claiming that the outcome may produce "rigged" results where Democrats cast multiple ballots. The heated debate generated many new state laws since the events in Florida during the 2000 election, producing a mélange of inconsistent registration and balloting procedures in states and localities across the United States. Legal appeals against the new statutes commonly claim that reforms to registration and voting processes, which either raise or lower the logistical costs of participation, will either heighten the risks of voter fraud or else suppress voting rights.

The evidence presented in this chapter suggests two main conclusions.

First, even after controlling for many factors that might influence expert's judgments, including their ideological and partisan leanings, state laws for registration and balloting are indeed related to the perceived performance of voter registration and balloting processes. In particular, the analysis suggests that *more lenient registration and balloting procedures used in a state are significantly associated with more accurate and inclusive electoral registers, according to expert evaluations*. At the same time, based on the analysis, *we found no proof that convenience procedures led to more ineligible electors being registered*, again according to expert judgments of the quality of state elections. From these findings, it does appear that the assumed trade-off between convenience and security is false; we were unable to demonstrate that more lenient procedures increased the risks of voter impersonation, identity theft, or other irregularities in the electoral roll.

Second, however, the impact of these state laws should not be exaggerated; *convenience state registration and balloting procedures do not affect the overall perceived performance of state elections*, as monitored through the standardized PEI index measuring more general evaluations of electoral integrity. This finding is not surprising in many ways. Although controversies about registration and balloting laws receive the most media attention in the United States, these procedures cannot account for the full electoral integrity score in each state.

This observation reinforces the necessity of broadening conceptualizations of electoral fraud and studying the entire electoral cycle, not just the end stages of the process. Cases around the world demonstrate that electoral integrity can also be undermined by partisan gerrymandering or by malapportionment favoring incumbents when drawing constituency boundaries.[56] Party and candidate registration processes may prove equally problematic, for example where independent candidates or new parties face high thresholds before they can gain ballot access.[57] Imbalanced campaign media coverage can also fail to provide a level playing field, and political finance regulations pose another range of challenges, especially where candidates need to accumulate large war chests to succeed.[58] Voting processes in polling places can be flawed, including issues of ballot irregularities and broken machines, while inaccurate counts or insecure ballot seals can undermine the vote tabulation process. The credibility of the outcome can suffer from undue delays in announcing the results or by lack of transparency and audit processes.

And, finally, election officials are vital to administering electoral processes and implementing the rules. Problems can commonly arise where authorities lack know-how capacity, technical resources, or a culture of impartiality. This study therefore sheds light on some of the reasons why US elections perform so poorly compared with other established democracies – but clearly each of the stages throughout the electoral cycle need to be taken into consideration for comprehensive explanations of patterns of electoral integrity. Expanding the analysis in the future to the performance of all 50 states in 2016 Presidential elections will allow these findings to be replicated and explored in further depth.[59]

PART IV

CONCLUSIONS: LESSONS LEARNED

10

Making Electoral Assistance Work Better

The decades since the early-1990s have been a period of remarkable growth in the assistance provided by the international community to the governance and civil society sector, including supporting elections as the foundation of liberal democracy. Electoral assistance covers a multitude of agencies, policies, and programs, whether providing support to legislators about the design, drafting, and revision of new electoral and quota laws; helping EMBs with the process of recruiting and training poll workers and their managers, implementing more convenient facilities for voter registration and balloting, and using digital technologies for tabulating results; strengthening the capacity of the independent judiciary to mediate in electoral disputes and prevent electoral malpractices; advising political parties about the rules used for the recruitment and nomination of candidates, the organization of campaigns, and the regulation of political funding; and working with multiple civil society organizations including supporting education for news workers in the independent media, civic education for citizens, and election watch activities by domestic observer NGOs.[1] These efforts have grown over the last quarter century, but electoral assistance and broader efforts in democracy promotion are encountering growing pushback from resurgent authoritarians abroad and doubts at home. It is now timely to take stock of several common types of interventions.

The collapse of the Soviet Union in late 1980s and early 1990s catalyzed heady optimism about the "end of history" and the triumph of liberal democracy, globalization, and free markets. Under the George W. Bush administration, the agenda of democracy promotion rose in prominence within the State Department and USAID programs.[2] Chapter 2 documented how bilateral development agencies and ministries of foreign affairs in European capitals expanded activities in this subsector, as did regional organizations, including the European Union, the Council of Europe, the Organization of American States, and the Organization for Security and Cooperation in Europe.[3] The turning point within the United Nations arguably came in 2002, when the UNDP, under the leadership of Lord Malloch Brown, created the Democratic Governance practice, which quickly became the largest sector within the organization, absorbing almost 50 percent of the UNDP budget by 2006, more than any other policy area, including poverty and economic development.[4]

During the last decade, however, the zeitgeist has swung in a more critical direction. The Biblical parable of the seven plentiful years followed by the seven lean years of famine seems particularly appropriate.[5] There are warning signs of increasing Western skepticism about the effectiveness of efforts at democracy promotion and state-building – which includes the provision of electoral assistance.[6] In 2005, after two decades of sustained progress, the number of democratic regimes around the globe started to stabilize or even retreat.[7] American and European doubts have been reinforced by the chaos and instability unleashed by the aftermath of Iraq and Afghanistan, the bitter fruits of the Arab uprisings and prolonged humanitarian crisis in Syria. These sentiments have been reinforced by populist disenchantment with globalization, symbolized by the outcome of the Brexit referendum favoring the UK's withdrawal from the European Union, as well as by the election of President Trump. Populist authoritarian parties, leaders, and movements have erratic electoral fortunes but they have also grown in popularity in many European countries, exemplified by the French National Front, the Austrian Freedom Party, the Swedish Democrats, the Swiss People's Party, and the Danish People's Party, among others. These parties appeal to feelings of xenophobic nationalism, fostering mistrust of the agencies of global governance, including the United Nations and European Union, and advocating withdrawal from international engagement and multinational cooperation. The success of these parties has increased pressure on European governments to reduce foreign aid budgets, especially those focused on programs of democracy and human rights rather than programs of security against terrorist threats. In Europe and Scandinavia, there are some clear signs of retrenchment, with aid budgets for democracy assistance abroad slashed and monies diverted to deal with the refugee crisis at home. In the United States, support for promoting democracy in other nations was a lower priority for US foreign policy under the Obama administration than under his predecessor.[8] The transactional realism of 'America First' guiding US foreign policy under the Trump administration promises to take these cuts much further. American public support for this goal has fallen since 9/11.[9] There is push-back among liberal cosmopolitans but the outcome of the 2016 US presidential election reflects a deepening mood of American isolationism and a weary and suspicious retreat from world leadership and global free trade, as indicated by the popular appeal of Donald Trump's nationalistic rhetoric. Meanwhile, there are growing indications of authoritarian pushback by Russia and more active resistance to attempts at democracy promotion, which is regarded by Putin as Western/American interference in sovereign nations.[10] The most dramatic evidence comes from the US intelligence community, which revealed active Russian engagement in cybersecurity threats, attempted hacking, and disinformation campaigns during the 2016 elections, a process designed to support the Trump candidacy and to delegitimize the electoral process.[11] Similar problems were reported in France and Germany.

Reflecting the skeptical mood among policymakers, Sarah Sunn Bush argued that many Western attempts at democracy promotion have become routine technical exercises, akin to rearranging the deck chairs on the Titanic, without acknowledging the broader political contexts.[12] These arguments echo the case for aid skeptics, led by William Easterly, who cautions gloomily that most large-scale development projects are doomed to fail.[13] He charges that decisions about the allocation of development aid are shaped primarily by the political, strategic, and commercial interests of the donors and what programs they can offer, rather than being driven by the urgent needs of the recipients. Substantial amounts of assistance are tied to the donor country's commercial, technical, and consultancy agencies, delivering goods and services, but limiting direct access by recipient countries. In general, development aid may also set up perverse incentives that undermine any beneficial consequences, including by lining the pockets of ruling elites and propping up dictators rather than trickling down to touch the lives of the poor.[14] For example, de Walle argues that foreign aid has made very little impact on overcoming poverty and stagnation in many of the world's poorest African societies, since resources have often kept repressive rulers in office and undermined local pressures for radical economic and political reforms.[15] Echoing these sentiments, one of the most seasoned observers, Thomas Carothers, worries that democracy assistance programs may be trapped by repeating an endless loop of routine approaches that fail to meet expectations.[16] At best, Peter Burnell argues that after twenty-five years of democracy support by the aid community, researchers still do not know enough about its value to provide useful practical guidance for policymakers.[17] Others warn that aid workers should follow the principle of physicians and "first do not harm." Mansfield and Snyder have repeatedly warned for many years that holding early elections in the initial stages of any transitions from authoritarianism often deepens conflict and instability, rather than ameliorating these risks.[18]

There is also prima facie evidence that, despite a quarter century of international electoral assistance, many contemporary contests around the world remain either deeply flawed or even failed.[19] Even in long-established democracies that have held elections for centuries, flaws in electoral procedures still occur, damaging public confidence in the honesty and democratic legitimacy of elections.[20]

A variety of panaceas are commonly proposed to overcome electoral problems, including reforming electoral systems, overhauling campaign finance laws, implementing term limits, and expanding the use of referenda and plebiscites. Some institutional patterns have been established with a high degree of confidence. For example, compared with majoritarian contests, comparative research suggests that in general, proportional representation electoral systems are usually associated with greater party competition, higher voter turnout, and the election of more women to parliament.[21] But the causality underlying these relationships remains complex to disentangle.[22] Bowler and Donovan warn that in practice, even in established democracies, attempts at electoral engineering have had limited success in achieving the aims of their proponents.[23] Unintended consequences commonly undermine well-intentioned institutional changes.[24] This suggests caution for hopes of equivalent electoral reforms succeeding in far less favorable conditions, such as in less democratic states with weak rule of law, widespread corruption, and authoritarian traditions. In short, the research literature suggests many reasons for skepticism about the value of international electoral assistance and the limits of domestic attempts at changing formal electoral laws and procedures.

How far popular skepticism about the impact of international engagement and populist arguments for isolationism will translate into shifts in developmental priorities remains unclear. In the short-term, this is unlikely to mean that the complex global network of international agencies, bilateral donors, regional organizations, and international NGOs that work to strengthen democracy and assist elections will abandoned long-term strategic plans, or that the United Nations general assembly will suddenly refused to endorse the series of biannual resolutions authorizing UN agencies to provide support for periodic or genuine elections.[25] There has not been a sudden dearth of local demand; for example, in 2015 UN-EAD received requests for electoral assistance from roughly one-third of all member states.[26] Today all but a handful of nation-states around the world hold elections (with varied some degree of competition) for the lower house of the national legislature or for executive office.[27] This tide shows no sign of retreating. Some contemporary military coups d'état or executive actions have delayed or temporarily suspended elections in several hybrid states, notably in Mali, Egypt, and Thailand, threatening democratic progress, but compared with earlier decades, the Center for Systemic Peace documents that the number of recent cases remains relatively rare.[28] Despite major constitutional crisis, the military generally remains in their barracks and, as in Benin in 2013, Burkina Faso in 2015, and Turkey in 2016, any attempted armed uprisings commonly quickly fail. Chapter 2 documented how electoral assistance was gradually institutionalized during the early-1990s to become an established subsector of development aid. The UN Sustainable Development Goals, endorsed by the world's governments as the blueprint for development from 2015 until 2030, includes targets for ensuring "... responsive, inclusive and representative decision-making at all levels" (16.7) and for developing "... effective, accountable and transparent institutions at all levels." (16.6)[29] The United Nations also continues to endorse "democracy, good governance, and the rule of law, as well an enabling environment at national and international levels, are essential for sustainable development."[30]

What does seem more likely, however, is that in the long-term, attempts at providing electoral assistance will face major challenges when seeking to strengthen electoral integrity. Difficulties multiply for contests held as part of the peace-building process in some of the world's hot spots, such as Afghanistan, Libya, and Iraq, where the riskiest contexts arise following attempted transitions from autocracy.[31]

In short, compared with other sectors of development and security, democracy promotion and electoral assistance agencies and programs are facing an increasingly chilly climate in the fight for legitimacy and resources. For example, Official Development Aid spending on the "government and civil society" sector (coded 151) is estimated to have risen dramatically from US$4.52bn in 1997 to a peak of $33.41bn in 2009, before falling back to $23.15bn in 2013.[32] There are indications that since then, several leading European donors have already started to adjust their priorities, shifting resources from humanitarian aid abroad to spending on the migration crisis at home.

This reinforces the importance of the question now confronting international organizations: have programs of electoral assistance been effective in achieving their goals? Do they deliver value for money? And if budgetary reductions are implemented, which programs should be prioritized and which dropped? Many positive examples are regularly published in annual reports by development agencies, but these are designed to provide positive images of the organizations, and it remains difficult to sort out the systematic evidence behind these claims.

Scholars focusing on the broader democracy promotion agenda remain divided in their assessments. On the one hand, muscular proponents, such as McFaul, argue that the United States and the development community both *can* and *should* foster the advance of democracy around the world, so as to strengthen accountable government, guarantee basic human rights, produce more prosperity, and improve security.[33] By contrast, critics of these policies contend that seeking to strengthen transitional elections from repressive autocracies heightens the risks of conflict, rather than resolving the underlying causes of violence and thereby building sustainable peaceful settlements.[34] Bush argues that US programs offering routine technical assistance programs, tinkering at the margins, have replaced more ambitious goals of radical regime change in authoritarian states.[35] Another critic, Lincoln Mitchell, warns that the US can never succeed by providing democracy assistance programs to civil society NGOs in authoritarian states, such as programs seeking to build independent journalism or human rights watch organizations, since rulers are unwilling to accept these reforms.[36]

Addressing Critics

To counter doubts, as the introduction to this book suggested, normative, instrumental, and pragmatic arguments can be advanced to provide reasons for maintaining and even redoubling investments in international programs of electoral assistance.

The normative case rests on fundamental rights and obligations established by the 1948 Universal Declaration of Human Rights and the long series of subsequent international conventions and treaties endorsed by the world's governments. Based on these ideals, the UN General Assembly has repeatedly passed a series of resolutions since 1991 recognizing that UN agencies and bureaus have a legitimate mandate to assist member states requesting financial, technical, or human resources to support electoral institutions and processes.[37] The capacity of the international community to offer assistance to states that request support for electoral laws, procedures, and processes has deepened with experience in recent decades. Moreover, despite evidence of growing popular disillusionment and frustration with the performance of governments and political institutions, there remains substantial worldwide support and enthusiasm for the ideals and principles of democracy and elections.[38]

The closely related but alternative instrumental argument for electoral assistance emphasizes the important consequences that are thought to flow from contests meeting international standards, especially for the way that competitive contests are at the heart of democratic legitimacy, electoral accountability, and civic participation. A growing body of evidence, presented in the previous books in this trilogy, demonstrates that flawed and failed contests which fail to meet international standards are deeply damaging, including by eroding public confidence in political institutions and satisfaction with the performance of democracy, weakening citizen participation through the ballot box, and catalyzing instability and conflict in fragile states.[39] Many commentators also emphasize the broader impact that democratic elections are believed to have for strengthening human welfare, economic development, and security.[40] This argument is exemplified by the work of Amartya Sen, buttressing the case for the intrinsic desirability of the democratic values of self-governance and human freedom, and the importance of electoral accountability and the free press for responsive leaders, processes of sustainable human development, and the avoidance of humanitarian disasters.[41]

Debates about the desirability of democratic elections as a fundamental human right and the consequences that flow from them continue to resonate; claims are far from settled. Without engaging directly in these debates in this volume, this book focuses instead upon scrutinizing a logically prior question concerning the *practicality* of international electoral assistance. It is important to raise hard-headed questions about the pragmatic utility of Western efforts to bolster free and fair contests, no matter how legitimate, well-meaning, and potentially important these interventions. There are reasons why electoral assistance programs provided by international organizations may produce results that are uncertain and ineffective, at best, and possibly counterproductive, at worst.[42] The pragmatic argument, buttressed by the evidence presented in this book, challenges skeptics by demonstrating that external support has the capacity to strengthen the integrity of elections.

Methods Evaluating the Impact of Democracy Promotion and Electoral Assistance

It is important to address skeptical arguments by trying to gather more comprehensive, systematic, and rigorous evidence about the effectiveness of electoral assistance programs and projects in order to assess what works in different contexts – and also to identify what often fails. Programs in electoral assistance have expanded sharply since 1990, so it is now timely to collect a report card on experience of these initiatives over the last 25 years. In general, program and project evaluations seek to learn from experience, to provide the basis for informed decision-making about policy priorities, to reinforce organizational accountability to oversight agencies, and to ensure that scarce resources are rationally allocated. The danger of failing to evaluate programs is that, as Thomas Carothers notes, democracy promotion and electoral assistance agencies repeat standard programs that fail to adapt and meet new challenges.[43]

At the same time, it must be acknowledged that complex theoretical and methodological challenges are raised in the attempt to develop a systematic and comprehensive scorecard concerning the overall effectiveness of electoral assistance programs, venturing beyond what has been established through previous illustrative case studies and also technically rigorous but narrowly defined project impact studies. Evaluations designed to strengthen electoral integrity would benefit from both clearer theories identifying the common risks and opportunities in each context – as well as more rigorous assessment methods integrated into the start of new projects.

Previous studies evaluating the effects of democracy promotion and electoral assistance programs have been conducted at progressively more granular levels of analysis, including by assessing: (i) the impact of overall levels of Official Development Assistance (ODA) on democratic governance in recipient states; (ii) the influence of spending by bilateral donors, like USAID, on programs in the sector of democratic governance; (iii) the outcomes arising from specific programs, such as those seeking to strengthen rule of law or provide media assistance; and (iv) the effect of implementing specific projects supported by international agencies in particular regions or countries, such as electoral observer monitoring missions, or reforms of electoral laws.[44]

Econometric cross-national and time-series analysis seek to provide the broadest picture about the observed relationship connecting overall levels of development assistance and the long-run process of democratization, facilitating valid generalizations across diverse societies and world regions. Despite an extensive body of research over many years, however, no agreement has emerged in the literature. Hence several studies support the "null-hypothesis"; for example, one of the most well-known early cross-national studies by Knack found no empirical evidence for the proposition that general levels of development aid promoted democracy in the long run.[45] Similarly Scott and Steel were unable to detect any positive effects on democracy arising from US National Endowment for Democracy (NED) annual grants during the 1990s.[46] Other scholars have detected harmful effects of aid on institutional quality and democratization, by encouraging inefficient public spending and increasing rent-seeking among corrupt officials.[47] This echoes the skeptical view of William Easterly who argues that there is no relation between aid and economic growth, so that aid may even have done more harm than good.[48]

By contrast, others have reported positive results; for example, a detailed and thorough analysis of USAID spending on democracy and governance from 1990 to 2003 by Finkel et al. found clear impacts of US foreign assistance on strengthening processes of democratization (measured by improvements in the Freedom House scores), using growth models.[49] The study reported that USAID spending on elections and political processes also had significant effects on democratization scores. Cross-national empirical and time-series panel analysis by Kersting and Kilby expanded the comparison to analyze the effects of aid from OECD donors and they reported that this had a modest effect on strengthening democratization, while democratic reforms were also found to be more likely to occur in countries when recipients faced the credible threat of conditional aid allocation.[50] These positive findings reflects the arguments of "development optimists" such as Jeffrey Sachs and Charles Kenny, who highlight impressive global gains in economic growth and human welfare over recent decades arising from international assistance.[51]

It is not surprising, however, that little consensus has emerged from this debate, and rival arguments continue to be heard, since regression analysis models of observational data remain highly sensitive to their theoretical assumptions and specifications, as well as the choice of cross-national coverage and time-series period, the selection of appropriate controls, and the treatment of missing observations. Given the difficulties of establishing robust linkages between general levels of aid and democratization in each country with any degree of confidence, and continuing debate among studies, it is safest to conclude that the jury still remains out on this question.

Multiple forms of evidence and techniques are utilized for program evaluations, ranging from diverse case studies drawing upon document reviews, surveys of participants, interviewers with stakeholders, and more anecdotal best-practice experiences, through various more or less controlled designs and econometric models applying regression models, to randomized control trials, regarded by many scholars as the gold standard at the top of the scientific hierarchy.[52] During recent decades, methods using observational data have been supplemented by growing use of randomized methods including *laboratory* experiments (controlling the treatment in highly artificial settings), *field* experiments (typically where researchers have less control of the specific type of project intervention but where treatments are randomized among groups to monitor effects), and *natural* experiments (taking advantage of pre/post changes in a treatment and control group in naturally occurring real-world phenomenon). A growing number of project evaluations using these techniques have been now been conducted and published in each sector of democratic governance, including a smaller subset using rigorous techniques of field experiments. Most of these experiments concern mass behavior, typically through the provision of information campaigns, to test the influence of civic education, media exposure, and mobilization campaigns on citizen's attitudes and behavior.[53] A growing body of field experiments have also been conducted to determine the impact of international observer missions on ballot box fraud,[54] to assess the effect on voter turnout of using different technologies to cast a ballot,[55] as well as to test the impact of natural experiments in electoral systems.[56]

By contrast to observational data, detailed studies of development projects using randomized control trials seek to provide more credible evidence by allowing researchers to identify the potential effect of specific types of interventions on a few key short- and medium-term outcomes, strengthening causal inferences and internal validity. These methods have been rapidly growing in popularity in development studies, including research on democratization.[57] Unfortunately, the gains in precision come at the loss of generalizability; such studies can provide little guidance about the long-term cumulative impact of projects or whether the specific findings on one case apply to other contexts, cultures, and populations. Although the research literature is expanding, we still lack a well-established body of randomized control trials testing the effects of democracy and electoral assistance programs across diverse societies, agencies, and types of programmatic interventions. Whatever the specific mix of methods deployed, however, it remains challenging to achieve effective, credible, and rigorous programmatic evaluations, based on valid and reliable evidence, especially where the results can be generalized across many diverse contexts. For all these reasons, this book employed a range of methods, using observational data, to counterbalance the strengths and limits of each approach. Chapters present comparative evidence demonstrating the pragmatic case for improving standards of electoral integrity through electoral assistance programs – while acknowledging when these efforts are constrained by both the risky underlying conditions in worst-case scenarios and the limits and capacities of particular agencies and types of programs.

Summarizing the Evidence for the Pragmatic Case

The pragmatic argument developed by this volume started with the premise that well-designed programs of technical electoral assistance can potentially achieve their specific goals, reduce malpractices, strengthen integrity, and thereby generally strengthen free and fair contests which reflect the genuine will of the people. How far was this claim supported by the evidence?

The book described the key international and regional agencies engaged in this sector. Activities by donors expanded substantially during the last quarter-century, as this sector moved from the margin to the mainstream of foreign aid. An important benchmark is that as a proportion of all Overseas Development Assistance (ODA) spending, the amount devoted to electoral assistance tripled from around 4 percent to 12 percent during the last decade. Estimates suggest that around $20 billion a year in ODA is invested in electoral assistance today. Programs typically used to strengthen electoral integrity include the sequential process of advocating reforms and providing technical advice for improving legal regulations, capacity building for implementing agencies, monitoring performance, and strengthening accountability and oversight mechanisms. Different agencies intervene strategically in different parts of this process, depending upon their capacities and mandate. Thus many international NGOs such as Transparency International, Amnesty International, IREX, Reporters without Borders, and Freedom House are engaged in the production of annual ranking indicators, "naming and shaming" countries for their records on human rights, censorship, or corruption, to catalyze reform pressures at home and abroad.[58] By contrast, regional organizations such as the OAS and OSCE are engaged in developing norms and conventions, sharing best practices and practical experience about democracy and elections among member states, and observing elections. And the major UN bureaus and agencies fulfil many functions in this sector, primarily working with governments in member states to expand the capacity of implementing agencies, such as Election Management Bodies, through providing technical advice, project support, and aid for local initiatives.

Using the common SWOT model, in Chapter 2 the effectiveness of electoral assistance provided by these agencies was predicted to be the product of their Strengths and Weaknesses, including their technical expertise, financial and human resources, and experience, coupled with the Opportunities and Threats facing each local context. The risks are especially important to determine the most strategic and effective interventions in contests where the international community seeks to support elections in the most difficult circumstances and hostile soil. Following the needs assessment and problem definition stage, evaluations need to identify the overall goals, targets and specific activities involved in any electoral assistance program. What, exactly, did the international agency and local actors do in programs seeking to strengthen civic engagement, improve campaign finance regulations, or reduce electoral conflict? The essential stage – and most difficult part of any rigorous policy evaluation – is then to gather and analyze systematic evidence which can help to determine how far particular program activities can be credibly associated with specific program outcomes that strengthen electoral integrity. Finally, it is also important to consider, although difficult to determine, whether programs had cumulative effects upon any longer-term societal impacts.

Drawing upon the previous volume in this trilogy, on *Why Elections Fail*, the risks and opportunities for electoral assistance in each society are shaped by structural socioeconomic conditions, the engagement of the international community, constitutional checks and balances preventing the abuse of power by the executive, and the culture and ethos in the public sector.[59] Each of these factors plays a role in whether electoral integrity or malpractices are common – and thus the challenges facing reformers.

On this basis, subsequent chapters examined several types of programs. Chapter 5 focused on the role of regional organizations in strengthening reforms to electoral laws and procedures, especially in their role as policy advisors. It has now become standard practice for the final reports issued by election observer mission to identify areas for improvement and to publish a series of concrete recommendations that are designed to encourage states to strengthen their electoral institutions, laws, and procedures in line with international treaties. Through this process, regional organizations highlight the electoral standards, obligations, and commitments that states should fulfil. Little is known with any certainty, however, about the consequences when regional organizations propose alternative steps that could be taken to improve electoral integrity in member states. Previous research has not established whether domestic stakeholders respond to these suggestions – or whether they are simply disregarded. Many obstacles may prevent the recommendations from being implemented, such as lack of financial resources and professional capacity, technical limitations and lack of time, challenging conditions such as outbreaks of instability and conflict, and political incumbents blocking change. Recommendations may be seen by domestic actors as inappropriate, unconvincing, or ineffective. Thus suggestions may well fall on deaf ears, in which case any shortcomings are likely to persist, and may even worsen.

The chapter presented new evidence suggesting several key findings. First, the agenda-setting stage of the policymaking process is indeed strongly influenced by the recommendations issued by regional organizational monitoring missions. Around half of the recommendations published in monitor's reports are subsequently implemented by member states, fully or partially. Given the many obstacles littering the pathway to any reform, this level suggests the effectiveness of electoral assistance programs. Of course the changes could have arisen without the intervention of the monitoring agency since they may echo and reflect dissatisfaction within each society among diverse stakeholders such as opposition parties and civil society organizations. Nevertheless, by highlighting salient problems and suggesting possible policy solutions, regional organizations contribute to the influence agenda-setting process. Secondly, the type of recommendations also mattered: the implementation rate was highest for proposals seeking to improve civic education, electoral laws, voter registration and electoral procedures, all activities occurring during the preelection stage of the electoral cycle. By contrast, policy advice concerning ways of overcoming problems of campaign media and political finance were less likely to be adopted. Procedural reforms and those recommending general principles and standards were also more likely to be enacted. This helps to identify important opportunities for international agencies seeking to encourage electoral reforms – and the limits of these proposals. Finally, confirming the international linkage theory, societies linked most strongly with the institutions of global governance implemented OAS recommendations most often. By contrast, many other institutional and structural factors, including levels of economic development and democratization, were neither significant advantages nor disadvantaged for reform. The overall conclusions from this evidence, therefore, are that the policy advisor role of regional organizations, sharing best practices, advocating improvements, and catalyzing the electoral reform agenda within member states, can make a significant contribution towards the implementation of legal and procedural electoral reforms.

Chapter 6 went on to consider the issue of women's empowerment and gender equality in elected and appointed public office. Ever since the Beijing declaration in 1995, international organizations and national governments around the world have repeatedly endorsed the aim of strengthening these goals. One of the primary ways that countries have sought to achieve this objective is through gender quotas, which have now been implemented in more than 100 countries worldwide. The worldwide spread of gender quota policies in recent decades has been a remarkable development; these statutes are more radical than many other alternative policies that are designed to strengthen equal opportunities in elected office, such as investing in training and capacity development for candidates or providing public funding for women. This phenomenon raises two questions considered in this book: What has driven the worldwide adoption of legal gender quota policies and, in particular, what has been the role of international forces and multilateral organizations in the diffusion process? And, equally important, have these policies proven effective by strengthening gender equality in representative bodies, which is a core dimension of women's rights and electoral integrity?

This chapter seeks to explain the adoption of gender quotas by the role of international organizations in this process, as well as impact of domestic political activists and the relative level of women's representation prior to the adoption and revision of gender quota policies. Models control for the role of structural conditions and mass cultural values. The results underline the importance of international diffusion as well as domestic advocates for the initial adoption of gender quotas. This reflects the process of norm diffusion in international human rights. The international community adopted the issue of gender equality in elected office, and the radical Beijing declaration from 1995 changed the 30 percent target, even if the controversial word "quotas" was not mentioned. The push for gender equality in elected office was reinforced by the 2000–2015 MDGs and their replacement by the SDGs. Insights into the causes of women's low political representation have gradually shifted from emphasizing supply-side factors (women's alleged lack of political interest, ambition, and competence) to blaming demand-side factors (including political parties and parliaments). Following international declarations, initiatives designed to strengthen women's participation agencies have been advocated by agencies such as UN Women, multilateral organizations such as the OSCE, International IDEA, IPU and OAS, and northern bilateral donors such as NORAD and SIDA. Consequently, many countries have adopted gender quotas, and today such measures are in use in a broad selection of political regimes, more often in democratic and authoritarian regime, less often in hybrid regimes. The successful example of gender quotas in several countries encouraged neighboring states with cultural ties to follow suit, exemplified by the influence of South Africa on other countries in the southern cone of Africa and the impact of Argentina on Latin American states. Women activists working in human rights NGOs and within political parties have been able to use global norms, technical assistance, and development aid to amplify demands that countries should take action to meet international standards. Comparative analyses have fostered an international competition between states to have a higher level of women's representation in parliament than at least their neighboring countries.

Moreover, the implementation of gender quotas has had an impact upon women's empowerment; almost half of the countries with quota laws have experienced a substantive increase in women's numerical representation in the first election after the adoption, an important achievement in its own right. During the recent wave of quota amendments, many countries with only weak results of their quota regulation have also strengthened their provisions, for example by introducing or tightening penalties for noncompliance, rank order rules or raising levels. Few countries have abandoned or weakened their quota laws, indicating that these policies have won widespread acceptance despite controversies around their adoption. Therefore, just as the previous chapter suggested that regional organizations have played an important role by encouraging electoral reforms, so the evidence on the adoption of gender quotas further confirms these patterns, with the important proviso that electoral assistance from the international community works best in conjunction with local stakeholders, combining to strengthen women's rights and inclusive electoral processes.

Other challenges to democracy and elections concerns major threats to freedom of information and the independent media. There are many types of interventions used by agencies concerned with the provision of media assistance, including how to strengthen values such as independence, diversity, freedom of expression, and pluralism, such as through implementing freedom of information laws, protecting the rights and security of journalists operating in risky environments, and investing in the infrastructure for digital communications. Chapter 7 focused upon the impact of programs of formal educational providing training for news workers as one of the most common types of activities by international organizations and domestic stakeholders. Evidence was drawn from one of the largest surveys of journalists in over 60 countries worldwide, as well as broader indices of media development. The evidence demonstrated that the predominant role orientations for journalists found in national media cultures (monitored through the surveys) are significantly associated with macrolevel indicators of the overall levels of electoral integrity in each country, freedom of the press, and democratization. In particular, where journalists regard their role as unofficial spokespersons for the regime authorities (like ministerial press officers, providing positive images of political leaders and supporting government policies), this damages the quality of levels of electoral integrity, press freedom, and processes of democratization. At the same time, however, the evidence considered in this chapter was unable to demonstrate that the predominant way that journalists see their work in any media culture was altered by formal college education and journalistic training programs. Role orientations may therefore be deeply embedded within national media cultures, and the product of levels of economic development and freedom of the press, rather than the product of formal college education. Further analysis of individual-level data is needed to examine this relationship more closely.

Chapter 8 compared the policies used in attempts to regulate political finance and, in particular, whether there was any evidence that the type and degree of legal regulations serve to strengthen electoral integrity, reduce corruption, and improve democratic governance. There have been many case studies considering these issues in particular countries but little recent systematic comparative research and no established consensus about which public policies have proved most effective in regulating political and campaign finance – and which have largely failed to meet their objectives.[60] The evidence suggests that when it comes to the question of what works, there is no single right mix of policies regulating political finance that fit countries with diverse institutional, cultural, and economic conditions. Instead, the decision to intervene in the flow of money into politics and the consequences of this intervention are affected by numerous contingent factors, some of which may be controlled and some of which lie beyond the control of policy makers and politicians. Nevertheless, the evidence also suggests several positive findings. First, practices in each country often do seem to reflect the legal framework, so that regulations are not merely a façade of window dressing to attract aid and investment. Laws matter. There was a significant correlation between de jure and de factor regulations. Secondly, there are many variations among all the types of campaign finance regulations, and the devil is often in the details when it comes down to the legal requirements and forms of implementation. Nevertheless, the regulations emphasizing public disclosure and transparency, which are some of the most popular reforms in recent years, also seem to generate the most positive impacts on the quality of campaign finance, electoral integrity, and democracy. At the same time, no single form of regulation of money in politics exists in most countries; instead, these rules are used in combination, for example emphasizing the importance of transparency as a quid pro quo for the introduction of public funding for political parties. The analysis also shows that, although there are some well-known exceptions, in general more heavily regulated systems of campaign finance also tend to be associated with better societal outcomes. Like other areas of electoral assistance offered by the international community, the findings provide further positive support buttressing the pragmatic argument.

Chapter 9 turned to the practical and technical challenges of implementing effective, comprehensive, and accurate processes of voter registration and balloting, an area which often receives requests to the United Nations and development agencies for electoral assistance and one where problems can arise even in long-established democracies. Unlike previous chapters, the study uses within-country comparisons across American states. This provides a suitable framework since there have been many reforms to state laws in recent years, while also allowing comparisons within broadly similar cultural, economic, and political conditions in American society. The chapter tests whether the logistical costs of registration and voting, as determined by state-level laws, influence the quality of state electoral performance when monitored through expert judgments. The evidence presented in this chapter suggests two main conclusions. First, even after controlling for many factors that might influence expert's judgments, including their ideological and partisan leanings, state laws for registration and balloting are indeed found to be related to the performance of voter registration and balloting processes. In particular, more lenient registration and balloting procedures used in a state are significantly associated with more accurate and inclusive electoral registers, according to expert evaluations. At the same time, the analysis found no proof that convenience procedures led to more ineligible electors being registered. These findings suggest that, according to the evidence, any assumptions about an inevitable trade-off between convenience and security is false; more lenient procedures did not increase the risks of voter impersonation, identity theft, or other irregularities in the electoral roll. At the same time, however, the impact of these state laws should not be exaggerated; convenience state registration and balloting procedures do not affect the overall performance of state elections, as monitored through the standardized PEI index measuring more general perceptions of electoral integrity. Controversies about registration and balloting laws receive considerable media attention in American, but these procedures are only one part of electoral integrity and other challenges influencing the overall quality of US contests and patterns of party competition, such as the widespread use of gerrymandered boundaries and the role of money in politics.

Summarizing the pragmatic case

New data presented throughout this book therefore demonstrates that electoral integrity has often been strengthened by a series of practical projects where international organizations and bilateral donors have supported the efforts of local stakeholders. The programs featured in successive chapters are not "cherry-picked" as success stories; instead they reflect cases where evidence is available concerning some of the most common types of interventions, whether seeking to reform electoral laws and procedures and to strengthen the capacity of agencies responsible for implementing these laws and monitoring their effectiveness. This includes the advocacy work reflected in hundreds of OAS election monitoring reports that have encouraged reforms to electoral laws and procedures in Latin America; technical assistance programs, such as handbooks and workshops supported by UN Women, International IDEA, the OSCE, and the Inter-parliamentary Union, spreading awareness of gender quotas laws which have served, in turn, to strengthen women's representation in many countries; education and professional training programs for journalists supported by international agencies such as the Open Society Foundation, the BBC Media Action and the Markle Foundation, which have helped to facilitate the growth of independent media; technical assistance offered by organizations such as Transparency international, International IDEA and IFES, providing information and sharing best practices concerning legal reforms regulating money in politics, especially disclosure and right to information policies; and US state reforms that seek to make voter registration and balloting processes more inclusive and convenient for all citizens.

Success should not be exaggerated. Not everything works, by any means. Electoral assistance is most effective, as Chapter 2 emphasized, where the strengths and weaknesses of international agencies and programs match the threats and opportunities on the ground. There are numerous risky cases such as Afghanistan where the international community provides support to local stakeholders, not because these contests provide the best prospects for success, but because United Nations agencies have a mandate to respond to requests from member states and the Security Council, irrespective of the severity of the challenges. If it was easy, in developing countries where democratic elections work well, then there is less need for their services. The last 25 years have deepened our knowledge about well-designed programs that improve the quality of elections, including through reforming electoral laws and procedures, strengthening gender equality in elected office, promoting independent media, increasing the transparency of campaign finance, and improving voter registration and balloting processes. These cases also exemplify projects that address issues where there is a broad consensus about global norms within the international community, based on international laws and human rights conventions and that often engage local public sector stakeholders (notably electoral management bodies and parliaments) with the authority to pass and implement legal reforms; and, finally, where international agencies, NGOs, and bilateral donors have the capacity to provide local stakeholders with resources, as well as giving technical assistance.

The book has only started to scrutinize some evidence for certain common types of intervention. Numerous other examples of related programs in this sector also deserve equal scrutiny, including training programs seeking to expand the human and technical capacity of Electoral Management Bodies, projects working to strengthen civic education and mobilize participation among citizens, initiatives aiming to improve electoral justice and mediation mechanisms in cases of electoral disputes, programs working to reduce the risks of conflict and violence in the campaign and its aftermath, and so on. There is a large research agenda remaining to be established by the next generation of scholars. The evidence-base for assessing the impact of all these types of interventions also needs to expand and use multiple methods, going beyond previous efforts to incorporate randomized experimental evaluations, surveys of participants and program managers, process-oriented case-studies, and other related techniques. Through this process, successful practices by multilateral organizations can be identified, while realistically acknowledging the serious risks of failure in many risky contexts, the continuing lack of hard evidence for many claims, and the limits of what external support alone can achieve without local stakeholder buy-in.

The trilogy of books has sought to deepen understanding of the importance of electoral integrity, the reasons why elections fail, and the challenges of electoral assistance – but much work still remains to be done. The difficulties facing this sector should not be underestimated, many major malpractices are common, and contests are often flawed, or even failed elections. But just because it's difficult, does not mean that international attempts to help local reformers in efforts to bolster electoral integrity should be reduced or even abandoned. Since 1948, the world has been committed to supporting free and fair contests reflecting the general will of the people. It would be a tragedy to undermine progress by slipping backwards, withdrawing from international engagement, ignoring appeals for support from local reformers, and thereby undermining opportunities to strengthen electoral integrity, prospects for democracy, and fundamental electoral rights to self-determination.

Technical Appendices

TECHNICAL APPENDIX 6A *Indicators and Variable Measures*

Category	Indicator	Measure	Year(s)	Source
DEPENDENT VARIABLE				
Gender quotas	Classification of the type of gender quota policies	1. Reserved seats for women 2. Legal gender quotas for lists of party candidates 3. If none of the above, then voluntary gender quotas for lists of party candidates in at least one of the three largest parties 4. None of the above	2014	Quota Project
Legal gender quotas	Adoption of any legal gender quota policies or reserved seat	1,2 above = yes (1); 4= No (0)	2014	Quota Project
EXPLANATORY VARIABLES				
International	Development aid spending	Aid for democratic participation & civil society (10-year average)	2013	AidData
International	Global diffusion	KOF Index of Globalization, 100-pts	2013	KOF/QoG
International	Regional adoption of quota policies	Mean number of states with any gender quota policy in a global region.	2014	Quota Project
International	Advocacy	Coded: Did women's organizations … advocate passing the first gender quota law? • International organizations, movements, donors	2014	Quota Project

TECHNICAL APPENDIX 6A *(continued)*

Category	Indicator	Measure	Year(s)	Source
Domestic political activists	Advocacy groups	Coded: Did women's organizations . . . advocate passing the first gender quota law? • Women/feminist NGOs • Women in some political parties • A woman's Commission or other equality policy state agency	2014	Quota Project
STRUCTURAL CONTROLS				
Socioeconomic	Level of economic development	Logged per capita GDP (in ppp constant US dollars)	2012	WDI
Socioeconomic	Female labor force participation rate	Women in labor force, ratio to Men	2012	WEF
Socioeconomic	Gender Ratio in School	Ratio of girls to boys in secondary level education	2013	WDI
Socioeconomic	Natural resources	Log total natural resources rents (as% of GDP)	2012	WDI
Political conditions	Contemporary level of democracy-autocracy	Freedom House/Imputed Polity	2013	QoG
Cultural values	Predominant religion	Predominant religious population in each society (Protestant, Catholic, Orthodox, Muslim, Other)	2014	CIA Yearbook

APPENDIX TABLE 9A *Classification of the Main Types of Convenience Election Laws Used in the United States*

Type	Mechanics	Coding	Source
Voter ID	The identification required to vote at the polling station varies across states, ranging from mandatory photo identification, to copies of a bill, bank statement, or government document showing name and address, to no identification at all.	0 – Some form of identification required to vote 1 – No identification required to vote	National Conference of State Legislative (NCSL) Election Law Database
Absentee Balloting	Absentee balloting allows voters to receive a ballot before the election day and return it before election day. Traditionally, an application for an absentee ballots could be submitted for a limited number of reasons, ranging from being physically unable to go to a polling station to living abroad. No-excuse absentee balloting allows any citizen to apply for an absentee ballot, with no reason required.	0 – Excuse needed for absentee ballot 1 – No excuse needed for absentee ballot	Election Administration and Voter Study (EAVS), Statutory Overview Report 2014
Vote by Mail	Voters receive a ballot in the mail before the election. Ballots can be returned via mail or dropped off at satellite locations or at elections office. Three states (Oregon, Colorado, and Washington) conduct all vote-by-mail elections.	0 – No mail-in voting 1 – Mail-in voting an option or the default method of casting a ballot	NCSL Election Law Database

APPENDIX TABLE 9A (*continued*)

Type	Mechanics	Coding	Source
In-person Early Voting	Voters have the option of casting a ballot in person early at a satellite location or at an election office. In some states an excuse is needed. In most jurisdictions, the same voting machinery is used for early in-person and Election Day balloting.	0 – No early voting option 1 – In-person early voting available	EAVS Statutory Overview Report 2014
Election Day Registration	Some states allow voters who are not registered prior to election day to register on election day.	0 – Election day registration not available 1 – election day registration available	NCSL Election Law Database
Online Registration	Some states have enacted online voter registration systems, which allow voters to check their status, amend their information, and/or register online.	0 – No online registration available 1 – Limited or full online registration available	NCSL Election Law Database
Felon Disenfranchisement	The voting rights of felons and incarcerated populations varies by state, often based on the nature of the felony.	0 – Most restricted felon disenfranchisement (all felonies, and some other crimes) 1 – Least restricted felon disenfranchisement (not all felonies result in disenfranchisement)	EAVS Statutory Overview Report 2014

Provisional Ballots	Provisional ballots are provided when the eligibility of a voter is questioned due to, for example, a lack of proper identification. Depending on the state, these ballots will be verified when the voter returns with ID, by matching signatures or by swearing an affidavit.	0 – No provisional ballots 1 – Provisional ballots allowed	NCSL Election Law Database
Registration under 18	In some states, those under the age of 18 can register to vote when they reach a certain age (usually 16 or 17), or if they will be 18 before the next election.	0 – No pre-registration 1 – Pre-registration available	NCSL Election Law Database
Voting Information Pamphlets	Some states are required by law to publish and distribute pamphlets containing voter information. The contents will vary by state.	0 – Voting Information pamphlets not required 1 – Voting information pamphlets required	NCSL Election Law Database
Sample Ballots	Some states are required by law to publish sample ballots. Their distribution will vary. Some states post these sample ballots at voting booths, others publish them in newspapers, and others still mail them to each household.	0 – Sample ballots not required 1 – Sample ballots required	NCSL Election Law Database

Sources:

- National Conference of State Legislative (NCSL) Election Law Database (http://www.ncsl.org/research/elections-and-campaigns/2011-2013-elections-legislation-database.aspx) contains a listing of election laws by state.

- 2014 Election Administration and Voting Survey (EAVS) Statutory Overview Report (http://www.eac.gov/assets/1/Page/2014_Statutory_Overview_Final-2015-03-09.pdf) compares state election laws and practices.

Notes

CHAPTER 1

1. Pippa Norris, Richard Frank, and Ferran Martinez i Coma. 2015. "Contentious elections: From votes to violence." In Pippa Norris, Richard Frank, and Ferran Martinez i Coma, eds., *Contentious Elections: From Ballots to Barricades*. New York: Routledge.
2. Pippa Norris. 2005. *Why Electoral Integrity Matters*. New York: Cambridge University Press; Pippa Norris. 2006. *Why Elections Fail*. New York: Cambridge University Press.
3. Pippa Norris and Ronald Inglehart. 2016. "Trump, Brexit and the Rise of Populism," John F. Kennedy School Faculty Research Paper. RWP16–026.
4. United Nations Development Programme. 2015. *UNDP in Focus 2014/2015: Time for Global Action*. New York: UNDP. www.undp.org/content/undp/en/home/librarypage/corporate/annual-report-2014-2015.html.
5. https://wwi.lib.byu.edu/index.php/Wilson's_War_Message_to_Congress.
6. http://avalon.law.yale.edu/wwii/atlantic.asp.
7. Michael Cox, Timothy J. Lynch, and Nicolas Bouchet. Eds. 2013. *US Foreign Policy and Democracy Promotion: From Theodore Roosevelt to Barack Obama*. New York: Routledge.
8. President Kennedy's Inaugural Address, January 20, 1961. www.jfklibrary.org/Research/Research-Aids/Ready-Reference/JFK-Quotations/Inaugural-Address.aspx.
9. Michael Cox, Timothy J. Lynch and Nicolas Bouchet. Eds. 2013. *US Foreign Policy and Democracy Promotion: From Theodore Roosevelt to Barack Obama*. New York: Routledge.
10. www.huffingtonpost.com/jamil-dakwar/un-issues-scathing-assess_b_7294792.html.
11. Francis Fukuyama. 2006. *The End of History and the Last Man*. New York: Simon & Schuster.
12. Lawrence Whitehead. 2009. "Losing the force? The dark side of democratization after Iraq." *Democratization* 16(2):215–242.
13. Jason Brownlee, Tarek Masoud, and Andrew Reynolds. 2015. *The Arab Spring: Pathways of Repression and Reform*. New York: Oxford University Press.

14. Robert Worth. 2016. *A Rage for Order: The Middle East in Turmoil, from Tahrir Square to ISIS*. New York: Farrar, Straus and Giroux. See also the comparison of states in the region in the Economist Intelligence Unit. 2017. *Democracy Index 2016*, pp. 42–44. www.eiu.com.
15. Michael Cox, Timothy J. Lynch, and Nicolas Bouchet. Eds. 2013. *US Foreign Policy and Democracy Promotion: From Theodore Roosevelt to Barack Obama.* New York: Routledge.
16. Michael Cox, Timothy J. Lynch, and Nicolas Bouchet. Eds. 2013. *US Foreign Policy and Democracy Promotion: From Theodore Roosevelt to Barack Obama.* New York: Routledge; Jeff Bridoux and Milja Kurki. 2016. *Democracy Promotion: A Critical Introduction*. New York: Routledge; Daniela Huber. 2015. *Democracy Promotion and Foreign Policy Identity and Interests in US, EU and Non-Western Democracies*. New York: Palgrave.
17. Thomas Carothers. 2012. *Democracy Policy Under Obama: Revitalization or Retreat?* Washington, DC: Carnegie Endowment for International Peace; Nicole Bibbins Sedaca and Nicolas Bouchet. 2014. *Holding Steady? US Democracy Promotion in a Changing World.* London: Chatham House. www.chathamhouse.org/sites/files/chathamhouse/home/chatham/public_html/sites/default/files/170214DemocracyPromotion.pdf.
18. Planned funding by fiscal year, democracy, human rights and governance. http://beta.foreignassistance.gov/categories/Democracy-Human-Rights-Governance.
19. Michael Ignatieff. Ed. 2005. *American Exceptionalism and Human Rights.* Princeton, NJ: Princeton University Press.
20. www.euractiv.com/section/development-policy/infographic/refugee-crisis-leads-to-boost-in-european-aid-spending/.
21. www.newsweek.com/ban-kimoon-refugees-reduction-development-aid-393324; Anne-Marie Helland, Gunilla Hallonste, Birgitte Qvist-Sørensen and Jouni Hemberg. 2015. *The End of Nordic Exceptionalism?* Oslo: Norwegian Church Aid. http://www.nca.no.
22. See, for example, Bruce Drake. 2013. "*Americans Put Low Priority on Promoting Democracy Abroad.*" Washington DC: The Pew Research Center. www.pewresearch.org/fact-tank/2013/12/04/americans-put-low-priority-on-promoting-democracy-abroad/.
23. www.people-press.org/2016/05/05/public-uncertain-divided-over-americas-place-in-the-world/.
24. Donald Trump. 27 April 2016. *Foreign Policy Speech*. www.donaldjtrump.com/press-releases/donald-j.-trump-foreign-policy-speech.
25. www.cnn.com/2017/01/20/politics/trump-inaugural-address/.
26. www.nytimes.com/interactive/projects/cp/opinion/election-night-2016/angela-merkels-warning-to-trump.
27. www.cnn.com/2017/01/20/politics/trump-inaugural-address/.
28. Thomas Carothers. 2017 "*Prospects for U.S. Democracy Promotion under Trump.*" Carnegie Endowment for International Peace. http://carnegieendowment.org/2017/01/05/prospects-for-u.s.-democracy-promotion-under-trump-pub-66588.
29. www.cnn.com/2017/01/27/politics/trump-approval-rating-quinnipiac-poll/index.html; www.gallup.com/poll/1597/confidence-institutions.aspx.
30. www.brennancenter.org/issues/restricting-vote.

31. See Richard L. Hasen, 2012. *The Voting Wars: From Florida 2000 to the Next Election Meltdown*. New Haven: Yale University Press; Pippa Norris. 2017. *Why American Elections Are Flawed (and how to Fix them)*. Ithaca: Cornell University Press.
32. Pippa Norris. 11 March 2016. "It's not just Trump. Authoritarian populism is rising across the West. Here's why." *Monkey Cage/Washington Post*. www.washingtonpost.com/news/monkey-cage/wp/2016/03/11/its-not-just-trump-authoritarian-populism-is-rising-across-the-west-heres-why/?utm_term=.afe2cd0ea8cb.
33. See also United Nations Development Programme. 2014. *The Longer-Term Impact of UNDP Electoral Assistance: Lessons Learned*. New York: UNDP.
34. See, for example, Zohid Askarov and Hristos Doucouliagos. 2013. "Does aid improve democracy and governance? A meta-regression analysis." *Public Choice* 157(3–4): 601–628; Altunbas, Yener and John Thornton. 2014. "The (small) blessing of foreign aid: further evidence on aid's impact on democracy." *Applied Economics* 46(32): 3922–3930; Sarah Blodget Bermeo. 2011. "Foreign aid and regime change: A role for donor intent." *World Development* 39(11): 2021–2031.
35. Thomas Carothers. 2002. "Taking stock of US democracy assistance." In Cox, Michael, G. John Ikenberry and Takashi Inoguchi, eds., *American Democracy Promotion*. Oxford: Oxford University Press.
36. Peter Burnell. 2011. *Promoting Democracy Abroad: Policy and Performance*. New Brunswick, NJ: Transaction Publishers. See also Richard Youngs. 2002. *The European Union and the Promotion of Democracy*. Oxford: Oxford University Press; Richard Youngs. Ed. 2006. *Survey of European Democracy Promotion Policies 2000–2006*. Madrid: Fride.
37. See Chapter 3.
38. Krishna Kumar. 2013. *Evaluating Democracy Assistance*. Boulder, CO: Lynne Rienner.
39. Sarah Sunn Bush. 2015. *The Taming of Democracy Assistance*. New York: Cambridge University Press.
40. Sarah Sunn Bush. 2015. *The Taming of Democracy Assistance*. New York: Cambridge University Press.
41. Jeroen de Zeeuw. 2005. "Projects do not create institutions: The record of democracy assistance in post-conflict societies." *Democratization* 12(4): 481–504.
42. Lincoln A. Mitchell. 2016. *The Democracy Promotion Paradox*. Washington DC: Brookings Institution Press.
43. Shaun Bowler and Todd Donovan. 2011. "The limited effects of election reforms on efficacy and engagement." *Australian Journal of Political Science* 47(1): 55–70; Shaun Bowler and Todd Donovan. 2013. *The Limits of Electoral Reform*. New York: Oxford University Press.
44. Jack Snyder. 2000. *From Voting to Violence: Democratization and Nationalist Conflict*. New York: Norton; Edward D. Mansfield and Jack Snyder. 2007. *Electing to Fight: Why Emerging Democracies Go to War*. Cambridge, MA: MIT Press; Dawn Brancati and Jack L. Snyder. 2011. "Rushing to the polls: The causes of premature post-conflict elections." *Journal of Conflict Resolution* 55(3): 469–492.

45. Dawn Brancati and Jack L. Snyder. 2011. "The Libyan rebels and electoral democracy: Why rushing to the polls could reignite civil war." *Foreign Affairs*.
46. Noah Coburn and Anna Larson. 2013. *Derailing Democracy in Afghanistan: Elections in an Unstable Political Landscape*. New York: Columbia University Press.
47. Joseph Nye. 2005. *Soft Power*. New York: Public Affairs.
48. Steven Levitsky and Lucan Way. 2010. *Competitive Authoritarianism: Hybrid Regimes After the Cold War*. New York: Cambridge University Press.
49. Amartya Sen. 1999. *Development as Freedom*. Oxford: Oxford University Press.
50. UN. 1966. *International Covenant of Civil and Political Rights*. www.ohchr.org/en/professionalinterest/pages/ccpr.aspx.
51. Domenico Tuccinardi. Ed. 2014. *International Obligations for Elections: Guidelines for Legal Frameworks*. International IDEA: Stockholm; Carter Center. 2014. *Elections Obligations and Standards Database: A Carter Center Manual. Atlanta*, Georgia: The Carter Center.
52. Thomas Carothers. 2007. "The 'sequencing' fallacy." *Journal of Democracy* 18(1): 12–27.
53. See, for example, the debate discussed in Pippa Norris. 2010. *Making Democratic Governance Work*. New York: Cambridge University Press.
54. Pippa Norris. 2014. *Why Electoral Integrity Matters*. New York: Cambridge University Press.
55. See also Sarah Birch. 2008. "Electoral institutions and popular confidence in electoral processes: a cross-national analysis." *Electoral Studies* 27 (2): 305–320; Sarah Birch. 2010. "Perceptions of electoral fairness and voter turnout." *Comparative Political Studies* 43 (12): 1601–1622.
56. See the Global Commission on Elections, Democracy and Security. 2012. *Deepening Democracy: A Strategy for Improving the Integrity of Elections Worldwide*. Sweden: IDEA; Joshua Tucker. "Enough! Electoral fraud, collective action problems, and post-communist colored revolutions." *Perspectives on Politics* 5(3): 535–551; Pippa Norris, Richard W. Frank and Ferran Martinez I Coma. Eds. *Contentious Elections: From Ballots to Barricades*. New York: Routledge.
57. UN Secretary General. 2015. *Strengthening the role of the United Nations in enhancing the effectiveness of the principle of periodic and genuine elections and the promotion of democratization*. UN General Assembly A/70/306.
58. Pippa Norris. 2010. *Making Democratic Governance Work*. New York: Cambridge University Press; Michael McFaul. 2010. *Advancing Democracy Abroad*. New York: Rowman & Littlefield; Larry Diamond. 1996. *Developing Democracy: Toward Consolidation*. Baltimore: Johns Hopkins University Press; Thomas Carothers. 1999. *Aiding Democracy Abroad: The Learning Curve*. Washington DC: Carnegie Endowment for International Peace.
59. Bueno de Mesquita, Bruce, Alistair Smith, Randolph M. Siverson, and James D. Morrow. 2003. *The Logic of Political Survival*. Cambridge: MIT Press; Christian Davenport. 2007. "State repression and political order." *Annual Review of Political Science* 10: 1–23; Christian Davenport. 2007. *State Repression and the Domestic Democratic Peace*. Cambridge: Cambridge University Press.
60. Morton H. Halperin, Joseph T. Siegle, and Michael M. Weinstein. 2010. *The Democracy Advantage: How Democracies Promote Prosperity and Peace*. New York: Routledge. 2nd edition; David S. Brown. 1999. "Democracy and

social spending in Latin America, 1980–92." *American Political Science Review* 93 (4): 779; David S. Brown. 1999. "Reading, writing, and regime type: Democracy's impact on primary school enrollment." *Political Research Quarterly* 52 (4): 681–707; David S. Brown and Wendy Hunter. 2004. "Democracy and human capital formation." *Comparative Political Studies* 37(7): 842–64; Stephan Haggard and Robert R. Kaufman. 2008. *Development, Democracy, and Welfare States: Latin America, East Asia, and Eastern Europe*. Princeton: Princeton University Press.

61. Adam Przeworski, Michael E. Alvarez, José Antonio Cheibub, and Fernando Limongi. 2000. *Democracy and Development: Political Institutions and Well-Being in the World, 1950–1990*. New York: Cambridge University Press; Yi Feng. 2003. *Democracy, Governance and Economic Growth: Theory and Evidence*. Cambridge, MA: The MIT Press; Jonathan Krieckhaus. 2004. "The regime debate revisited: A sensitivity analysis of democracy's economic effect." *British Journal of Political Science* 34 (4): 635–655; Hristos Doucouliagos and Mehmet Ali Ulubasoglu. 2008. "Democracy and economic growth: A meta-analysis." *American Journal of Political Science* 52(1): 61–83.
62. Bruce M. Russett. 1993. *Grasping the Democratic Peace: Principles for a Post-Cold War World*. Princeton: Princeton University Press, p.11; Michael W. Doyle. 2005. "Three Pillars of the Liberal Peace." *American Political Science Review*, 99: 463–466.
63. Pippa Norris. 2010. *Making Democratic Governance Work*. New York: Cambridge University Press.
64. UNDP. 2012. *Evaluation of UNDP Contribution to Strengthening Electoral Systems and Processes*. New York: UNDP.
65. For details, see Domenico Tuccinardi. Ed. 2014. *International Obligations for Elections: Guidelines for Legal Frameworks*. International IDEA: Stockholm; Carter Center. 2014. *Elections Obligations and Standards Database: A Carter Center Manual*. Atlanta, Georgia: The Carter Center www.cartercenter.org/des-search/des/Introduction.aspx; The Network of Europeans for Electoral and Democracy Support (NEEDS) Compendium of International Standards for Elections provides a comprehensive list of each country to which international and regional obligations has signed up and/or ratified http://web.needsproject.eu/fi les/Compendium_of_Int_Standards_3_EN.pdf.
66. UN Secretary General. 2015. *Strengthening the role of the United Nations in enhancing the effectiveness of the principle of periodic and genuine elections and the promotion of democratization*. UN General Assembly A/70/306.
67. See, for example, Fabrice Edouard Lehoucq and Iván Molina Jiménez. 2002. *Stuffing the Ballot Box: Fraud, Electoral Reform, and Democratization in Costa Rica*. New York: Cambridge University Press; Beatriz Magaloni. 2006. *Voting for Autocracy: Hegemonic Party Survival and Its Demise in Mexico*. Cambridge: Cambridge University Press; Andreas Schedler. Ed. 2006. *Electoral Authoritarianism: The Dynamics of Unfree Competition*. Boulder and London: Lynne Rienner; Jason Brownlee. 2007. *Authoritarianism in an Age of Democratization*. New York: Cambridge University Press; Valerie J. Bunce and Sharon L. Wolchik. 2011. *Defeating Authoritarian Leaders in Post-Communist Countries*. New York: Cambridge University Press; Steven Levitsky and Lucan Way. 2010. *Competitive Authoritarianism: Hybrid Regimes After the Cold*

War, New York: Cambridge University Press; Andreas Schedler. 2012. *The Politics of Uncertainty Sustaining and Subverting Electoral Authoritarianism*. CIDE: Mexico City; Alberto Simpser. 2013. *Why Parties and Governments Manipulate Elections: Theory, Practice and Implications*. New York: Cambridge University Press.

68. Thomas Carothers. 2015. "Democracy aid at 25: Time to choose." *Journal of Democracy* 26(1): 59–73.
69. Pippa Norris. 2014. *Why Electoral Integrity Matters*. New York: Cambridge University Press; Pippa Norris. 2015. *Why Elections Fail*. New York: Cambridge University Press.
70. International IDEA. 2012. *The Integrity of Elections: The Role of Regional Organizations*. Stockholm: International IDEA.
71. Judith Kelley. 2008. "Assessing the complex evolution of norms: the rise of international election monitoring." *International Organization* 62(2): 221–255; Judith Kelley. 2009. "D-Minus Elections: The politics and norms of international election observation." *International Organization* 63 (4): 765-787; Judith Kelley. 2009. "The more the merrier? The effects of having multiple international election monitoring organizations." *Perspectives on Politics* 7: 59–64; Judith Kelley. 2010. "Election observers and their biases." *Journal of Democracy* 21: 158–172; Judith Kelley. 2012. "The international influences on elections in transition states." *Annual Review of Political Science* 15; Judith Kelley. 2012. *Monitoring Democracy: When International Election Observation Works and Why It Often Fails*. Princeton, NJ: Princeton University Press; Susan. D. Hyde. 2007. "Experimenting in democracy promotion: international observers and the 2004 presidential elections in Indonesia." *Perspectives on Politics* 8(2): 511–527; Susan. D. Hyde. 2007. "The observer effect in international politics: evidence from a natural experiment." *World Politics* 60(1): 37–63; Susan. D. Hyde. 2011. *The Pseudo-Democrat's Dilemma*. Ithaca: Cornell University Press.
72. Joseph M. Colomer. 2004. *Handbook of Electoral System Choice*. New York: Palgrave Macmillan; Pippa Norris. 2006. *Electoral Engineering*. New York: Cambridge University Press; Michael Gallagher and Paul Mitchell. Eds. 2008. *The Politics of Electoral Systems*. Oxford: Oxford University Press; Alan Renwick. 2011. *The Politics of Electoral Reform: Changing the Rules of Democracy*. New York: Cambridge University Press.
73. Kristof Jacobs and Monique Leyenaar. 2011. "A conceptual framework for major, minor, and technical electoral reform." *West European Politics* 34(3): 495–513.
74. Joseph M. Colomer. 2004. *Handbook of Electoral System Choice*. New York: Palgrave Macmillan.
75. Matthew Golder. 2005. "Democratic electoral systems around the world, 1946–2000." *Electoral Studies* 24(2): 103–121.
76. Drude Dahlerup. Ed. 2006. *Women, Quotas, and Politics*. London: Routledge; Pippa Norris and Mona Lena Krook. 2012. *Gender equality in Elected Office: A Six-Point Action Plan*. Warsaw: OSCE; Mona Lena Krook. 2009. *Quotas for Women in Politics*. New York: Oxford University Press; Frank C. Thames, and Margaret S Williams. 2013. *Contagious Representation: Women's Political Representation in Democracies Around the World*. New York: NYU Press.

77. Inter-parliamentary Union. www.ipu.org *Women in National Parliaments*, last referenced March 2016.
78. *The Gender Quota Database*. GQD: Release 1.0 May 2014. Stockholm: University of Stockholm.
79. Andrew Reynolds. 2011. "Reserved seats in national legislatures: A research note." *Legislative Studies Quarterly*. 30(2): 301–310.
80. Pippa Norris. 2015. *Why Elections Fail*. Chapter 5. New York: Cambridge University Press.
81. Sarah Birch. Electoral Malpractices. New York: Oxford University Press; Alessandro Nai. 2017. "The Fourth Estate: why and how traditional news media provide fair coverage of elections." In Pippa Norris and Alessandro Nai, eds., *Watchdog Elections*. New York: Oxford University Press.
82. Pippa Norris. Ed. 2010. *Public Sentinel: News Media and the Governance Agenda*. Washington DC: The World Bank.
83. Jessica Noske-Turner. 2014. "Evaluating the impacts of media assistance: Problems and principles." *Global Media Journal*. 4(2): 1–21.
84. Pippa Norris and Andrea Abel Van Es. Eds. 2016. *Checkbook Politics: Political Finance in Comparative Perspective*.
85. For the International IDEA database, see Elin Falguera, Samuel Jones, and Magnus Ohman. 2014. *Funding of Political Parties and Election Campaigns: A Handbook on Political Finance*. Stockholm: International IDEA.
86. Andre Blais and Daniel Rubenson. 2013. "The source of turnout decline: New values or new contexts?" *Comparative Political Studies* 46 (1): 95–117.
87. Paul Gronke, Eva Galanes-Rosenbaum, and Peter A. Miller. 2008. "Convenience voting." *Annual Review of Political Science* 11: 437–455. For reviews of voting facilities, see Ivor Crewe. 1981. "Electoral Participation." In Austin Ranney and David Butler, eds., *Democracy at the Polls*. Washington, DC: American Enterprise Institute for Public Policy Research.
88. Pippa Norris. 2004. "Will new technology boost turnout?" In *Electronic Voting and Democracy: A Comparative Analysis*. Edited by Norbert Kersting and Harald Baldersheim. London: Palgrave, pp.193–225; Pippa Norris. 2005. "E-voting as the magic bullet for European parliamentary elections?" In Alexander Trechsel and Fernando Mendez, eds. *The European Union and E-voting*. London: Routledge, pp. 60–91; Shaun Bowler and Todd Donovan. 2011. "The limited effects of election reforms on efficacy and engagement." *Australian Journal of Political Science* 47(1): 55–70; Michael J. Hanmer. 2009. *Discount Voting: Voter Registration Reforms and Their Effects*. New York: Cambridge University Press.
89. Adam Berinsky. 2005. "The perverse consequences of electoral reform in the United States." *American Politics Research* 33 (4): 471–491.
90. Barry C. Burden, David T. Canon, Kenneth R. Mayer, and Donald P. Moynihan. 2011. "Election laws, mobilization, and turnout: The unanticipated consequences of election reform." *American Journal of Political Science* 58: 95–109.
91. Mona Lena Krook. 2009. *Quotas for Women in Politics: Gender and Candidate Selection Reform Worldwide*. New York: Oxford University Press; Sarah Sunn Bush. 2011. "International politics and the spread of quotas for women in legislatures." *International Organization* 65(1): 103–137.

CHAPTER 2

1. Michael Cox, Timothy J. Lynch, and Nicolas Bouchet. Eds. 2013. *US Foreign Policy and Democracy Promotion: From Theodore Roosevelt to Barack Obama*. New York: Routledge; Jeff Bridoux and Milja Kurki. 2016. *Democracy Promotion: A Critical Introduction*. New York: Routledge; Daniela Huber. 2015. *Democracy Promotion and Foreign Policy Identity and Interests in US, EU and Non-Western Democracies*. New York: Palgrave.
2. www.un.org/undpa/en/elections.
3. Maria Rosaria Macchiaverna and Mario Giuseppe Varrenti. 2012. *Study on Performance Indicators for Electoral Assistance projects developed within the context of the EC-UNDP Partnership on Electoral Assistance*. Brussels: European Commission.
4. Joseph Nye. 2005. *Soft Power: The Means to Success in World Politics*. New York: PublicAffairs.
5. Daniella Donno. 2013. *Defending Democratic Norms*. New York: Oxford University Press.
6. www.africanews.com/2016/06/24/drc-un-extends-sanctions-pushes-for-respect-of-electoral-calendar/.
7. Steven Levitsky and Lucan A. Way. 2006. "Linkage versus leverage: Rethinking the international dimension of regime change." *Comparative Politics* 38(4): 379–400; Steven Levitsky and Lucan A. Way. 2010. *Competitive Authoritarianism: Hybrid Regimes After the Cold War*, New York: Cambridge University Press.
8. See, for example, G. Bingham Powell. 2000. *Elections as Instruments of Democracy*. New Haven, CT: Yale University Press.
9. For more detail see, for example, Pippa Norris, Ferran Martinez i Coma, Alessandro Nai and Max Groemping. 2016. *The Year in Elections, 2015*. Sydney: University of Sydney. www.electoralintegrityproject.com.
10. Pippa Norris. 2014. *Why Electoral Integrity Matters*. New York: Cambridge University Press.
11. Thomas Edward Flores and Irfan Nooruddin. 2016. *Elections in Hard Times: Building Stronger Democracies in the 21st Century*. New York: Cambridge University Press.
12. David Hirschmann. 1998. "Improving crisis management in the imperfect world of foreign electoral assistance." *Public Administration and Development* 18(1): 23–36.
13. Fabio Bargiacchi, Mette Bakken, Paul Guerin, and Ricardo Godhinho Gomes. 2011. *The Electoral Cycle Approach*. Instituti per Gli Studi di Politica Internzaionale. Working Paper.
14. Joshua Muravchik. 1992. *Exporting Democracy*. Washington DC: AEI Press; Michael Cox, John Ikenberry and Takashi Inoguchi. Eds. 2000. *American Democracy Promotion: Impulses, Strategies, and Impacts*. New York: Oxford University Press.
15. Samuel Huntington. 1995. *The Third Wave*. Oklahoma: University of Oklahoma Press.
16. The estimate is calculated from the Cross-National Time-Series (CNTS) dataset, produced by Databanks International, originally developed by Arthur S. Banks. www.databanksinternational.com/.

17. As of July 2015, five independent nation-states (defined by membership of the United Nations) lack any de jure constitutional provisions for direct elections for the lower house of parliament: Brunei Darussalam, China, Qatar, UAE, and Saudi Arabia. Another three states have constitutional provisions for such contests but they have not yet held any such elections since independence or within the last thirty years. Pippa Norris, Ferran Martinez i Coma, Alesandro Nai, and Max Groemping. 2015. *The Year in Elections, mid-2015 update.* Sydney: University of Sydney. Technical Appendix.
18. Joshua Kurlantzick. 2014. *Democracy in Retreat: The Revolt of the Middle Class and the Worldwide Decline of Representative Government.* New Haven, CT: Yale University Press; Larry Diamond and Marc F. Plattner. Eds. 2015. *Democracy in Decline?* Baltimore: Johns Hopkins University Press.
19. Pippa Norris. 2017. "Is Western democracy backsliding?" *Journal of Democracy* 28(2): online. http://journalofdemocracy.org/online-exchange-%E2%80%9Cdemocratic-deconsolidation%E2%80%9D.
20. The Varieties of Democracy project. www.v-dem.net; The Economist Intelligence Unit. 2017. *Democracy Index 2016: Revenge of the Deplorables.* www.eiu.com; Arch Puddington and Tyler Roylance. 2016. "Anxious dictators, wavering democracies: Global freedom under pressure." *Freedom House: Freedom in the World 2016.* www.freedomhouse.org.
21. See Inken van Borzyskowski. 2016. "Resisting democracy assistance: Who seeks and receives technical election assistance?" *Review of International Organizations* 11 (2): 247–282.
22. Michael Cox, Timothy J. Lynch and Nicolas Bouchet. Eds. 2013. *US Foreign Policy and Democracy Promotion: From Theodore Roosevelt to Barack Obama.* New York: Routledge; Jeff Bridoux and Milja Kurki. 2016. *Democracy Promotion: A Critical Introduction.* New York: Routledge; Daniela Huber. 2015. *Democracy Promotion and Foreign Policy Identity and Interests in US, EU and Non-Western Democracies.* New York: Palgrave.
23. Michael Schroeder. 2013. "The politics of change: The evolution of UN electoral services, 1989–2006." *Global Governance.* 19(2): 207–226.
24. For the full text of the series of resolutions, see www.un.org/wcm/content/site/undpa/main/issues/elections/resolutions. For the most recent (2012) resolution, see www.un.org/wcm/webdav/site/undpa/shared/undpa/pdf/N1146860.pdf.
25. For a discussion, see Thomas Carothers. 1999. *Aiding Democracy Abroad: The Learning Curve.* Washington DC: The Brookings Institution; Amichai Magen, Thomas Risse and Michael A. McFaul. Eds. 2013. *Promoting Democracy and the Rule of Law: American and European Strategies.* New York: Palgrave Macmillan.
26. UN-Department of Political Affairs. *Annual Report* 2015. New York: United Nations.
27. The Millennium Development Declaration. 2000. www.un.org/millennium/declaration/ares552e.htm. It is worth noting, however, that no specific target was set to monitor this value. The Sustainable Development Goals, designed to replace the MDGs from 2015–2030, refer to target 16.7 of ensuring "... responsive, inclusive and representative decision-making at all levels" and target 16.6 "develop effective, accountable and transparent institutions at all levels." No reference is made to democracy or elections per se.

28. Thomas Carothers. 1999. *Aiding Democracy Abroad*. Washington DC: The Brookings Institution.
29. United Nations. 2015. "Democracy and the United Nations." www.un.org/en/globalissues/democracy/democracy_and_un.shtml.
30. UN Secretary General. 2015. Strengthening the role of the United Nations in enhancing the effectiveness of the principle of periodic and genuine elections and the promotion of democratization. UN General Assembly A/70/306.
31. www.un.org/undpa/en/elections.
32. www.un.org/undpa/en/elections.
33. See Craig N. Murphy. 2006. *The United Nations Development Programme: A Better Way?* New York: Cambridge University Press.
34. See UNDP. www.undp.org/content/undp/en/home/ourwork/democraticgovernance/focus_areas/focus_electoral.html.
35. United Nations Development Programme. 2012. *Evaluation of UNDP Contribution to Strengthening Electoral Systems and Processes*. New York: UNDP.
36. Daniel Calingaert, Arch Puddington, and Sarah Repucci. 2014. "The democracy support deficit: Despite progress, major countries fall short." In *Supporting Democracy Abroad: An Assessment of Leading Powers*. Washington DC: Freedom House.
37. See, for example, 80 member organizations linked to the Network of Democracy Research Institutes coordinated with NED. www.ned.org/ideas/network-of-democracy-research-institutes-ndri/ndri-member-institutes/.
38. OECD/DAC. 2014. *Development assistance flows for government and peace, 2014*. Paris: OECD/DAC.
39. Official Development Aid spending on the "government and civil society" sector is estimated to have risen from US$5.54bn in 1995 to $29.69bn in 2009, before falling back to $16.04bn in 2012. (AIDData. http://aiddata.org/dashboard Consulted August 2016.
40. *UNDP Annual Report 2011/12*. New York: UNDP. www.undp.org/content/dam/undp/library/corporate/UNDP-in-action/2012/English/UNDP-AnnualReport_ENGLISH.pdf. It should be noted that this level of spending on democratic governance has been shrinking in recent years, from around $1.4bn in 2009 down to $US1bn (24 percent of the overall UNDP budget) in 2013.
41. National Research Council. 2008. *Improving Democracy Assistance: Building Knowledge Through Evaluations and Research*. Washington DC: National Academies Press, p .1.
42. U.S. Agency for International Development (USAID), 2014. *Foreign Operations FY 2013 Performance Report*. Washington DC: USAID. www.usaid.gov/sites/default/files/documents/1870/USAID_FY2013_APR.pdf.
43. UK Department for International Development (DFID). 2013. *Annual Report and Accounts 2012–13*. London: The Stationery Office. www.gov.uk/government/uploads/system/uploads/attachment_data/file/208445/annual-report-accounts2013-13.pdf.
44. Amichai Magen, Thomas Risse and Michael A. McFaul. Eds. 2013. *Promoting Democracy and the Rule of Law: American and European Strategies*. New York: Palgrave Macmillan.
45. Peter Burnell. Ed. 2010. *Democracy Assistance: International Co-operation for Democratization*. London: Routledge.

46. Eric C. Bjornlund. 2004. *Beyond Free and Fair: Monitoring Elections and Building Democracy*. Washington DC: Woodrow Wilson Center Press; Guy S. Goodwin-Gill. 2006. *Free and Fair Elections*. 2nd edition. Geneva: Inter-parliamentary Union; John Hardin Young. 2009. *International Election Principles: Democracy and the Rule of Law*. Chicago: American Bar Association.
47. See, for example, International IDEA. 2004. *Handbook on the Funding of Political Parties and Election Campaigns*. Stockholm: International IDEA; Organization of American States/International IDEA. 2005. *Funding of Political Parties and Election Campaigns in the Americas*. OAS/International IDEA; Wall, Alan, et al. 2006. *Electoral Management Design: The International IDEA Handbook*. Sweden: International IDEA; Magnus Öhman and Hani Zainulbhai. 2011. *Political Finance Regulation: The Global Experience*. Washington, DC: IFES.
48. International IDEA. 2002. *International Electoral Standards: Guidelines for Reviewing the Legal Framework for Elections*. Stockholm: International IDEA.
49. United Nations. 1948. Universal Declaration of Human Rights www.un.org/en/documents/udhr/.
50. www.un.org/wcm/content/site/undpa/main/issues/elections/resolutions.
51. www.un.org/wcm/content/site/undpa/main/issues/elections/resolutions.
52. UNDP. 2012. *Evaluation of UNDP Contribution to Strengthening Electoral Systems and Processes*. New York: UNDP.
53. UNDP Global Programme for Electoral Cycle Support. http://web.undp.org/eu/UNDP_Global_Programme_for_Electoral_Cycle_Support%20.shtml.
54. See, for example, the ACE Electoral Knowledge Network http://aceproject.org/; R. Michael Alvarez and Thad E. Hall. 2008. "Building secure and transparent elections through standard operating procedures." *Public Administration Review* 68 (5): 828–838.
55. Michael R. Alvarez and Thad E. Hall. 2006. "Controlling democracy: The principal agent problems in election administration." *Policy Studies Journal* 34(4): 491–510; Michael R. Alvarez, Hall, Thad E. and Llewellyn Morgan. 2008. "Who should run elections in the United States?" *Policy Studies Journal* 36(3): 325–346; Michael R. Alvarez and Thad E. Hall. 2008. "Building secure and transparent elections through standard operating procedures." *Public Administration Review* 68 (5): 828-838; Atkeson, Lonna Rae, Bryant, Lisa Ann, and Hall, Thad E. 2010. "A new barrier to participation: Heterogeneous application of voter identification policies." *Electoral Studies* 29(1): 66–73; Robert S. Montjoy, 2008. "The public administration of elections." *Public Administration Review* 68 (5): 788–799; Robert S. Montjoy, 2010. "The changing nature ... and costs ... of election administration." *Public Administration Review* 70(6): 867–875; Michael R. Alvarez, Lonna Rae Atkeson and Thad Hall. 2012. *Evaluating Elections: A Handbook of Methods and Standards*. New York: Cambridge University Press.
56. Paul Gronke, Eva Galanes-Rosenbaum, Peter A. Miller, and Daniel Toffey. 2008. "Convenience voting." *Annual Review of Political Science*. 11: 437–55.
57. Shaheen Mozaffar and Andreas Schedler. 2002. "The comparative study of electoral governance: Introduction." *International Political Science Review* 23(1): 5–27; Jonathan Hartlyn, Jennifer Mccoy, and Thomas M. Mustillo, 2008. "Electoral governance matters: Explaining the quality of elections in contemporary Latin America." *Comparative Political Studies* 41(1): 73–98.

58. Global Commission on Elections, Democracy and Security. 2012. *Deepening Democracy: A Strategy for improving the Integrity of Elections Worldwide.* Sweden: IDEA.
59. Emily Beaulieu. 2014. *Electoral Protests and Democracy in the Developing World.* New York: Cambridge University Press.
60. Susan B. Hyde. 2011. *The Pseudo-Democrat's Dilemma.* Ithaca: Cornell University Press; Judith Kelley. 2012. *Monitoring Democracy: When International Election Observation Works and Why It Often Fails.* Princeton, NJ: Princeton University Press.
61. Judith Kelley. 2008. "Assessing the complex evolution of norms: the rise of international election monitoring." *International Organization* 62(2): 221–255; Judith Kelley. 2009. "D-Minus Elections: The politics and norms of international election observation." *International Organization* 63 (4): 765–787; Judith Kelley. 2009. "The more the merrier? The effects of having multiple international election monitoring organizations." *Perspectives on Politics* 7: 59–64; Judith Kelley. 2010. "Election observers and their biases." *Journal of Democracy* 21: 158–172; Judith Kelley. 2012. "The international influences on elections in transition states." *Annual Review of Political Science* 15; Judith Kelley. 2012. *Monitoring Democracy: When International Election Observation Works and Why It Often Fails.* Princeton, NJ: Princeton University Press; Susan. D. Hyde. 2007. "Experimenting in democracy promotion: international observers and the 2004 presidential elections in Indonesia." *Perspectives on Politics* 8(2): 511-27; Susan. D. Hyde. 2007. "The observer effect in international politics: evidence from a natural experiment." *World Politics* 60(1): 37–63; Susan. D. Hyde. 2011. *The Pseudo-Democrat's Dilemma.* Ithaca: Cornell University Press.
62. See, for example, www.openelectiondata.net/en/guide/electoral-integrity/public-confidence/ "Public confidence in each step of an election process is critical to the integrity of the election. Citizens not only have a right to participate in elections, they have a right to know for themselves whether the electoral process is valid. Access to information about each phase of the election process is fundamental to creating and reinforcing public confidence in elections."
63. The Open Society Foundation: www.opensocietyfoundations.org/topics/freedom-information.
64. Alan Wall et al. 2006. *Electoral Management Design: The International IDEA Handbook.* Sweden: International IDEA, p. 24.
65. Archon Fung, Mary Graham, David Weil. Eds. 2008. *Full Disclosure: The Perils and Promise of Transparency.* New York: Cambridge University Press.
66. John Gaventa and Rosemary McGee. 2013. "The impact of transparency and accountability initiatives." *Development Policy Review* 31: S3–S28; Anuradha Joshi. 2013. "Do they work? Assessing the impact of transparency and Accountability Initiatives in Service Delivery." *Development Policy Review* 31: 29–48; Stephen Kosack and Archon Fung. 2014. "Does transparency improve governance?" *Annual Review of Political Science* 27: 65–87.
67. www.ly.undp.org/content/libya/en/home/operations/projects/democratic_governance/project_sample3.html.
68. IFES Election Guide. www.electionguide.org/elections/id/2798/.

CHAPTER 3

1. OECD-DAC Glossary. 2002.
2. Iqbal Dhaliwal and Caitlin Tulloch. 2012. "From research to policy: using evidence from impact evaluations to inform development policy." *Journal of Development Effectiveness* 4(4): 515–536; Krishna Kumar. 2012. *Evaluating Democracy Assistance*. Boulder, CO: Lynne Rienner.
3. D. L. Sackett, W. C. Rosenberg, J. A. M. Gray, R. B. Haynes, and W. S. Richardson. 1996. "Evidence based medicine: What it is and what it isn't." *British Medical Journal*, 312: 71–72.
4. Michael Woolcock. 2009. "Towards a plurality of methods in project evaluation: A contextualized approach to understanding impact trajectories and efficacy." *Journal of Development Effectiveness* 1(1): 1–14.
5. Joseph Schumpeter. 1943. *Capitalism, Socialism and Democracy*. London: George Allen & Unwin.
6. David Held. 2006. *Models of Democracy*. 3rd ed. Palo Alto, CA: Stanford University Press.
7. Pippa Norris. 2014. *Why Electoral Integrity Matters*. New York: Cambridge University Press.
8. Emily Beaulieu. 2014. *Electoral Protest and Democracy in the Developing World*. New York: Cambridge University Press; Pippa Norris, Richard Frank and Ferran Martinez i Coma. Eds. 2014. *Contentious Elections*. New York: Routledge.
9. Jennifer Gandhi, and Ellen Lust-Okar. 2009. "Elections under authoritarianism." *Annual Review of Political Science* 12: 403–422; Milan W. Svolik, 2012. *The Politics of Authoritarian Rule*. New York: Cambridge University Press.
10. Pippa Norris, Ferran Martinez i Coma, Alessandro Nai and Max Groemping. 2016. *The Year in Elections, 2015*. Sydney: University of Sydney.
11. G. Bingham Powell. 2000. *Elections as Instruments of Democracy*. New Haven, CT: Yale University Press; G. Bingham Powell. 2014. "Why elections matter." In Lawrence LeDuc, Richard Niemi, and Pippa Norris, eds., *Comparing Democracies*. London: Sage.
12. www.oecd.org/dac/effectiveness/parisdeclarationandaccraagendaforaction.htm.
13. Rachel Glennerster and Kudzai Takavarasha. 2013. *Running Randomized Evaluations: A Practical Guide*. Princeton, NJ: Princeton University Press.
14. Krishna Kumar. 2012. *Evaluating Democracy Assistance*. Boulder, CO: Lynne Rienner.
15. Thomas Carothers. 2015. "Democracy aid at 25: Time to choose." *Journal of Democracy* 26(1): 59–73.
16. Development Assistance Committee, the Organization for Economic Cooperation and Development's (OECD-DAC). 2014. *Development Assistance Flows for Governance and Peace, 2014*. Paris: OECD.
17. OECD-DAC estimates (Table 19) of ODA spending in 2013 (the latest year available) by major purpose. www.oecd.org/dac/stats/data.htm.
18. Arch Puddington. 2013. "Countering the critics of democracy promotion." https://freedomhouse.org/blog/countering-critics-democracy-promotion.
19. Larry Diamond and Marc F. Plattner. Eds. 2015. *Democracy in Decline?* Baltimore: Johns Hopkins University Press.

20. Thomas Risse and Nelli Babayan. 2015. "Democracy promotion and the challenges of illiberal regional powers: introduction to the special issue." *Democratization* 22 (3): 381–399.
21. See Christian von Soest. 2015. "Democracy prevention: The international collaboration of authoritarian regimes." *European Journal of Political Research* 54(4): 623–638; Jakob Tolstrup. 2015. "Black knights and elections in authoritarian regimes: Why and how Russia supports authoritarian incumbents in post-Soviet states." *European Journal of Political Research* 54 (4): 673–690; Lucan A. Way. 2015. "The limits of autocracy promotion: The case of Russia in the 'near abroad'." *European Journal Of Political Research*. 54(4): 691–706.
22. For proponents of democracy promotion, see Morton Halperin, Joseph T. Siegle and Michael M. Weinstein. 2010. *The Democracy Advantage: How Democracies Promote Prosperity and Peace*. 2nd edition. New York: Routledge; Michael McFaul. 2010. *Advancing Democracy Abroad*. New York: Rowman and Littlefield. For more skeptical arguments, see Zoltan Barany and Robert G. Moser, 2009. *Is Democracy Exportable?* New York: Cambridge University Press.
23. Jakob Tolstrup. 2015. "Black knights and elections in authoritarian regimes: Why and how Russia supports authoritarian incumbents in post-Soviet states." *European Journal of Political Research* 54 (4): 673–690.
24. Thomas Carothers. 2015. "Democracy aid at 25: Time to choose." *Journal of Democracy* 26(1): 59–73.
25. Robert D. Kaplan. 1997. "Was democracy just a moment?" *Atlantic Monthly*, December. pp. 55–80.
26. Fareed Zakaria. 1997. "The Rise of Illiberal Democracy." *Foreign Affairs*, 76(6): 22–43.
27. Thomas Carothers. 2015. "Democracy Aid at 25: Time to choose." *Journal of Democracy* 26(1): 59–73.
28. A transcript of Donald Trump's meeting with *The Washington Post* editorial board, 21 March 2016. www.washingtonpost.com/blogs/post-partisan/wp/2016/03/21/a-transcript-of-donald-trumps-meeting-with-the-washington-post-editorial-board/.
29. Ronald Inglehart and Pippa Norris. 2016. *Trump, Brexit, and the Rise of Populism: Economic Have-Nots and Cultural Backlash*. HKS Working Paper No. RWP16–026.
30. Krishna Kumar. 2013. *Evaluating Democracy Assistance*. Boulder, CO: Lynne Rienner.
31. Krishna Kumar. 2012. *Evaluating Democracy Assistance*. Boulder, Co: Lynne Rienner.
32. For comparisons underlying these cases, see Pippa Norris, Ferran Martinez i Coma, Alessandro Nai and Max Groemping. 2016. *The Year in Elections, 2015*. Sydney: University of Sydney.
33. See R. Michael Alvarez, Lonna Rae Atkeson and Thad Hall. 2013. *Evaluating Elections: A Handbook of Methods and Standards*. New York: Cambridge University Press. For the methods used by the UNDP, see UNDP Evaluation Office. 2012. *Evaluation of UNDP Contribution to Strengthening Electoral Systems and Processes*. NY: UNDP.

34. See Pippa Norris, Ferran Martinez i Coma, and Max Grömping. February 2015. *The Expert Survey of Perceptions of Electoral Integrity, Release 3 (PEI-3)*. Sydney, University of Sydney. www.electoralintegrityproject.com.
35. Christopher Pollitt and G. Bouckaert. 2004. *Public Management Reform. A Comparative Analysis*. 2nd edition. New York, NY: Oxford University Press.
36. See Maria Rosaria Macchiaverna and Mario Giuseppe Varrenti. 2012. *Study on Performance Indicators for Electoral Assistance projects developed within the context of the EC-UNDP Partnership on Electoral Assistance*. Brussels: European Union. www.eidhr.eu/files/dmfile/StudyonPerformanceindicatorsforelectoralassistanceprojects.pdf.
37. Judith Kelley. 2010. *Quality of Elections Data Codebook*. http://sites.duke.edu/kelley/data/; Sarah Birch. 2012. Electoral Malpractice. www.essex.ac.uk/government/electoralmalpractice/index.htm.
38. See, for example, the Quality of Government Institute.
39. Susan D. Hyde and Nikolay Marinov. *Codebook for National Elections across Democracy and Autocracy (NELDA) 3rd release*, 10 November 2011.
40. Pippa Norris. 2015. *Why Elections Fail*. New York: Cambridge University Press.
41. www2.ohchr.org/english/law/ccpr.htm.
42. www.cartercenter.org/des-search/des/Default.aspx.
43. John Hardin Young. 2009. *International Election Principles: Democracy and the Rule of Law*. Chicago: American Bar Association.
44. For details about the Sustainable Development Goals, see www.un.org/sustainabledevelopment/sustainable-development-goals/.
45. United Nations. 2015. *The Millennium Development Goals Report 2014*. UN: New York. www.un.org/millenniumgoals/2014%20MDG%20report/MDG%202014%20English%20web.pdf.
46. See www.gatesfoundation.org/What-We-Do.
47. Krishna Kumar. 2012. *Evaluating Democracy Assistance*. Boulder, CO: Lynne Rienner.
48. http://oe.cd/parisdeclarationeval.
49. Christopher Pollitt and G. Bouckaert. 2004. *Public Management Reform. A comparative Analysis*. 2nd edition. New York, NY: Oxford University Press.
50. See International IDEA. *Programme and Budget 2012–14*. IDEA: Stockholm. www.idea.int/upload/Int-IDEA-Programme-Budget-2012-2014.pdf.
51. David Osborne and T. Gaebler. 1992. *Reinventing Government*. Reading, MA: Addison-Wesley.
52. USAID. 2014. *Foreign Operations FY 2013 Performance Report*. Washington DC: USAID.
53. R. Pawson. 2006. *Evidence-based policy. A realist perspective*. London, UK: Sage; G. Bevan and Christopher Hood. 2006. "What's measured is what matters: Targets and gaming in the English public health care system." *Public Administration* 84: 517–538; D. Wilson, B. Croxson and A. Atkinson. 2006. "'What gets measured gets done': Head-teachers response to the English secondary school performance management system." *Policy Studies* 27: 153–171.
54. www.oecd.org/dac/evaluation/dcdndep/49247821.pdf.
55. United Nations. *Fourth World Conference on Women: Beijing Declaration*. www.un.org/womenwatch/daw/beijing/platform/declar.htm.

56. Peter Triantafillou. 2015. "The Political implications of performance management and evidence-Based Policymaking." *American Review of Public Administration* 45 (2): 167–181.
57. See, for example, National Democratic Institute. 2005. "Middle East Women's Campaign Training." http://pdf.usaid.gov/pdf_docs/pdacf909.pdf.
58. USAID. June 2014. "*Performance Evaluation of USAID Electoral Assistance to Kenya from January 2008–August 2013*." Washington DC: USAID. http://pdf.usaid.gov/pdf_docs/paoojvsb.pdf.
59. See USAID. June 2014. "*Performance Evaluation of USAID Electoral Assistance to Kenya from January 2008–August 2013*." Washington DC: USAID. http://pdf.usaid.gov/pdf_docs/paoojvsb.pdf.
60. The USAID evaluation report concludes cautiously: "USAID made a significant financial contribution to the elections and IPs appreciated the flexibility of USAID's support; however, there were not adequate systems in place to measure program contribution." USAID. June 2014. "*Performance Evaluation of USAID Electoral Assistance to Kenya from January 2008–August 2013*." Washington DC: USAID. http://pdf.usaid.gov/pdf_docs/paoojvsb.pdf, p. 13.
61. The Electoral Commission. 2002. *Modernising Elections: A strategic evaluation of the 2002 electoral pilot schemes*. London: The Electoral Commission. www.electoralcommission.org.uk.
62. Pippa Norris. 2004. "Will new technology boost turnout?" In *Electronic Voting and Democracy: A Comparative Analysis*. Edited by Norbert Kersting and Harald Baldersheim. London: Palgrave, pp.193–225.
63. Michael Woolcock. 2009. "Towards a plurality of methods in project evaluation: A contextualized approach to understanding impact trajectories and efficacy." *Journal of Development Effectiveness* 1(1): 1–14.
64. Joel D. Barkan. 1993. "Kenya: Lessons from a flawed election." *Journal of Democracy* 4(3): 85–99.
65. www.usaid.gov/what-we-do/democracy-human-rights-and-governance.
66. UK Department for International Development (DFID). 2013. *Annual Report and Accounts 2012–13*. London: The Stationery Office. www.gov.uk/government/uploads/system/uploads/attachment_data/file/208445/annual-report-accounts2013-13.pdf.
67. Indran A. Naidoo Director, UNDP Evaluation Office. "Foreword," p iii. In United Nations Development Programme. 2012. *Evaluation of UNDP Contribution to Strengthening Electoral Systems and Processes*. New York: UNDP.
68. Morton H. Halperin, Joseph T. Siegle, and Michael M. Weinstein. 2010. *The Democracy Advantage: How Democracies Promote Prosperity and Peace*. New York: Routledge. 2nd edition; Michael McFaul. 2010. *Advancing Democracy Abroad*. New York: Rowman & Littlefield; Larry Diamond. 1996. *Developing Democracy: Toward Consolidation*. Baltimore: Johns Hopkins University Press; Thomas Carothers. 1999. *Aiding Democracy Abroad: The Learning Curve*. Washington DC: Carnegie Endowment for International Peace.
69. Morton H. Halperin, Joseph T. Siegle, and Michael M. Weinstein. 2010. *The Democracy Advantage: How Democracies Promote Prosperity and Peace*. New York: Routledge. 2nd edition.

70. Thomas Carothers. 1999. *Aiding Democracy Abroad*. Washington DC: Carnegie Endowment for International Peace (chapter 5); Larry Diamond. 1999. *Developing Democracy: Toward Consolidation*. Baltimore: John Hopkins University Press.
71. Francis Fukuyama. 2004. *State-Building: Governance and World Order in the 21st Century*. NY: Cornell University Press; Simon Chesterman. 2004. *You, the People: The United Nations, Transitional Administration, and State-building*. New York: Oxford University Press; James D. Fearon and David D. Laitin. 2004. "Neo-trusteeship and the problem of weak states." *International Security* 29(4): 5–43; Stephen Krasner. 2004. "Sharing sovereignty: New institutions for collapsed and failing states." *International Security* 29(2): 85–120; Roland Paris. 2004. *At War's End: Building Peace After Civil Conflict*. Cambridge: Cambridge University Press.
72. An annual ranked Fragile States Index is published by the Fund for Peace, see. www.fundforpeace.org/global/?q=fsi. The 2014 Index ranked South Sudan, Somalia, and the Central African States in the top positions.
73. Francis Fukuyama. 2011. *The Origins of Political Order: From Pre-human Times to the French Revolution*. New York: Farrar, Straus & Giroux.
74. See Roland Paris and Timothy D. Sisk. 2009. Ed. *The Dilemmas of State-building*. New York: Routledge.
75. Dawn Brancati and Jack L. Snyder. 2011. "Rushing to the Polls: The causes of early post- conflict elections." *Journal of Conflict Resolution*. 55(3): 469–492; Dawn Brancati and Jack L. Snyder. 2013. "Time to kill: The impact of election timing on post-conflict stability." *Journal of Conflict Resolution* 57(5): 822–850.
76. Krishna Kumar. 2012. *Evaluating Democracy Assistance*. Boulder, CO: Lynne Rienner.
77. United Nations Development Programme. 2014. *The Longer-Term Impact of UNDP Electoral Assistance: Lessons Learned*. New York: UNDP.
78. A.A. Goldsmith. 2001. "Foreign aid and statehood." *International Organization* 55 (1): 123–148; Styephen Knack. 2004. "Does foreign aid promote democracy?" *International Studies Quarterly* 48: 251–266; Simeon Djankov, Jose G. Montalvo, and Marta Reynal-Querol. 2008. "The curse of aid." *Journal of Economic Growth* 13: 169–194; Sarah Blodgett Bermeo. 2011. "Foreign aid and regime change: A role for donor intent." *World Development* 39(11): 2021–2031; Steven E. Finkel, Aníbal Pérez-Liñán, Mitchell A. Seligson, 2007. "The effects of U.S. foreign assistance on democracy building, 1990–2003." *World Politics* 59 (1): 404–439.
79. See Pippa Norris. 2012. *Making Democratic Governance Work*. New York: Cambridge University Press.
80. Roger C. Riddell. 2007. *Does Aid Really Work?* New York: Oxford University Press.
81. Mansfield, Edward D., and Jon C. Pevehouse. 2006. "Democratization and International Organizations." *International Organization* 60(1): 137–167.
82. The Pew Charitable Trust. 2014. *Election Performance Index: Methodology*. www.pewtrusts.org/~/media/Assets/2014/04/07/EPI_methodology.pdf.
83. See, for example, Robert F. Bauer and Benjamin L. Ginsberg, et al., 2014. *The American Voting Experience: Report and Recommendations of the Presidential Commission on Election Administration*. Washington, DC.

84. Devra C. Moehler, 2010. "Democracy, governance, and randomized development assistance." *Annals of the American Academy of Political and Social Science*, 628: 30–46.
85. www.usaid.gov/evaluation/usaid-forward-evaluation-reports.
86. http://e-gap.org/.

CHAPTER 4

1. Pippa Norris, Richard W. Frank and Ferran Martínez i Coma. Eds. 2015. *Contentious Elections: From Ballots to the Barricades.* New York: Routledge.
2. Emily Beaulieu. 2014. *Electoral Protest and Democracy in the Developing World.* New York: Cambridge University Press.
3. Estimates are derived from Susan D. and Nicola Marinov. 2012. *Codebook for National Elections across Democracy and Autocracy (NELDA) 1945–2010.* Version 3. http://hyde.research.yale.edu/nelda/.
4. Ursula E. Daxecker and Gerald Schneider. 2014. "Electoral monitoring." In Pippa Norris, Richard W. Frank and Ferran Martínez i Coma, eds., *Advancing Electoral Integrity.* New York: Oxford University Press.
5. See, for example, Reporters without Borders *2016 Index of Press Freedom*, https://rsf.org/en/ranking.
6. Walter R. Mebane Jr. 2012. "Comment on 'Benford's Law and the detection of election fraud.'" *Political Analysis.* 19(3): 269–272; J. M. Montgomery, S. Olivella, Potter J. D., Crisp B. F. 2015. "An informed forensics approach to detecting vote irregularities." *Political Analysis.* 23(4): 488–505.
7. Mary Meyer and Jane Booker. 2001. *Eliciting and Analyzing expert Judgment: A Practical Guide.* Society for Industrial and Applied Mathematics.
8. See Geraldo L. Munck, 2009. *Measuring Democracy: A Bridge Between Scholarship and Politics.* Baltimore: The Johns Hopkins Press; Andreas Schedler. 2012. "Judgment and measurement in political science." *Perspectives on Politics* 10(1): 21–36; Ferran Martinez i Coma and Richard W. Frank. 2014. "Expert judgments." In Pippa Norris, Richard W. Frank, and Ferran Martinez i Coma, eds., *Advancing Electoral Integrity*, chapter 4. New York: Oxford University Press; Todd Landman and Edzia Carvalho. 2010. *Measuring Human Rights.* London: Routledge; Kevin E. Davis, Angelina Fisher, Benedict Kingsbury, and Sally Engle Merry. Eds. 2015. *Governance by Indicators.* Oxford: Oxford University Press; Transparency International *Corruption Perception Index.* www.transparency.org/research/cpi/overview.
9. For details, see the Varieties of Democracy project, see https://v-dem.net/.
10. Marco R. Steenbergen and Gary Marks. 2007. "Evaluating expert judgments." *European Journal of Political Research* 46: 347–366.
11. Kevin E. Davis, Angelina Fisher, Benedict Kingsbury, and Sally Engle Merry. Eds. 2015. *Governance by Indicators.* Oxford: Oxford University Press.
12. See Pippa Norris, Jørgen Elklit and Andrew Reynolds. 2014. "Methods and evidence." In Pippa Norris, Richard W. Frank, and Ferran Martinez i Coma, eds., *Advancing Electoral Integrity*, chapter 3. New York: Oxford University Press.

13. Mary Meyer and Jane Booker. 2001. *Eliciting and Analyzing Expert Judgment: A Practical Guide*. Society for Industrial and Applied Mathematics.
14. See also, Andreas Schedler. 2002. "The menu of manipulation." *Journal of Democracy* 13(2): 36–50.
15. Pippa Norris and Andrea Abel van Es. 2015. *Checkbook Elections? Political Finance in Comparative Perspective*. New York: Oxford University Press.
16. Pippa Norris, Ferran Martinez i Coma and Richard W. Frank. 2014. "Assessing the quality of elections." *Journal of Democracy* 24(4): 124–135; Ferran Martínez i Coma and Carolien van Ham. 2015, "Can experts judge elections? Testing the validity of expert judgments for measuring election integrity." *European Journal of Political Research* 54: 305–325.
17. Pippa Norris, Ferran Martínez i Coma and Richard Frank. 2013. "Assessing the quality of elections." *Journal of Democracy* 24(4): 124–135; Pippa Norris, Richard W. Frank, and Ferran Martínez i Coma. 2014. Eds. *Advancing Electoral Integrity*. New York: Oxford University Press.
18. Carolien van Ham. 2015. "Getting elections right? Measuring electoral integrity." *Democratization* 22(4): 714–737.
19. Jan Teorell, Stefan Dahlberg, Sören Holmberg, Bo Rothstein, Felix Hartmann, and Richard Svensson. January 2016. *The Quality of Government Standard Dataset*, version Jan16. University of Gothenburg: The Quality of Government Institute, www.qog.pol.gu.se.
20. *Varieties of Democracy* (V-DEM), Country-Year Dataset, released January 2016. https://v-dem.net/en/.
21. The PEI Index was correlated with the Cingranelli and Richards' index of electoral self-determination rights (R = .63***, N.137), the Economist Intelligence Unit measure of Electoral Processes and Pluralism (R = .71***, N.129), and the Bertelsmann Transformation Index of Free and Fair Elections (R = .64***, N.98). For more details, see Jan Teorell, Stefan Dahlberg, Sören Holmberg, Bo Rothstein, Anna Khomenko, and Richard Svensson. 2016. *The Quality of Government Standard Dataset*, version Jan16. University of Gothenburg: The Quality of Government Institute. QoGStdJan16, www.qog.pol.gu.se.
22. For further methodological tests, see Ferran Martínez i Coma and Carolien van Ham. 2015, "Can experts judge elections? Testing the validity of expert judgments for measuring election integrity." *European Journal of Political Research* 54: 305–325.
23. Pippa Norris. 2016. *Why Elections Fail*. New York: Cambridge University Press; Pippa Norris. 2017. "Electoral integrity and electoral systems." In Erik S. Herron, Robert J. Pekkanen, and Matthew S. Shugart, eds., *The Oxford Handbook of Electoral Systems*. New York: Oxford University Press.
24. UK Electoral Commission. 2013. *Electoral fraud in the UK: Evidence and Issues Paper*. London: UK Electoral Commission. www.electoralcommission.org.uk; Alistair Clark and Toby S. James. 2017. "Poll Workers." In Pippa Norris and Alessandro Nai, eds., *Watchdog Elections: Transparency, Accountability and Integrity*. New York: Oxford University Press.
25. Richard L. Hasen, 2012. *The Voting Wars: From Florida 2000 to the Next Election Meltdown*. New Haven: Yale University Press.
26. www.ncsl.org/research/elections-and-campaigns/voter-id-history.aspx.

27. Pippa Norris. 2017. *Why American Elections Are Flawed (and How to Fix Them)*. Ithaca: Cornell University Press.
28. Office of the Director of National Intelligence. January 2016. *Background to "Assessing Russian Activities and Intentions in Recent US Elections": The Analytic Process and Cyber Incident Attribution*. https://assets.documentcloud.org/documents/3254237/Russia-Hack-Report.pdf
29. www.nbcnews.com/politics/politics-news/nsa-chief-potential-russian-hacking-u-s-elections-concern-n647491.
30. Lorraine Carol Minnite. 2010. *The Myth of Voter Fraud*. Ithaca: Cornell University Press; Richard L. Hasen, 2012. *The Voting Wars: From Florida 2000 to the Next Election Meltdown*. New Haven: Yale University Press; Tova Andrea Wang. 2012. *T he Politics of Voter Suppression: Defending and Expanding Americans' Right to Vote*. Ithaca: Cornell University Press; Thad E. Hall. 2013. "US voter registration reform." *Electoral Studies*. 32(4): 589–596.
31. The National Conference on State and Local Legislatures (NCSL). www.ncsl.org/research/elections-and-campaigns/voter-id.aspx.
32. Robert F. Bauer and Benjamin L. Ginsberg, et al, 2014. *The American Voting Experience: Report and Recommendations of the Presidential Commission on Election Administration* Washington DC. www.supportthevoter.gov/.
33. Pippa Norris and Andrea Abel van Es. Eds. 2016. *Checkbook Elections? Political Finance in Comparative Perspective*. New York: Oxford University Press.
34. Lisa Handley and Bernard Grofman. Eds. 2008. *Redistricting in Comparative Perspective*. New York: Oxford University Press.
35. Gallup Polls. 15–16 August 2016. *About Six in 10 Confident in Accuracy of U.S. Vote Count*. www.gallup.com.
36. See Michael Pal. 2014. "Canadian Election Administration on Trial: The 'Robocalls' case and the Opitz decision." Paper presented at EIP/MEDW workshop prior to the IPSA World Congress, Montreal 18 July 2014.
37. OSCE/ODIHR. 5 February 2016. *Canada Parliamentary Elections 19 October 2015 OSCE/ODIHR Election Assessment Mission Final Report*. Warsaw: OSCE/ODIHR. www.osce.org/odihr/elections/220661?download=true.
38. www.canada.ca/en/campaign/electoral-reform/learn-about-canadian-federal-electoral-reform/mydemocracyca-online-digital-consultation-engagement-platform.html.
39. www.un.org/apps/news/story.asp?NewsID=52256#.VqHI6rcU9Fo.
40. OSCE/ODIHR. 2015. *Estonia Parliamentary Elections 1 March 2015 OSCE/ODIHR Election Expert Team Final Report*. Warsaw: OSCE/ODIHR.
41. OSCE/ODIHR. 2015. *Republic of Poland Parliamentary Elections 25 October 2015 OSCE/ODIHR Election Assessment Mission Report*. Warsaw: OSCE/ODIHR.
42. Ferran Martinez i Coma, Pippa Norris and Richard W. Frank. "Integridad en las elecciones de America 2012–2014." [Integrity of the elections in America 2012–2014], *America Latina Hoy* 70: 37–54.
43. Jorge I. Dominguez and Michael Shifter. Eds. 2003. *Constructing Democratic Governance in Latin America*. Baltimore: Johns Hopkins Press; Daniel H. Levine and Jose E. Molina. Eds. 2011. *The Quality of Democracy in Latin America*. Boulder, CO: Lynne Rienner.

44. www.ibtimes.com/haiti-elections-2015-presidential-candidates-key-issues-dates-violence-concerns-how-2154324.
45. www.reuters.com/article/us-haiti-election-idUSKCN0QE09H20150809.
46. Frances Robles. 21 Jan 2015. "U.S. presses for Haiti run-off vote amid fears of violence and fraud." *The New York Times.*
47. IFES. *Election Guide*. Washington DC: IFES. www.electionguide.org/elections/id/2593/.
48. www.npr.org/sections/goatsandsoda/2015/01/12/376138864/5-years-after-haiti-s-earthquake-why-aren-t-things-better.
49. Pippa Norris. 2016. "Electoral integrity in East Asia." *Routledge Handbook on Democratization in East Asia.* Co-ed Tun-jen Cheng and Yun-han Chu. Routledge: New York.
50. Zoltan Barany. 2016. "Moving toward Democracy: The 2015 Parliamentary Elections in Myanmar." *Electoral Studies.* 42(3): 75–77. DOI: 10.1016/j.electstud.2016.02.005
51. European Union. 2015. *Election Observation Mission Republic of the Union of Myanmar*. www.eueom.eu/files/pressreleases/english/101115-eueom-ps_en.pdf.
52. IFES. Election Guide. Washington DC: IFES. www.electionguide.org/elections/id/2746/.
53. National Democratic Institute (NDI). 2014. *Preliminary Statement of the Observer Delegation to Tunisia's 2014 Legislative Elections.* Washington, DC: NDI.
54. Instance Supérieure Indépendante pour les Elections (ISIE). 2014. *Les Résultats Préliminaires du Deuxième Tour de la Présidentielle.* Tunis, December 22, 2014.
55. European Union. 2014. *Union Europeenne Mission D'observation Electorale Tunisie 2014. Deuxième tour des élections présidentielles.* Brussels: EU.
56. The Carter Center. 2014. "Carter Center Preliminary Statement on Tunisia's Second Round of Presidential Elections." Atlanta: Carter Center.
57. www.theguardian.com/world/2014/feb/03/afghanistan-election-guide-candidates-list.
58. www.tolonews.com/en/election-2014/13875-24-polling-centers-of-414-will-be-open-on-elections-day-moi.
59. www.theguardian.com/world/2014/feb/03/afghanistan-election-guide-candidates-list.
60. National Democratic Institute. 2010. "Despite Violence, Voters in Afghanistan Show Commitment to Democratic Process, NDI Finds." Washington DC: NDI. http://afghanistanelectiondata.org/node/69.
61. http://edition.cnn.com/2016/01/22/middleeast/iran-elections/.
62. IFES. *Election Guide*. Washington DC: IFES.
63. www.hrw.org/news/2016/01/24/iran-threats-free-fair-elections.
64. www.nytimes.com/aponline/2016/01/20/world/middleeast/ap-ml-iran-elections.html.
65. www.reuters.com/article/us-iran-election-candidates-idUSKCN0V419V.
66. www.nytimes.com/aponline/2016/01/20/world/middleeast/ap-ml-iran-elections.html.
67. http://edition.cnn.com/2016/01/22/middleeast/iran-elections/.
68. www.reuters.com/article/us-iran-election-candidates-idUSKCN0V419V.

69. www.nytimes.com/aponline/2016/01/20/world/middleeast/ap-ml-iran-elections .html.
70. edition.cnn.com/2016/01/22/middleeast/iran-elections/.
71. www.usatoday.com/story/news/world/2016/01/26/iranian-president-tours-europea-sign-big-trade-deals/79339580/.
72. www.syriahr.com/en/.
73. www.bbc.com/news/world-middle-east-26116868.
74. http://sputniknews.com/middleeast/20151218/1031952062/syria-parliamentary-elections.html.
75. www.theguardian.com/world/2015/oct/26/syrias-assad-open-to-early-presidential-elections-only-if-terrorists-defeated-first.
76. www.theguardian.com/world/2015/oct/26/syrias-assad-open-to-early-presidential-elections-only-if-terrorists-defeated-first.
77. https://en.wikipedia.org/wiki/Plurality-at-large_voting.
78. www.voanews.com/a/syria-assad-election/3276726.html.
79. www.nytimes.com/2016/04/14/world/middleeast/syrian-parliamentary-elections-highlight-divisions-and-uncertainty.html.
80. www.ipu.org/wmn-e/classif.htm.
81. www.reuters.com/article/us-mideast-crisis-syria-idUSKCN0XA2C5.
82. www.voanews.com/a/assad-rules-out-syrian-elections-with-foreign-observers/2932940.html.
83. Max Grömping and Ferran Martínez i Coma. 2015. "*Electoral Integrity in Africa.*" Germany: Hans Seidel Foundation.
84. www.article19.org/resources.php/resource/37788/en/ethiopia-2015-elections:-an-opportunity-to-change-course-and-increase-freedom-of-expression.
85. www.aljazeera.com/indepth/opinion/2015/04/elections-ethiopian-style-150430084220440.html.
86. http://eeas.europa.eu/delegations/ethiopia/press_corner/all_news/news/2015/elections26022015.htm.
87. www.reuters.com/article/us-ethiopia-election-idUSKBN0OB1ST20150526.
88. Jason Mosley. May 22, 2015. "Ethiopia's elections are just an exercise in controlled political participation." *The Guardian*. www.theguardian.com/global-development/2015/may/22/ethiopia-elections-controlled-political-participation.
89. www.reuters.com/article/2015/06/29/us-burundi-election-idUSKCN0P90H820150629.
90. www.eueom.eu/files/pressreleases/english/communique-de-presse-moeue-burundi-28052015_fr.pdf.
91. *The Independent*. July 25, 2015. "Burundi elections: President Pierre Nkurunziza wins third term in poll denounced by opposition and international observers." www.independent.co.uk/news/world/africa/burundis-president-wins-third-term-in-election-denounced-by-opposition-and-international-observers-10415501.html.
92. See Samuel Decalo. 1997. "Benin: First of the New Democracies." In John F. Clarke and David E. Gardiner, eds., *Political Reform in Francophone Africa*, pp. 41–61. Boulder, CO: Westview Press.
93. Freedom House. 2016. *Freedom in the World, 2016*. www.freedomhouse.org.
94. www.bbc.com/afrique/region/2016/02/160212_benin.
95. www.electionguide.org/elections/id/2893/.

96. www.reuters.com/article/us-benin-election-idUSKBN0TL25620151202#Swod51 bgcJXdb3DT.97.
97. www.elombah.com/index.php/reports/6148-preliminary-declaration-runoff-benin-election.
98. www.electionguide.org/elections/id/2893/.
99. www.elombah.com/index.php/reports/6148-preliminary-declaration-runoff-benin-election.
100. Freedom House. 2016. *Freedom in the World, 2016.* www.freedomhouse.org.
101. www.eueom.eu/files/pressreleases/english/300315prps-nigeria_en.pdf.
102. Pippa Norris. 2015. *Why Elections Fail.* New York: Cambridge University Press.
103. The Quality of Government dataset. www.qog.pol.gu.se/.
104. The Ace Project: http://aceproject.org/.
105. For a discussion, Sarah Birch. 2012. *Electoral Malpractice.* Oxford: Oxford University Press; van Ham, Carolien. 2015. "Getting elections right? Measuring electoral integrity." *Democratization.* 22(4): 714–737.
106. Seymour Martin Lipset. 1959. "Some social requisites of democracy: Economic development and political legitimacy." *American Political Science Review.* 53: 69–105. See also Seymour Martin Lipset. 1960. *Political Man: The Social Basis of Politics.* New York: Doubleday; Seymour Martin Lipset, Kyoung-Ryung Seong and John Charles Torres. 1993. "A comparative analysis of the social requisites of democracy." *International Social Science Journal.* 45(2): 154–175; Seymour Martin Lipset and Jason M. Lakin. 2004. *The Democratic Century.* Oklahoma: The University of Oklahoma Press.
107. Seymour Martin Lipset. 1959. "Some social requisites of democracy: Economic development and political legitimacy." *American Political Science Review.* 53: 75.
108. J. Krieckhaus. 2004. "The regime debate revisited: A sensitivity analysis of democracy's economic effect." *British Journal of Political Science* 34 (4): 635–655.
109. Netina Tan. 2013. "Electoral engineering and hegemonic party resilience in Singapore." *Electoral Studies.* 32(4): 632–643.
110. See, for example, Michael L. Ross. 2001. "Does oil hinder democracy?" *World Politics* 53: 325–361; N. Jensen and L. Wantchekon. 2004. "Resource wealth and political regimes in Africa." *Comparative Political Studies* 37, 816–841; Carles Boix. 2003. *Democracy and Redistribution.* Cambridge: Cambridge University Press; M.L. Ross. 2004. "How do natural resources influence civil war? Evidence from thirteen cases." *International Organization* 58 (1): 35–67; Stephen Haber and Victor Menaldo. 2011. "Do natural resources fuel authoritarianism? A reappraisal of the resource curse." *American Political Science Review* 105(1): 1–26; Michael L. Ross. 2013. *The Oil Curse: How Petroleum Wealth Shapes the Development of Nations.* Princeton, NJ: Princeton University Press.
111. Paul Collier and Nicholas Sambanis. Eds. 2005. *Understanding Civil War.* Washington DC: World Bank; M. Humphreys. 2005. "Natural resources, conflict, and conflict resolution – Uncovering the mechanisms." *Journal of Conflict Resolution* 49 (4): 508–537; Richard Snyder. 2006. "Does lootable wealth breed disorder? A political economy of extraction framework." *Comparative Political Studies* 39 (8): 943–968.
112. For balanced overviews of the debate about globalization, see David Held, Anthony McGrew, David Goldblatt, and Jonathan Perraton. 1999. *Global*

transformations: Politics, Economics, and Culture. Stanford, CA: Stanford University Press. Chapter 7; Anthony McGrew and David Held. Eds. 2007. *Globalization Theory: Approaches and Controversies*. Cambridge: Polity.

113. David Held and Anthony McGrew. 2007. *Globalization/Anti-Globalization: Beyond the Great Divide* Cambridge: Polity; Jens Bartelson. 2000. "Three concepts of globalization." *International Sociology* 15(2): 180–196.
114. Valerie Bunch and Sharon l. Wolchik. 2006. "International diffusion and post-communist electoral revolutions." *Communist and Post-Communist Studies* 39 (3): 283–304; Joshua Tucker. 2007. "Enough! Electoral fraud, collective action problems, and post-communist colored revolutions." *Perspectives on Politics* 5(3): 535–551.
115. UNDP. 2004. *Arab Human Development Report 2004*. New York: UNDP/Oxford University Press.
116. Jon C. Pevehouse. 2004. *Democracy from Above: Regional Organizations and Democratization*. New York: Cambridge University Press; Harvey Starr and Christina Lindborg. 2003. "Democratic dominoes: diffusion approaches to the spread of democracy in the international system." *Journal of Conflict Resolution* 35 (2): 356–381; Barbara Wejnart. 2005. "Diffusion, development and democracy, 1800–1999." *American Sociological Review*. 70 (1): 53–81.
117. The African Union. hwww.africaunion.org/root/au/Documents/Treaties/text/Charter%20on%20Democracy.pdf.
118. Karen Elizabeth Smith. 2003. *European Union Foreign Policy in a Changing World*. Oxford: Polity Press; Richard Youngs. 2002. *The European Union and the Promotion of Democracy*. Oxford: Oxford University Press.
119. Pippa Norris. 2015. *Why Elections Fail*. New York: Cambridge University Press.
120. Pippa Norris. 2017. "Electoral integrity and electoral systems." In Erik S. Herron, Robert J. Pekkanen, and Matthew S. Shugart, eds., the *Oxford Handbook of Electoral Systems*. New York: Oxford University Press.
121. R. Michael Alvarez, Lonna Rae Atkeson and Thad Hall. 2012. *Evaluating Elections: A Handbook of Methods and Standards*. New York: Cambridge University Press.
122. Pippa Norris. 2015. *Why Elections Fail*. New York: Cambridge University Press.

CHAPTER 5

1. See Pippa Norris. 2004. *Electoral Engineering*. New York: Cambridge University Press.
2. Kenneth Benoit. 2004. "Models of electoral system change." *Electoral Studies*, 23:3, 363–389; Gideon Rahat and Reuvan Hazan. "The barriers to electoral system reform: A synthesis of alternative approaches." *West European Politics*. 34(3): 478–494; Alan Renwick. 2010. *Changing the Rules of Democracy: The Politics of Electoral Reform*. Cambridge: Cambridge University Press.
3. Pippa Norris. 2011. "Cultural explanations of electoral reform: A policy cycle model." *West European Politics*, 34:3, 531–550.
4. We are most grateful for the cooperation of the Organization of American States in the Democratic Diffusion project. For details, see www.electoralintegrityproject.com.

5. Raul Cordenillo and Andrew Ellis. Eds. 2012. *The Integrity of Elections: The Role of Regional Organizations*. Stockholm: International IDEA.
6. Susan. D. Hyde. 2011. *The Pseudo-Democrat's Dilemma*. Ithaca: Cornell University Press; Judith Kelley. 2012. *Monitoring Democracy: When International Election Observation Works and Why It Often Fails*. Princeton, New Jersey: Princeton University Press; Daniella Donno. 2013. *Defending Democratic Norms*. New York: Oxford University Press.
7. OAS General Secretariat. 2013. *The 2007–2012 Electoral Cycle in The Americas*. Washington DC: OAS. www.oas.org/es/sap/docs/deco/CicloElectoral_e.pdf
8. OAS General Secretariat. 2013. *The 2007–2012 Electoral Cycle in The Americas*. Washington DC: OAS. www.oas.org/es/sap/docs/deco/CicloElectoral_e.pdf
9. www.osce.org/odihr/elections/193741.
10. UN. 2005. *Declaration of Principles for International Election Observation*. New York: United Nations. www.ndi.org/files/1923_declaration_102705_0.pdf.
11. Ursula E. Daxecker and Gerald Schneider. 2014. "Electoral monitoring." In Pippa Norris, Richard W. Frank and Ferran Martinez I Coma, eds., *Advancing Electoral Integrity*. New York: Oxford University Press.
12. Sharon F. Lean. 2007. "Democracy assistance to domestic election monitoring organizations: Conditions for success." *Democratization*, 14(2): 289–312; Sharon F. Lean. Ed. 2012. *Civil Society and Electoral Accountability in Latin America*. New York: Palgrave; Max Grömping. 2017. "Domestic election monitors." In Pippa Norris and Alexandre Nai, eds., *Election Watchdogs*.
13. www.gndem.org/members.
14. http://enemo.eu/member.htm.
15. www.ndi.org.
16. See GNDEM. *Declaration of Global Principles for Nonpartisan Election Observation and Monitoring by Citizen Organizations*. www.gndem.org/declaration-of-global-principles.
17. See Sharon F. Lean. 2012. *Civil Society and Electoral Accountability in Latin America*. New York: Palgrave Macmillan.
18. Makulilo Alexander Boniface. 2011. "'Watching the watcher': an evaluation of local election observers in Tanzania." *Journal of Modern African Studies* 49(2): 241–262.
19. Ursula E. Daxecker. 2012. "The cost of exposing cheating: International election monitoring, fraud, and post-election violence in Africa." *Journal of Peace Research* 49(4): 503–516.
20. Susan. D. Hyde. 2011. *The Pseudo-Democrat's Dilemma*. Ithaca: Cornell University Press; Daniella Donno. 2013. *Defending Democratic Norms*. New York: Oxford University Press. 2012.
21. Susan. D. Hyde. 2011. *The Pseudo-Democrat's Dilemma*. Ithaca: Cornell University Press; Judith Kelley. 2012. *Monitoring Democracy: When International Election Observation Works and Why It Often Fails*. Princeton, NJ: Princeton University Press; Daniella Donno. 2013. *Defending Democratic Norms*. New York: Oxford University Press.
22. Susan D. Hyde. 2007. "Experimenting in democracy promotion: International observers and the 2004 presidential elections in Indonesia." *Perspectives on Politics* 8(2): 511–527; Susan D. Hyde. 2007. "The observer effect in international politics: Evidence from a natural experiment." *World Politics* 60(1): 37–63; Nahomi Ichino and Matthias Schuendeln. 2012. "Deterring or displacing

electoral irregularities? Spillover effects of observers in a randomized field experiment in Ghana." *Journal of Politics* 74(1): 292–307; Fredrik M. Sjoberg. 2014. "Autocratic adaptation: The strategic use of transparency and the persistence of election fraud." *Electoral Studies* 33: 233–245.

23. Thomas Carothers. 1997. "The observers observed." *Journal of Democracy*. 8 (3): 17–31; Judith Kelley. 2010. "Election observers and their biases." *Journal of Democracy* 21: 158–172.
24. Ursula E. Daxecker and Gerald Schneider. 2014. "Electoral monitoring." In Pippa Norris, Richard W. Frank and Ferran Martinez i Coma, eds., *Advancing Electoral Integrity*. New York: Oxford University Press.
25. Pippa Norris and Max Gromping. 2017. *The Perceptions of Electoral Integrity Rolling Expert Survey* (PEI-5.0). www.electoralintegrityproject.com.
26. Pippa Norris and Max Gromping. 2017. *The Perceptions of Electoral Integrity Rolling Expert Survey* (PEI-5.0). www.electoralintegrityproject.com.
27. Nahomi Ichino and Matthias Schuendeln. 2012. "Deterring or displacing electoral irregularities? Spillover effects of observers in a randomized field experiment in Ghana." *Journal of Politics* 74(1): 292–307.
28. Daniella Donno. 2013. *Defending Democratic Norms*. New York: Oxford University Press; Daniella Donno. 2010. "Who is punished? Regional intergovernmental organizations and the enforcement of democratic norms." *International Organization* 64(4): 593–625.
29. Susan. D. Hyde. 2011. *The Pseudo-Democrat's Dilemma*. Ithaca: Cornell University Press; Judith Kelley. 2012. *Monitoring Democracy: When International Election Observation Works and Why It Often Fails*. Princeton, NJ: Princeton University Press; Daniella Donno. 2013. *Defending Democratic Norms*. New York: Oxford University Press.
30. Christopher Hood and David Heald. Eds. 2006. *Transparency: The Key to Better Governance?* Oxford: British Academy/Oxford University Press; S. Kosack, C. Tolmie, an C. Griffin. 2010. *From the Ground Up: Improving Government Performance with Independent Monitoring Organizations*. Washington DC: Brookings Institute Press; John Gaventa and Rosemary McGee. 2013. "The impact of transparency and accountability initiatives." *Development Policy Review* 31: S3–S28; Anuradha Joshi. 2013. "Do They Work? Assessing the Impact of Transparency and Accountability Initiatives in Service Delivery." *Development Policy Review* 31: 29–48.
31. See, for example, www.openelectiondata.net/en/guide/electoral-integrity/public-confidence/. "Public confidence in each step of an election process is critical to the integrity of the election. Citizens not only have a right to participate in elections, they have a right to know for themselves whether the electoral process is valid. Access to information about each phase of the election process is fundamental to creating and reinforcing public confidence in elections."
32. The Open Society Foundation. www.opensocietyfoundations.org/topics/freedom-information.
33. www.openelectiondata.net/en/.
34. Alan Wall et al. 2006. *Electoral Management Design: The International IDEA Handbook*. Sweden: International IDEA, p. 24.

35. John C. Pevehouse. 2002. "With a little help from my friends? Regional organizations and the consolidation of democracy." *American Journal of Political Science* 46(3): 611–626.
36. See, for example, www.oas.org/en/spa/deco/pro_estudios.asp.
37. ACE Electoral Knowledge Network. www.ACEProject.org.
38. John C. Pevehouse. 2002. "With a little help from my friends? Regional organizations and the consolidation of democracy." *American Journal of Political Science* 46(3): 611–626.
39. Pippa Norris. 2015. *Why Elections Fail.* New York: Cambridge University Press.
40. Pippa Norris and Ronald Inglehart. 2009. *Cosmopolitan Communications.* New York: Cambridge University Press.
41. Valerie J. Bunce and Sharon L. Wolchik. 2006. "Favorable conditions and electoral revolutions." *Journal of Democracy* 17: 5–18; Valerie J. Bunce and Sharon L. Wolchik. 2011. *Defeating Authoritarian Leaders in Post-Communist Countries.* New York: Cambridge University Press.
42. Noah Coburn and Anna Larson. 2013. *Derailing Democracy in Afghanistan: Elections in an Unstable Political Landscape.* New York: Columbia University Press.
43. OAS. 2011. *Promotion and Strengthening of Democracy: Follow-Up to The Inter-American Democratic Charter.* (AG/RES. 2694, 2011).
44. Organization for Security and Cooperation in Europe (OSCE). 2016. *Handbook on the Follow-up of Electoral Recommendations.* Warsaw: OSCE/ODIHR.
45. Betilde Munoz-Pogassian, Sara Mia Noguera and Tyler Finn. 2013. "OAS Electoral Observation Missions: 50 Years Contributing to the Strengthening of Democratic Systems in the Region." In *The 2007–2012 Electoral Cycle in the Americas: A review by the OAS General Secretariat.* Washington DC: OAS. See also the Organization for Security and Cooperation in Europe (OSCE). 2016. *Handbook on the Follow-up of Electoral Recommendations.* Warsaw: OSCE/ODIHR. Chapter 6.
46. Andrew Cooper and Thomas Legler. 2006. *Intervention Without Intervening? The OAS Defense and Promotion of Democracy in the Americas.* New York: Palgrave Macmillan; Hawkins, Darren and Shaw, Carolyn. 2008. "Legalising norms of democracy in the Americas." *Review Of International Studies* 34(3): 459–480; Amichai Magen, Thomas Risse, and Michael A McFaul. Eds. 2009. "Introduction: American and European Strategies to Promote Democracy – Shared Values, Common Challenges, Divergent Tools?" Promoting Democracy and The Rule of Law: American and European Strategies.
47. Organization for Security and Cooperation in Europe (OSCE). 2016. *Handbook on the Follow-up of Electoral Recommendations.* Warsaw: OSCE/ODIHR.
48. Kristof Jacobs and Monique Leyenaar. 2011. "A conceptual framework for major, minor, and technical electoral reform." *West European Politics* 34(3): 495–513.
49. For details, see Matthew Soberg Shugart and Martin P. Wattenberg. Eds. 2003. *Mixed-Member Electoral Systems: The Best of Both Worlds?* New York: Oxford University Press; Michael Gallagher and Paul Mitchell. Eds. 2005. *The Politics of Electoral Systems.* Oxford: Oxford University Press.
50. Arend Lijphart. 1994. *Electoral Systems and Party Systems: A Study of Twenty-Seven Democracies, 1945–1990.* Oxford: Oxford University Press.
51. Richard S. Katz. 1997. *Democracy and Elections.* New York: Oxford University Press; pp. 60–61.

52. Monique Leyenaar and Reuvan Hazan. "Reconceptualizing Electoral Reform." *West European Politics* 34(3): 437–455.
53. www.parliament.uk/about/how/elections-and-voting/voting-systems/.
54. Pippa Norris. 2016. "Electoral integrity and electoral systems." In Erik S. Herron, Robert J. Pekkanen, and Matthew S. Shugart, eds., *Oxford Handbook of Electoral Systems*. New York: Oxford University Press.
55. See, however, Ferran Martinez i Coma. Forthcoming. "International observers and electoral reforms." In Pippa Norris and Alessandro Nai, eds., *Election Watchdogs*.
56. Maxwell McCombs and Donald Shaw. 1972. "The agenda-setting function of the mass media." *Public Opinion Quarterly* 36(2)176–187; James W. Dearing and Everett Rogers. 2006. *Agenda-setting*. London: Sage Publications.
57. Stuart Soroka and Christopher Wlezian. 2010. *Degrees of Democracy*. New York: Cambridge University Press.
58. Maxwell McCombs. 2014. *Setting the Agenda: Mass Media and Public Opinion*. Cambridge: Polity Press. 2nd edition.
59. Matthew S. Shugart and Martin P. Wattenberg. Eds. 2001. *Mixed Member Electoral Systems: The Best of Both Worlds?* New York: Oxford University Press; Joseph M. Colomer. Ed. 2004. *Handbook of Electoral System Choice*. New York: Palgrave Macmillan; Michael Gallagher and Paul Mitchell. Eds. 2005. *The Politics of Electoral Systems*. Oxford: Oxford University Press.
60. Noah Coburn and Anna Larson. 2013. *Derailing Democracy in Afghanistan: Elections in an Unstable Political Landscape*. New York: Columbia University Press.
61. Mona Lena Krook. 2009. *Quotas for Women in Politics: Gender and Candidate Selection Reform Worldwide*. New York: Oxford University Press.
62. Damien Bol, Jean-Benoit Pilet and Pedro Riera. 2015. "The international diffusion of electoral systems." *European Journal of Political Research* 54: 384–410.
63. Pippa Norris. 2015. *Why Elections Fail*. New York: Cambridge University Press.
64. Daniel Levine and Jose E. Molina. 2011. *The Quality of Democracy in Latin America*. Boulder, CO: Lynne Rienner.
65. Judith Kelley. 2013. *The Good, the Bad, and the Ugly: Rethinking Election Monitoring*. Stockholm: International IDEA.
66. For more details, see Pippa Norris and Andrea Abel van Es. 2016. *Checkbook Elections*. New York: Oxford University Press.
67. http://globalization.kof.ethz.ch/media/filer_public/2016/03/03/variables_2016.pdf.
68. See, for example, Pippa Norris. 1997. "Choosing Electoral Systems." *International Political Science Review* 18(3): 297–312; David Farrell. 1997. *Comparing Electoral Systems*. London: Prentice Hall/Harvester Wheatsheaf; Gary Cox. 1997. *Making Votes Count*. New York and London: Cambridge University Press; Andrew Reynolds and Ben Reilly. 1997. *The International IDEA Handbook of Electoral System Design*. Stockholm: International Institute for Democracy and Electoral Assistance; Arend Lijphart. 1994. *Electoral Systems and Party Systems: A Study of Twenty-Seven Democracies, 1945–1990*. Oxford: Oxford University Press; Richard S. Katz. 1997. *Democracy and Elections*. New York: Oxford University Press; G. Bingham Powell, Jr. 2000. *Elections as Instruments of Democracy*. Yale University Press; Pippa Norris. 2004. *Electoral Engineering*. Cambridge: Cambridge University Press.

69. See Raul Cordenillo and Andrew Ellis. Eds. 2012. *The Integrity of Elections: The Role of Regional Organizations*. Stockholm: International IDEA; Mansfield, Edward D. and Jon C. Pevehouse. 2008. "Democratization and the varieties of international organizations." *Journal Of Conflict Resolution* 52(2): 269–294.

CHAPTER 6

1. Inter-Parliamentary Union. *Women in National Parliaments*, www.ipu.org last referenced August 2016.
2. European Commission. *Women and Men in Decision-making*, consulted third quarter 2016. http://ec.europa.eu/justice/gender-equality/gender-decision-making/database/index_en.htm. For more details, see Miki Caul Kittilson. 2006. *Challenging Parties, Changing Parliaments: Women and Elected Office in Contemporary Western Europe*. Columbus: Ohio State University Press.
3. Drude Dahlerup and Lenita Freidenvall. 2005. "Quotas as a fast track to equal representation for women." *International Feminist Journal of Politics* 7(1): 26–48; Drude Dahlerup. Ed. 2006. *Women, Quotas, and Politics*. London: Routledge; Mona Lena Krook. 2009. *Quotas for Women in Politics*. New York: Oxford University Press; Tripp and Kang 2007; Thames and Williams 2013.
4. Lena Wängnerud. 2009. "Women in parliaments: Descriptive and substantive representation." *Annual Review of Politics*. 12: 51–69.
5. Susan Franceschet, Mona Lena Krook, Jennifer M. Piscopo and Drude Dahlerup. Eds. 2012. *The Impact of Gender Quotas*. New York: Oxford University Press.
6. Drude Dahlerup and Lenita Freidenvall. 2005. "Quotas as a fast track to equal representation for women." *International Feminist Journal of Politics* 7(1): 26–48; Drude Dahlerup Ed. 2006. *Women, Quotas, and Politics*. London: Routledge; Mona Lena Krook. 2009. *Quotas for Women in Politics*. New York: Oxford University Press.
7. http://iknowpolitics.org/en.
8. *The Gender Quota Database*. GQD: Release 1.0 May 2014. Stockholm: University of Stockholm. See also the *Atlas of Electoral Gender Quotas* (2014). International IDEA, Stockholm University and the Inter-Parliamentary Union. Available at www.idea.int. For details, see www.quotaproject.org/. The May 2014 update of the Global Quota Web site was published as the *Atlas of Electoral Gender Quotas*, June 2014 and this is available from www.idea.int. The database excludes quotas at subnational level or in the Upper House. Overall 110 countries are classified with gender quotas for the lower house of the national legislature. Of these, two-thirds (63 percent) have also adopted legal gender quotas for local elections. Among the countries with bicameral legislatures, more than half (55 percent) have also adopted such quotas for their Upper House.
9. Jennifer Lawless. 2012. *Becoming a Candidate: Political Ambition and the Decision to Run for Office*. New York: Cambridge University Press.
10. Pippa Norris and Mona Lena Krook. 2011. *Gender Equality in Elected Office: A Six-Step Action Plan*. Warsaw: Organization for Security and Cooperation in Europe.

11. Jean Grugel. 1999. *Democracy Without Borders: Transnationalisation and Conditionality in New Democracies.* London: Routledge; Beth Simmons. 2009. *Mobilizing for Human Rights: International Law in Domestic Politics.* New York: Cambridge University Press; Sarah Sunn Bush. 2011. "International politics and the spread of quotas for women in legislatures." *International Organization* 65(1): 103–137.
12. Rawwida Bakshe and Wendy Harcourt, eds. 2015. *The Oxford Handbook of Transnational Feminist Movements.* New York: Oxford University Press.
13. Inter-Parliamentary Union. *Women in National Parliaments.* www.ipu.org
14. www.quotaproject.org.
15. Thomas Carothers. 1999. *Aiding Democracy Abroad.* Washington DC: Carnegie Endowment for International Peace; Beth Simmons. 2009. *Mobilizing for Human Rights: International Law in Domestic Politics.* New York: Cambridge University Press; Peter Burnell. 2011. *Promoting Democracy Abroad: Policy and Performance.* New Brunswick, New Jersey: Transaction Publishers.
16. Pippa Norris and Ronald Inglehart. 2009. *Cosmopolitan Communications: Cultural Diversity in a Globalized World.* New York: Cambridge University Press.
17. Susan Franceschet and Jennifer M. Piscopo. 2013. "Equality, democracy, and the broadening and deepening of gender quotas." Politics & Gender 9 (3): 310–316; Frank C. Thames and Margaret S. Williams. 2013. *Contagious Representation: Women's Political Representation in Democracies Around the World.* New York: NYU Press.
18. Yvonne Galligan et al. 2007. *Gender Politics and Democracy in Post-socialist Europe.* Opladen: Barbara Budrich Publishers; Pippa Norris, and Mona Lena Krook. 2011. *Gender Equality in Elected Office: A Six-Step Action Plan.* Warsaw: Organization for Security and Cooperation in Europe.
19. Pippa Norris. 2012. *Gender Equality in Elected Office in Asia-Pacific: Six Actions to Expand Women's Empowerment.* Bangkok: UNDP.
20. Drude Dahlerup and Monique Leyenaar. 2013. *Breaking Male Dominance in Old Democracies.* Oxford: Oxford University Press; Pamela Paxton, Melanie Hughes, and Jennifer Green. 2006. "The International Women's Movement and Women's Political Representation, 1893–2003." *American Sociological Review* 71:898–920.
21. Lenita Freidenvall, et al. 2006. "The Nordic countries: an incremental model." In Drude Dahlerup, ed., *Women, Quotas and Politics*, pp. 55–82. London: Routledge; Sarah Childs. 2004. *New Labour Women MPs.* London: Routledge.
22. Sarah Sunn Bush. 2011. "International politics and the spread of quotas for women in legislatures. " *International Organization* 65 (1): 103–137.
23. Pippa Norris. 2007. "Opening the door: Women leaders and constitution-building in Iraq and Afghanistan." In Barbara Kellerman, ed., *Women Who Lead*, pp. 197–226. New York: Jossey Bass; Drude Dahlerup. 2014. *Women's Under-Representation in Politics in the New Democracy of Bhutan – The Need for New Strategies. Available at Danish Institute for Parties and Democracy*, www.dipd.dk.
24. Seymour Martin Lipset. 1959. "Some social requisites of democracy: Economic development and political legitimacy." *American Political Science Review* 53: 69–105; Seymour Martin Lipset. 1960. *Political Man: The Social Basis of Politics.* New York: Doubleday.

25. Torbin Iversen and Frances Rosenbluth. 2008. "Work and Power: The Connection between Female Labor Force Participation and Female Political Representation." *Annual Review of Political Science* 11: 479; Kay L. Schlozman, 1999. "'What happened at work today?' A multistage model of gender, employment, and political participation." *Journal of Politics* 61: 29.
26. Michael L. Ross, 2008. "Oil, Islam and Women." *American Political Science Review* 102(1): 107–123.
27. Richard E. Matland, 1998. "Women's representation in national legislatures: Developed and developing countries." *Legislative Studies Quarterly* 23(1): 109–125.
28. Lenita Freidenvall and Drude Dahlerup. Eds. 2013 Update. *Electoral Gender Quota Systems and their Implementation in Europe*. Brussels: European Parliament, PE 493.011; Lenita Freidenvall et al. 2006. "The Nordic countries: An incremental model." In Drude Dahlerup, ed., *Women, Quotas and Politics*, pp 55–82. London: Routledge.
29. Ronald Inglehart and Pippa Norris. 2003. *Rising Tide*. New York: Cambridge University Press.
30. Didier Ruedin. 2012. "The representation of women in national parliaments: A cross-national comparison." *European Sociological Review* 28(1): 96–109.
31. Pippa Norris and Ronald Inglehart. 2012. *Sacred and Secular*. 2nd edition. New York: Cambridge University Press.
32. Pippa Norris and Ronald Inglehart. 2012. *Sacred and Secular*. 2nd edition. New York: Cambridge University Press.
33. Drude Dahlerup. 2009. "Women in Arab Parliaments: Can gender quotas contribute to democratization?" *Al- Raida*, 126–127(3): 28–38.
34. Miki Caul Kittlison. 2006. *Challenging Parties, Changing Parliaments*. Columbus: Ohio State University Press.
35. Kathleen M. Fallon, Liam Swiss, and J. Viterna. 2012. "Resolving the Democracy Paradox Democratization and Women's Legislative Representation in Developing Nations, 1975 to 2009." *American Sociological Review*, 77(3): 380–408; Frank C. Thames, and Margaret S Williams. 2013. *Contagious Representation: Women's Political Representation in Democracies Around the World*. New York: NYU Press.
36. Daniel Stockemer. 2014. "Women's descriptive representation in developed and developing countries." *International Political Science Review*: 36(4): 393–408.
37. Mona Lena Krook. 2014. "Electoral gender quotas: A conceptual analysis." *Comparative Political Studies* 47 (9): 1268–1293.
38. Andrew Reynolds. 2011. "Reserved seats in national legislatures: A research note." *Legislative Studies Quarterly*. 30(2): 301–310.
39. Petra Meier. 2014. "Quotas for advisory committees, business and politics: Just more of the same?" *International Political Science Review* 35(1): 106–118.
40. Joni Lovenduski, and Pippa Norris. Eds. 1993. *Gender and Party Politics*. London: Sage; Pippa Norris and Joni Lovenduski. 1995. *Political Representation in the British Parliament*. Cambridge: Cambridge University Press.
41. Hanane Darhour and Drude Dahlerup. 2013. "Sustainable representation of women through gender quotas: A decade of experiences in Morocco." *Women's Studies International Forum*, 41 (2): 132–42.

42. The Global Database of Quotas for Women, was developed by the University of Stockholm and International IDEA, later joined by the Inter-Parliamentary Union. See www.quotaproject.org; Atlas of Electoral Gender Quotas. 2014.
43. KOF Index of Globalization http://globalization.kof.ethz.ch/.
44. Analyzed from www.AidData.org.
45. Two countries, Venezuela and Italy, abolished their quota laws, leaving 78 countries with quota laws as of May 2014.
46. Gail Lapidus. 1975. "Political mobilization, participation and leadership: Women in Soviet politics." *Comparative Politics* 8: 90–118; Sharon L. Wolchik, 1981. "Eastern Europe." In Joni Lovenduski and Jill Hills, eds., *The Politics of the Second Electorate*. London: Routledge and Kegan Paul; Richard E. Matland and K. Montgomery. Eds. 2003. *Women's Access to Political Power in Post-Communist Europe*. Oxford: Oxford University Press.
47. Hanane Darhour and Drude Dahlerup. 2013. "Sustainable representation of women through gender quotas: A decade of experiences in Morocco." *Women's Studies International Forum*, 41 (2):132–142.
48. Sarah Sunn Bush. 2011. "International politics and the spread of quotas for women in legislatures." *International Organization* 65 (1): 103–137.
49. Mala Htun and Mark P. Jones. 2002. "Engendering the Right to Participate in Decision-making: Electoral Quotas and Women's Leadership in Latin America." In Nikki Craske and Maxine Molyneux, eds., *Gender and the Politics of Rights and Democracy in Latin America*, pp. 32–56. London: Palgrave.
50. Pippa Norris and Mona Lena Krook. 2011. *Gender Equality in Elected Office: A Six-Step Action Plan*. Warsaw: Organization for Security and Cooperation in Europe.
51. www.quotaproject.org. Pippa Norris and Mona Lena Krook. 2011. *Gender Equality in Elected Office: A Six-Step Action Plan*. Warsaw: Organization for Security and Cooperation in Europe.
52. Torbin Iversen and Frances Rosenbluth. 2008. "Work and power: The connection between female labor force participation and female political representation." *Annual Review of Political Science* 11: 479.
53. Michael L. Ross. 2008. "Oil, Islam and women." *American Political Science Review* 102(1):107–123.
54. Leslie A. Schwindt-Bayer. 2009. "Making quotas work: The effect of gender quota laws on the election of women." *Legislative Studies Quarterly* 34(1): 5–28; Leslie A. Schwindt-Bayer. 2012. *Political Power and Women's Representation in Latin America*. New York: Oxford University Press.

CHAPTER 7

1. Reporters Without Borders. *2016 World Press Freedom Index*. https://rsf.org/en/deep-and-disturbing-decline-media-freedom.
2. www.cpj.org/.
3. Jennifer Dunham. 2016. *Press Freedom in 2016: The Battle for the Dominant Message*. Washington, DC: Freedom House. https://freedomhouse.org/report/freedom-press/freedom-press-2016.

4. Pippa Norris, Ferran Martinez i Coma, Alessandro Nai, and Max Gromping. 2016. *The Year in Elections, 2015*. Sydney: University of Sydney. See this book, Figure 4.4.
5. See, for example, The World Bank's Communication for Governance and Accountability Program (CommGAP). http://siteresources.worldbank.org/EXTGOVACC/Resources/CommGAPBrochureweb.pdf.
6. Monroe Price. 2002. *Mapping Media Assistance*. Oxford: Centre for Socio-Legal Studies.
7. Beate Josephi. "Journalism education," Chapter 4. In The Handbook of Journalism Studies edited by Karin Wahl-Jorgensen and Thomas Hanitzsch. London: Routledge; Bob Franklin and Donica Mensing. Eds. 2011. *Journalism Education, Training and Employment*. London: Routledge.
8. See the World of Journalism project, www.worldsofjournalism.org.
9. See, for example, www.comminit.com/global/spaces-frontpage.
10. Joseph Nye. 2005. *Soft Power*. New York: Public Affairs.
11. www.unesco.org/new/en/communication-and-information/freedom-of-expression/extrabudgetary-projects-on-freedom-of-expression/.
12. https://ec.europa.eu/digital-single-market/en/media-freedom-and-pluralism.
13. Peter Cary. 2013. *U.S. Government Funding for Media: Trends and Strategies*. Washington, DC: CIMA.
14. Eduardo González Cauhapé–Cazaux and Shanthi Kalathil. March 2015. *Official Development Assistance for Media: Figures and Findings*. CIMA and the OECD/DAC. www.oecd.org/dac/governance-peace/publications/documentuploads/CIMA.pdf.
15. www.AidDATA.org, AidData 3.0.
16. Eduardo González Cauhapé–Cazaux and Shanthi Kalathil. March 2015. *Official Development Assistance for Media: Figures and Findings*. CIMA and the OECD/DAC. www.oecd.org/dac/governance-peace/publications/documentuploads/CIMA.pdf. These authors estimate that in total ODA allocated across several categories to "media support" represented nearly 0.4 percent of total sector allocable ODA.
17. Eduardo González Cauhapé–Cazaux and Shanthi Kalathil. March 2015. *Official Development Assistance for Media: Figures and Findings*. CIMA and the OECD/DAC. www.oecd.org/dac/governance-peace/publications/documentuploads/CIMA.pdf.
18. Monroe Price. 2002. *Mapping Media Assistance*. Oxford: Centre for Socio-Legal Studies.
19. Krishna Kumar. 2006. *Promoting Independent Media: Strategies for Democracy Assistance*. Boulder, CO: Lynne Rienner.
20. www.USAID.org.
21. Krishna Kumar. 2004. "USAID's Media Assistance: Policy and Programmatic Lessons." Policy and Program Coordination Evaluation Working Paper 16. Washington, DC: USAID.
22. www.mediasupport.org.
23. See for example http://gijn.org/resources/grants-and-fellowships/.
24. David E. Kaplan. 2012. *Empowering Independent Media, U.S. Efforts to Foster Free and Independent News Around the World*. 2nd edition. Washington, DC: National Endowment for Democracy/Center for International Media Assistance.
25. See for example https://wjec.net/member-organizations/.

26. For comparative overviews, see Philip Gaunt. 1992, *Making the Newsmakers*. Paris: UNESCO; Slavko Splichal and Colin Sparks. 1994. *Journalists for the 21st Century*. Norwood, NJ: Ablex Publications; David Weaver. 1998. *The Global Journalist: News People Around the World*, Creskill, NJ: Hampton; Romy Frohlich and Christine Holtz-Bacha. 2003. *Journalism Education in Europe and North America*. New York: Hampton Press; Daniel Hallin and Paolo Mancini. 2004. *Comparing Media Systems*; Hugo de Burgh. Ed. 2005. *Making Journalists*. New York: Routledge.
27. Bob Franklin and Donica Mensing. Eds. 2011. *Journalism Education, Training and Employment*. London: Routledge.
28. Charles C. Self. June 2015. "Global journalism education: A missed opportunity for media development." *CIMA Insights*. Washington, DC: Center for International Media Assistance. www.cima.ned.org/wp-content/uploads/2015/06/CIMA-Global-Journalism-Education.pdf.
29. Biddle, B.J. 1979. *Role Theory: Expectations, Identities, and Behaviors*. New York: Academic Press.
30. For a discussion, see Pamela J. Shoemaker and Stephen D. Reese. 1996. *Mediating the Message*. New York: Longman Publishers.
31. Denis McQuail. 1992. *Media Performance: Mass Communication and the Public Interest*. London: Sage; Pippa Norris and Sina Odugbemi. 2010. "Evaluating media performance." In Pippa Norris, ed., 2010. *Public Sentinel: News Media and the Governance Agenda*. Washington, DC: The World Bank; Jessica Noske-Turner. 2014. "Evaluating the impacts of media assistance: Problems and principles." Global Media Journal. 4(2): 1–21.
32. Thomas Hanitzsch et al. 2011. "Mapping journalism cultures across nations: A comparative study of 18 countries. " *Journalism Studies* 12(3): 273–293;.
33. David H. Weaver. Ed. 1998. *The Global Journalist: News People Around the World*. Cresskill, NJ: Hampton Press.
34. For a review, see Thomas Hanitzsch and Wolfgang Donsbach. 2012. "Comparing journalism cultures." In Frank Esser and Barbara Pfetsch, eds. *Comparing Political Communication: Theories, Cases, and Challenges*, pp. 251–270. New York: Cambridge University Press.
35. Richard Gunther and Anthony Mughan. Eds. 2000. *Democracy and the Media: A Comparative Perspective*. New York: Cambridge University Press; Monroe Price, Beata Rozumilowicz, and Stefaan G. Verhulst. Eds. 2001. *Media Reform: Democratizing Media, Democratizing the State*. London: Routledge; S. Pasti. 2005. "Two generations of contemporary Russian journalists." European Journal of Communication 20 (1): 89–115; Katrin Voltmer. Ed. 2006. *Mass Media and Political Communication in New Democracies*. London: Routledge.
36. Michael Schudson. 2001. "The objectivity norm in American journalism." Journalism 2(2): 149–170.
37. D. M. White. 1950. "The gatekeeper: A case study in the selection of news." *Journalism Quarterly* 27: 383–90; M. Janowitz. 1975. "Professional models in journalism: Gatekeeper and advocate." *Journalism Quarterly* 52 (4): 618.
38. Organization for Security and Cooperation in Europe (OSCE/ODIHR). 2012. *Handbook on Media Monitoring for Election Observation Missions*. Warsaw: OSCE/ODIHR.

39. See, for example, Wolfgang Donsbach. 1995. "Lapdogs, watchdogs and junkyard dogs." *Media Studies Journal* 9 (4): 17–30; Bart Cammaerts and Nico Carpentier. Eds. 2007. *Reclaiming the Media: Communication Rights and Democratic Media Roles*. London: Intellect Inc.
40. www.niemanwatchdog.org/index.cfm?fuseaction=about.Mission_Statement.
41. B. Fjaestad and P.G. Holmlov. 1976. "The Journalist's View." *Journal of Communication* 2: 108–14; J. W. L. Johnstone, E. J. Slawski, and W. W. Bowman. 1976. *The News People*. Urbana, IL: University of Illinois Press; David Weaver and C. G. Wilhoit. 1986. *The American Journalist*. Bloomington: University of Indiana Press; Renate Köcher. 1986. "Bloodhounds or missionaries: Role definitions of German and British journalists." *European Journal of Communication* 1(1): 43–64; Thomas Hanitzsch, Folker Hanusch, and Corinna Lauerer. "Setting the agenda, influencing public opinion, and advocating for social change: Determinants of journalistic interventionism in 21 countries." Journalism Studies 17(1): 1–20.
42. Thomas Hanitzsch. 2007. "Deconstructing journalism culture: Toward a universal theory." *Communication Theory*. 17(4): 367–385.
43. J. Ramaprasad and N. N. Hamdy. 2006. "Functions of Egyptian journalists: Perceived importance and actual performance." *International Communication Gazette* 68 (2): 167–185.
44. Krishna Kumar. 2004. *USAID's Media Assistance. Policy and Programmatic Lessons*. PPC Evaluation Working Paper No. 16. Washington, DC: USAID; International Programme for the Development of Communication. 2006. *Evaluation Reports on Selected Projects*. CI-2006/WS/5. Intergovernmental Council, IPDC; Pippa Norris. Ed. 2010. *Public Sentinel: News Media and the Governance Agenda*. Washington, DC: The World Bank; Anya Schiffrin and Michael Behrman. 2011. "Does training make a difference? Evaluating journalism training programs in sub-Saharan Africa." *Journalism & Mass Communication*, Winter: 340–360.
45. Jessica Noske-Turner. 2014. "Evaluating the impacts of media assistance: Problems and principles." *Global Media Journal*. 4(2): 1–21.
46. Tara Susman-Peña. 2012. *Making Media Development More Effective*. Washington, DC: CIMA/National Endowment for Democracy.
47. David E. Kaplan. 2012. *Empowering Independent Media, U.S. Efforts to Foster Free and Independent News Around the World*. 2nd edition. Washington, DC: National Endowment for Democracy/Center for International Media Assistance.
48. Krishna Kumar. 2004. *USAID's Media Assistance. Policy and Programmatic Lessons*. Washington, DC: USAID.
49. David E. Kaplan. 2012. *Global Investigative Journalism: Strategies for Support. A Report to the Center for International Media Assistance*. Washington, DC: CIMA/National Endowment for Democracy.
50. Monroe Price. 2002. *Mapping Media Assistance*. Oxford: Centre for Socio-Legal Studies.
51. Steve Buckley, Kreszentia Duer, Toby Mendel, and Seán Ó Siochrú. 2008. *Broadcasting, Voice, and Accountability*. Washington, DC: World Bank Group.
52. Pippa Norris. 2015. *Why Elections Fail*. Chapter 5. NY: Cambridge University Press; Sarah Birch. *Electoral Malpractices*. NY: Oxford University Press; Alessandro Nai. 2017. "The Fourth Estate: Why and how traditional news media

provide fair coverage of elections." In Pippa Norris and Alessandro Nai, eds., *Watchdog Elections*. New York: Oxford University Press.

53. Sarah Birch and Carolien van Ham. 2014. "Getting Away with Foul Play? How Oversight Institutions Strengthen Election Integrity." ECPR General Conference, University of Glasgow, 3–6 September 2014.
54. Pippa Norris. 2015. *Why Elections Fail*. Chapter 5. New York: Cambridge University Press.
55. Chappell Lawson. 2003. *Building the Fourth Estate: Democratization and the Rise of a Free Press in Mexico*. Berkeley: University of California Press; Ellen Mickiewicz. 1997. *Changing Channels: Television and the Struggle for Power in Russia*. New York: Oxford University Press; Ellen Mickiewicz. 2008. *Television, Power, and the Public in Russia*. New York: Cambridge University Press; Pippa Norris. Ed. 2010. *Public Sentinel: News Media and the Governance Agenda*. *Washington*, DC: The World Bank.
56. Reporters Without Borders. *World Press Freedom Index, 2016*. https://rsf.org/en/ranking.
57. See, for example, Daniel C. Hallin and Paolo Mancini. 2004. *Comparing Media Systems: Three Models of Media and Politics*. Cambridge and New York: Cambridge University Press; Daniel C. Hallin and Polo Mancini. Eds. 2012. *Comparing Media Systems Beyond the Western World*. New York: Cambridge University Press; David H. Weaver and Wei Wu. Eds. 1998. *The Global Journalist: News People Around the World*. Cresskill, NJ: Hampton Press; Thomas E. Patterson and Wolfgang Donsbach. 1996. "News decisions: Journalists as partisan actors." *Political Communication* 13 (4): 455–468.
58. Mark Deuze. 2002. "National news cultures: A comparison of Dutch, German, British, Australian and U.S. journalists." *Journalism & Mass Communication Quarterly* 79 (1): 134–149.
59. Wolfgang Donsbach. 1983. "Journalists' conceptions of their audience: Comparative Indicators for the Way British and German Journalists Define their Relations to the public." *Gazette* 32: 19–36; Renate Kocher. 1986. "Bloodhounds or missionaries: Role definitions of German and British journalists." *European Journal of Communication* 1 (2): 43–64; Anthony Delano and John Henningham. 1995. *The News Breed: British Journalists in the 1990s*. London: School of Media, London College of Printing and Distributive Trades; John Henningham. 1996. "Australian journalists' professional and ethical values." *Journalism & Mass Communication Quarterly* 73 (2): 206–18; Thomas E. Patterson and Wolfgang Donsbach. 1996. "News Decisions: Journalists as Partisan Actors." *Political Communication* 13 (4): 455–468; Wolfgang Donsbach and Thomas E. Patterson. 2004. "Political news journalists: Partisanship, professionalism, and political roles in five countries." In Frank Esser and Barbara Pfetsch, eds., *Comparing Political Communication: Theories, Cases, and Challenges*, 251–270. New York: Cambridge University Press.
60. H. G. Herscovitz. 2004. "Brazilian journalists' perceptions of media roles, ethics, and foreign influences on Brazilian journalism." *Journalism Studies* 5 (1): 71–86; Thomas Hanitzsch. 2005. "Journalists in Indonesia: Educated but timid watchdogs." *Journalism Studies* 6: 493–508; J. Ramaprasad. 2001. "A profile of journalists in post-independence Tanzania." *Gazette* 63: 539–556; J. Ramaprasad and N. N. Hamdy. 2006. "Functions of Egyptian journalists: Perceived importance

and actual performance." *International Communication Gazette* 68 (2): 167–185; J. Ramaprasad and J.D. Kelly. 2003. "Reporting the news from the world's rooftop: A survey of Nepalese journalists." *Gazette* 65: 291–315; Wei Wu, David Weaver, and O. V. Johnson. 1996. "Professional roles of Russian and U.S. Journalists: A comparative study." *Journalism & Mass Communication Quarterly* 73: 534; J. Ramaprasad and S. Rahman. 2006. "Tradition with a twist: A survey of Bangladeshi journalists." *International Communication Gazette* 68 (2): 148–65; Jian-Hua Zhu, David Weaver, Ven-hwei Lo, Chongshan Chen, and Wei Wu. 1997. "Individual, organizational, and societal influences on media role perceptions: A comparative study of journalists in China, Taiwan, and the United States." *Journalism & Mass Communication Quarterly* 74 (2): 84–96.

61. The author is most grateful to the contributors of the project. See the World of Journalism project, www.worldsofjournalism.org.
62. Thomas Hanitzsch. 2007. "Deconstructing Journalism Culture: Towards a Universal Theory." *Communication Theory* 17 (4): 367–385. See also the World of Journalism project, www.worldsofjournalism.org.
63. Derived from the Quality of Government dataset, January 2016. http://qog.pol.gu.se.
64. Freedom House. *Freedom of the Press.* https://freedomhouse.org/report/freedom-press/freedom-press-2016.
65. Derived from the Quality of Government dataset, January 2016. Http://qog.pol.gu.se.
66. This included the Reporters Without Borders annual measure of press freedom, as well as the analysis of the Freedom House sub-indices measuring political pressures and economic influences over the media contents.
67. Sarah Birch and Carolien van Ham. 2014. "Getting Away with Foul Play? How Oversight Institutions Strengthen Election Integrity." ECPR General Conference, University of Glasgow, 3–6 September 2014; Pippa Norris. 2015. *Why Elections Fail.* Chapter 5. New York: Cambridge University Press.
68. Pippa Norris. Ed. 2010. *Public Sentinel: News Media and the Governance Agenda.* Washington, DC: The World Bank.

CHAPTER 8

1. Richard Hason. 2016. *Plutocrats United: Campaign Money, the Supreme Court, and the Distortion of American Elections.* New Haven, CT: Yale University Press
2. The Center for Responsive Politics. www.opensecrets.org/.
3. Suzanne Mulcahy. 2012. *Money, Politics, Power: Corruption Risks in Europe.* Transparency International.
4. Donatella Della Porta and Alberto Vannucci. 1999. *Corrupt Exchanges: Actors, Resources, and Mechanisms of Political Corruption.* New York: Aldine de Gruyter.
5. www.transparency.org/cpi2014/results.
6. www.worldbank.org/en/topic/governance/brief/anti-corruption.
7. For recent comparative overviews, see Jonathan Mendilow. Ed. 2012. *Money, Corruption, and Political Competition in Established and Emerging Democracies.* Lexington Books: Lanham, MD; Pippa Norris and Andrea Abe van Es. Eds. 2016. *Checkbook Elections? Political Finance in Comparative Perspective.* New York:

Oxford University Press; Robert G. Boatright. Ed. 2015. *The Deregulatory Moment? A Comparative Perspective on Changing Campaign Finance Laws*. Michigan: University of Michigan Press.

8. James D. Wolfensohn. October 1, 1996. *Corruption and Development*. Annual Meetings Address President, The World Bank. http://web.worldbank.org/.
9. www.unodc.org/unodc/en/treaties/CAC/signatories.html.
10. www.worldbank.org/projects.
11. World Bank. 2016. *Making Politics Work for Development: Harnessing Transparency and Citizen Engagement*. Policy Research Report. Washington, DC: World Bank. http://documents.worldbank.org/curated/en/268021467831470443/pdf/106337-revised-PUBLCI-Making-Politics-Work-for-Development.pdf.
12. See Magnus Ohman. 2012. *Political Finance Regulations Around the World: An Overview of the IDEA Database*. Stockholm: IDEA Publications Office; International IDEA. *Political Finance Database*. Stockholm: IDEA. www.idea.int/political-finance/index.cfm.
13. Magnus Ohman and Hani Zainulbhai. 2009. *Political Finance Regulation: The Global Experience*. Washington, DC: International Foundation for Electoral Systems.
14. www.europarl.europa.eu/news/en/news-room/20140317IPR39131/new-rules-on-funding-eu-political-parties-and-foundations.
15. Organization of American States. 2012. *Observing Political-Electoral Financing Systems: A Manual for OAS Electoral Observation Missions*. Washington, DC: OAS. www.oas.org/es/sap/deco/pubs/manuales/MOE_Manual_e.PDF.
16. For reviews, see Susan Rose-Ackerman and Bonnie J. Palifka. 2016. *Corruption and Government: Causes, Consequences, and Reform*. 2nd edition. New York: Cambridge University Press; Alina Mungiu-Pippidi. 2015. *The Quest for Good Governance*. New York: Cambridge University Press.
17. *UN Human Rights and Elections: A Handbook on the Legal, Technical and Human Aspects of Elections*. New York: United Nations.
18. Eswararan Sridharan and Milan Vaishnav. 2016. "India." In Pippa Norris and Andrea Abe van Es, eds., *Checkbook Elections? Political Finance in Comparative Perspective*. New York: Oxford University Press.
19. Alejandro Trelles and Miguel Carreras. 2012. "Bullets and votes: Violence and electoral participation in Mexico." *Journal of Politics in Latin America*, 4(2): 89–123.
20. Michael Pinto-Duschinsky. 2002. "Financing politics: A global view." *Journal of Democracy*, 13: 69–86.
21. Reginald Austin and Maja Tjernstrom. 2003. *Funding of Political Parties and Election Campaigns*. Stockholm: International IDEA; Magnus Ohman. 2012. *Political Finance Regulations Around the World: An Overview of the IDEA Database*. Stockholm: IDEA Publications Office; International IDEA. Political Finance Database. Stockholm: IDEA. www.idea.int/political-finance/index.cfm.
22. www.undp.org/content/undp/en/home/ourwork/democraticgovernance/global_programmes/global_programmeforelectoralcyclesupport/programme_scope_and strategy.html.
23. Pippa Norris and Andrea Abe van Es. Eds. 2016. *Checkbook Elections? Political Finance in Comparative Perspective*. New York: Oxford University Press.

24. Christopher Hood and David Heald. Eds. 2006. *Transparency: The Key to Better Governance?* Oxford: British Academy/Oxford University Press; John Gaventa and Rosemary McGee. 2013. "The impact of transparency and accountability initiatives." *Development Policy Review* 31: S3–S28; Anuradha Joshi. 2013. "Do they work? Assessing the impact of transparency and accountability initiatives in service delivery." *Development Policy Review* 31: 29–48; Stephen Kosack and Archon Fung. 2014. "Does transparency improve governance?" *Annual Review of Political Science* 27: 65–87.
25. John Samples. 2006. *The Fallacy of Campaign Finance Reform*. Chicago: University of Chicago Press.
26. http://rti.gov.in/.
27. John M. Ackerman, and Irma E. Sandoval-Ballesteros. 2006. "The global explosion of freedom of information laws." *Administrative Law Review* 58(1): 85–130; Ann Florini. Ed. 2007. *The Right to Know: Transparency for an Open World*. New York: Columbia University Press.
28. www.rti-rating.org/. See also, www.freedominfo.org/.
29. OAS. *Inter-American Democratic Charter of the Organization of American States*, article 5. OAS: Washington, DC.
30. Council of Europe. *Guidelines and Explanatory Report on Political Parties* (Paragraph 2.20); Council of Europe. *Guidelines for Financing Political Parties and Election Campaigns*.
31. www.unodc.org/documents/treaties/UNCAC/Publications/Convention/08-50026_E.pdf
32. www.opensecrets.org.
33. Archon Fung, Mary Graham, David Weil. Eds. 2008. *Full Disclosure: The Perils and Promise of Transparency*. New York: Cambridge University Press.
34. Jonathan Fox. 2007. "The uncertain relationship between transparency and accountability." *Development in Practice* 17(4): 663–671.
35. J. Licht de Fine. 2011. "Do we really want to know? The potentially negative effect of transparency in decision-making on perceived legitimacy." *Scandinavian Political Studies* 34(3): 183–201.
36. Stephen Kosack and Archon Fung. 2014. "Does transparency improve governance?" *Annual Review of Political Science* 27: 65–87.
37. Jane Mayer. 2016. *Dark Money: The Hidden History of the Billionaires Behind the Rise of the Radical Right*. New York: Doubleday.
38. UK Electoral Commission. www.electoralcommission.org.uk/__data/assets/pdf_file/0004/173074/UKPGE-Part-3-Spending-and-donations.pdf.
39. www.electoralcommission.org.uk/__data/assets/pdf_file/0011/109388/2010-UKPGE-Campaign-expenditure-report.pdf.
40. SADC. *Norms and Standards for Elections in the SADC Region*. Paragraph 3(i). Johannesburg: SADC.
41. European Commission. *Handbook for EU Election Observers*. Brussels: European Union.
42. Stephen Levitsky and Lucan Way, 2010. *Competitive Authoritarianism: Hybrid Regimes After the Cold War*, New York: Cambridge University Press.
43. Kevin Casas-Zamora. 2005. *Paying for Democracy: Political Finance and State Funding for Parties*. Colchester, UK: ECPR; Karl-Heinz Nassmacher. 2009. *The Funding of Party Competition: Political Finance in 25 Democracies*;

Michael Ross. 2011. The *Politics of Party Funding*. Oxford: Oxford University Press. Baden-Baden: Nomos.

44. See Magnus Ohman. "Sweden." In Pippa Norris and Andrea Abe van Es. Eds. 2016. *Checkbook Elections? Political Finance in Comparative Perspective*. New York: Oxford University Press.
45. For more details, see Magnus Ohman. 2012. *Political Finance Regulations Around the World: An Overview of the IDEA database*. Stockholm: IDEA Publications Office; International IDEA. *Political Finance Database*. Stockholm: IDEA. www .idea.int/political-finance/index.cfm.
46. Anthony Corrado and Thomas E. Mann. 2014. *Party Polarization and Campaign Finance*. Research Paper, Brookings Institution Center for Effective Public Management.
47. The Money, Politics, and Transparency (MPT) indices were developed by Global Integrity and the Electoral Integrity Project. For more details, see http://moneypoli ticstransparency.org.
48. Shaun Bowler and Todd Donovan. 2013. *The Limits of Electoral Reform*. New York: Oxford University Press.
49. Richard Katz and Peter Mair. 1995. "Changing models of party organization and party democracy: The emergence of the cartel party." *Party Politics* 1: 5–28.
50. For more details about all these case studies, see Pippa Norris and Andrea Abe van Es. Eds. 2016. *Checkbook Elections? Political Finance in Comparative Perspective*. New York: Oxford University Pres s.
51. Each type of regulation is a ratio ranging between zero and one, indicating the ratio of the number of laws a country has with respect to a particular type of regulation to the total number of laws possible (as defined by International IDEA's database) for any particular type of regulation.
52. For details, see Chapter 4 and www.electoralintegrityproject.com.
53. Daniel Treisman. 2007. "What have we learned about the causes of corruption from ten years of cross-national empirical research?" *Annual Review of Political Science*, 10: 211–244.
54. Further analysis, including a more comprehensive range of variables and additional tests, in presented in Pippa Norris and Andrea Abel van Es. 2016. "Does regulation work," Chapter 12. In Pippa Norris and Andrea Abe van Es, eds., *Checkbook Elections? Political Finance in Comparative Perspective*. New York: Oxford University Press.
55. John M. Ackerman, and Irma E. Sandoval-Ballesteros. 2006. "The global explosion of freedom of information laws."*Administrative Law Review* 58(1): 85–130; Ann Florini. Ed. 2007. *The Right to Know: Transparency for an Open World*. New York: Columbia University Press.
56. Richard Katz and Peter Mair. 1995. "Changing models of party organization and party democracy: The emergence of the cartel party." *Party Politics* 1: 5–28; Richard Katz, 1996. "Party organizations and finance." In Lawrence LeDuc, Richard Niemi, and Pippa Norris, eds., *Comparing Democracies*. London: Sage.
57. Pippa Norris and Andrea Abe van Es. Eds. 2016. *Checkbook Elections? Political Finance in Comparative Perspective*. New York: Oxford University Press.

CHAPTER 9

1. Robert F. Bauer and Benjamin L. Ginsberg, et al., 2014. *The American Voting Experience: Report and Recommendations of the Presidential Commission on Election Administration*. Washington, DC. For more details, see www.supportthevoter.gov.
2. Robert F. Bauer and Benjamin L. Ginsberg, et al., 2014. *The American Voting Experience: Report and Recommendations of the Presidential Commission on Election Administration*. Washington, DC. For more details, see www.supportthevoter.gov.
3. The Pew Charitable Trust. 2014. *Election Performance index*. www.pewtrusts.org/en/multimedia/data-visualizations/2014/elections-performance-index#intro. Data from 2008 to 2012 are currently available.
4. The Pew Charitable Trust. Nov. 6, 2014. "State Election Sites Crashed on Election Day." www.pewtrusts.org/en/about/news-room/news/2014/11/06/where-did-voters-look-to-find-their-polling-places.
5. *The Hartford Current*. Nov. 9, 2014. "Anatomy of a flawed election." www.courant.com/community/hartford/hc-hartford-voting-problems-p-20141108-story.html#page=2.
6. *Chicago Sun Times*. Nov. 4, 2014. "Calls to election judges a 'serious attempt to disrupt' voting." http://chicago.suntimes.com/chicago-politics/7/71/154384/calls-to-election-judges-a-serious-attempt-to-disrupt-voting.
7. *The Washington Post*. Nov. 4, 2014. "Voting machine problems in Newport News, Va. Beach." www.washingtonpost.com/local/virginians-deciding-senate-congressional-races/2014/11/4/33164a92-63f9-11e4-ab86-46e1d35_story.html.
8. *Bloomberg Politics*. Nov. 4, 2014. "Your Guide to 2014 Midterm Election Voting Problems." www.bloomberg.com/politics/articles/2014-11-4/your-guide-to-2014-midterm-election-voting-problems.
9. *The New York Times*. Nov. 4, 2014. "As New Rules Take Effect, Voters Report Problems in Some States." www.nytimes.com/2014/11/5/us/election-tests-new-rules-on-voting.html.
10. Anthony J. McGann, Charles Anthony Smith, Michael Latner, and Alex Keena. 2016. *Gerrymandering in America*. New York: Cambridge University Press.
11. Lisa Handley and Bernard Grofman. Eds. 2008. *Redistricting in Comparative Perspective*. New York: Oxford University Press.
12. Richard L. Hasen, 2012. *The Voting Wars: From Florida 2000 to the Next Election Meltdown*. New Haven: Yale University Press. This is updated by the Brennan Center. www.brennancenter.org/voting-restrictions-first-time-2016.
13. Thomas Patterson. 2016. "Media coverage of the 2016 election." https://shorensteincenter.org/research-media-coverage-2016-election/.
14. Pippa Norris. 2014. *Why Electoral Integrity Matters*. New York: Cambridge University Press; Emily Beaulieu. 2014. *Electoral Protests and Democracy in the Developing World*. New York: Cambridge University Press.
15. See, for example, Bruce E. Cain, Todd Donovan, and C. Tolbert. 2008. *Democracy in the States: Experimentation in Election Reform*. Washington, DC: Brookings Institution Press; R. Michael Alvarez and Bernard Grofman, Eds. 2014. *Election Administration in the United States*. New York: Cambridge University Press.

16. For a discussion, see Ferran Martinez i Coma and Carolien Van Ham. 2015. "Can experts judge elections? Testing the validity of expert judgments for measuring election integrity." *European Journal of Political Research* 54 (2): 35–325.
17. See Pippa Norris. 2015. *Why Elections Fail.* New York: Cambridge University Press. See Chapter 2, Table 2.4.
18. Pippa Norris, Ferran Martinezi Coma and Max Groemping. 2015. *The Year in Elections, 2014.* Sydney: The Electoral Integrity Project, University of Sydney, 9.
19. Richard L. Hasen. 2012. *The Voting Wars: From Florida 2000 to the Next Election Meltdown.* New Haven: Yale University Press.
20. Paul Gronke, Eva Galanes-Rosenbaum, and Peter A. Miller. 2008. "Convenience voting." *Annual Review of Political Science* 11: 437–455. It should be noted that convenience voting facilities for citizens differ from reforms modernizing electoral procedures, which are designed to make electoral administration easier for managers, such as the use of electronic machines rather than paper ballots.
21. Anthony Downs. 1957. *An Economic Theory of Voting.* New York: Harper.
22. Electoral Assistance Commission. 2015. *The 2014 EAC Election Administration and Voting Survey Comprehensive Report.* www.eac.gov/research/election_administration_and_voting_survey.aspx.
23. See, for example, Louis Massicotte, Andre Blais and Antoine Yoshinaka. 2004. *Establishing the Rules of the Game.* Toronto: University of Toronto Press.
24. Electoral Assistance Commission. 2015. *The 2014 EAC Election Administration and Voting Survey Comprehensive Report.* www.eac.gov/research/election_administration_and_voting_survey.aspx.
25. M. Qvortup. 2005. "First past the postman: Voting by mail in comparative perspective." *Political Quarterly*, 76 (3):414–419; S. Luechinger, M. Rosinger and A. Stutzer. 2007. "The impact of postal voting on participation: Evidence for Switzerland." *Swiss Political Science Review*, 13, 167–172; Colin Rallings, Michael Thrasher, and G. Borisyuk. "Much ado about not very much: The electoral consequences of postal voting at the 2005 British General Election." *British Journal of Politics & International Relations* 12(2): 223–238.
26. Kaat Smets and Carolien van Ham. 2013. "The embarrassment of riches? A meta-analysis of individual-level research on voter turnout." *Electoral Studies* 32(2): 344–359.
27. Steven J. Rosenstone and Raymond E. Wolfinger. 1978. "The effect of registration laws on voter turnout." *American Political Science Review*, 72: 27–45.
28. Francis Fox Piven and Richard A. Cloward. 1988. *Why Americans Don't Vote.* New York: Pantheon.
29. Barry C. Burden, David T. Canon, Kenneth R. Mayer, and Donald P. Moynihan. 2011. "Election laws, mobilization, and turnout: The unanticipated consequences of election reform." *American Journal of Political Science* 58: 95–119.
30. Adam J. Berinsky. 2005. "The perverse consequences of electoral reform in the United States." *American Politics Research* 33 (4): 471–491; Benjamin Highton. 2004. "Voter Registration and Turnout in the United States." *Perspectives on Politics* 2 (September): 57–65; Marjorie Randon Hershey. 2009. "What we know about Voter-ID laws, registration, and turnout." *PS-Political Science & Politics* 42 (1): 87–91.
31. Michael J. Hanmer. 2009. *Discount Voting: Voter Registration Reforms and Their Effects.* New York: Cambridge University Press; Shaun Bowler and Todd Donovan.

2011. "The limited effects of election reforms on efficacy and engagement." *Australian Journal of Political Science* 47(1): 55–57; Pippa Norris. 2004. "Will new technology boost turnout?" In *Electronic Voting and Democracy: A Comparative Analysis*. Edited by Norbert Kersting and Harald Baldersheim. London: Palgrave, pp.193–225.

32. Barry C. Burden, David T. Canon, Kenneth R. Mayer, and Donald P. Moynihan. 2014. "Election laws, mobilization, and turnout: The unanticipated consequences of election reform." *American Journal of Political Science* 58 (1): 95–119; Adam J. Berinsky. 2005. "The perverse consequences of electoral reform in the United States." *American Politics Research* 33 (4): 471–491.
33. Barry C. Burden, David T. Canon, Kenneth R. Mayer, and Donald P. Moynihan. 2014. "Election laws, mobilization, and turnout: The unanticipated consequences of election reform." *American Journal of Political Science* 58 (1): 95–119.
34. Lonna Rae Atkeson, R. Michael Alvarez, and Thad E. Hall et al. 2014. "Balancing Fraud Prevention and Electoral Participation: Attitudes Toward Voter Identification." *Social Science Quarterly* 95(5): 1381–1398.
35. Debate about the extent of electoral fraud is heated. Thus some estimates find incidents of electoral fraud in recent US elections to be trivial or nonexistent. See, for example, Lorraine Carol Minnite. 2010. *The Myth of Voter Fraud*. Ithaca: Cornell University Press. Others counter that the threats are real. See, for example, Jesse T. Richman, Gulshan A. Chattha, and David C. Earnest. 2014. "Do non-citizens vote in US elections?" *Electoral Studies* 36: 149–157.
36. National Conference of State Legislative (NCSL) Election Law Database. 2014. *History of Voter ID*. www.ncsl.org/research/elections-and-campaigns/voter-id-history.aspx
37. Fredric Charles Schaffer. 2008. *The Hidden Costs of Clean Election Reform*. Cornell: Cornell University Press.
38. J.F. Benson. 2009. "Voter fraud or voter defrauded? Highlighting an inconsistent consideration of election fraud." *Harvard Civil Rights: Civil Liberties Law Review* 44 (1): 1–42; Richard K. Scher. 2001. *The Politics of Disenfranchisement: Why Is It So Hard to Vote in America?* New York: M.E. Sharpe.
39. Keith G. Bentele, and Erin E. O'Brien. 2013. "Jim Crow 2.0? Why States Consider and Adopt Restrictive Voter Access Policies." *Perspectives On Politics* 11(4): 1088–1116; C.L. Brians and Bernard Grofman. 2010. "Election day registration's effect on US voter turnout." *Social Science Quarterly*, 82: 17–18; M.J. Fenster. 1994. "The impact of allowing day of registration voting on turnout in US elections from 1960–1992." *American Politics Quarterly*, 22: 74–87; Benjamin Highton. 1997. "Easy registration and voter turnout." *Journal of Politics*, 59: 565–575; Stephen Knack. 1995. "Does 'motor voter' work?" *Journal of Politics*, 57: 796–811; Stephen Knack. 1999. "Drivers wanted: Motor voter and the election of 1996." *PS Online*: 237–243.
40. Craig C. Donsanto and Nancy L. Simmons. 2007. *Federal prosecutions of electoral offences*. 7th ed. Washington, DC: US Department of Justice. www.justice.gov/sites/default/files/criminal/legacy/2013/9/3/electbook-57.pdf.
41. Lorraine Carol Minnite. 2010. *The Myth of Voter Fraud*. Ithaca: Cornell University Press; R. Michael Alvarez and Frederick J. Boehmke. 2008. "Correlates of fraud:

Studying state election fraud allegations." In R. Michael Alvarez, Thad Hall, and Susan Hyde, Eds. 2008. *Election Fraud*. Washington, DC: Brookings Institution Press.

42. See, for example, Mikhail Myagkov, Peter C. Ordeshook, and Dimitri Shakin. 2009. *The Forensics of Election Fraud: Russia and Ukraine*. New York: Cambridge University Press; Christian Breunig and Achim Goerres. 2011. "Searching for electoral irregularities in an established democracy: Applying Benford's Law tests to Bundestag elections in Unified Germany." *Electoral Studies* 3(3): 534–545; Gonzalo Castaneda. 2011. "Benford's law and its applicability in the forensic analysis of electoral results." *Politica Y Gobierno* 18(2): 297–329; Luis Pericchi and David Torres. 2011. "Quick anomaly detection by the Newcomb-Benford Law, with applications to electoral processes data from the USA, Puerto Rico and Venezuela." *Statistical Science* 26(4): 52–516; Walter R. Mebane, Jr. 2012. "Comment on Benford's Law and the detection of election fraud." *Political Analysis* 19(3): 269–272; Bernd Beber and Alexandra Scacco. 2012. "What the numbers say: A digit-based test for election fraud." *Political Analysis* 2(2): 211–234; Jimenez, Raul and Manuel Hidalgo. 2014. "Forensic Analysis of Venezuelan Elections during the Chavez Presidency." *Plos One* 9(6): 2–29.
43. Shaun Bowler, Thomas Brunell, Todd Donovan, and Paul Gronke. 2015. "Election administration and perceptions of fair elections." *Electoral Studies* 38:1–9.
44. See Pippa Norris, Richard W. Frank, and Ferran Martinez i Coma. Eds. 2014. *Advancing Electoral Integrity*. Oxford: Oxford University Press.
45. R. Michael Alvarez, Lonna Rae Atkeson, and Thad Hall. 2012. *Evaluating Elections: A Handbook of Methods and Standards*. New York: Cambridge University Press.
46. See Barry C. Burden and Charles Stewart III. Eds. 2014. *The Measure of American Elections*. New York, New York: Cambridge University Press.
47. Pippa Norris. 2014. "Does the world agree about standards of electoral integrity? Evidence for the diffusion of global norms." Special issue of *Electoral Studies* 32(4): 576–588.
48. Emily Beaulieu. 2014. "From Voter ID to Party ID: How political parties affect perceptions of election fraud in the U.S." *Electoral Studies* 35: 24–32; Paul Gronke. 2014. "Voter confidence as a metric of election performance." In Barry C. Burden and Charles Stewart III, eds., *The Measure of American Elections*. New York, New York: Cambridge University Press; Bowler, Shaun, Thomas Brunell, Todd Donovan, and Paul Gronke. 2015. "Election administration and perceptions of fair elections." *Electoral Studies* 38:1–9; Pippa Norris. 2014. *Why Electoral Integrity Matters*. New York: Cambridge University Press.
49. It should be noted that a subsequent surveys covering all 50 states, in PEI-US-2016, was unavailable at the time of writing but this data will be used for future research. See Pippa Norris, Holly Ann Garnett, and Max Gromping. 2017. *Perceptions of Electoral Integrity: The 2016 American Presidential Elections*. www.electoralintegrityproject.com.
50. Pippa Norris, Richard W. Frank, and Ferran Martinez i Coma. 2014. "Measuring electoral integrity: A new dataset." *PS Politics and Political Science* 47(4): 789–798. For details, see www.electoralintegrityproject.com.
51. National Conference of State Legislative (NCSL) Election Law Database. www.ncsl.org/research/elections-and-campaigns/voter-id-history.aspx.

52. Electoral Assistance Commission. 2015. *The 2014 EAC Election Administration and Voting Survey Comprehensive Report*. www.eac.gov/research/election_administration_and_voting_survey.aspx.
53. Robert Bickel. 2007. *Multilevel Analysis for Applied Research: It's Just Regression!* New York: The Guilford Press.
54. Stephen W. Raudenbush and Anthony S. Bryk. 2002. *Hierarchical Linear Models*. 2nd edition. Thousand Oaks: Sage; Andrew Gelman and Jennifer Hill. 2007. *Data Analysis Using Regression and Multilevel/Hierarchical Models*. New York: Cambridge University Press.
55. It should be noted that no controls were introduced for education, since there was no variance among experts.
56. Pippa Norris. 2015. *Why Elections Fail*. New York: Cambridge University Press.
57. Scot Schraufnagel. 2011. *Third Party Blues: The Truth and Consequences of Two-Party Dominance*. New York: Routledge.
58. Pippa Norris and Andrea Abel van Es. 2016. *Checkbook Elections: Political Finance in Comparative Perspective*. New York: Oxford University Press.
59. For an initial look at the PEI-US 2016 data, see Pippa Norris, Holly Ann Garnett, and Max Groemping. 2016. "Electoral integrity in all 50 US states, ranked by experts." *Vox* 24 December 2016.

CHAPTER 10

1. See, for example, http://aceproject.org.
2. Amichai Magen, Thomas Risse, and Michael A. McFaul. Eds. 2013. *Promoting Democracy and the Rule of Law: American and European Strategies*. New York: Palgrave Macmillan; Michael Cox, Timothy J. Lynch and Nicolas Bouchet. Eds. 2013. *US Foreign Policy and Democracy Promotion: From Theodore Roosevelt to Barack Obama*. New York: Routledge.
3. Richard Youngs. 2001. *The European Union and the Promotion of Democracy*. Oxford: Oxford University Press; Peter Burnell. 2011. *Promoting Democracy Abroad: Policy and Performance*. New Brunswick, NJ: Transaction Publishers; Richard Youngs. Ed. 2006. *Survey of European Democracy Promotion Policies 2000–2006*. Madrid: Fride; Jeff Bridoux and Milja Kurki. 2016. *Democracy Promotion: A Critical Introduction*. New York: Routledge; Daniela Huber. 2015. *Democracy Promotion and Foreign Policy Identity and Interests in US, EU and Non-Western Democracies*. New York: Palgrave.
4. Craig N. Murphy. 2006. *The United Nations Development Programme: A Better Way?* New York: Cambridge University Press; Michael Schroeder. 2013. "The politics of change: The evolution of UN electoral services, 1989–2006." *Global Governance*. 19(2): 207–226.
5. King James Bible: "And the seven thin and ill-favoured kine that came up after them *are* seven years; and the seven empty ears blasted with the east wind shall be seven years of famine." Genesis 41:27
6. Robert Kagan. 2008. *The Return of History and the End of Dreams*. London: Atlantic Books; Nuno Severiano Teixeira. Ed. 2008. *The International Politics of Democratization: Comparative perspectives* London: Routledge.

7. Joshua Kurlantzick. 2014. *Democracy in Retreat: The Revolt of the Middle Class and the Worldwide Decline of Representative Government*. New Haven, CT: Yale University Press; Larry Diamond and Marc F. Plattner. Eds. 2015. *Democracy in Decline?* Baltimore: Johns Hopkins University Press; Arch Puddington and Tyler Roylance. 2016. "Anxious dictators, wavering democracies: Global freedom under pressure." *Freedom House: Freedom in the World 2016*. www.freedomhouse .org.
8. Thomas Carothers. 2012. *Democracy Policy Under Obama: Revitalization or Retreat?* Washington, DC: Carnegie Endowment for International Peace; Nicole Bibbins Sedaca and Nicolas Bouchet. 2014. *Holding steady? US Democracy Promotion in a Changing World*. London: Chatham House; Thomas Carothers. 2017. *Prospects for Democracy Promotion under Trump*. Washington, DC: Carnegie Endowment for International Peace.
9. Bruce Drake. 2013. *Americans Put Low Priority on Promoting Democracy Abroad.* Washington, DC: The Pew Research center. www.pewresearch.org/fact-tank/2013/ 12/04/americans-put-low-priority-on-promoting-democracy-abroad/
10. Arch Puddington and Tyler Roylance. 2016. "Anxious dictators, wavering democracies: Global freedom under pressure." *Freedom House: Freedom in the World 2016*. www.freedomhouse.org.
11. National Intelligence Council. 6 January 2017. *Background to "Assessing Russian activities and Intentions in Recent U.S. elections."* www.dni.gov/files/documents/I CA_2017_01.pdf.
12. Sarah Sunn Bush. 2015. *The Taming of Democracy Assistance: Why Democracy Promotion Does Not Confront Dictators*. New York: Cambridge University Press.
13. William Easterly. 2001. *The Elusive Quest for Growth*. Cambridge, MA: MIT Press. William Easterly. 2006. *The White Man's Burden*. New York: Penguin; Dambisa Moyo. 2010. *Dead Aid: Why Aid Is Not Working and How There Is a Better Way for Africa*. New York: Farrar, Straus and Giroux.
14. Roger Riddell. 2007. *Does Foreign Aid Really Work?* New York: Oxford University Press.
15. Nicholas van de Walle. 2005. *Overcoming Stagnation in Aid-Dependent Countries.* Washington, DC: Center for Global Development.
16. Thomas Carothers. 2015. "Democracy Aid at 25: Time to Choose." *Journal of Democracy* 26(1): 59–73.
17. Peter Burnell. Ed. 2000. *Democracy Assistance: International Co-Operation for Democratization*. London: Frank Cass.
18. Edward D. Mansfield and Jack Snyder. 2007. *Electing to Fight: Why Emerging Democracies go to War*. Cambridge, MA: MIT Press.
19. See Pippa Norris, Ferran Martinez i Coma, Alessandro Nai, and Max Groemping. 2016. *The Year in Elections, 2015*. Sydney: University of Sydney.
20. Pippa Norris. 2017. *Why American Elections Are Flawed (and How to Fix Them)*. Ithaca: Cornell University Press.
21. Pippa Norris. 2004. *Electoral Engineering*. New York: Cambridge University Press.
22. Kenneth Benoit. 2007. "Electoral laws as political consequences: Explaining the origins and change of electoral institutions." *Annual Review of Political Science*. 10: 363–390.
23. Shaun Bowler and Todd Donovan. 2013. *The Limits of Electoral Reform*. New York: Oxford University Press.

24. Adam J. Berinsky. 2004. “The perverse consequences of electoral reform in the United States.” *American Politics Research* 33(4): 471–491; Barry C. Burden, David T. Canon, Kenneth R. Mayer, and Donald P. Moynihan. 2011. “Election laws, mobilization, and turnout: The unanticipated consequences of election reform.” *American Journal of Political Science* 58: 95–109.
25. UN Secretary General. 2015. *Strengthening the role of the United Nations in enhancing the effectiveness of the principle of periodic and genuine elections and the promotion of democratization*. UN General Assembly A/70/306.
26. UN-Department of Political Affairs. *Annual Report 2015*. New York: United Nations; Inken van Borzyskowski. 2016. “Resisting democracy assistance: Who seeks and receives technical election assistance?” *Review of International Organizations* 11(2): 247–282.
27. As of July 2015, out of 193 member states of the United Nations, five lack de jure constitutional provisions for direct elections for the lower house of parliament: Brunei Darussalam, China, Qatar, UAE, and Saudi Arabia. Another three states (Eritrea, Somalia, and South Sudan) have constitutional provisions in place for such contests, but they have not yet held any such elections since independence or within the last thirty years. There are a few other cases, such as Thailand, where regularly scheduled elections have been temporarily suspended by the regime. Pippa Norris, Ferran Martinez i Coma, Alesandro Nai, and Max Groemping. 2015. *The Year in Elections, 2015*. Sydney: University of Sydney. Technical Appendix.
28. Center for Systemic Peace. *Coup d’état 1946–2015*. www.systemicpeace.org/inscr data.html.
29. www.un.org/sustainabledevelopment/sustainable-development-goals/.
30. www.un.org/sustainabledevelopment/sustainable-development-goals/.
31. Thomas Edward Flores and Irfan Nooruddin. 2016. *Elections in Hard Times: Building Stronger Democracies in the 21st Century*. New York: Cambridge University Press.
32. AidData. http://aiddata.org/dashboard. Consulted January 2017.
33. Michael McFaul. 2010. *Advancing Democracy Abroad*. New York: Rowman and Littlefield.
34. Edward D. Mansfield and Jack Snyder. 2007. *Electing to Fight: Why Emerging Democracies go to War*. Cambridge, MA: MIT Press.
35. Sarah Sunn Bush. 2015. *The Taming of Democracy Assistance*. New York: Cambridge University Press.
36. Lincoln A. Mitchell. 2016. *The Democracy Promotion Paradox*. Washington, DC: Brookings Institution Press.
37. n.org/wcm/webdav/site/undpa/shared/undpa/pdf/N1146860.pdf.
38. Pippa Norris. 2013. *Democratic Deficit*. New York: Cambridge University Press.
39. Pippa Norris. 2014. *Why Electoral Integrity Matters*. New York: Cambridge University Press.
40. See, for example, Evelyn Huber, Thomas Mustillo, and John D. Stevens. 2008. “Politics and social spending in Latin America.” *Journal of Politics* 70 (2): 420–436; David Stasavage. 2005. “Democracy and education spending in Africa.” *American Journal of Political Science* 49 (2): 348–358; Pippa Norris. 2010. *Making Democratic Governance Work*. New York: Cambridge University Press.

41. Amartya Sen. 1999. *Development as Freedom*. Oxford: Oxford University Press. For a counter argument, however, see Pippa Norris. 2012. *Making Democratic Governance Work*. New York: Cambridge University Press.
42. Jeroen de Zeeuw. 2005. "Projects do not create institutions: The record of democracy assistance in post-conflict societies." *Democratization* 12(4): 481–504.
43. Thomas Carothers. 2015. "Democracy aid at 25: Time to choose." *Journal of Democracy* 26(1): 59–73.
44. See, for example, Thomas Carothers. 1999. *Aiding Democracy Abroad*. Washington, DC: Carnegie Endowment for International Peace; Jean Grugel. 1999. *Democracy Without Borders: Trans-nationalisation and Conditionality in New Democracies*. London: Routledge; Peter Burnell. Ed. 2000. *Democracy Assistance: International Co-Operation for Democratization*. London: Frank Cass; James Manor. 2007. *Aid that Works: Successful Development in Fragile States*. Washington, DC: The World Bank; Ted Piccone and Richard Youngs. Eds. 2006. *Strategies for Democratic Change: Assessing the Global Response*. Washington, DC: Democracy Coalition Project; Joseph Wright. 2009. "How foreign aid can foster democratization in authoritarian regimes." *American Journal of Political Science* 53(3): 552–571; Krishna Kumar. 2012. *Evaluating Democracy Assistance*. Boulder, Co: Lynne Rienner; Pippa Norris. 2012. *Making Democratic Governance Work*. New York: Cambridge University Press.
45. Stephen Knack. 2004. "Does foreign aid promote democracy?" *International Studies Quarterly* 48: 251–266.
46. James M. Scot and Carie A. Steele. 2005. "Assisting democrats or resisting dictators? The nature of democracy support by the United States National Endowment for Democracy, 1990–1999." *Democratization* 12(4): 439–460. See, however, a subsequent study by the authors which found a positive effect from USAID democracy aid disbursements; James M. Scot and Carie A. Steele. 2011. "Sponsoring democracy: the United States and democracy aid in the developing world, 1988–2001." *International Studies Quarterly* 55: 47–69.
47. Simone Djankov, Jose Montalvo, and Marta Reynal-Querol. 2008. "The curse of aid." *Journal of Economic Growth* 13: 169–194.
48. William Easterly. 2006. *The White Man's Burden: Why the West's Efforts to Aid the Rest Have Done so Much Ill and so Little Good*. New York: Penguin.
49. Steven E. Finkel, Pérez-Liñán, Aníbal, Mitchell A. Seligson, 2007. "The effects of U.S. foreign assistance on democracy building, 1990–2003." *World Politics* 59 (1): 404–439.
50. Erasmus Kersting and Christopher Kilby. 2014. "Aid and democracy redux." *European Economic Review* 67: 125–143.
51. Jeffrey Sachs. 2005. *The End of Poverty: How We Can Make It Happen in Our Lifetime*. London: Penguin; Charles Kenny. 2012. *Getting Better: Why Global Development Is Succeeding, and How We Can Improve the World Even More*. New York: Basic Books.
52. D. L. Sackett, W. C. Rosenberg, J. A. M. Gray, R. B. Haynes, and W. S. Richardson. 1996. "Evidence based medicine: What it is and what is isn't." *British Medical Journal*, 312: 71.
53. Devra C. Moehler, 2010. "Democracy, governance, and randomized development assistance." *Annals of the American Academy of Political and Social Science*, 628: 30–46; James N. Druckman, Donald P. Green, James H. Kuklinski, and

Arthur Lupia. Eds. 2011. *Cambridge Handbook of Experimental Political Science*. New York: Cambridge University Press; Rebecca B. Morton and Kenneth C. Williams. 2010. *Experimental Political Science and the Study of Causality: From Nature to the Lab*. New York: Cambridge University Press.

54. See, for example, Susan. D. Hyde. 2007. "Experimenting in democracy promotion: International observers and the 2004 presidential elections in Indonesia." *Perspectives on Politics* 8(2): 511-527; Nahomi Ichino and Matthias Schuendeln. 2012. "Deterring or displacing electoral irregularities? Spillover effects of observers in a randomized field experiment in Ghana." *Journal of Politics* 74(1): 292–307; Fredrik Sjoberg. 2012. "Making voters count: Evidence from field experiments about the efficacy of domestic election observation." Harriman Institute Working Paper 1.
55. Pippa Norris. 2004. "Will new technology boost turnout?" In Norbert Kersting and Harald Baldersheim, eds., *Electronic Voting and Democracy: A Comparative Analysis*. London: Palgrave, pp.193–225.
56. Marcus Drometer and Rincke Johannes. 2009. "The impact of ballot access restrictions on electoral competition: Evidence from a natural experiment." *Public Choice* 138(3–4): 461–474; Kentaro Fukumoto and Yusaku Horiuchi. 2011. "Making outsiders' votes count: Detecting electoral fraud through a natural experiment." *American Political Science Review* 105(3): 586–603; Thad Dunning. 2012. *Natural Experiments in the Social Sciences*. New York: Cambridge University Press.
57. Devra C. Moehler. 2010. "Democracy, governance, and randomized development assistance." *Annals of the American Academy of Political and Social Science* 628: 30–46.
58. Alexander Cooley and Jack Snyder. Eds. 2015. *Ranking the World*. New York: Cambridge University Press.
59. Pippa Norris. 2016. *Why Elections Fail*. New York: Cambridge University Press.
60. For recent comparative overviews, see Jonathan Mendilow. Ed. 2012. *Money, Corruption, and Political Competition in Established and Emerging Democracies*. Lexington Books: Lanham, MD; Pippa Norris and Andrea Abek van Es. Eds. 2016. *Checkbook Elections? Political Finance in Comparative Perspective*. New York: Oxford University Press; Robert G. Boatright. Ed. 2015. *The Deregulatory Moment? A Comparative Perspective on Changing Campaign Finance Laws*. Michigan: University of Michigan Press.

Select Bibliography

Aaken, Anne van. 2009. "Independent Election Management Bodies and international election observer missions: Any impact on the observed levels of democracy? A Conceptual Framework." *Constitutional Political Economy* 20(3–4): 296–322.

Abbink, Jon. 2000. "Introduction: Rethinking democratization and election observation." In Jon Abbink and G. Hesseling, eds. *Election Observation and Democratization in Africa*. New York: St. Martin's Press, pp. 1–17.

Acemoglu, Daron and James A. Robinson. 2005. *Economic Origins of Dictatorship or Democracy*. New York: Cambridge University Press.

Ākhatāra, Muhāmmada Iẏāhaiẏā. 2001. *Electoral Corruption in Bangladesh*. Burlington, VT: Ashgate.

Albaugh, Ericka A. 2011. "An autocrat's toolkit: adaptation and manipulation in 'democratic' Cameroon." *Democratization* 18(2): 388–414.

Alesina, Alberto and Enrico Spolaore. 2003. *The Size of Nations*. Cambridge, MA: MIT Press.

Al-Fattal Eeckelaert, Rouba. 2016. *Transatlantic Trends in Democracy Promotion: Electoral Assistance in the Palestinian Territories*. New York: Routledge.

Alihodzic, Sead. 2016. "The mechanics of democracy promotion tools: Bridging the knowledge-to-practice gap." *Development In Practice* 26(4): 431–443.

Allen, H. W. and K. W. Allen. 1981. "Voting fraud and data validity." In J.M. Clubb, W. H. Flanigan, and H. Zingale, eds., *Analyzing Electoral History*. Beverley Hills, CA: Sage, pp. 153–193.

Alston, L. J. and A. A. Gallo. "Electoral fraud, the rise of Peron and demise of checks and balances in Argentina." *Explorations in Economic History* 47(2): 179–197.

Altunbas, Yener and John Thornton. 2014. "The (small) blessing of foreign aid: Further evidence on aid's impact on democracy." *Applied Economics* 46(32): 3922–3930.

Alvarez, R. Michael, Lonna Atkeson, and Thad E. Hall. Eds. 2012. *Confirming Elections: Creating Confidence and Integrity through Election Auditing*. New York: Palgrave Macmillan.

Alvarez, R. Michael, Lonna Rae Atkeson, and Thad Hall. 2012. *Evaluating Elections: A Handbook of Methods and Standards*. New York: Cambridge University Press.
Alvarez, R. Michael, Lonna Rae Atkeson, Thad Hall, and Andrew J. Lotempio. 2002. "Winning, losing and political trust in America." *British Journal of Political Science* 32(2): 335–351.
Alvarez, R. Michael, José Antonio Cheibub, Fernando Limongi, and Adam Przeworski. 1996. "Classifying political regimes." *Studies in International Comparative Development* 31: 3–36.
Alvarez, R. Michael and Bernard Grofman. Eds. 2014. *Election Administration in the United States: The State of Reform After Bush v. Gore*. New York: Cambridge University Press.
Alvarez, R. Michael and Thad E. Hall. 2006. "Controlling democracy: The principal agent problems in election administration." *Policy Studies Journal* 34(4): 491–510.
Alvarez, R. Michael and Thad E. Hall. 2008. "Building secure and transparent elections through standard operating procedures." *Public Administration Review* 68(5): 828–838.
Alvarez, R. Michael, Thad Hall, and Susan Hyde. 2008. Eds. *Election Fraud*. Washington DC: Brookings Institution Press.
Alvarez, R. Michael, Hall, Thad E., and Llewellyn, Morgan H. 2008. "Are Americans confident their ballots are counted?" *Journal of Politics* 70 (3): 754–766.
Alvarez, R. Michael, Thad E. Hall, and Llewellyn Morgan. 2008. "Who should run elections in the United States?" *Policy Studies Journal* 36(3): 325–346.
Anderson, Christopher J. 1995. *Blaming the Government*. New York: Oxford University Press.
Anderson, Christopher J., Andre Blais, Shaun Bowler, Todd Donovan, and Ola Listhaug. 2005. *Losers' Consent: Elections and Democratic Legitimacy*. New York: Oxford University Press.
Anderson, Christopher J. and Christine A. Guillory. 1997. "Political institutions and satisfaction with democracy." *American Political Science Review* 91(1): 66–81.
Anderson, Christopher and Silvia Mendes. 2006. "Learning to Lose: Election Outcomes, Democratic Experience and Political Protest Potential." *British Journal of Political Science* 36(1): 91–111.
Anderson, Christopher J. and Y. V. Tverdova. 2001. "Winners, losers, and attitudes about government in contemporary democracies." *International Political Science Review* 22: 321–338.
Anderson, Christopher J. and Yuliya V. Tverdova. 2003. "Corruption, political allegiances, and attitudes toward government in contemporary democracies." *American Journal of Political Science* 47(1): 91–109.
Andrews, Matt. 2013. *The Limits of Institutional Reform in Development*. New York: Cambridge University Press.
Anglin, Douglas G. 1995. "International monitoring of the transition to democracy in South Africa, 1992–1994." *African Affairs*, 9(377): 519–543.
Anglin, Douglas G. 1998. "International election monitoring: The African experience." *African Affairs* 97: 471–495.
Ansolabehere, Stephen 2009. "Effects of identification requirements on voting: Evidence from the experiences of voters on election day." *PS: Political Science & Politics*, 42: 127–130.

Ansolabehere, Stephen, Eitan Hersh, and Kenneth Shepsle. 2012. "Movers, stayers, and registration: Why age is correlated with registration in the U.S." *Quarterly Journal of Political Science* 7 (4): 333–363.

Arrington, Theodore S. 2010. "Redistricting in the US: A review of scholarship and plan for future research." *Forum: A Journal of Applied Research in Contemporary Politics* 8(2).

Arriola, Leonardo R. 2012. *Multi-Ethnic Coalitions in Africa: Business Financing of Opposition Election Campaigns*. New York: Cambridge University Press.

Askarov, Zohid and Hristos Doucouliagos. 2013. "Does aid improve democracy and governance? A meta-regression analysis." *Public Choice* 157(3–4): 601–628.

Askarov, Zohid and Hristos Doucouliagos. 2015. "Development aid and growth in transition countries." *World Development* 66: 383–399.

Atkeson, Lonna Rae; R. Michael Alvarez, and Thad E. Hall et al. 2014. "Balancing Fraud Prevention and Electoral Participation: Attitudes Toward Voter Identification." *Social Science Quarterly* 95(5): 1381–1398.

Atkeson, Lonna Rae, R. Michael Alvarez, and Thad E. Hall. 2015. "Voter Confidence: How to Measure It and How It Differs from Government Support." *Election Law Journal* 14 (3): 207–219.

Atkeson, Lonna Rae, Lisa Ann Bryant, and Thad E. Hall, 2010. "A new barrier to participation: Heterogeneous application of voter identification policies." *Electoral Studies* 29(1): 66–73.

Atkeson, Lonna Rae, Yann P. Kerevel, R. Michael Alvarez, and Thad E. Hall. 2014. "Who asks for voter identification? Explaining poll-worker discretion." *The Journal of Politics* 76(4): 944–957.

Atkeson, Lonna Rae and K. L. Saunders. 2007. "The effect of election administration on voter confidence: A local matter?" *PS: Political Science & Politics* 40: 655–660.

Atwood, Richard. 2012. *How the EU can support peaceful post-election transitions of power: lessons from Africa*. Directorate-General for External Policies of the Union, Directorate B Policy Department, European Parliament, Brussels.

Austin, Reginold and Maja Tjernstrom. Eds. 2003. *Funding of Political Parties and Election Campaigns*. Stockholm: International IDEA.

Bader, Max and Carolien van Ham. 2015. "What explains regional variation in election fraud? Evidence from Russia: A research note." *Post-Soviet Affairs* 31(6): 514–528.

Baker, B. 2002. "When to call black white: Zimbabwe's electoral reports." *Third World Quarterly* 23 (6): 1145–1158.

Balule, Badala Tachilisa. 2008. "Election management bodies in the SADC region: An appraisal of the independence of Botswana's independent electoral commission." *South African Journal on Human Rights* 24: 104–122.

Banducci, Susan A. and Jeffrey A. Karp. 1999. "Perceptions of fairness and support for Proportional Representation." *Political Behavior* 21(3): 217–238.

Banerji, Abhijit V., Esther Duflo, Clement Imbert, Rohini Pande, Michael Walton, and Bibhu Prasad Mohapatra. 2014. "An impact evaluation of information disclosure on elected representatives' performance: Evidence from rural and urban India." *3ie Impact Evaluation Report 11*. www.3ieimpact.org/media/filer_public/2014/08/20/ie11_voter_education.pdf.

Bardall, Gabrielle. "Election violence monitoring and the use of new communication technologies." *Democracy & Society*. 7(2): 8.

Barkan, Joel D. 1993. "Kenya: Lessons from a flawed election." *Journal of Democracy* 4(3): 85–99.

Barkan, Joel D. 2013. "Technology is not democracy." *Journal of Democracy*. 24(3): 156–165.

Barnes, Tiffany D. and Emily Beaulieu. 2014. "Gender stereotypes and corruption: How candidates affect perceptions of election fraud." *Politics & Gender* 10(3): 365–391.

Barro, Robert. 1999. "Determinants of democracy." *Journal of Political Economy* 107(6): 158–193.

Basedau, Matthais, Gero Erdman, and Andreas Mehler. 2007. *Votes, Money and Violence: Political Parties in Sub-Saharan Africa*. Sweden: Nordiska Afrikainstitutet. http://urn.kb.se/resolve?urn=urn:nbn:se:nai:diva-492.

Bauer, Robert F. and Benjamin L. Ginsberg, et al., 2014. *The American Voting Experience: Report and Recommendations of the Presidential Commission on Election Administration*. Washington, DC.

Beaulieu, Emily. 2014. *Electoral Protests and Democracy in the Developing World*. New York: Cambridge University Press.

Beaulieu, Emily. 2014. "From Voter ID to Party ID: How political parties affect perceptions of election fraud in the U.S." *Electoral Studies* 35: 24–32.

Beaulieu, Emily and Susan D. Hyde. 2009. "In the shadow of democracy promotion: Strategic manipulation, international observers, and election boycotts." *Comparative Political Studies* 42(3): 392–415.

Beber, Bernd and Alexandra Scacco. 2012. "What the numbers say: A digit-based test for election fraud." *Political Analysis* 20(2): 211–234.

Bekoe, Dorina. Ed. 2012. *Voting in Fear: Electoral Violence in Sub-Saharan Africa*. Washington, DC: United States Institute of Peace.

Benoit, Kenneth. 2007. "Electoral Laws as Political Consequences: Explaining the Origins and Change of Electoral Institutions." *Annual Review of Political Science*. 10: 363–390.

Benson, J. F. 2009. "Voter fraud or voter defrauded? Highlighting an inconsistent consideration of election fraud." *Harvard Civil Rights-Civil Liberties Law Review* 44 (1): 1–42.

Berinsky, Adam J. 2004. "The perverse consequences of electoral reform in the United States." *American Politics Research* 33(4): 471–491.

Berinsky, Adam J., Nancy Burns, and Michael W. Traugott. 2001. "Who votes by mail? A dynamic model of the individual-level consequences of voting-by-mail systems." *Public Opinion Quarterly* 65(2): 178–197.

Berman, Eli, Michael Callen, Clark Gibson, and James D. Long. 2014. "Election fairness and government legitimacy in Afghanistan." National Bureau of Economic Research Working Paper 19949. www.nber.org/papers/w19949.

Bermeo, Nancy. "Interests, inequality, and illusion in the choice for fair elections." *Comparative Political Studies* 43(8–9): 1119–1147.

Bermeo, Sarah Blodgett. 2011. "Foreign aid and regime change: A role for donor intent." *World Development* 39(11): 2021–2031.

Bhasin, Tavishi and Jennifer Gandhi. 2013. "State repression in authoritarian elections." *Electoral Studies* 32(4): 620–631.

Birch, Sarah. 2007. "Electoral systems and electoral misconduct." *Comparative Political Studies* 40(12): 1533–1556.

Birch, Sarah. 2008. "Electoral institutions and popular confidence in electoral processes: A cross-national analysis." *Electoral Studies* 27 (2): 305–320.
Birch, Sarah. 2010. "Perceptions of electoral fairness and voter turnout." *Comparative Political Studies* 43(12): 1601–1622.
Birch, Sarah. 2011. *Electoral Malpractice*. Oxford: Oxford University Press.
Birch, Sarah. 2012. *Electoral Malpractice*. www.essex.ac.uk/government/electoralmalpractice/index.htm.
Bishop, Sylvia and Anke Hoeffler. 2014. "Free and fair elections: A new database." Oxford: *Center for the Study of African Economies (CSAE) Working Paper* WPS/2014–14.
Bjornlund, Eric C. 2004. *Beyond Free and Fair: Monitoring Elections and Building Democracy*. Washington DC: Woodrow Wilson Center Press.
Bjornskov, C. "How does social trust lead to better governance? An attempt to separate electoral and bureaucratic mechanisms." *Public Choice* 144 (1-2): 323–346.
Bland, Gary, Andrew Green, and Toby Moore. 2012. "Measuring the quality of election administration." *Democratization*. 1–20.
Blaydes, Lisa. 2011. *Elections and Distributive Politics in Mubarak's Egypt*. New York: Cambridge University Press.
Boatright, Robert G. Ed. 2011. *Campaign Finance: The Problems and Consequences of Reform*. New York: IDebate Press.
Bochsler, Daniel. 2012. "A quasi-proportional electoral system 'only for honest men'? The hidden potential for manipulating mixed compensatory electoral systems." *International Political Science Review* 33(4): 401–420.
Boda, M.D. 2005. "Reconsidering the 'free and fair' question." *Representation* 41(3), 155–160.
Bogaards, Matthijs. 2013. "Reexamining African Elections." *Journal of Democracy* 24(4):151–160.
Bogaards, Matthijs, Matthias Basedau, and Christof Hartmann, 2010. "Ethnic party bans in Africa: An introduction." *Democratization* 17(4): 599–617.
Boix, Carles, Michael K. Miller, and Sebastian Rosato. "A Complete Dataset of Political Regimes, 1800–2007." *Comparative Political Studies*. Forthcoming.
Boniface, Makulilo Alexander. 2011. "'Watching the watcher': an evaluation of local election observers in Tanzania." *Journal of Modern African Studies* 49(2): 241–262.
Boone, Catherine. 2011. "Politically allocated land rights and the geography of electoral violence: The case of Kenya in the 1990s." *Comparative Political Studies* 44(10): 1311–1342.
Borzyskowski, Inken van. 2016. "Resisting democracy assistance: Who seeks and receives technical Election Assistance?" *Review of International Organizations* 11(2): 247–282.
Bowler, Shaun, Thomas Brunell, Todd Donovan, and Paul Gronke. 2015. "Electoral administration and perceptions of fair elections." *Electoral Studies*. 38(2): 1–9.
Bowler, Shaun and Todd Donovan. 2011. "The limited effects of election reforms on efficacy and engagement." *Australian Journal of Political Science* 47(1): 55–70.
Bowler, Shaun and Todd Donovan. 2013. *The Limits of Electoral Reform*. New York: Oxford University Press.
Brancati, Dawn and Jack L. Snyder. 2011. "Rushing to the polls: The causes of premature post-conflict elections." *Journal of Conflict Resolution* 55(3): 469–492.

Bratton, Michael and Nicholas van de Walle. 1997. *Democratic Experiments in Africa: Regime Transitions in Comparative Perspective*. New York: Cambridge University Press.

Bratton, Michael, Robert Mattes, and E. Gyimah-Boadi. 2005. *Public Opinion, Democracy and Market Reform in Africa*. Cambridge: Cambridge University Press.

Bratton, Michael. 2008. "Vote buying and violence in Nigerian election campaigns." *Electoral Studies* 27(4): 621–632.

Breunig, Christian and Goerres, Achim. 2011. "Searching for electoral irregularities in an established democracy: Applying Benford's Law tests to Bundestag elections in Unified Germany." *Electoral Studies* 30(3): 534–545.

Bratton, Michael. Ed. 2013. *Voting and Democratic citizenship in Africa*. Boulder, CO: Lynne Rienner Publishers.

Bräutigam, Deborah and Stephan Knack. 2004. "Foreign aid, institutions, and governance in Sub-Saharan Africa." *Economic Development and Cultural Change* 52: 255–285.

Bridoux, Jeff and Milja Kurki. 2016. *Democracy Promotion: A Critical Introduction*. New York: Routledge.

Brown, Nathan J. Ed. 2011. *The Dynamics of Democratization: Dictatorship, Development and Diffusion*. Baltimore: Johns Hopkins University Press.

Brownlee, Jason. 2007. *Authoritarianism in an Age of Democratization*. New York: Cambridge University Press.

Brownlee, Jason. 2008. "Bound to rule: Party institutions and regime trajectories in Malaysia and the Philippines." *Journal of East Asian Studies* 8(1): 89–118.

Brownlee, Jason. 2009. "Portents of pluralism: How hybrid regimes affect democratic transitions." *American Journal of Political Science* 53 (3): 515–532.

Brownlee, Jason, 2011. "Executive elections in the Arab world: When and how do they matter?" *Comparative Political Studies* 44(7): 807–828.

Brusco, V., M. Nazareno, and S.C. Stokes. 2004. "Vote buying in Argentina." *Latin American Research Review*, 39(2), 66–88.

Buckley, Sam. 2011. *Banana Republic UK? Vote rigging, fraud and error in British elections since 2001*. Open Rights Group.

Bunce, Valerie J. and Sharon L. Wolchik. 2006. "Favorable conditions and electoral revolutions." *Journal of Democracy* 17: 5–18.

Bunce, Valerie J. and Sharon L. Wolchik. 2010. "Defeating dictators: Electoral change and stability in competitive authoritarian regimes." *World Politics* 62(1): 43–86.

Bunce, Valerie J. and Sharon L. Wolchik. 2011. *Defeating Authoritarian Leaders in Post-Communist Countries*. New York: Cambridge University Press.

Burch, Patricia E. and Carolyn J. Heinrich. 2015. *Mixed Methods for Policy Research and Program Evaluation*. Sage Publications.

Burden, Barry C., David T. Canon, Kenneth R. Mayer, and Donald P. Moynihan. 2011. "Election laws, mobilization, and turnout: The unanticipated consequences of election reform." *American Journal of Political Science* 58: 95–109.

Burden, Barry C., David T. Canon, Kenneth R. Mayer, and Donald P. Moynihan. 2011. "Early voting and election day registration in the Trenches: Local officials' perceptions of election reform." *Election Law Journal* 10: 89–102.

Burden, Barry C. and Jacob R. Neiheisel. 2013. "Election administration and the pure effect of voter registration on turnout." *Political Research Quarterly* 66:77–90.

Burden, Barry C. and Charles Stewart III. Eds. 2014. *The Measure of American Elections*. New York: Cambridge University Press.
Burnell, Peter. 2008. "Promoting Democracy." In Daniele Caramani, ed., *Comparative Politics*, Oxford: Oxford University Press.
Burnell, Peter. 2011. *Promoting Democracy Abroad: Policy and Performance*. New Brunswick, NJ: Transaction Publishers.
Bush, Sarah Sunn. 2011. "International politics and the spread of quotas for women in legislatures." *International Organization* 65(1): 103–137.
Bush, Sarah Sunn. 2015. *The Taming of Democracy Assistance: Why Democracy Promotion Does Not Confront Dictators*. New York: Cambridge University Press.
Butler, David and Bruce E. Cain. 1992. *Congressional Redistricting: Comparative and Theoretical Perspectives*. New York: Macmillan.
Cain, Bruce. E., Donovan, Todd, and Tolbert, C. J. 2008. *Democracy in the States: Experimentation in Election Reform*. Washington, DC: Brookings Institution Press.
Calimbahin, Cleo. 2011. "Exceeding (low) expectations: Autonomy, bureaucratic integrity, and capacity in the 2010 elections." *Philippine Political Science Journal* 32(55): 103–126.
Calingaert, D. 2006. "Election Rigging and How to Fight It." *Journal of Democracy* 17(3): 138–151.
Calingaert, Daniel, Arch Puddington, and Sarah Repucci. 2014. "The democracy support deficit: Despite progress, major countries fall short." In *Supporting Democracy Abroad: An Assessment of Leading Powers*. Washington, DC: Freedom House.
Callahan, W. A. 2000. *Poll Watching, Elections and Civil Society in South-East Asia*. Burlington, VT: Ashgate.
Callahan, W. A. 2005. "The discourse of vote buying and political reform in Thailand." *Pacific Affairs* 78(1): 95–99.
Callen, Michael, Clark C. Gibson, Danielle F. Jung, and James D. Long. 2015. "Improving electoral integrity with information and communications technology." *Journal of Experimental Political Science* 3(1): 4–17.
Campbell, Tracy. 2006. *Deliver the Vote: A History of Election Fraud, an American Political Tradition 1742–2004*. New York: Basic Books.
Cantu, Francisco. 2014. "Identifying Irregularities in Mexican Local Elections." *American Journal of Political Science* 58(4): 936–951.
Cantu, Francisco and Garcia-Ponce, Omar. 2015. "Partisan losers' effects: Perceptions of electoral integrity in Mexico." *Electoral Studies* 39:1–14.
Carey, Sabine. 2007. "Violent dissent and rebellion in Africa." *Journal of Peace Research* 44(1): 1–39.
Carman, Christopher, Mitchell, James, and Johns, Robert. 2008. "The unfortunate natural experiment in ballot design: The Scottish Parliamentary elections of 2007." *Electoral Studies* 27(3): 442–459.
Carothers, Thomas. 1997. "The observers observed." *Journal of Democracy*. 8 (3): 17–31.
Carothers, Thomas. 1999. *Aiding Democracy Abroad*. Washington DC: The Brookings Institution.
Carothers, Thomas. 2002. "The end of the transition paradigm." *Journal of Democracy* 13 (1): 5–21.

Carothers, Thomas. 2015. "Democracy aid at 25: Time to choose." *Journal of Democracy* 26(1): 59–73.
Carothers, Thomas and Diane de-Gramont. 2013. *Development Aid Confronts Politics: The Almost Revolution*. Washington, DC: Carnegie Endowment for International Peace.
Carriquiry, Alicia L. 2011. "Election forensics and the 2004 Venezuelan Presidential recall referendum as a case study." *Statistical Science* 26(4): 471–478.
Carroll, David J. and Avery Davis-Roberts. 2013. "The Carter Center and election observation: An obligations-based approach for assessing elections." *Election Law Journal* 12(1): 87–93.
Carter Center. *Database of Obligations for Democratic Elections*. Carter Center: Atlanta. www.cartercenter.org/des-search/des/Introduction.aspx.
Casas-Zamora, Kevin. 2004. *Paying for Democracy*. Essex: ECPR Press.
Case, William. 2011. "Electoral authoritarianism and backlash: Hardening Malaysia, oscillating Thailand." *International Political Science Review* 32(4): 438–457.
Castaneda, Gonzalo. 2011. "Benford's law and its applicability in the forensic analysis of electoral results." *Politica Y Gobierno* 18(2): 297–329.
Castaneda, Gonzalo and I. Ibarra. "Detection of fraud with agent-based models: The 2006 Mexican election." *Perfiles Latinoamericanos* 18(36):43–69.
Catterberg, Gabriella and Alejandro Moreno. 2006. "The individual bases of political trust: Trends in new and established democracies." *International Journal of Public Opinion Research* 18(1): 31–48.
Cederman, Lars-Erik, Kristian S. Gleditsch, and Simon Hug. 2012. "Elections and civil war." *Comparative Political Studies* 46(3) 387–417.
Celestino, Mauricio Rivera and Gleditsch, Kristian Skrede. 2013. "Fresh carnations or all thorn, no rose? Nonviolent campaigns and transitions in autocracies." *Journal of Peace Research* 50(3): 385–400.
Chaisty, Paul and Steven Whitefield. 2013. "Forward to democracy or back to authoritarianism? The attitudinal bases of mass support for the Russian election protests of 2011–2012." *Post-Soviet Affairs* 29(5): 387–403.
Chand, Vikram. 1997. "Democratisation from the outside in: NGO and international efforts to promote open elections." *Third World Quarterly*, 18(3): 543–61.
Chang, Eric C. C. 2005. "Electoral Incentives for Political Corruption under Open-List Proportional Representation." *The Journal of Politics* 67(3): 716–730.
Chaturvedi, Ashish. 2005. "Rigged elections with violence." *Public Choice* 125(1–2): 189–202.
Cheeseman, Nic, Gabrielle Lynch, and Justin Willis. 2014. "Democracy and its discontents: understanding Kenya's 2013 elections." *Journal of Eastern African Studies* 8(1): 2–24.
Cheibub, Jose Antonio, Jennifer Gandhi, and James Raymond Vreeland. 2010. "Democracy and dictatorship revisited." *Public Choice* 143(1–2): 67–101.
Chernykh, Svitlana. 2014. "When do political parties protest election results?" *Comparative Political Studies* 47(10): 1359–1383.
Chernykh, Svitlana and Milan W. Svolik. 2015. "Third-party actors and the success of democracy: How electoral commissions, courts, and observers shape incentives for electoral manipulation and post-election protests." *The Journal of Politics* 77(2): 407–420.

Cho, Youngho, and Yong C. Kim. 2015. "Procedural justice and perceived electoral integrity: The case of Korea's 2012 presidential election." *Democratization*. 23(7): 1180–1197.
Cingranelli, David L., David L. Richards, and K. Chad Clay. 2013. *The Cingranelli-Richards (CIRI) Human Rights Dataset*. www.humanrightsdata.org.
Clark, Alistair. 2014. "Funding capacity in electoral democracy: Insights from electoral administration." PSA Annual Conference, Manchester, April 2014.
Clark, Alistair. 2015. "Public administration and the integrity of the electoral process in British elections." *Public Administration* 93(1): 86–102.
Coburn, Noah and Anna Larson.2013. *Derailing Democracy in Afghanistan: Elections in an Unstable Political Landscape*. New York: Columbia University Press.
Collier, David and Steven Levitsky. 1997. "Democracy with Democracy with Adjectives: Conceptual Innovation in Comparative Research." *World Politics*. 49(3): 430–451.
Collier, Paul. 2009. *Wars, Guns and Votes: Democracy in Dangerous Places*. New York: HarperCollins.
Collier, Paul and Anke Hoeffler. 1998. "On economic causes of civil war." *Oxford Economic Papers – New Series* 50(4): 563–573.
Collier, Paul and Anke Hoeffler. 2002. "On the incidence of civil war in Africa." *Journal of Conflict Resolution* 46(1): 13–28.
Collier, Paul and Anke Hoeffler. 2004. "Greed and grievance in civil war." *Oxford Economic Papers-New Series* 56(4): 563–595.
Collier, Paul, Anke Hoeffler, and Dominic Rohner. 2009. "Beyond greed and grievance: feasibility and civil war." *Oxford Economic Papers-New Series* 61(1): 1–27.
Collier, Paul, Anke Hoeffler, and Nicholas Sambanis. 2005. "The Collier-Hoeffler model of civil war onset and the case study project research design. In Paul Collier and Nicolas Sambanis, eds. *Understanding Civil War*. Washington, DC: The World Bank.
Collier Paul, Anke Hoeffler, and Mans Soderbom. 2008. "Post-conflict risks." *Journal of Peace Research* 45 (4): 461–478.
Collier, Paul and Pedro Vicente. 2011. "Violence, bribery and fraud: The political economy of elections in Sub-Saharan Africa." *Public Choice*. 153(1): 1–31.
Colton, Timothy J. 2000. *Transitional Citizens: Voters and What Influences Them in the New Russia*. Cambridge, MA: Harvard University Press.
Cooley, Alexander and Jack Snyder. Eds. 2015. *Ranking the World: Grading States as a Tool of Global Governance*. New York: Cambridge University Press.
Coppedge, Michael. 2012. *Democratization and Research Methods*. New York: Cambridge University Press.
Cox, Michael, G. John Ikenberry, and Takashi Inoguchi. Eds. 2002. *American Democracy Promotion*. Oxford: Oxford University Press.
Cox, Michael, Timothy J. Lynch, and Nicolas Bouchet. Eds. 2013. *US Foreign Policy and Democracy Promotion: From Theodore Roosevelt to Barack Obama*. New York: Routledge.
Craig, Stephen C., Michael D. Martinez, and Jason Gainous 2006. "Winners, losers, and election context: Voter responses to the 2000 presidential election." *Political Research Quarterly* 59(4): 579–592.
Crawford, Gordon, 2003. "Promoting democracy from without: Learning from within (Part I)." *Democratization*, 10(1): 77–98.

Crewe, Ivor. 1981. "Electoral Participation." In Austin Ranney and David Butler, eds. *Democracy at the Polls.* Washington, DC: American Enterprise Institute for Public Policy Research.
Cruz, R. C. 2001. "Voting for the unexpected: Electoral fraud and political struggle in Costa Rica (1901–1948)." *Journal of Latin American Studies* 33: 893–94.
Curtice, John. 2013. "Politicians, voters and democracy: The 2011 UK referendum on the Alternative Vote." *Electoral Studies* 32(2): 215–223.
Dahl, Robert A. 1971. *Polyarchy: Participation and Opposition.* New Haven: Yale University Press.
D'Anieri, Paul. Ed. 2010. *Orange Revolution and Aftermath: Mobilization, Apathy, and the state in Ukraine.* Baltimore: Johns Hopkins University Press.
Darnolf, Staffan. 2011. *Assessing Electoral Fraud in New Democracies: A New Strategic Approach.* Washington, DC International Foundation for Electoral Systems: White Paper Series Electoral Fraud.
Davenport, Christian. 1997. "From ballots to bullets: An empirical assessment of how national elections influence state uses of political repression." *Electoral Studies* 6(4): 517–540.
Davenport, Christian. 2007. "State repression and political order." *Annual Review of Political Science* 10: 1–23.
Davenport, Christian. 2007. *State Repression and the Domestic Democratic Peace.* New York: Cambridge University Press.
Davenport, Christian and Molly Inman. 2012. "The state of state repression research since the 1990s." *Terrorism and Political Violence* 24(4): 619–634.
Davis-Roberts, Avery and David J. Carroll. 2010. "Using International Law to Assess Elections." *Democratization.* 17(3): 416–441.
Daxecker, Ursula E. 2012. "The cost of exposing cheating: International election monitoring, fraud, and post-election violence in Africa." *Journal of Peace Research* 49(4): 503–516.
Daxecker, Ursula E. and Gerald Schneider. 2014. "Electoral monitoring." In Pippa Norris, Richard W. Frank, and Ferran Martinez i Coma, eds. *Advancing Electoral Integrity*, New York: Oxford University Press.
de Sousa, Luis and Marcelo Moriconi. 2014. "Why voters do not throw the rascals out? A conceptual framework for analysing electoral punishment of corruption." *Crime Law and Social Change* 60(5): 471–502.
Debrah, Emmanuel. 2011. "Measuring governance institutions' success in Ghana: The case of the Electoral Commission, 1993–2008." *African Studies* 70(1): 25–45.
Deckert, Joseph, Mikhail Myagkov, and Peter C. Ordeshook. 2011. "Benford's Law and the detection of election fraud." *Political Analysis* 19: 245–268.
Denver, David, R. Johns, and C. Carman. 2009. "Rejected ballot papers in the 2007 Scottish Parliament Election: The voters' perspective." *British Politics* 4(1): 3–21.
Dercon, Stefan and Gutierrez-Romero, Roxana. 2012. "Triggers and characteristics of the 2007 Kenyan electoral violence." *World Development* 40(4): 731–744.
Diamond, Larry. 2002. "Thinking about hybrid regimes." *Journal of Democracy* 13(2): 21–35.
Diamond, Larry and Leonardo Morlino. 2004. "Quality of Democracy: An Overview." *Journal of Democracy* 15(4): 20–31.
Diamond, Larry and Marc F. Plattner. Eds. 2015. *Democracy in Decline?* Baltimore: Johns Hopkins University Press.

Dietrich, Simone and Joseph Wright. 2015. "Foreign aid allocation tactics and democratic change in Africa." *Journal of Politics* 77(1): 216–234.
Djankov, Simeon, Jose G. Montalvo, and Marta Reynal-Querol. 2008. "The curse of aid." *Journal of Economic Growth* 13: 169–194.
Doherty, David, and Jennifer Wolak. 2012. "When do the ends justify the means? Evaluating procedural fairness." *Political Behavior* 34(2): 301–323.
Donno, Daniella. 2010. "Who is punished? Regional intergovernmental organizations and the enforcement of democratic norms." *International Organization* 64(4): 593–625.
Donno, Daniela. 2013. "Elections and democratization in authoritarian regimes." *American Journal of Political Science* 57(3): 703–716.
Donno, Daniella. 2013. *Defending Democratic Norms*. New York: Oxford University Press.
Donno, Daniella and Nasos Roussias. 2012. "Does cheating pay? The effect of electoral misconduct on party systems." *Comparative Political Studies*. 45(5): 575–605.
Donno, Daniella and Alberto Simpser. 2012. "Can international election monitoring harm governance?" *Journal of Politics*. 74(2): 501–513.
Donsanto, C. C. 2008. "Corruption in the electoral process under U.S. federal law." In R. Michael Alvarez, Thad E. Hall and Susan Hyde, eds., *Election Fraud: Detecting and Deterring Electoral Manipulation*. Washington, DC: Brookings Institute.
Downs, Anthony. 1957. *An Economic Theory of Democracy*. New York: Harper and Row.
Doyle, Michael W and Nicolas Sambanis. 2000. "International peace-building: A theoretical and quantitative analysis." *American Political Science Review* 94 (4): 779–801.
Drometer, Marcus and Rincke Johannes. 2009. "The impact of ballot access restrictions on electoral competition: Evidence from a natural experiment." *Public Choice* 138(3–4): 461–474.
Druckman, James N., Donald P. Green, James H. Kuklinski, and Arthur Lupia. Eds. 2011. *Cambridge Handbook of Experimental Political Science*. New York: Cambridge University Press.
Dunning, Thad. 2004. "Conditioning the effects of aid: Cold War politics, donor credibility, and democracy in Africa." *International Organization* 58(2): 409–423.
Dunning, Thad. 2011. "Fighting and voting: Violent conflict and electoral politics." *Journal of Conflict Resolution* 55(3): 327–339.
Dunning, Thad. 2012. *Natural Experiments in the Social Sciences*. New York: Cambridge University Press.
Eisenstadt, T. A. 2004. "Catching the state off guard: Electoral courts, campaign finance, and Mexico's separation of state and ruling party." *Party Politics* 10(6): 723-45.
Eisenstadt, T.A. 2004. *Courting Democracy in Mexico: Party Strategies and Electoral Institutions*. New York: Cambridge University Press.
Ekman, Joakim. 2009. "Political participation and regime stability: A framework for analyzing hybrid regimes." *International Political Science Review* 30(1): 7–31.
Elklit, Jørgen. 1999. "Electoral institutional change and democratization: You can lead a horse to water, but you can't make it drink." *Democratization* 6 (4): 28–51.

Elklit, Jørgen and Andrew Reynolds. 2002. "The impact of election administration on the legitimacy of emerging democracies: A new comparative politics research agenda." *Commonwealth & Comparative Politics* 40 (2): 86–119.

Elklit, Jørgen and Andrew Reynolds. 2005. "A framework for the systematic study of election quality." *Democratization* 12 (2): 147–162.

Elklit, Jørgen and Svend-Erik Skaaning. *Coding Manual: Assessing Election and Election Management Quality*, 2011. www.democracy-assessment.dk/start/page.asp?page=22.

Elklit, Jørgen and Palle Svensson. 1997. "What makes elections free and fair?" *Journal of Democracy* 8(3): 32–46.

Estevez, Federico, Eric Magar, and Guillermo Rosas. 2008. "Partisanship in non-partisan electoral agencies and democratic compliance: Evidence from Mexico's Federal Electoral Institute." *Electoral Studies* 27(2): 257–271.

European Commission. 2007. *Compendium of International Standards for Elections*. 2nd ed. Brussels: European Commission, Brussels: EC/NEEDS.

Evrensel, Astrid. Ed. 2010. *Voter registration in Africa: A comparative analysis*. Johannesburg: EISA.

Ewing, Keith. 2009. *The Funding of Political Parties in Britain*. Cambridge: Cambridge University Press.

Fall, Ismaila Madior, Mathias Hounkpe, Adele L. Jinadu, and Pascal Kambale. 2011. *Election Management Bodies in West Africa: A Comparative Study of the Contribution of Electoral Commissions to the Strengthening of Democracy*. Johannesberg: Open Society Institute.

Fawn, Rick. 2006. "Battle over the box: International election observation missions, political competition and retrenchment in the post-Soviet space." *International Affairs* 82(6): 1133–1153.

Fell, Dafydd. 2005. *Party Politics in Taiwan: Party Change and the Democratic Evolution of Taiwan, 1991–2004*. London: Routledge.

Ferree, Karen E., Clark C. Gibson, James D. Long. 2014. "Voting behavior and electoral irregularities in Kenya's 2013 Election" *Journal of Eastern African Studies*, 8(1): 153.

Fife, Brian L. 2010. *Reforming the Electoral Process in America*. Santa Barbara, CA: Praeger.

Finkel, Evgeny and Yitzhak M. Brudny. 2012. "No more colour! Authoritarian regimes and colour revolutions in Eurasia." *Democratization* 19(1): 1–14.

Finkel, Steven E. 2014. "The impact of adult civic education programmes in developing democracies." *Public Administration and Development* 34(3): 168–180.

Finkel, Steven E., Aníbal Pérez-Liñán, Mitchell A. Seligson, 2007. "The effects of U.S. foreign assistance on democracy building, 1990–2003." *World Politics* 59(1): 404–439.

Finnemore, Martha and Kathryn Sikkink. 1998. "International norm dynamics and political change." *International Organization* 52(3): 887–917.

Fish, Steven and Matthew Kroenig. 2009. *The Handbook of National Legislatures: A Global Survey*. New York: Cambridge University Press.

Fisher, Jeff. 2002. *Electoral Conflict and Violence*. Washington, DC: IFES.

Fisher, Jonathan. 2013. "The limits – and limiters – of external influence: donors, the Ugandan Electoral Commission and the 2011 elections." *Journal of Eastern African Studies* 7(3) 471–491.

Fisher, Jonathan. 2015. "Does it work?" – Work for whom? Britain and Political Conditionality since the Cold War." *World Development* 75: 13–25.

Fishkin, Joseph. 2011. "Equal citizenship and the individual right to vote." *Indiana Law Journal* 86(4): 1289–1360.

Fjelde, Hanne and Harvard Hegre. 2014. "Political corruption and institutional stability." *Studies in Comparative International Development* 49(3): 267–299.

Flores, Thomas Edward and Irfan Nooruddin. 2012. "The effect of elections on post-conflict peace and reconstruction." *Journal of Politics* 74(2): 558–570.

Flores, Thomas Edward and Irfan Nooruddin. 2016. *Elections in Hard Times: Building Stronger Democracies in the 21st Century*. New York: Cambridge University Press.

Forest, Benjamin. 2012. "Electoral redistricting and minority political representation in Canada and the United States." *Canadian Geographer* 56(3): 318–338.

Foweraker, Joseph and R. Krznaric. 2002. "The uneven performance of third wave democracies: Electoral politics and the imperfect rule of law in Latin America." *Latin American Politics and Society* 44(3): 29–60.

Franklin, Mark. 2004. *Voter Turnout and the Dynamics of Electoral Competition in Established Democracies since 1945*. New York: Cambridge University Press.

Franzese, R. J. 2002. "Electoral and partisan cycles in economic policies and outcomes." *Annual Review of Political Science* 5: 369–421.

Frazer, Jendayi E. and E. Gyimah-Boadi. Eds. 2011. *Preventing Electoral Violence in Africa*. Pittsburgh: Carnegie Mellon University.

Fukumoto, Kentaro and Yusaku Horiuchi. 2011. "Making outsiders' votes count: Detecting electoral fraud through a natural experiment." *American Political Science Review* 105(3): 586–603.

Fund, John H. 2004. *Stealing Elections: How Voter Fraud Threatens Our Democracy*. San Francisco, CA: Encounter Books.

Fung, Archon. 2011. "Popular election monitoring." In Heather Gerken, Guy-Uriel E. Charles, and Michael S. Kang, eds., *Race, Reform and Regulation of the Electoral Process: Recurring Puzzles in American Democracy*. New York: Cambridge University Press.

Gallagher, Michael and Paul Mitchell. Eds. 2005. *The Politics of Electoral Systems*. Oxford: Oxford University Press.

Gandhi, Jennifer. 2008. *Political Institutions under Dictatorship*. New York: Cambridge University Press.

Gandhi, Jennifer and Ellen Lust-Okar. 2009. "Elections under authoritarianism." *Annual Review of Political Science* 12: 403–422.

Gazibo, Mamoudou. 2006. "The forging of institutional autonomy: A comparative study of Electoral Management Commissions in Africa." *Canadian Journal of Political Science* 39(3): 611–633.

Geddes, Barbara. 1999. "What do we know about democratization after twenty years?" *Annual Review of Political Science* 2: 115–144.

Geddes, Barbara, Joseph Wright, and Erica Frantz. 2014. "Autocratic Regimes and Transitions." *Perspectives on Politics*. 12(2): 313–331.

Geddes, Barbara, Joseph Wright, and Erika Frantz. 2014. "Autocratic Regimes Codebook: Version 1.2." http://dictators.la.psu.edu/.

Geisler, G. 1993. "Fair – what has fairness got to do with it? Vagaries of election observations and democratic standards." *Journal of Modern African Studies* 31 (4): 613–637.

Gelman, Andrew and Gary King. 1994. "Enhancing democracy through legislative redistricting." *American Political Science Review* 88(3): 541–559.
George, Alexander L. and Andrew Bennett, 2005. *Case Studies and Theory Development in the Social Sciences*. Massachusetts: MIT Press.
Gerber, Alan S. and Donald Green. 2012. *Field Experiments: Design, Analysis and Interpretation*. New York: W. W. Norton.
Geys, Benny. 2006. "Explaining voter turnout: A review of aggregate-level research." *Electoral Studies* 25(4): 637–663.
Gilardi, Fabrizio. 2008. *Delegation in the Regulatory State: Independent Regulatory Agencies in Western Democracies*. UK: Edward Elgar.
Gilbert, Leah and Mohseni Payam. 2011. "Beyond authoritarianism: The conceptualization of hybrid regimes." *Studies in Comparative International Development* 46(3): 270–297.
Gingerich, D. W. 2009. "Ballot structure, political corruption, and the performance of proportional representation." *Journal of Theoretical Politics* 21(4): 509–541.
Glennerster, Rachel and Kudzai Takavarasha. 2013. *Running Randomized Evaluations: A Practical Guide*. Princeton, NJ: Princeton University Press.
Global Commission on Elections, Democracy and Security. 2012. *Deepening Democracy: A Strategy for improving the Integrity of Elections Worldwide*. Sweden: IDEA.
Global Governance 19(2): 207–226.
Goldsmith, A. A. 2001. "Foreign aid and statehood." *International Organization* 55(1): 123–148.
Gomez, Edmund Terence. 2012. "Monetizing politics: Financing parties and elections in Malaysia." *Modern Asian Studies* 46: 1370–1397.
Goodnow, Regina, Robert G. Moser, and Tony Smith. 2014. "Ethnicity and electoral manipulation in Russia Electoral Studies." 36: 15–27.
Goodwin-Gill, Guy. S. 2006. *Free and Fair Elections*. 2nd ed. Geneva: Inter-parliamentary Union.
Gosnell, Herbert F. 1968. *Machine Politics: Chicago Model*. 2nd ed. Chicago and London: University of Chicago Press.
Green, Donald P., Brian R. Calfano, and Peter M. Aronow. 2014. "Field experimental designs for the study of media effects." *Political Communication*, 31(1), 168–180.
Greenberg, Ari and Robert Mattes. 2013. "Does the quality of elections affect the consolidation of democracy?" In Michael Bratton, ed., *Voting and Democratic Citizenship in Africa*. Boulder: Lynne Rienner Publishers.
Greene, Kenneth F. 2007. *Why Dominant Parties Lose: Mexico's Democratization in Comparative Perspective*. New York: Cambridge University Press.
Grömping, Max. 2012. "Many Eyes of Any Kind? Comparing Traditional and Crowd-sourced Monitoring and their Contribution to Democracy." Paper presented at the Second International Conference on International Relations and Development, July 2012 in Thailand.
Grömping, Max. 2017. "Domestic election monitors." In Pippa Norris and Alexandre Nai, eds., *Election Watchdogs*. New York: Oxford University Press.
Gronke, Paul. 2013. "Are we confident in voter confidence? Conceptual and methodological challenges in survey measures of electoral integrity." Paper presented at the Workshop on Challenges of Electoral Integrity, Harvard University 2–3 June 2013.

Gronke, Paul, Eva Galanes-Rosenbaum, and Peter Miller. 2007. "Early voting and turnout." *PS: Political Science and Politics* 40(4): 639–645.
Gronke, Paul, Eva Galanes-Rosenbaum, Peter A. Miller, and Daniel Toffey. 2008. "Convenience voting." *Annual Review of Political Science*. 11: 437–55.
Gronke, Paul and Daniel Krantz Toffey. 2008. "The psychological and institutional determinants of early voting." *Journal of Social Issues* 64(3): 503–524.
Grose, Christian R. 2014. "Field experimental work on political institutions." *Annual Review of Political Science* 17: 355–370.
Gunlicks, Arthur B. Ed. 1993. *Campaign and Party Finance in North America and Western Europe*. Boulder: Westview Press.
Gunther, Richard, Paul A. Beck, Pedro C. Magahaes, and Alejandro Moreno. Eds. 2016. *Voting in Old and New Democracies*. New York: Routledge.
Gustafson, Marc. 2010. "Elections and the probability of violence in Sudan." *Harvard International Law Journal Online* 51: 47–62.
Gutierrez-Romero, Roxana. 2014. "An inquiry into the use of illegal electoral practices and effects of political violence and vote-buying." *Journal of Conflict Resolution* 58(8): 1500–1527.
Hadenius, Axel and Jan Teorell. 2007. "Pathways from authoritarianism." *Journal of Democracy* 18(1): 143–156.
Hafner-Burton, Emilie M., Susan D. Hyde, and Ryan S. Jablonski. 2014. "When do governments resort to election violence?" *British Journal of Political Science* 44(1): 149–179.
Hale, Henry E. 2011. "Formal constitutions in informal politics: Institutions and democratization in post-Soviet Eurasia." *World Politics* 63(4): 581–617.
Hall, Thad. 2011. "Voter opinions about election reform: Do they support making voting more convenient?" *Election Law Journal* 10(2): 73–87.
Hall, Thad E., J. Quin Monson, and Kelly D. Patterson. 2009. "The human dimension of elections: How poll workers shape public confidence in elections." *Political Research Quarterly* 62(3): 507–522.
Hamm, Keith E. and Robert E. Hogan 2008. "Campaign finance laws and decisions in state legislative candidacy elections." *Political Research Quarterly* 61(3): 458–467.
Handley, Lisa and Bernie Grofman. Eds. 2008. *Redistricting in Comparative Perspective*. New York: Oxford University Press.
Handlin, Samuel. 2015. "Observing incumbent abuses: Improving measures of electoral and competitive authoritarianism with new data." *Democratization*. 24(1): 41–60.
Hanham, Harry J. 1959. *Elections and Party Management: Politics in the Time of Disraeli and Gladstone*. London: Longmans.
Hanmer, Michael J. 2009. *Discount Voting: Voter Registration Reforms and Their Effects*. New York: Cambridge University Press.
Hanmer, Michael J. and Michael W. Traugott. 2004. "The impact of vote-by-mail on voter behavior." *American Politics Research*, 32: 375–405.
Hanretty, Chris and Christel Koop. 2012. "Shall the law set them free? The formal and actual independence of regulatory agencies." *Regulation & Governance* 7(2): 195–214.
Hartlyn, Jonathan, Jennifer McCoy, and Thomas Mustillo. 2008. "Electoral governance matters: Explaining the quality of elections in contemporary Latin America." *Comparative Political Studies* 41: 73–98.

Hasen, Richard L. 2012. *The Voting Wars: From Florida 2000 to the Next Election Meltdown*. New Haven: Yale University Press.
Hasseling, Gerti and Jon Abbink. Eds. 2000. *Election Observation and Democratization in Africa*. New York: Palgrave Macmillan.
Hausmann, Ricardo and Rigobon Roberto. 2011. "In search of the black swan: Analysis of the statistical evidence of electoral fraud in Venezuela." *Statistical Science* 26(4): 543–563.
Heidenheimer, Arnold J., Michael Johnston, and V.T. Levine. Eds. 1990. *Political Corruption: A Handbook*. New Brunswick, NJ: Transaction Publishers.
Heinzelman, Jessica and Patrick Meier. 2012. "Crowdsourcing for human rights monitoring: Challenges and opportunities for verification." In John Lannon, ed.,, *Human Rights and Information Communication Technologies: Trends and Consequences of Use*. Hershey, Pa.: IGI Global.
Hermet, Guy, Richard Rose, and Alain Rouquié. Eds. 1978. *Elections without Choice*. London: Macmillan.
Herrnson, Paul, Richard G. Niemi, and Michael J. Hanmer, 2012. "The impact of ballot type on voter errors." *American Journal of Political Science* 56(3): 716–730.
Herrnson, Paul S., Richard G. Niemi, Michael J. Hanmer, Benjamin B. Bederson, Frederick G. Conrad, and Michael W. Traugott. 2008. *Voting Technology: The Not-So-Simple Act of Casting a Ballot*. Washington: Brookings.
Herron, Erik S. 2009. *Elections and Democracy After Communism?* New York: Palgrave Macmillan.
Herron, Erik S. 2010. "The effect of passive observation methods on Azerbaijan's 2008 presidential election and 2009 referendum." *Electoral Studies* 29(3): 417–424.
Hershey, Marjorie Randon. 2009. "What we know about voter ID Laws, registration, and turnout." *PS: Political Science & Politics*, 42: 87–91.
Hicken, A. 2007. "Institutional incentives: Do candidate-centered electoral rules encourage vote buying?" In Frederic C. Schaffer, ed., *Elections for Sale: The Causes and Consequences of Vote Buying*. Boulder, CO: Lynne Rienner Publishers.
Hicken, Allen, Stephen Leider, Nico Ravanilla, and Dean Yang. 2015. "Measuring Vote-Selling: Field Evidence from the Philippines." *American Economic Review: Papers and Proceedings*, May 2015.
Hicks, William D., McKee, Seth C., Sellers, Mitchell D., and Smith, Daniel A. 2015. "A Principle or a Strategy? Voter Identification Laws and Partisan Competition in the American States." *Political Research Quarterly* 68(1): 18–33.
Hicks, William D., McKee, Seth C., Sellers, Mitchell D., et al. 2015. "A Principle or a Strategy? Voter Identification Laws and Partisan Competition in the American States." *Political Research Quarterly* 68(1): 18–33.
Hillman, Ben. 2013. "Public administration reform in post-conflict societies: Lessons from Aceh, Indonesia." *Public Administration and Development* 33(1): 1–14.
Hirschmann, David. 1998. "Improving crisis management in the imperfect world of foreign electoral assistance." *Public Administration and Development* 18(1): 23–36.
Hoglund, Kristine. 2009. "Electoral violence in conflict-ridden societies: Concepts, causes, and consequences." *Terrorism and Political Violence* 21(3): 412–427.
Hoglund, Kristine and Jarstad, Anna K. 2011. "Toward electoral security: Experiences from KwaZulu-Natal." *Africa Spectrum* 46(1): 33–59.

Honohan, Iseult and Derek Hutcheson. 2015. "Transnational citizenship and access to electoral rights: Defining the demos in European states." In Johan A. Elkink and David M. Farrell. *The Act of Voting: Identities, Institutions and Locale*. London: Routledge.

Howard, Marc Morjé, and Philip G. Roessler. 2006. "Liberalizing electoral outcomes in competitive authoritarian regimes." *American Journal of Political Science* 50(2): 365–381.

Howell, Patrick and Florian Justwan. 2013. "Nail-biters and no-contests: The effect of electoral margins on satisfaction with democracy in winners and losers." *Electoral Studies* 32(2): 334–343.

Hubbard, Glenn and Tim Kane. 2013. "In defense of Citizens United: Why campaign finance reform threatens American democracy." *Foreign Affairs* 92(4): 126–133.

Huber, Daniela. 2015. *Democracy Promotion and Foreign Policy Identity and Interests in US, EU and Non-Western Democracies*. New York: Palgrave.

Huntington, Samuel. 1993. *The Third Wave: Democratization in the late twentieth century*. Oklahoma: University of Oklahoma Press.

Hyde, Susan. D. 2007. "Experimenting in democracy promotion: International observers and the 2004 presidential elections in Indonesia." *Perspectives on Politics* 8(2): 511–527.

Hyde, Susan. D. 2007. "The observer effect in international politics: Evidence from a natural experiment." *World Politics* 60(1): 37–63.

Hyde, Susan. D. 2011. *The Pseudo-Democrat's Dilemma*. Ithaca: Cornell University Press.

Hyde, Susan D. and Nikolay Marinov. 2012. *Codebook for National Elections across Democracy and Autocracy (NELDA) 1945–2010*. Version 3. http://hyde.research.yale.edu/nelda/.

Hyde, Susan D. and Nikolay Marinov. 2012. "Which elections can be lost?" *Political Analysis*. 20(2): 191–210.

Hyde, Susan D. and Nikolay Marinov. 2014. "Information and self-enforcing democracy: The role of international election observation." *International Organization* 68(2): 329–359.

Hyde, Susan D. and Kevin Pallister. 2015. "Electoral administration, electoral observation, and election quality." In Jennifer Gandhi, Rubén Ruiz-Rufino, eds., *The Routledge Handbook of Comparative Political Institutions*. New York: Routledge.

Ichino, Nahomi and Matthias Schuendeln. 2012. "Deterring or displacing electoral irregularities? Spillover effects of observers in a randomized field experiment in Ghana." *Journal of Politics* 74(1): 292–307.

International IDEA. 2002. *International Electoral Standards: Guidelines for Reviewing the Legal Framework for Elections*. Stockholm: International IDEA.

International IDEA. 2004. *Handbook on the Funding of Political Parties and Election Campaigns*. Stockholm: International IDEA.

Jablonski, Ryan. 2013. "How aid targets votes: The impact of electoral incentives on foreign aid distribution." *World Politics* 66(02): 293–330. https://ncgg.princeton.edu/IPES/2013/papers/S215_rm1.pdf.

Jacobs, Kristof and Monique Leyenaar. 2011. "A conceptual framework for major, minor, and technical electoral reform." *West European Politics* 34(3): 495–513.

James, Toby S. 2010. "Electoral administration and voter turnout: Towards an international public policy continuum." *Representation* 45(4): 369–389.

James, Toby S. 2010. "Electoral modernisation or elite statecraft? Electoral administration in the U.K. 1997–2007." *British Politics*, 5(2): 179–201.
James, Toby S. 2012. *Elite Statecraft and Election Administration: Bending the Rules of the Game*. Basingstoke: Palgrave.
Jimenez, Raul and Manuel Hidalgo. 2014. "Forensic analysis of Venezuelan elections during the Chavez presidency." *Plos One* 9(6): 20–29.
Jockers, Heinz, Dirk Kohnert, and Nugent, Paul. 2010. "The successful Ghana election of 2008: A convenient myth?" *Journal of Modern African Studies* 48(1): 95–115.
Johansson, Anders C. 2015. "On the challenge to competitive authoritarianism and political patronage in Malaysia." *Asian-Pacific Economic Literature* 29(2): 47–67.
Johnson, Michael. 2013. "More than necessary, less than sufficient: Democratization and the control of corruption." *Social Research*. 80(4): 20–29.
Johnson, Michael. 2014. *Corruption, Contention, and Reform: The Power of Deep Democratization*. Cambridge and New York: Cambridge University Press.
Jones, Douglas W. and Barbara Simons. 2012. *Broken Ballots: Will Your Vote Count?* Chicago: University of Chicago Press.
Joshi, Madhav. 2013. "Inclusive institutions and stability of transition toward democracy in post-civil war states." *Democratization* 20(4): 743–770.
Kaare Strøm. 2000. "Delegation and accountability in parliamentary democracies." *European Journal of Political Research* 37(3): 261–290.
Kairys, David. 2013. "The contradictory messages of Rehnquist-Roberts era speech law: Liberty and justice for some." *University of Illinois Law Review* 1: 195–220.
Kalandadze, Katya and Orenstein, Mitchell A. 2009. "Electoral protests and democratization beyond the color revolutions." *Comparative Political Studies* 42(11): 1403–1425.
Kang, M.S. 2005. "The hydraulics and politics of party regulation." *Iowa Law Review* 91(1): 131–187.
Karlan, Dean and Jacob Appel. 2011. *More than Good Intentions: How the New Economics Is Helping to Solve Global Poverty*. New York: Dutton.
Katz, Richard S. 2005. "Democratic principles and judging 'free and fair.'" *Representation* 41(3): 161–179.
Kaya, Ruchan and Bernhard, Michael. 2013. "Are elections mechanisms of authoritarian stability or democratization? Evidence from Post-communist Eurasia." *Perspectives on Politics* 11(3): 734–752.
Keefer, Philip and R. Vlaicu. 2008. "Democracy, credibility, and clientelism." *Journal of Law Economics & Organization* 24(2): 371–406.
Kelley, Judith. 2008. "Assessing the complex evolution of norms: The rise of international election monitoring." *International Organization* 62(2): 221–255.
Kelley, Judith. 2009. "D-Minus Elections: The politics and norms of international election observation." *International Organization* 63(4): 765–787.
Kelley, Judith. 2009. "The more the merrier? The effects of having multiple international election monitoring organizations." *Perspectives on Politics* 7: 59–64.
Kelley, Judith. 2010. "Election observers and their biases." *Journal of Democracy* 21: 158–172.
Kelley, Judith. 2010. *Quality of Elections Data Codebook*. http://sites.duke.edu/kelley/data/.
Kelley, Judith. 2011. "Do international election monitors increase or decrease opposition boycotts?" *Comparative Political Studies* 44(11): 1527–1556.

Kelley, Judith. 2012. *Monitoring Democracy: When International Election Observation Works and Why It Often Fails*. Princeton, N.J.: Princeton University Press.

Kelley, Judith. 2012. "The international influences on elections in new multiparty states." *Annual Review of Political Science* 15: 203–220.

Kelley, Judith. *Project on International Election Monitoring*. http://sites.duke.edu/kelley/data/.

Kendall-Taylor, Andrea. 2012. "Purchasing Power: Oil, Elections and Regime Durability in Azerbaijan and Kazakhstan." *Europe-Asia Studies* 64(4): 737–760.

Kerr, Nicholas. 2014. "Public perceptions of election quality in Africa: A cross-national analysis.' In Pippa Norris, Richard Frank, and Ferran Martinez I Coma, eds., *Advancing Electoral Integrity*. New York: Oxford University Press.

Kersting, Erasmus and Christopher Kilby. 2014. "Aid and democracy redux." *European Economic Review* 67: 125–143.

Keyssar, Alexander. 2009. *The Right to Vote: The Contested History of Democracy in the United States*. Revised 2nd ed. New York: Basic Books.

King, Gary. 1990. "Electoral responsiveness and partisan bias in multiparty democracies." *Legislative Studies Quarterly*, 15(2).

Kitschelt, Herbert and Steven L. Wilkinson. Eds. 2007. *Patrons, Clients and Policies*. New York: Cambridge University Press.

Klassen, Andrew James. 2014. *Perceptions of Electoral Fairness*. Unpublished PhD thesis. Canberra, Australian National University.

Klein, A. "The puzzle of ineffective election campaigning in Japan." *Japanese Journal of Political Science* 12: 57–74.

Klein, Richard L. and Patrick Merloe. 2001. *Building Confidence in the Voter Registration Process: An NDI Monitoring Guide*. Washington DC: National Democratic Institute for International Affairs (NDI).

Knack, Stephen, 2004. "Does foreign aid promote democracy?" *International Studies Quarterly* 48: 251–266.

Koehler, Kevin. 2008. "Authoritarian elections in Egypt: Formal institutions and informal mechanisms of rule." *Democratization* 15(5): 974–990.

Kornblith, Miriam. 2013. "Chavism after Chavez?" *Journal of Democracy*. 24(4): 136–150.

Koss, Michael. 2008. "The convergence of party funding regimes in Western Europe: Towards an analytical framework." *Osterreichische Zeitschrift Fur Politikwissenschaft* 37(1): 63–69.

Koss, Michael. 2011. *The Politics of Party Funding*. Oxford: Oxford University Press.

Kovalov, Maksym. 2014. "Electoral manipulations and fraud in parliamentary elections: The case of Ukraine." *East European Politics And Societies* 28(4): 781–807.

Krasner, Stephen D. and Weinstein, Jeremy M. 2014. "Improving governance from the outside in." *Annual Review of Political Science* 17: 123–145.

Krook, Mona Lena. 2009. *Quotas for Women in Politics: Gender and Candidate Selection Reform Worldwide*. New York: Oxford University Press.

Kropf, Martha and David C. Kimball. 2012. *Helping America Vote: The Limits of Election Reform*. New York: Routledge.

Kumar, Krishna. 1998. *Post-Conflict Elections, Democratization, and International Assistance*. Boulder, Co: Lynne Rienner.

Kumar, Krishna. 2013. *Evaluating Democracy Assistance*. Boulder, CO: Lynne Rienner.

Kunicova, J. and Susan Rose-Ackerman. 2005. "Electoral rules and constitutional structures as constraints on corruption." *British Journal of Political Science* 35 (4): 573–606.
Kuntz, Philipp and Mark R. Thompson. 2009. "More than just the final straw stolen elections as revolutionary triggers." *Comparative Politics* 41(3): 253–261.
Kurlantzick, Joshua. 2014. *Democracy in Retreat: The Revolt of the Middle Class and the Worldwide Decline of Representative Government*. New Haven, CT: Yale University Press.
Landman, Todd and Edzia Carvalho. 2010. *Measuring Human Rights*. London: Routledge.
Lanning, K. 2008. "Democracy, voting, and disenfranchisement in the United States: A social psychological perspective." *Journal of Social Issues* 64(3): 431–446.
Lasthuizen, Karin, Leo Huberts, and Leonie Heres. 2011. "How to measure integrity violations." *Public Management Review* 13(3): 383–408.
Laycock, Samantha, Alan Renwick, Daniel Stevens, and Jack Vowles. 2013. "The UK's electoral reform referendum of May 2011." *Electoral Studies* 32(2): 211–214.
Lean, Sharon F. 2007. "Democracy assistance to domestic election monitoring organizations: Conditions for success." *Democratization* 14(2): 289–312.
Lean, Sharon F. Ed. 2012. *Civil Society and Electoral Accountability in Latin America*. New York: Palgrave.
Leduc, Lawrence, Richard Niemi, and Pippa Norris. Eds. 2010. *Comparing Democracies 3: Elections and Voting in the 21st Century*. London: Sage.
Leemanna, Lucas and Daniel Bochsler. 2014. "A systematic approach to study electoral fraud." *Electoral Studies* 35(3): 33–47.
Lehoucq, Fabrice Edouard. 2002. "Can parties police themselves? Electoral governance and democratization." *International Political Science Review* 23(1): 29–46.
Lehoucq, Fabrice Edouard. 2003. "Electoral fraud: Causes, types, and consequences." *Annual Review of Political Science* 6: 233–256.
Lehoucq, Fabrice Edouard and Iván Molina Jiménez. 2002. *Stuffing the Ballot Box: Fraud, Electoral Reform, and Democratization in Costa Rica*. New York: Cambridge University Press.
Lehoucq, Fabrice Edouard and Kiril Kolev. 2015. "Varying the Un-Variable: Social Structure, Electoral Formulae, and Election Quality." *Political Research Quarterly* 68(2): 1–13.
Lessig, Lawrence. 2011. *Republic, Lost*. New York: Twelve.
Levine, Dov. 2016. "When the great power gets a vote: The effects of great power electoral interventions on election results." *International Studies Quarterly*, 60(2): 189–202.
Levitsky, Steven and Lucan A. Way. 2002. "The rise of competitive authoritarianism." *Journal of Democracy*. 13(2): 51–66.
Levitsky, Steven and Lucan A. Way. 2006. "Linkage versus leverage – Rethinking the international dimension of regime change." *Comparative Politics* 38(4):379.
Levitsky, Steven and Lucan Way. 2010. *Competitive Authoritarianism: Hybrid Regimes After the Cold War*. New York: Cambridge University Press.
Levitsky, Steven and Lucan A. Way. 2010. "Why democracy needs a level playing field." *Journal of Democracy* 21(1): 57–68.
Leyenaar, Monique and Hazan, Reuven Y. 2011. "Reconceptualising electoral reform." *West European Politics* 34(3): 437–455.

Lijphart, Arend. 1994. *Electoral Systems and Party Systems: A Study of Twenty-Seven Democracies, 1945–1990*. New York: Oxford University Press.

Lindberg, Staffan. I. 2005. "Consequences of electoral systems in Africa: A preliminary inquiry." *Electoral Studies* 24(1): 41–64.

Lindberg, Staffan.2006. *Democracy and Elections in Africa*. Baltimore, Md.: Johns Hopkins University Press.

Lindberg, Staffan I. 2006. "The surprising significance of African elections." *Journal of Democracy* 17(1): 139–151.

Lindberg, Staffan. Ed. 2009. *Democratization by Elections: A New Mode of Transition*. Baltimore, MD: Johns Hopkins University Press.

Lindberg, Staffan I. 2013. "Confusing Categories, Shifting Targets." *Journal of Democracy* 24(4): 161–167.

Lindberg, Staffan I and Minion K.C. Morrison. 2013. "Are African Voters Really Ethnic or Clientelistic? Survey Evidence from Ghana." Political Science Quarterly 123(1): 95–122.

Liow, Joseph Chinyong. 2012. "March 2008 general election: Understanding the new media factor." *Pacific Review* 25(3): 293–315.

Little, Andrew T. 2012. "Elections, fraud, and election monitoring in the shadow of revolution. *Quarterly Journal of Political Science* 7(3): 249–283.

Lo, B. B. 2003. "Russian elections: Uncivil state." *World Today* 59(11): 22–24.

López-Pintor, Rafael, 2000. *Electoral Management Bodies as Institutions of Governance*, New York: United Nations Development Programme.

López-Pintor, Rafael. 2006. *Getting to the CORE: On the Cost of Registration and Elections*. New York: UNDP.

López-Pintor, Rafael. 2010. *Assessing Electoral Fraud in New Democracies: A Basic Conceptual Framework*. Washington DC: The International Foundation for Electoral Systems, IFES.

Ludwig, Robin and Edwards McMahon. June 2014. *An assessment of BRIDGE*. P31.

Lukinova, Evgeniya, Mikhail Myagkov, and Peter C. Ordeshook. 2011. "Ukraine 2010: Were Tymoshenko's cries of fraud anything more than smoke?" *Post-Soviet Affairs* 27(1): 37–63.

Lust-Okar, Ellen. 2000. "Legislative politics in the Arab world: The resurgence of democratic institutions." *International Journal of Middle East Studies* 32(3): 420–422.

Lust-Okar, Ellen. 2004. "Divided they rule: The management and manipulation of political opposition." *Comparative Politics* 36(2): 159–179.

Lust-Okar, Ellen and Amaney Jamal. 2002. "Rulers and rules: Reassessing the influence of regime type on electoral law formation." *Comparative Political Studies* 35(3): 337–366.

Lynch, Gabrielle and Gordon Crawford. 2011. "Democratization in Africa 1990–2010: An assessment." *Democratization* 18(2): 275–310.

Macchiaverna, Maria Rosaria and Mario Giuseppe Varrenti. 2012. *Study on Performance Indicators for Electoral Assistance projects developed within the context of the EC-UNDP Partnership on Electoral Assistance*. Brussels: European Commission.

Magaloni, Beatriz. 2006. *Voting for Autocracy: Hegemonic Party Survival and Its Demise in Mexico*. Cambridge: Cambridge University Press.

Magaloni, Beatriz. 2008. "Credible power-sharing and the longevity of authoritarian rule." *Comparative Political Studies* 41(4–5): 715–741.
Magaloni, Beatriz. 2010. "The game of electoral fraud and the ousting of authoritarian rule." *American Journal of Political Science* 54(3): 751–765.
Magen, Amichi, Thomas Risse, and Michael A. McFaul. Eds. 2013. *Promoting Democracy and the Rule of Law: American and European Strategies*. New York: Palgrave Macmillan.
Mainwaring, Scott and Aníbal Pérez-Liñán. 2014. *Democracies and Dictatorships in Latin America: Emergence, Survival, and Fall*. New York: Cambridge University Press.
Makulilo, Alexander Boniface. 2011. "'Watching the watcher': An evaluation of local election observers in Tanzania." *Journal of Modern African Studies* 49(2): 241–262.
Maldonaldo, Arturo and Mitchell A. Seligson. 2014. "Electoral Trust in Latin America." In Pippa Norris, Richard W. Frank, and Ferran Martinez iComa, eds., *Advancing Electoral Integrity*. New York: Oxford University Press.
Mansfield, Edward D. and Jack Snyder. 2007. *Electing to Fight: Why Emerging Democracies Go to War*. Cambridge, MA: MIT Press.
Mares, Isabela and Zhu, Boliang. 2015. "The production of electoral intimidation: Economic and political incentives." *Comparative Politics* 48(1):23–40.
Martinez i Coma, Ferran and Richard W. Frank. 2014. "Expert judgments." In Pippa Norris, Richard W. Frank, and Ferran Martinez I Coma, eds., *Advancing Electoral Integrity*. New York: Oxford University Press.
Martínez i Coma, Ferran and Carolien van Ham. 2015. "Can experts judge elections? Testing the validity of expert judgments for measuring election integrity." *European Journal of Political Research*, 54: 305–325.
Mattes, Robert et al. 2016. "Parties, elections, voters and democracy." In Richard Gunther, Paul A. Beck, Pedro C. Magahaes, and Alejandro Moreno, eds., *Voting in Old and New Democracies*. New York: Routledge.
McAllister, Ian. 2014. "Corruption and confidence in Australian political institutions." *Australian Journal of Political Science* 49(2): 174–185.
McAllister, Ian and Stephen White, 2011. "Public perceptions of electoral fairness in Russia." *Europe-Asia Studies* 63(4): 663–683.
McAllister, Ian and Stephen White. 2015. "Electoral integrity and support for democracy in Belarus, Russia and Ukraine." *Journal of Elections, Public Opinion and Parties* 25(2): 78–96.
McCann, J. A. and Jorge I. Dominguez. 1998. "Mexicans react to electoral fraud and political corruption: An assessment of public opinion and voting behavior." *Electoral Studies* 17(4): 483–503.
McDonald, Michael P. 2004. "A comparative analysis of redistricting institutions in the United States, 2001–02." *State Politics and Policy Quarterly* 4: 371–395.
McDonald, Michael P. and Samuel Popkin. 2001. "The myth of the vanishing voter." *American Political Science Review* 95(4): 963–974.
McFaul, Michael. 2009. *Advancing Democracy Abroad*. New York: Rowman and Littlefield.
McFaul, Michael and N. Petrov. 2004. "What the elections tell us." *Journal of Democracy* 15(3): 20–31.
McGrath, Amy. 1997. *Corrupt Elections: Ballot Rigging in Australia*. Sydney, NSW: H. S. Chapman Society.

Mebane, Walter R. Jr. 2012. "Comment on 'Benford's Law and the detection of election fraud.'" *Political Analysis* 19(3): 269–272.

Meyer, M. and J. Booker. 1991. *Eliciting and Analyzing Expert Judgment: A Practical Guide*. London: Academic Press.

Michalik, Susanne. 2015. *Multiparty Elections in Authoritarian Regimes: Explaining their Introduction and Effects* (Studien zur Neuen Politischen Ökonomie). Springer.

Mickiewicz, Ellen. 1997. *Changing Channels: Television and the Struggle for Power in Russia*. New York: Oxford University Press.

Mickiewicz, Ellen. 2008. *Television, Power, and the Public in Russia*. New York: Cambridge University Press.

Minnite, Lorraine Carol. 2010. *The Myth of Voter Fraud*. Ithaca: Cornell University Press.

Mitchell, Lincoln A. 2016. *The Democracy Promotion Paradox*. Washington DC: Brookings Institution.

Moehler, Devra C. 2009. "Critical citizens and submissive subjects: Elections losers and winners in Africa." *British Journal of Political Science* 39(2): 345–366.

Moehler, Devra C. 2010. "Democracy, governance, and randomized development assistance." *Annals of the American Academy of Political and Social Science*, 628: 30–46.

Moehler, Devra C. and Staffan I. Lindberg. 2009. "Narrowing the legitimacy gap: Turnovers as a cause of democratic consolidation." *Journal of Politics* 71(4): 1448–1466.

Molina, I., and Fabrice Edouard Lehoucq. 1999. "Political competition and electoral fraud: A Latin American case study." *Journal of Interdisciplinary History* 30(2): 199.

Moller, Jorgen and Svend-Erik. Skaaning. 2010. "Post-communist regime types: Hierarchies across attributes and space." *Communist and Post-Communist Studies* 43(1): 51–71.

Moller, Jorgen and Svend-Erik Skaaning. 2010. "Beyond the radial delusion: conceptualizing and measuring democracy and non-democracy." *International Political Science Review* 31(3): 261–283.

Montjoy, Robert S. 2008. "The public administration of elections." *Public Administration Review* 68 (5): 788–799.

Montjoy, Robert S. 2010. "The changing nature ... and costs ... of election administration." *Public Administration Review* 70(6): 867–875.

Morse, Yonatan L. 2012. "The era of electoral authoritarianism." *World Politics* 64(1): 161–198.

Morse, Yonatan L. 2015. "From Single-Party to Electoral Authoritarian Regimes: The Institutional Origins of Competitiveness in Post-Cold War Africa." *Comparative Politics* 48(1): 126–135.

Morton, Rebecca B. and Kenneth C. Williams. 2010. *Experimental Political Science and the Study of Causality: From Nature to the Lab*. New York: Cambridge University Press.

Moyo, Dambisa. 2010. *Dead Aid: Why Aid Is Not Working and How There Is a Better Way for Africa*. New York: Farrar, Straus and Giroux.

Mozaffar, Shaheen. 2002. "Patterns of electoral governance in Africa's emerging democracies." International *Political Science Review* 23(1): 85–101.

Mozaffar, Shaheen and Andreas Schedler. 2002. "The comparative study of electoral governance: Introduction." *International Political Science Review* 23(1): 5–27.

Munck, Geraldo L. 2009. *Measuring Democracy: A Bridge between Scholarship and Politics*. Baltimore: Johns Hopkins University Press.
Munck, Geraldo L. and Jay Verkuilen. 2002. "Conceptualizing and measuring democracy: Evaluating alternative indices." *Comparative Political Studies* 35(1): 5–34.
Munck, Geraldo L. and Jay Verkuilen. 2002. "Generating better data: A response to discussants." *Comparative Political Studies* 35(1): 52–57.
Murphy, Craig N. 2006. *The United Nations Development Programme: A Better Way?* New York: Cambridge University Press.
Myagkov, Mikhail and Peter C. Ordeshook. 2008. "Ukraine's 2007 parliamentary elections free and fair, or fraud once again?" *Problems of Post-Communism* 55(6): 33–41
Myagkov, Mikhail and Peter C. Ordeshook. 2005. "The trail of votes in Ukraine's 1998, 1999, and 2002 elections." *Post-Soviet Affairs* 21(1): 56–71.
Myagkov, Mikhail, Peter C. Ordeshook, and Dimitri Shakin. 2005. "Fraud or fairytales: Russia and Ukraine's electoral experience." *Post-Soviet Affairs* 21(2): 91–131.
Myagkov, Mikhail, Peter C. Ordeshook, and Dimitri Shakin. 2009. *The Forensics of Election Fraud: Russia and Ukraine*. New York: Cambridge University Press.
Nagle, J. C. 2004. "How not to count votes." *Columbia Law Review* 104(6): 1732–1763.
Nassmacher, Karl-Heinz. 2001. Ed. *Foundations for Democracy: Approaches to Comparative Political Finance*. Baden-Baden: Nomos.
Nassmacher, Karl-Heinz. 2009. *The Funding of Party Competition: Political Finance in 25 Democracies*. Berlin: Nomos.
National Democratic Institute. 2005. *Money in Politics: A Study of Party Financing Practices in 22 Countries*. Washington DC: National Democratic Institute.
Nazzarine, S. R. 2003. "A faceless name in the crowd: Freedom of association, equal protection, and discriminatory ballot access laws." *University of Cincinnati Law Review* 72(1): 309–361.
Neiheisel, Jacob R. and Burden, Barry C. 2012. "The impact of election day registration on voter turnout and election outcomes." *American Politics Research* 40(4): 636–664.
Neiheisel, Jacob R. and Barry C. Burden. 2012. "The impact of election day registration on voter turnout and election outcomes." *American Politics Research* 40: 636–664.
Newell, James. *The Politics of Italy: Governance in a Normal Country*. New York: Cambridge University Press.
Norris, Pippa. Ed. 1999. *Critical Citizens*. Oxford: Oxford University Press.
Norris, Pippa. 2003. *Democratic Phoenix*. New York: Cambridge University Press.
Norris, Pippa. 2004 *Electoral Engineering: Voting Rules and Political Behavior*. New York: Cambridge University Press.
Norris, Pippa. 2004. "Will new technology boost turnout?" In Norbert Kersting and Harald Baldersheim, eds., *Electronic Voting and Democracy: A Comparative Analysis*. London: Palgrave, pp. 193–225.
Norris, Pippa. 2008. *Driving Democracy: Do Power-Sharing Institutions Work?* New York: Cambridge University Press.
Norris, Pippa. Ed. 2010. *Public Sentinel: News Media and the Governance Agenda*. Washington, DC: The World Bank.
Norris, Pippa. 2011. "Cultural explanations of electoral reform: A policy cycle model." *West European Politics* 34(1): 531–550.

Norris, Pippa. 2011. *Democratic Deficit: Critical Citizens Revisited*. New York: Cambridge University Press.
Norris, Pippa. 2012. *Making Democratic Governance Work: How Regimes Shape Prosperity, Welfare and Peace*. New York: Cambridge University Press.
Norris, Pippa. 2013. "Does the world agree about standards of electoral integrity? Evidence for the diffusion of global norms." Special issue of *Electoral Studies* 32(4): 576–588.
Norris, Pippa. 2013. "The new research agenda studying electoral integrity." *Special issue of Electoral Studies* 32(4): 563–575.
Norris, Pippa. 2014. "Electoral integrity and political legitimacy." In Lawrence LeDuc, Richard Niemi, and Pippa Norris, eds., *Comparing Democracies* 4, London: Sage.
Norris, Pippa. 2014. *Why Electoral Integrity Matters*. New York: Cambridge University Press.
Norris, Pippa. 2016. "Electoral integrity in East Asia." In Tun-jen Cheng and Yun-han Chu, eds., *Routledge Handbook on Democratization in East Asia*. New York: Routledge.
Norris, Pippa. 2017. "Electoral integrity and electoral systems." In Erik S. Herron, Robert J. Pekkanen, and Matthew S. Shugart, eds., *Oxford Handbook of Electoral Systems*. New York: Oxford University Press.
Norris, Pippa. 2017. "Electoral integrity and voting behavior." In Mark Franklin et al., eds., *Routledge Handbook on Voting Behavior and Public Opinion*. New York: Routledge.
Norris, Pippa. 2017. "Electoral transitions: Stumbling out of the gate." In Mohammad-Mahmoud Ould Mohamedou and Timothy D. Sisk, eds., *Democratization in the 21st Century: Reviving Transitology*. Routledge, pp. 49–74.
Norris, Pippa and Andrea Abel van Es. 2016. *Checkbook Elections: Political Finance in Comparative Perspective*. New York: Oxford University Press.
Norris, Pippa, Ferran Martinez i Coma, and Richard W. Frank. 2013. "Assessing the quality of elections." *Journal of Democracy*. 24(4): 124–135.
Norris, Pippa, Ferran Martinez i Coma, Max Grömping, and Alessandro Nai. 2015. *Perceptions of Electoral Integrity (PEI-4.5)* doi: 10.7910/DVN/LYO57K, Harvard Dataverse, V4.5.
Norris, Pippa, Ferran Martinez i Coma, Alessandro Nai, and Max Groemping. 2016. *The Expert Survey of Perceptions of Electoral Integrity*. www.electoralintegrityproject.com.
Norris, Pippa, Richard W. Frank, and Ferran Martinez i Coma. Eds. 2014. *Advancing Electoral Integrity*. New York: Oxford University Press.
Norris, Pippa, Richard W. Frank, and Ferran Martinez i Coma. 2014. "Measuring electoral integrity: A new dataset." *PS Politics and Political Science* 47(4): 789–798.
Norris, Pippa, Richard W. Frank, and Ferran Martinez i Coma. Eds. 2015. *Contentious Elections: From Ballots to Barricades*. New York: Routledge.
Norris, Pippa, Holly Ann Garnett, and Max Groemping. 2016. "Electoral integrity in all 50 US states, ranked by experts." *Vox* 24 December 2016.
Norris, Pippa, Holly Ann Garnett, and Max Gromping. 2017. *Perceptions of Electoral Integrity: The 2016 American Presidential Elections*. www.electoralintegrityproject.com.
Norris, Pippa and Ronald Inglehart. 2009. *Cosmopolitan Communications: Cultural Diversity in a Globalized World*. New York: Cambridge University Press.
Norris, Pippa and Ronald Inglehart. 2016. "Trump, Brexit and the Rise of Populism." Faculty Research paper, Harvard's Kennedy School of Government.

Norris, Pippa and Alessandro Nai. Eds. 2017. *Election Watchdogs: Transparency, Accountability, and Integrity*. New York: Oxford University Press.

Noske-Turner, Jessica. 2014. "Evaluating the impacts of media assistance: Problems and principles." *Global Media Journal* 4(2): 1–21.

Nou, J. 2009. "Privatizing democracy: promoting election integrity through procurement contracts." *Yale Law Journal* 118 (4): 744–793.

Nunnally, Shayla C. 2011. "(Dis)counting on democracy to work: Perceptions of electoral fairness in the 2008 presidential election." *Journal of Black Studies* 42(6): 923–942.

Nyblade, B., and S. R. Reed. "Who cheats? Who loots? Political competition and corruption in Japan, 1947–1993." *American Journal of Political Science* 52(4):926–941.

Obi, Cyril. 2011. "Taking back our democracy? The trials and travails of Nigerian elections since 1999." *Democratization* 18(2): 366–387.

Öhman, Magnus and Hani Zainulbhai. 2011. *Political Finance Regulation: The Global Experience*. Washington, DC: IFES. www.ifes.org/files/Political_Finance_Regulation_The_Global_Experience.pdf.

O'Leary, Cornelius. 1962. *The Elimination of Corrupt Practices in British Elections, 1968–1911*. Oxford: Oxford University Press.

Omotola, J. S. "Elections and democratic transition in Nigeria under the Fourth Republic." *African Affairs* 109 (437): 535–553.

Onapajo, Hakeem. 2014. "Violence and Votes in Nigeria: The Dominance of Incumbents in the Use of Violence to Rig Elections" *Africa Spectrum*, 49(2): 27–51.

Opitz, Christian, Fjelde, Hanne, and Hoglund, Kristine. 2013. "Including peace: The influence of electoral management bodies on electoral violence." *Journal of Eastern African Studies* 7(4): 713–731.

Organization of American States General Secretariat. 2013. *The 2007–2012 Electoral Cycle in the Americas*. Washington DC: OAS. www.oas.org/es/sap/docs/deco/CicloElectoral_e.pdf.

Organization for Security and Cooperation in Europe. 2007. *Handbook for Long-Term Election Observers: Beyond Election Day Observation*. Warsaw: OSCE/ODIHR.

Organization for Security and Cooperation in Europe (OSCE). 2010. *Election Observation Handbook*. Warsaw: OSCE/ODIHR. 6th ed.

Organization for Security and Cooperation in Europe (OSCE). 2016. *Handbook on the Follow-up of Electoral Recommendations*. Warsaw: OSCE/ODIHR.

Organization of American States/International IDEA. 2005. *Funding of Political Parties and Election Campaigns in the Americas*. OAS/International IDEA.

Orozco-Henríquez, Jesús. 2010. *Electoral Justice: The International IDEA Handbook*. Stockholm: International IDEA.

Ottaway, Marina. 2003. *Democracy Challenged: The Rise of Semi-Authoritarianism* Washington DC: Carnegie Endowment for International Peace.

Overton, Spencer. 2006. *Stealing Democracy: The New Politics of Voter Suppression*. New York: Norton.

Panov, Petr and Cameron Ross. 2013. "Sub-National Elections in Russia: Variations in United Russia's Domination of Regional Assemblies." *Europe-Asia Studies* 65(4): 737–752.

Paris, Roland. 2004. *At War's End: Building Peace After Civil Conflict*. Cambridge: Cambridge University Press.

Pastor, Robert A. 1999. "A brief history of electoral commissions." In Andreas Schedler, Larry Diamond, and Marc F. Plattner, eds., *The Self-restraining State: Power and Accountability in New Democracies*. Boulder, CO: Lynne Rienner, p. 75–82.

Pastor, Robert A. 1999. "The role of electoral administration in democratic transitions." *Democratization* 6(4): 1–27.

Pastor, Robert A., Robert Santos, and Alison Prevost. 2011. "Voting and ID requirements: A survey of registered voters in three states." *American Review of Public Administration* 40(4): 461–481.

Paxton, Pamela, Kenneth A. Bollen, Deborah M. Lee, and HyoJuong Kim. 2003. "A half-century of suffrage: New data and a comparative analysis." *Studies in Comparative International Development* 38: 93–122.

Pericchi, Luis and Torres, David. 2011. "Quick anomaly detection by the Newcomb-Benford Law, with applications to electoral processes data from the USA, Puerto Rico and Venezuela." *Statistical Science* 26(4): 502–516.

Pernelle, A. Smits and Francois Champagne, 2008. "An assessment of the theoretical underpinnings of practical participatory evaluation." *American Journal of Evaluation* 29: 427.

Persily, N. 2001. "Candidates *v.* parties: The constitutional constraints on primary ballot access laws." *Georgetown Law Journal* 89(7): 2181–2225.

Pevehouse, Jon C. 2002. "With a little help from my friends? Regional organizations and the consolidation of democracy." *American Journal of Political Science* 46(3): 611–626.

Piccone, Ted and Richard Youngs. Ed. 2006. *Strategies for Democratic Change*. Washington, DC: Democratic Coalition Project.

Pinto-Duschinsky, Michael. 2005. "Financing politics: a global view." *Journal of Democracy* 13(4): 69–86.

Pinto-Duschinsky. Michael. 2014. *Electoral Omission*. London: Policy Exchange.

Piven, Frances Fox, L. Minnite, and M. Groarke. 2009. *Keeping Down the Black Vote*. London: The New Press.

Popova, Marina. 2006. "Watchdogs or attack dogs? The role of the Russian Courts and the Central Election Commission in the resolution of electoral disputes." *Europe-Asia Studies* 58 (3): 391–414.

Post, Robert C. 2014. *Citizens Divided: Campaign Finance Reform and the Constitution*. Cambridge, MA: Harvard University Press.

Powell, G. Bingham. 2000. *Elections as Instruments of Democracy*. New Haven, CT: Yale University Press.

Powell, G. Bingham. 2004. "Political representation in comparative politics." *Annual Review of Political Science* 7: 273–296.

Powell, G. Bingham. 2004. "The chain of responsiveness." *Journal of Democracy* 15(4): 91–105.

Powell, G. Bingham. 2014. "Why elections matter." In Lawrence LeDuc, Richard Niemi, and Pippa Norris, eds., *Comparing Democracies 4*. London: Sage.

Power, Timothy J. and Matthew MacLeod Taylor. *Corruption and Democracy in Brazil: The Struggle for Accountability*, Notre Dame, Ind.: University of Notre Dame Press.

Przeworski, Adam, Michael E. Alvarez, Jose Antonio Cheibub, and Fernando Limongi. 2000. *Democracy and Development: Political Institutions and Well-Being in the World, 1950–1990*. New York: Cambridge University Press.

Puddington, Arch and Tyler Roylance. 2016. "Anxious dictators, wavering democracies: Global freedom under pressure." *Freedom House: Freedom in the World 2016*. www.freedomhouse.org.

Quimpo, N. G. 2009. "The Philippines: Predatory regime, growing authoritarian features." *Pacific Review* 22(3): 335–353.

Qvortup, M. 2005. "First past the postman: Voting by mail in comparative perspective." *Political Quarterly*, 76(3): 414–419.

Rahat, Gideon and Hazan, Reuven Y. 2011. "The barriers to electoral system reform: A synthesis of alternative approaches." *West European Politics* 34(3): 478–494.

Rallings, Colin, Michael Thrasher, and G. Borisyuk. "Much ado about not very much: The electoral consequences of postal voting at the 2005 British General Election." *British Journal of Politics & International Relations* 12(2): 223–238.

Regan, P. M., Frank, R. W., and Clark, D. H. 2009. "Political institutions and elections: New datasets." *Conflict Management and Peace Science*, 26(3): 320–337.

Reilly, Benjamin. 2002. "Post-conflict elections: Constraints and dangers." *International Peacekeeping* 9(2): 118.

Reilly, Benjamin. 2004. "Elections in Post-conflict Societies." In Edward Newman and Roland Rich, eds., *The UN Role in Promoting Democracy: Between Ideals and Reality*. Tokyo: United Nations University Press.

Reynolds, Andrew. 2011. *Designing Democracy in a Dangerous World*. New York: Oxford University Press.

Reynolds, Andrew and M. Steenbergen. 2006. "How the world votes: The political consequences of ballot design, innovation and manipulation." *Electoral Studies* 25(3): 570–598.

Richman, Jesse T., Gulshan A. Chattha, and David C. Earnest. 2014. "Do non-citizens vote in US elections? *Electoral Studies* 36: 149–157.

Riddell, Roger C. 2007. *Does Aid Really Work?* New York: Oxford University Press.

Risse, Thomas and Nelli Babayan. 2015. "Democracy promotion and the challenges of illiberal regional powers: Introduction to the special issue." *Democratization* 22(3): 381–399.

Robertson, Graeme. 2015. "Political orientation, information, and perceptions of election fraud: Evidence from Russia." *British Journal of Political Science* 45(1): 29–51.

Rolfe, Meredith. 2012. *Voter Turnout*. New York: Cambridge University Press.

Romanelli, Raffaele. Ed. 1998. *How Did They Become Voters? The History of Franchise in Modern European Representation*. The Hague: Kluwer Law.

Rosas, Guillermo. 2010. "Trust in elections and the institutional design of electoral authorities: Evidence from Latin America." *Electoral Studies* 29(1): 74–90.

Rose, Richard, William Mishler, and Christian Haerpfer. 1998. *Democracy and Its Alternatives: Understanding Post-Communist Societies*. Baltimore: Johns Hopkins University Press.

Rose, Richard and William Mishler. 2009. "How do electors respond to an "unfair" election? The experience of Russians." *Post-Soviet Affairs* 25(2): 118–136.

Rose, Richard, William Mishler, and Neil Monroe. 2011. *Popular Support for an Undemocratic Regime: The Changing Views of Russians*. New York: Cambridge University Press.

Rose, Richard and Neil Munro. 2002. *Elections Without Order: Russia's Challenge to Vladimir Putin*. Cambridge: Cambridge University Press.

Rose, Richard and Neil Munro. 2009. *Parties and Elections in New European Democracies*. Colchester: ECPR Press.
Rosenstone, Steve and Mark Hansen. 1993. *Mobilization, Participation and Democracy in America*. New York: Macmillan.
Ross, Michael L. 2013. *The Oil Curse: How Petroleum Wealth Shapes the Development of Nations*. Princeton, N.J.: Princeton University Press.
Rothstein, Bo. 2009. "Creating political legitimacy: Electoral democracy versus quality of government." *American Behavioral Scientist* 53(3): 311–330.
Samples, John Curtis. 2006. *The Fallacy of Campaign Reform*. Chicago: University of Chicago Press.
Santa-Cruz, Arturo. 2005. "Constitutional structures, sovereignty, and the emergence of norms: The case of international election monitoring." *International Organization* 59(03): 663–693.
Santiso, C. and A. Loada. 2003. "Explaining the unexpected: Electoral reform and democratic governance in Burkina Faso." *Journal of Modern African Studies* 41(3): 395–419.
Scarrow, Susan. 2004."Explaining political finance reforms: Competition and context." *Party Politics* 10: 653–675.
Scarrow, Susan. 2007. "Political finance in comparative perspective." *Annual Review of Political Science* 10: 193–210.
Schaffer, Fredric Charles. 2002. "Might cleaning up elections keep people away from the polls? Historical and comparative perspectives." *International Political Science Review* 23(1): 69–84.
Schaffer, Fredric Charles. Ed. 2007. *Elections for Sale: The Causes and Consequences of Vote Buying*. Boulder and London: Lynne Rienner.
Schaffer, Fredric Charles. 2008. *The Hidden Costs of Clean Election Reform*. Cornell: Cornell University Press.
Schaffer, Frederic Charles and Tova Andrea Wang. 2009. "Is everyone else doing it? Indiana's Voter identification law in international perspective." *Harvard Law & Policy Review*, 3: 397–413.
Schedler, Andreas. 1999. "Civil society and political elections: A culture of distrust?" *Annals of the American Academy of Political and Social Science* 565: 126–141.
Schedler, Andreas. 2002. "The menu of manipulation." *Journal of Democracy* 13(2): 36–50.
Schedler, Andreas. Ed. 2006. *Electoral Authoritarianism: The Dynamics of Unfree Competition*. Boulder and London: Lynne Rienner.
Schedler, Andreas. 2010. "Authoritarianism's last line of defense." *Journal of Democracy* 21(1): 69–80.
Schedler, Andreas. 2012. "Judgment and measurement in political science." *Perspectives on Politics* 10(1): 21–36.
Schedler, Andreas. 2012. *The Politics of Uncertainty Sustaining and Subverting Electoral Authoritarianism*. CIDE: Mexico City.
Scher, Richard K. 2010. *The Politics of Disenfranchisement: Why Is It So Hard to Vote in America?* New York: M. E. Sharpe.
Schmeets, Hans. Ed. 2010. *International Election Observation and Assessment of Elections*. The Hague: Statistics Netherlands.
Schraufnagel, Scot. 2011. *Third Party Blues: The Truth and Consequences of Two-Party Dominance*. New York: Routledge.

Schroeder, Michael. 2013. "The politics of change: The evolution of UN electoral services, 1989–2006." *Global Governance*. 19(2): 207–226.
Schuler, Ian. 2008. "SMS as a tool in election observation." *Innovations* 3(2): 143–157.
Schumpeter, Joseph. 1942. *Capitalism, Socialism and Democracy*. London: George Allen & Unwin.
Scott, James M and Ralph G. Carter. 2016. "Promoting democracy in Latin America: Foreign policy change and US democracy assistance, 1975–2010." *Third World Quarterly* 37(2): 299–320.
Seeberg, Merete Bech. 2014. "State capacity and the paradox of authoritarian elections." *Democratization* 21(7): 1265–1285.
Sekhon, Jasjeet S. and Titiunik, Rocio. 2012. "When natural experiments are neither natural nor experiments." *American Political Science Review* 106(1): 35–57.
Selway, Joel and Kharis Templeman. 2012. "The Myth of Consociationalism? Conflict Reduction in Divided Societies." *Comparative Political Studies* 45(12): 1542–1571.
Serritzlew, Soren, Kim Mannemar Sonderskov, and Gert Tinggaard Svendsen. 2014. "Do corruption and social trust affect economic growth? A review." *Journal of Comparative Policy Analysis* 16(2): 121–139.
Severiano Teixeira, Nuno. Ed. 2008. *The International Politics of Democratization: Comparative perspectives*. London: Routledge.
Seymour, Charles. 1970. *Electoral Reform in England and Wales: The Development and Operation of the Parliamentary Franchise 1832–1885*. London: David and Charles, reprint.
Shah, Seema. 2015. "Free and fair? Citizens' assessments of the 2013 general election in Kenya." *Review of African Political Economy* 42(143): 44–61.
Sharafutdinova, Gulnaz. *Political Consequences of Crony Capitalism inside Russia*. Notre Dame, Ind.: University of Notre Dame Press.
Shock, David R. 2008. "Securing a line on the ballot: Measuring and explaining the restrictiveness of ballot access laws for non-major party candidates in the United States." *Social Science Journal* 45(1): 48–60.
Simmons, Beth A. 2009. *Mobilizing for Human Rights: International Law in Domestic Politics*. New York: Cambridge University Press.
Simpser, Alberto. 2012. "Does electoral manipulation discourage voter turnout? Evidence from Mexico." *Journal of Politics* 74(3): 782–795.
Simpser, Alberto. 2013. *Why Parties and Governments Manipulate Elections: Theory, Practice and Implications*. New York: Cambridge University Press.
Sisk, Timothy and Andrew Reynolds. Eds. 1998. *Elections and Conflict Management in Africa*. Washington DC: US Institute of Peace Press.
Sjoberg, Fredrik. 2012. "Making voters count: Evidence from field experiments about the efficacy of domestic election observation." Harriman Institute Working Paper 1.
Sjoberg, Fredrik M. 2014. "Autocratic adaptation: The strategic use of transparency and the persistence of election fraud." *Electoral Studies* 33: 233–245.
Slater, Dan. 2010. *Ordering Power: Contentious Politics and Authoritarian Leviathans in Southeast Asia*. New York: Cambridge University Press.
Smets, Kaat and Carolien van Ham. 2013. "The embarrassment of riches? A meta-analysis of individual-level research on voter turnout." *Electoral Studies* 32(2): 344–359.
Smith, Lahra. 2009. "Explaining violence after recent elections in Ethiopia and Kenya." *Democratization* 16(5): 867–897.

Smith, Rodney. 2016. "Confidence in voting channels in Australia." *Australian Journal of Political Studies* 51(1): 68–75.
Snyder, Jack. 2000. *From Voting to Violence: Democratization and Nationalist Conflict*. New York: Norton.
Spinelli, Antonio. 2011. *Strategic Planning for Effective Electoral Management: A practical guide for election management bodies to conduct a strategic planning exercise*. Washington, DC: IFES.
Steenbergen, Marco R., and Gary Marks. 2007. "Evaluating expert judgments." *European Journal of Political Research* 46: 347–366.
Stewart, J. 2006. "A banana republic? The investigation into electoral fraud by the Birmingham Election Court." *Parliamentary Affairs* 59 (4): 654–667.
Stockemer, Daniel, Bernadette LaMontagne, and Lyle Scruggs. 2013. "Bribes and ballots: The impact of corruption on voter turnout in democracies." *International Political Science Review* 34(1): 74–90.
Stokes, Susan, Thad Dunning, Marcelo Nazareno, and Valeria Brusco. 2013. *Brokers, Voters, and Clientelism: The Puzzle of Distributive Politics*. New York: Cambridge University Press.
Straus, Scott and Charles Taylor. 2012. "Democratization and electoral violence in Sub-Saharan Africa, 1990–2008." In Dorina Bekoe, ed., *Voting in Fear: Electoral Violence in Sub-Saharan Africa*. United States Institute of Peace: Washington, DC
Straus, Scott. 2011. "'It's sheer horror here': Patterns of violence during the first four months of Cote d'Ivoire's post-electoral crisis." *African Affairs* 110(440): 481–489.
Straus, Scott, 2012. "Wars do end! Changing patterns of political violence in sub-Saharan Africa." *African Affairs* 111(443): 179–201.
Straus, Scott and Charlie Taylor. 2012. "Democratization and electoral violence in Sub-Saharan Africa, 1990–2008." In Dorina A. Bekoe, ed., *Voting in Fear*. Washington, DC: United States Institute of Peace.
Streb, Matthew J. Ed. 2004. *Law and Election Politics*. 2nd ed. New York: Routledge.
Stroh, Alexander. 2010. "Electoral rules of the authoritarian game: Undemocratic Effects of proportional representation in Rwanda." *Journal of Eastern African Studies* 4(1): 1–19.
Strøm, Kaare, Wolfgang C. Müller, and Torbjörn Bergman. 2003. *Delegation and Accountability in Parliamentary Democracies*. New York: Oxford University Press.
Struwig, Jare, Benjamin J. Roberts, and Elme Vivier. 2011. "A vote of confidence: election management and public perceptions." *Journal of Public Administration*, 46(3): 1122–1138.
Svolik, Milan W. 2012. *The Politics of Authoritarian Rule*. New York: Cambridge University Press.
Tan, Netina. 2013. "Electoral engineering and hegemonic party resilience in Singapore." *Electoral Studies* 32(4): 632–643.
Tancangco, Luzviminda G. 1992. *The Anatomy of Electoral Fraud: Concrete Bases for Electoral Reforms*. Manila: MJAGM: Distributor Matrix.
Tay, Louis, Mitchel N. Herian, and Ed Diener. 2014. "Detrimental Effects of Corruption and Subjective Well-Being: Whether, How, and When." *Social Psychological and Personality Science* 5(7): 751–759.
Taylor, Charles, Jon Pevehouse, and Scott Straus. 2013. "Perils of Pluralism: Electoral Violence and Competitive Authoritarianism in Sub-Saharan Africa." Simons Papers in

Security and Development 23, School for International Studies, Simon Fraser University.
Taylor, Steven L. 2009. *Voting Amid Violence: Electoral Democracy in Colombia*. Northeastern University Press.
Teorell, Jan. 2010. *Determinants of Democratization*. New York: Cambridge University Press.
Thomas, Paul G. and Lorne R. Gibson. 2014. *Comparative Assessment of Central Electoral Agencies*. Elections Canada.
Thompson, Mark R. and Philipp Kuntz. 2004. "Stolen elections: The case of the Serbian October." *Journal of Democracy* 15(4): 159–172.
Thompson, Mark R. and Philipp Kuntz, 2009. "More than just the final straw: Stolen elections as revolutionary triggers." *Comparative Politics* 41(3): 253–272.
Tierney, Michael J., Daniel L. Nielson, Darren G. Hawkins, J. Timmons Roberts, Michael G. Findley, Ryan M. Powers, Bradley Parks, Sven E. Wilson, and Robert L. Hicks. 2011. "More Dollars than Sense: Refining our knowledge of development finance using AidData." *World Development* 39(11): 1891–1906.
Tolstrup, Jakob. 2015. "Black knights and elections in authoritarian regimes: Why and how Russia supports authoritarian incumbents in post-Soviet states." *European Journal of Political Research* 54(4): 673–690.
Trenschel, Alexander and Fernando Mendez. Eds. 2005. *The European Union and e-voting*. London: Routledge.
Triantafillou, Peter. 2015. "The political implications of performance management and evidence-based policymaking." *American Review of Public Administration* 45(2): 167–181.
Tuccinardi, Domenico. Ed. 2014. *International Obligations for Elections: Guidelines for Legal Frameworks*. International IDEA: Stockholm.
Tucker, Joshua. 2007. "Enough! Electoral fraud, collective action problems, and post-communist colored revolutions." *Perspectives on Politics* 5(3): 535–551.
Tyler, Tom R. 1984. "The role of perceived injustice in defendants' evaluations of their courtroom experience." *Law & Society Review* 18(1): 51–74.
Tyler, Tom R. 1990. *Why People Obey the Law*. New Haven: Yale University Press.
Tyler, Tom R. 1994. "Governing amid diversity: The effect of fair decision-making procedures on the legitimacy of government." *Law & Society Review* 28(4): 809–831.
Tyler, Tom R., Jonathan D. Casper, and Bonnie Fisher. 1989. "Maintaining allegiance toward political authorities: The role of prior attitudes and the use of fair procedures." *American Journal of Political Science* 33(3): 629–652.
Tyler, Tom R., Kenneth A. Rasinski, and Kathleen M. McGraw. 1985. "The influence of perceived injustice on the endorsement of political leaders." *Journal of Applied Social Psychology* 15(8): 700–725.
Ugues, Jr, Antonio. 2010. "Citizens' views on electoral governance in Mexico." *Journal of Elections, Public Opinion & Parties*, 20(4): 495–527.
Ugues, Jr, Antonio. 2014. "Electoral management in Central America." In Pippa Norris, Richard W. Frank, and Ferran Martinez i Coma, eds., *Advancing Electoral Integrity*. New York: Oxford University Press.
Ugues, Jr, Antonio and D.X.M. Vidal. 2015. "Public evaluations of electoral institutions in Mexico: A analysis of the IFE and TRIFE in the 2006 and 2012 elections." *Electoral Studies* 40: 231–244.

UK Electoral Commission. 2014. *Electoral Fraud in the UK: Final Report and Recommendations*. London: UK Electoral Commission.

United Nations. 2005. *Declaration of Principles for International Election Observation and Code of Conduct for International Elections Observers*. New York: United Nations. www.cartercenter.com/documents/2231.pdf.

United Nations Development Programme. 2007. *UN Electoral Assistance Implementation Guide*. New York: UNDP.

United Nations Development Programme. 2011. *Understanding Electoral Violence in Asia*. UNDP Asia-Pacific Regional Center.

United Nations Development Programme. 2012. *Evaluation of UNDP Contribution to Strengthening Electoral Systems and Processes*. New York: UNDP.

United Nations Development Programme. 2014. *The Longer-Term Impact of UNDP Electoral Assistance: Lessons Learned*. New York: UNDP. www.undp.org/content/undp/en/home/librarypage/democratic-governance/electoral_systemsandprocesses/11-the-longer-term-impact-of-undp-electoral-assistance–lessons.html.

United Nations Development Programme/IFES. 2005. *Getting to the CORE. A Global Survey on the Cost of Registration and Elections*. New York: UNDP.

United Nations General Assembly resolution 63/163. April 12, 2012. "*Strengthening the role of the United Nations in enhancing periodic and genuine elections and the promotion of democratization.*"

U.S. Agency for International Development (USAID), 2014. *Foreign Operations FY 2013 Performance Report*. Washington, DC: USAID. www.usaid.gov/sites/default/files/documents/1870/USAID_FY2013_APR.pdf.

Vachudova, Milada Anna. 2005. *Europe Undivided*: Oxford: Oxford University Press.

van der Walle, Nicholas. 2003. "Presidentialism and clientelism in Africa's emerging party systems." *The Journal of Modern African Studies* 41(02):297–321. doi: dx.doi.org/10.1017/S0022278X03004269.

van Ham, Carolien. 2012. *Beyond Electoralism? Electoral fraud in third wave regimes 1974–2009*. PhD Thesis. Florence: European University Institute.

van Ham, Carolien. 2015. "Getting elections right? Measuring electoral integrity." *Democratization*. 22(4): 714–737.

van Ham, Carolien and Staffan Lindberg. 2015. "When guardians matter most: Exploring the conditions under which electoral management body institutional design affects election integrity." *Irish Political Studies* 30(4):454–481.

van Ham, Carolien and Staffan I. Lindberg. 2015. "From sticks to carrots: Electoral manipulation in Africa, 1986–2012." *Government and Opposition* 50(3): 521–548.

Verba, Sidney, and Norman Nie. 1972. *Participation in America: Political Democracy and Social Equality*. New York: Harper and Row.

Verba, Sidney, Norman Nie, and Jae-on Kim. 1978. *Participation and Political Equality: A Seven-Nation Comparison*. New York: Cambridge University Press.

Verba, Sidney, Kay Schlozman, and Henry E. Brady. 1995. *Voice and Equality: Civic Voluntarism in American Politics*. Cambridge, MA: Harvard University Press.

Vicente, Pedro and Leonard Wantchekon. 2009. "Clientelism and vote buying: Lessons from field experiments in African elections." *Oxford Review of Economic Policy* 25(2): 292–305.

Vickery, Chad and Erica Shein. 2012. "Assessing electoral fraud in new democracies." IFES: Washington, DC. www.ifes.org/~/media/Files/Publications/White%20PaperReport/2012/Assessing_Electoral_Fraud_Series_Vickery_Shein.pdf.

Volkov, Denis. 2012. "The protesters and the public." *Journal of Democracy* 23(3): 55–62.
von Soest, Christian. 2015. "Democracy prevention: The international collaboration of authoritarian regimes." *European Journal of Political Research* 54(4): 623–638.
Wahmn, Michael, Jan Teorell, and Axel Hadenius. 2013. "Authoritarian regime types revisited: updated data in comparative perspective." *Contemporary Politics* 19(1): 19–34.
Wall, Alan, Andrew Ellis, Ayman Ayoub, Carl W. Dundas, Joram Rukambe, and Sara Staino. 2006. International IDEA. 2006. *Electoral Management Design: The International IDEA Handbook*. Sweden: International IDEA.
Wand, Jonathan, Gary King, and Olivia Lau. 2011. "Anchors: Software for Anchoring Vignettes Data." *Journal of Statistical Software* 42(3): 1–25. http://j.mp/m5tITE.
Wand, J.N., K.W. Shotts, J.S. Sekhon, Walter Mebane, M.C. Herron, and Henry E. Brady. 2001. "The butterfly did it: The aberrant vote for Buchanan in Palm Beach County, Florida." *American Political Science Review* 95(4): 793–810.
Wang, Tova Andrea. 2012. *The Politics of Voter Suppression: Defending and Expanding Americans' Right to Vote*. Ithaca: Cornell University Press.
Wang, Tova Andrea. 2014. *Voter Identification Requirements and Public International Law: An Examination of Africa and Latin America*. Atlanta: The Carter Center.
Way, Lucan A. 2015. "The limits of autocracy promotion: The case of Russia in the "near abroad." *European Journal of Political Research*. 54(4): 691–706.
Weghorst, Keith R. and Staffan I. Lindberg. 2011. "Effective opposition strategies: Collective goods or clientelism?" *Democratization* 18(5): 1193–1214.
Weidmann, Nils B. and Michael Callen. 2013. "Violence and election fraud: Evidence from Afghanistan." *British Journal of Political Science* 43(1): 53–75.
Welsh, Bridget. 2015. "Elections in Malaysia: Voting behaviour and electoral integrity." In M.L. Weiss, ed., the *Routledge Handbook Of Contemporary Malaysia*. London: Routledge, pp. 11–21.
Welsh, Brigitte. 2013. "Malaysia's elections: A step backward." *Journal of Democracy*. 24(4): 136–150.
White, Stephen and Ian McAllister. 2014. "Did Russia (Nearly) have a Facebook Revolution in 2011? Social Media's Challenge to Authoritarianism." *Politics* 34(1): 72–84.
White, Stephen and Ian McAllister. 2014. "Electoral integrity and support for democracy in Belarus, Russia, and Ukraine." *Journal of Elections, Public Opinion and Parties*.
White, Stephen. "Non-competitive elections and national politics: The USSR Supreme Soviet elections of 1984." *Electoral Studies* 4(3): 215–229.
White, Stephen. 2011. "Elections Russian-Style." *Europe-Asia Studies* 63(4): 531–556.
Whitehead, Laurence. 2002. *The International Dimensions of Democratization: Europe and the Americas*. Oxford: Oxford University Press.
Wigell, M. 2008. "Mapping 'Hybrid Regimes': Regime types and concepts in comparative politics." *Democratization* 15(2): 230–250.
Wilking, Jennifer R. 2011. "The portability of electoral procedural fairness: Evidence from experimental studies in China and the United States." *Political Behavior* 33(1): 139–159.
Wilkinson, Steven. 2006. *Votes and Violence: Electoral Competition and Ethnic Riots in India*: New York: Cambridge University Press.

Willis, Justin and Atta el Battahani. 2010. "'We changed the laws': Electoral practice and malpractice in Sudan since 1953." *African Affairs* 109(435): 191–212.
Wilson, Kenneth. 2012. "How Russians view electoral fairness: A qualitative analysis." *Europe-Asia Studies* 64(1): 145–168.
Wise, Charles R. 2001. "Electoral administration in crisis: An early look at lessons from Bush versus Gore." *Public Administration Review* 61(2): 131–139.
Wlezien, Christopher and Stuart Soroka. 2012. "Political Institutions and the Opinion–Policy Link." *West European Politics* 35(6): 1407–1432.
Wong, Chin-Huat, Chin James, and Othman Norani. 2010. "Malaysia: towards a topology of an electoral one-party state." *Democratization* 17(5): 920–949.
Woolcock, Michael. 2009. "Towards a plurality of methods in project evaluation: A contextualized approach to understanding impact trajectories and efficacy." *Journal of Development Effectiveness* 1(1): 1–14.
Young, John Hardin. 2009. *International Election Principles: Democracy and the Rule of Law*. Chicago: American Bar Association.
Youngs, Richard. Ed. 2002. *The European Union and the Promotion of Democracy*. Oxford: Oxford University Press.
Youngs, Richard. Ed. 2006. *Survey of European Democracy Promotion Policies 2000–2006*. Madrid: Fride.
Ziblatt, Daniel. 2009. "Shaping democratic practice and the causes of electoral fraud: The case of nineteenth century Germany." *American Political Science Review* 103(1): 1–21.

Index